The HOUSE PLANT ENCYCLOPEDIA

The HOUSE PLANT ENCYCLOPEDIA

Ingrid Jantra and Ursula Krüger

Translated by Maya Anyas and Joan Campbell

North American Consultant:
Sam Benvie, Hons. B.Sc. (Bio.), Dip. L.A.T.

KEY PORTER BOOKS

Picture Credits

Copyright © 1997 by Mosaik Verlag GmbH

Canadian Cataloguing in Publication Data

Jantra, Ingrid.
    The houseplant encyclopedia

ISBN 1-55013-795-6

1. House plants - Encyclopedias. I. Kruger, Ursula.
II. Title

SB419.J36   1997   635.9'65   C96-931764-6

Key Porter Books Limited
70 The Esplanade
Toronto, Ontario
Canada M5E 1R2

Printed and bound in Germany

97 98 99 00 6 5 4 3 2 1

CONTENTS

Contents

Greener Living with Plants

Greener living with plants—who wouldn't want that? Flowering and leafy plants give us so many opportunities to create an agreeable living environment. They delight us with the beauty of their decorative form, their color, their perfume. Happy are those who possess a garden they can transform into a piece of paradise. Yet, it is also possible to create green and flowering oases—spaces that will make you the envy of all—in and around the house: in living rooms, on landings, on small and large balconies and patios, and in greenhouses and conservatories. With plants from temperate, tropical, and subtropical regions—familiar to us as room, balcony, tub, and garden-room plants—this is no magic trick, provided that you learn their needs, cultivate them appropriately, and understand how to use their beauty to best advantage.

Step by step to success

This richly illustrated guide, in color throughout, introduces you step by step to the care of plants, and offers you a multitude of suggestions, tips, and ideas for decorating with leafy and flowering plants in and around your own house.

First, we explain what you must consider before you decide to buy plants. Then we offer easily understandable basic information about the habitat and lifestyle of plants. (You will be amazed at how fascinating botany can be!) Next, you will learn all you need to know about the prerequisites for growth: about light, air, water, fertilizer, soil, plant health, and propagation.

Those seeking quick information will find it in the colored boxes scattered throughout the text.

Plant splendor in pots, tubs, and hanging planters

The color of the boxes is used to highlight the sections summarizing the practical information that follow every major topic, making them quick and easy to find. Drawings are provided to illustrate countless practical tasks or the individual steps involved in watering, fertilizing, repotting, propagating, pruning, training, and over-wintering. Colored drawings illustrating symptoms make possible instant identification of pests or diseases that have

affected your plants to help you determine what countermeasures to take.

The motto Living Greener, Living Better introduces a chapter that should inspire you to decorate creatively with plants. It is truly amazing what decorative effects can be achieved with plants, indoors and out! Allow yourself to be surprised by novel decorating ideas and suggestions for planting. A brief Glossary containing the most important technical terms will

useful plants from the tropics.

Also, because we wish not only to stimulate your interest but also to satisfy it, the book concludes with a section that lists important addresses and sources for plants and items related to their care.

Who doesn't dream of such a plant idyll? It embodies both the bright, everyday world and romanticism, the vitality of summer and the joy of life. Naturally, a little work is needed to achieve this magical combination of blooming plants, but the rewards are simply incomparable.

increase your gardening know-how, and serve as a useful guide to terms used in the major section of the book: an extensive series of plant portraits of the most beautiful plants, alphabetically arranged.

Care plans for more than 1000 varieties

Central to this guide is an extensive plant encyclopedia. Its 250-odd pages describe more than 1000 of the best-known and best-loved varieties of plants for the house,

garden room, balcony, and patio. Plants are listed alphabetically by their internationally recognized botanical names, and each is illustrated by at least one picture. For every plant, there is a description and a detailed care plan. In addition, the book deals with and provides care plans for less familiar species of plants: new varieties that have not yet established themselves, "old" plants that are making a comeback, botanical rarities and curiosities, as well as

I f you want to enjoy your room and balcony plants for any length of time, you must give them a location comparable to their original environment. The most important factors are light and temperature. Most of our houseplants prefer a light, though not necessarily sunny, location, one that is warm and where the air is not too dry. Some, however, prefer an environment that is partly shady, warm, and humid. It is up to you to determine for yourself which room in your home corresponds to the particular requirements of any plant.

Houseplants on a windowsill create a cheerful atmosphere in a room. This book will tell you how to care for your green friends.

Some Preliminary Thoughts about Location

In a home, there are many places for plants: on the balcony, patio, and windowsill, in the rooms themselves, and in the garden room. Suitable species can be found for almost every location.

All plants are able, for a time, to withstand a warmer or colder, lighter or darker placement than the one that corresponds perfectly to their natural needs. Yet in order for them to thrive, you must find them a location that approaches their natural habitat to the greatest extent possible. Every house offers several different potential locations.

Living rooms

In most cases, it is the living room, the place where you spend the greatest amount of time, that you will choose to beautify with plants.

LIGHT. Light, temperature, and humidity play a major role in the life of plants. This is why you should first determine the quality of light in every location where plants might be placed. It is best not to depend on your eyes alone. Human beings tend to judge a location to be reasonably light when it is actually too dark for plants. With small measuring instruments (light meters) you can check the light intensity at the chosen location (→ Light, page 36).

Remember, too, that light quality is not constant throughout the year. For example, if a large leafy tree is standing in front of a south window, the windowsill will be warm in the summertime, but not necessarily light and sunny. In the winter, on the other hand, when the tree has no leaves, the sun will shine directly onto the plants. A north window on the upper floor of an apartment house is often lighter than a west window on the ground floor that is shaded by evergreens or a large rhododendron. Covered balconies, thin curtains, or even houses across the street significantly cut down the light level inside. As well, the amount of light varies with the length of days over the annual cycle. Most tropical houseplants are used to twelve hours of daylight and darkness, and suffer because they don't get enough light for several months in our temperate climate.

The size of the window also plays a part. In the wild, light reaches plants from all sides, but in a window it comes to them from one side only. Most plants should

therefore be turned occasionally, so that they do not become lopsided. (The larger the window, however, the wider the angle of incidence.)

TEMPERATURE. Temperature is just as important as light. If plants are in the right location from the perspective of their lighting needs, the temperature is generally suitable from spring to fall. It is in winter that problems arise. The temperature may drop too much in unheated rooms, but be too high in the heated living room. In the case of plants that are used to "warm feet," large, floor-standing specimens do well with under-floor heating, while those in pots can tolerate a radiator under the windowsill. Many plants, however, suffer from lack of humidity during this period. If all the rooms in a home are heated, plants that need a rest period at low temperatures are particularly hard hit.

Kitchens and bathrooms

Kitchens and bathrooms are often overlooked in the quest for suitable locations. Given appropriate lighting conditions, plants that need an even temperature and high humidity throughout the year can thrive in these locations. Humidity is higher in the kitchen and bathroom than in the other rooms, and the temperature is also generally warmer.

In addition to herbs on the windowsill, blossoming summer plants and hanging planters are attractive decorations for the kitchen. However, many plants cannot tolerate mist that contains fat. Suitable plants for such conditions have leathery leaves that can be wiped off.

In a bathroom with good natural

The various locations for house, balcony, and tub plants

light, ferns do especially well. A richly varied picture can be created using a number of standing and hanging types. If there is enough space, bamboo or Swiss cheese plant (*Monstera deliciosa*) look very decorative.

Bedrooms

A light, cool bedroom that is heated in winter, and in which the temperature occasionally sinks to 50°F (10°C), is ideal for plants that need—or can withstand—low winter temperatures. Examples of plants that will do well here all year long are grape ivy (*Cissus*), fatshedera (*x Fatshedera lizei*), schefflera (*Schefflera*), and indoor linden (*Sparmannia africana*).

Halls and stairwells

Draft-free halls and stairwells may be good locations for large plants when the windowsill can no longer accommodate them. As these spaces are usually cooler than the other rooms, particularly in winter, they are also suitable as winter quarters for tub plants and those that require a rest period at a low temperature. In the case of rented apartments, however, you will need to ask the landlord and the neighbors for permission before setting out your plants.

Open plant windows

These differ from normal plant windows in that the plants grow in a large box or container that is deeper than a windowsill, and extends the entire breadth of the window. If the side walls and ceiling are drawn into the planting, one really looks into green.

Closed plant windows

Some of the most beautiful plants simply cannot accommodate

Plant lights augment natural light in dark corners.

themselves to the climate of our living rooms. Their environment must be warm, damp, and light. These requirements can only be met in a kind of greenhouse—a closed plant window. Transforming an existing window into a closed plant window, however, does involve numerous construction steps and considerable expense. In rental apartments, permission will seldom be granted; the chances are better in condominiums. The best thing, undoubtedly, is to incorporate a plant window into construction plans for a new home. Ideally, it should be located on the west or east side of the house, linked to the electrical and water supplies, and have the plant container built in. Temperature, ventilation, and

humidity should be regulated automatically. If the plant window faces south, a blind on the exterior is essential to provide shade. The expense is only worth it if the window is large and if one has a lot of time for the care of costly plant treasures. Such windows need attention daily. In this artificial living space, small omissions can easily lead to large catastrophes, because fungi are quick to proliferate and pests multiply at breakneck speed.

If you place an epiphyte branch as a decorative element in the closed plant window, the "rainforest look" is almost perfect.

No plant can survive without light. If there is insufficient natural light in a given location, plant lights can help. These are lights with a spectral distribution comparable to the natural light that is essential for plants. Ordinary lamps will not do the trick.

Which Plants Go Where?

Plants do particularly well in light garden rooms, but only if the glass does not heat up too much. Preventive shading and regular airing are absolutely essential.

Plants in sealed containers (terrariums)

More modest than plant windows but equally charming are sealed plant display units, which are available in various sizes, from small glass cases to large stands with heating and lighting. These work on the principle of the "Wardian case" (→ page 27). Because water circulation, photosynthesis, and respiration take care of themselves in a space that is closed almost all the time, such units do not require daily care. Plants suited to them need hardly any nutrients, especially as they are meant to remain small enough to fit into their limited space. Should they grow too large for their small containers, the circulation will be disturbed, making it necessary for you to give them water occasionally or remove the large plants. Of course, withered leaves and blooms must also be removed immediately.

Plants appropriate for these containers are those that prefer a warm, humid atmosphere, are weak growers, and develop slowly.

Garden rooms

The garden room or solarium is the optimal location for plants because it offers more light than any other room in the house. Those who use it as a green living room and heat it in the winter can cultivate all warmth-loving plants. In contrast, an unheated porch or frost-free glass shelter is ideal for Mediterranean species and, naturally, also makes the perfect place to overwinter plants.

Balconies and patios

All considerations that apply to interior rooms are also relevant to the out-of-doors: How light is it? At

Garden rooms are heaven for plants.

what time of day, and for how long, does it get the sun? Does the heat get trapped? Is the balcony or patio roofed? Is it often windy?

How sunny a balcony is depends on the latitude and the surroundings. Narrow streets, high houses, or trees can throw long shadows and make even a south-facing balcony in a generally warm but partially shaded location uncongenial for plants. Unobstructed east and west balconies with sunshine from dawn to mid-morning and from mid-afternoon until sunset are ideal locations for most plants. A north-facing balcony offers relatively unfavorable growing conditions. Covered balconies or loggias have both advantages and drawbacks: rain and wind damage are avoided,

but warmth is trapped. On roof decks and apartment balconies, wind and rain often become a problem.

When designing balconies and patios it is also essential to take structural considerations into account. Plants, tubs, and boxes, soil, furniture and people can add up to a heavy load. In general, the load must not exceed 55 lb. per square foot (250 kg per m^2). You should also always make prior application to the landlord to discover what restrictions there are as regards planting, the installation of boxes, or other alterations.

14

PLACEMENT AND PURCHASE

Below, you will find some examples of plants that grow best in certain kinds of locations (for many of these plants, more details about location and care may be found in the plant portraits, starting on page 126).

Plants for sunny, warm, dry locations

In south-, east-, or west-facing windows, and in garden rooms, it can be extremely sunny for many hours of the day. Examples of plants suited to these locations are *Aeonium, Agave, Aloe variegata, Aporocactus flagelliformis, Astrophytum, Beaucarnea, Callistemon citrinus, Cephalocereus senillis, Chamaerops humilis, Cordyline australis, Cycas, Echeveria, Eucalyptus, Nerium oleander, Phoenix,* and *Strelitzia.*

Plants for partly shady, warm, humid locations

The natural habitats of these plants are the virgin forests of the tropics and subtropics. Suitable, among others, are *Aglaonema, Alocasia, Anthurium, Asplenium nidus, Miltonia, Phyllitis, Rhipsalis, Scirpus,* and *Streptocarpus.*

Plants for shady, cool locations

A very few plants do not object to being placed, literally, "in a corner." These are plants from the cool mountain forests of tropical and subtropical regions. Just the same, you should occasionally give them a lighter (though not sunnier) location for several weeks. These plants include *Aspidistra elatior, Fuchsia, Hedera, Pteris cretica,* and *Soleirolia.*

Plants for light, cool locations

The plants that thrive in light hallways, studies, stairwells, or on glassed-in balconies originate in the higher mountain areas of the warmer climatic zones, as well as in the Mediterranean region. Occasional direct sun does them no harm. In the summer, they appreciate a period on the balcony or patio. Examples are *Abutilon, Ampelopsis brevipedunculata, Araucaria heterophylla, Browallia, Campanula, Citrus, Cytisus, Euonymus japonicus, Fatsia japonica, Grevillea robusta,* and *Rhododendron* hybrids.

Plants for sheltered locations

Roofed balconies, atrium courtyards, and patios sheltered at the side offer security to wind-sensitive plants. Among these are *Abutilon, Arbutus unedo, Aristolochia macrophylla, Begonia, Bougainvillea, Campanula, Campsis radicans, Caryopteris x clandonensis, Cuphea ignea, Dahlia, Datura, Ensete ventricosum, Fuchsia, Heliotropium arborescens, Hibiscus rosa-sinensis, Lagerstroemia indica, Lathyrus odoratus, Plumbago auriculata, Salvia splendens, Thunbergia alata,* and *Tropaeolum peregrinum.*

Plants sensitive to rain

Plants from dry regions dislike a damp climate; in other species, rain ruins the blooms. A sheltering roof is desired particularly by *Abutilon, Aeonium arboreum, Aucuba japonica, Calceolaria integrifolia, Calliandra tweedii, Capparis spinosa, Chamaerops humilis, Cycas revoluta, Gazania, Gomphrena globosa, Heliotropium arborescens, Hibiscus rosa-sinensis, Impatiens, Mesembryanthemum criniflorum, Nerium oleander, Petunia, Plumbago auriculata, Portulaca grandiflora, Salvia splendens, Schizanthus wisentonensis* hybrids, *Senecio bicolor,* and *Yucca.*

Plants requiring epiphyte supports

Plants that grow on trees in nature do best on an epiphyte support or branch in the damp, warm environment of a plant window or terrarium. Examples are ferns and many types of bromeliads and orchids.

A shady window is the right location for fatshedera (x *Fatshedera lizei*) and many types of fern such as squirrel's foot fern (*Davallia mariesii*) and bird's nest fern (*Asplenium nidus*). Pygmy palm (*Chamaedorea elegans*) also does well here.

Plants suitable for a shady window

Plants That Need Careful Handling

Many of the beautiful plants that we want around us are dangerous. They contain elements that irritate the skin or that may even be poisonous to the touch. Above all, allergy sufferers must take special care. But do not let this ruin the joy you take in such plants. It is just a matter of dealing with them properly:

- Wear rubber gloves and, above all, avoid getting any plant juices into eyes, mouth, or open wounds.
- If there are small children in the home, it is best to avoid dangerous plants until the children are old enough to understand the dangers.
- Pets, too, are not always as clever as we think. Cats and birds love to nibble on green plants, and, unfortunately, now and then on poisonous ones.

Sometimes only particular varieties or species need special caution; at other times, an entire plant family. In some plants, the irritants are confined to certain parts, while in others the whole plant is poisonous.

 All poisonous plants are marked with the death's-head symbol in the plant portraits.

Plants containing skin irritants
All *Euphorbiaceae* contain varying concentrations of whitish sap that irritate the skin. To this family belong such much-loved plants as poinsettia (*Euphorbia pulcherrima*), Christ plants (*Euphorbia milii*), croton (*Codiaeum variegatum*), and acalypha (*Acalypha*).

If plants are wounded, a bit of the latex gets onto the skin easily. This may produce eczema.

Some of the *Araceae* found among houseplants also contain a poisonous sap, for example

> ### First aid in case of poisoning
>
> - If children have swallowed parts of a plant, you must find a doctor at once—even if no symptoms have yet appeared. Take the plant with you, or note its botanical name.
>
> - If you become ill, it is best to go to a clinic right away. Take along specimens of the broken plant or, in case of diarrhea, of the feces, along with the suspect plant.
>
> - Should immediate medical attention be unavailable, you must stimulate vomiting (by putting a finger down your throat). Give children a drink of warm water.
>
> - Never drink milk. It binds the fatty poisons and encourages the body to take up more poison.
>
> - Many cities have poison centers. Check the telephone book or call the police emergency number.
>
> - Keep calm and give as precise information as possible about the kind and timing of the poisoning.

dieffenbachia (*Dieffenbachia*), Chinese evergreen (*Aglaonema*), flamingo flower (*Anthurium*), Swiss cheese plant (*Monstera deliciosa*), philodendron (*Philodendron*), and calla lily (*Zantedeschia*). Seeping out of cuts, this sap causes major swellings and acute pain on the mucous membrane of mouth and throat, and produces conjunctivitis and changes of the cornea in the eye.

Amaryllis-like plants (*Liliaceae*), too, contain sap that can produce nausea, vomiting, and diarrhea. Well-known representatives of this family are the tulip, narcissus, hyacinth, amaryllis, and clivia.

- Always wash your hands thoroughly if plant injuries have let sap or cell juices ooze out.
- Do not rub your eyes while working with these plants.

Plants with poisonous parts
Known for their poisonous qualities are the *Solanaceae*. Among many others, these include *Browallia*, *Brunfelsia*, *Capsicum*, and *Solanum pseudocapsicum*. Its orange-colored berries, like those of clivia, are particularly dangerous for children, who often cannot resist temptation and put the fruit in their mouths. The berries produce nausea, vomiting, and stomach pains, followed by sleepiness and widening of the pupils. Most cases of plant poisoning are caused by *Solanum pseudocapsicum*.

PLACEMENT AND PURCHASE

Many plants, such as roses and cacti, can defend themselves very well. Palms, too—for example, the Mediterranean palm—protect themselves with thorns. Caution is advised!

The stems of Mediterranean palms (Chamaerops humilis) *are covered with thorns.*

Also extremely dangerous are the *Apocynaceae.* Popular representatives of this family are oleander (*Nerium oleander*), *Allamanda, Carissa, Catharanthus roseus, Dipladenia,* and Madagascar palms (*Pachypodium*). These plants taste very bitter and initially cause nausea. They contain substances that affect the functioning of the heart, but are dangerous only if a large number of blooms or leaves are eaten. Just the same, be very careful around this plant family—especially with children. Although one seldom makes contact with the subterranean portions of these plants, it is important to know whether it is necessary to look out for poisonous substances when repotting. It is life-threatening for children to eat the

tubers of *Gloriosa superba* or *Colchicum autumnale.*

Plants that cause allergies

An allergy to primulas can be very troublesome. People with such an allergy may experience irritation or skin infections at the lightest contact with *Primula abconica* (and even more so with *Primula malacoides*). Secretions from the fine hairs on the leaves and stems of this species cause extreme reactions in many people. Primulas are not poisonous, however. A similar material is contained in the corms of *Cyclamen persicum,* but one usually doesn't come into contact with these.

Injuries from plants

Nature has given certain plants

very effective defenses, equipping them with thorns, prickles, and sharp ends.

Everyone will have experienced how painful cactus thorns in the skin can be. Yucca, as well as many species of agave and aloe, have hard points on their leaves that produce skin abrasions and wounds if you bump into them while repotting, or are not careful enough when moving the plants. Children playing near them can hurt themselves seriously—for example, by getting the sharp points in their eyes.

Poisonous Plants at a Glance

Adenium obesum

Plants dangerous to pets

Plants that endanger humans can also be dangerous to our pets. That is true of cats, dogs, caged birds, rabbits, hamsters, guinea pigs—any pets that roam freely in the home. If cats are not allowed outdoors every day to satisfy their need for grass, they will begin to nibble the houseplants, including the poisonous ones. It is wrong to believe that animals know instinctively what is good for them and what is not. Always put a bowl of cat grass on the windowsill for your room tigers. They love to nibble on umbrella sedge, which does not endanger them, and

The strongest poisons in the world are produced by plants. A particularly poisonous specimen is the *Adenium obesum*, which belongs to the *Apocynaceae* family. It is absolutely essential to avoid contact with its latex.

There are plants that are poisonous in all their parts, others that have only poisonous leaves or fruits, and still others that contain poisonous latex. The table below lists the best-known house, balcony, and container plants, and directs attention to their dangerous parts.

Botanical Name	English Name	Dangerous Parts
Acalypha hispida	Acalypha	Latex
Adenium obesum	Adenium	Latex
Ageratum houstonianum	Ageratum	All parts
Aglaonema	Chinese evergreen	All parts
Allamanda cathartica	Allamanda	All parts
Alocasia	Alocasia	All parts
Anthurium scherzerianum	Flamingo flower	All parts
Asparagus	Asparagus	Berries
Aucuba japonica	Aucuba	Berries
Begonia semperflorens hybrids	Wax begonia hybrids	All parts
Browallia	Browallia	All parts
Brunfelsia	Brunfelsia	All parts
Buxus sempervirens	Box	Leaves
Capsicum annuum	Red pepper	All parts
Carissa macrocarpa	Natal palm	All parts, except fruits
Cassia	Cassia	All parts
Catharanthus roseus	Catharanthus	All parts
Cestrum	Cestrum	All parts
Clivia miniata	Clivia/Kafir lily	All parts, particularly berries
Codiaeum variegatum	Leaf croton	Latex
Colchicum autumnale	Autumn crocus	All parts
Convallaria majalis	Lily of the valley	Berries
Cycas revoluta	Sago palm	All parts
Cytisus	Broom	All parts
Datura	Angel's trumpet	All parts
Dieffenbachia	Dieffenbachia	All parts
Dipladenia	Dipladenia	All parts

which is sufficiently robust to constantly replace the damage with new shoots. Prickly specimens also hurt animals. Chasing flies at a window has netted many a cat prickles instead of booty. The small wounds often need many weeks to heal.

Dogs, too, get hurt—for example, by the points of agaves. Because both dogs and cats will drink any water, they are also endangered by plant remedies and fertilizers that have been dissolved in leftover plant water.

As every pet owner knows, cats love plants and need greens for their digestion. Outdoors, they eat grass, but inside, if no cat grass is available, they occasionally attack houseplants.

No danger for Pussy—grape ivy (Cissus rhombifolia) *is not poisonous.*

Botanical Name	English Name	Dangerous Parts
Euphorbia milii	Euphorbia	Latex
Gloriosa superba	Glory lily	Tubers
Haemanthus	Blood lily	Bulbs
Hedera helix	English Ivy	Berries and leaves
Heliotropium arborescens	Heliotrope	All parts
Hippeastrum	Amaryllis	All parts
Hoya	Wax plant	All parts
Hyacinthus	Hyacinth	Bulbs
Iris	Iris	All parts
Jathropha podagrica	Nettle spurge	All parts
Lantana	Lantana	All parts
Lathyrus odoratus	Sweet pea	Seeds
Lilium	Lily	Bulbs
Lonicera	Honeysuckle	Berries
Monstera deliciosa	Swiss cheese plant	All parts
Narcissus	Narcissus	Bulbs
Nerium oleander	Oleander	All parts
Pachypodium	Pachypodium	Stem and leaves
Petunia	Petunia	All parts
Philodendron	Philodendron	All parts
Primula obconica	Primrose	All parts
Ricinus communis	Castor bean	Seeds
Senecio bicolor	Senecio	All parts
Solanum pseudocapsicum	Jerusalem cherry	All parts, especially berries
Trachelospermum jasminoides	Star jasmine	Latex
Tulip	Tulip	Bulbs
Zantedeschia	Calla lily	All parts

Tips for Buying Plants

Houseplants are available nowadays on nearly every street corner. All the buyer needs to do is choose. Nevertheless, we recommend that you purchase good-quality plants from a professional nursery. There you can assume that the plants will be healthy and cared for according to the needs of their species, and that the salespeople will be trained and qualified to advise you in your choice. As well, there are firms that specialize in certain groups of plants, such as orchids, bromeliads, palms, rain-forest plants, carnivorous plants, cacti and succulents, or container plants, and that will either sell plants on a cash-and-carry basis or ship them to you. Catalog sales are accompanied by some risks: you cannot choose the plant yourself and also can't be certain what it has experienced on its way to you. The various associations of plant lovers will be delighted to recommend reliable sources to you.

Good-quality summer flowers for the balcony, and annuals, are obtainable from weekly markets or directly from a garden center.

Good plant or bad?

Often, it is not easy to tell the quality of plants on offer. In addition to the general appearance of the plants, the outward circumstances in the nursery can be an important factor. Plants should be presented in clean pots, have clean leaves, and be labeled with brief instructions for care.

Here are a few tips on what to look out for when buying:
- The plant should be straight, have clean and firm leaves, and show new growth.
- Yellow or blotchy leaves and withered plant parts indicate pests. Turn over several leaves, as pests often hide underneath.
- Flowering plants should show many buds. Never buy fully blooming plants; they won't give you pleasure for long.
- Limp, shriveled leaves are usually a sign of lack of water. If the soil feels damp, however, this indicates root rot. In this event, do not buy the plant!
- Don't choose the biggest and cheapest plants. Younger, smaller plants adapt better and more quickly to a new environment.

Environmental conditions

Before buying a plant for house or balcony, be very clear about the living conditions you are able to offer it. For example, it makes no sense to seek a plant for a light, cool location when such a spot is not available. Before buying a container plant, you must also think about its winter placement.

PLANTS THAT CAN TOLERATE A DARK, COOL LOCATION IN WINTER: *Agapanthus praecox, Clerodendrum bungei, Erythrina crista galli, Haemanthys* hybrids, *Hedychium gardnerianum, Plumbago auriculata, Punica granatum.*

PLANTS NEEDING A LIGHT, COLD, WINTER LOCATION: *Acca sellowiana, Agave americana, Anisodontea capensis, Araucaria, Arbutus unedo, Callistemon, Chrysanthemum frutescens, Cistus, Cycas revoluta,* Hebe-Andersonii hybrids, *Laurus nobilis, Metrosideros excelsa, Nerium oleander, Tibouchina urvilleana, Viburnum tinus.*

PLANTS NEEDING A LIGHT, TEMPERATE, WINTER LOCATION: *Abutilon, Bougainvillea, Brugmansia, Cassia didymobotrya, Cestrum, Citrus limon, Cuphea ignea, Datura, Ensete, Fremontodendron californicum, Fuchsia, Hibiscus rosa-sinensis, Lantana Camara* hybrids, *Musa, Solanum rantonnetii, Tecomaria capensis, Tecomaria stans.*

PLANTS NEEDING A LIGHT, WARM LOCATION IN WINTER: All warmth-loving tropical houseplants.

Care immediately after purchase

Before plants reach your windowsill, they have endured a long, exhausting journey. In the greenhouses of plant nurseries they live in an ideal environment. Light, temperature, humidity, watering, fertilizer—all correspond to their optimal desires throughout the year. What a shock it is to be packed up, loaded into a truck or other means of transport, and stored in a wholesale gardener's warehouse. There, the flower dealers buy the green commodity, load it once more into cars, and place it in their warehouse or salesroom. Finally, you come along, have your plants wrapped, and transport the new purchase to your home. For the plants, all this means repeated changes in temperature and humidity, unaccustomed watering, and, possibly, lack of light. To overcome this stress requires much energy. Do not expect your new houseplant to demonstrate maximum growth performance or bud formation on the first day. Before that can happen, it must get used to its new environment.

Plants cope best with being moved in the spring or early summer. At this time, there is the least difference between the greenhouse atmosphere, outside temperatures, and conditions at home. Do not buy expensive houseplants in the winter, and

On page 376 we list some gardening firms, several of them specializing in certain groups of plants. The selection makes no claim to completeness, nor can we assume any responsibility for the quality of the supplies.

PLACEMENT AND PURCHASE

especially never from outdoor sales stands or weekly markets. Should a winter purchase be unavoidable, the plant must be carefully wrapped in many layers of newspaper and taken home by the quickest route. Unpack it immediately so that it gets air again and can spread out. To acclimatize plants, give them an initial location that is light but not too warm.

Summer flowers for the balcony and patio, which are offered very early in spring, were also started in a greenhouse and cannot put up very well with cool spring air and hot sunshine. Plant your boxes, but place your flower decorations in a spot protected from the wind and sun for several days.

Check the soil before reaching for the watering can. Too much moisture around the roots increases the plant's stress level. Only when the root ball is dry should you water thoroughly. Exactly when it is necessary to start fertilizing also cannot be determined precisely. If new shoots do not appear after about two weeks, put some liquid fertilizer in the watering can.

In garden centers and well-run florists, plants experience an optimal environment, with the correct temperature, light, and humidity.

A large variety of house, balcony, and container plants is available from garden centers and florists.

Plants with Particular Needs

Some like it hot and dry, others cool and damp. Some grow on the ground, others on trees. Among houseplants, there are many "specialists." These include bromeliads, ferns, orchids, palms, succulents, and cacti.

In the plant realm, there are several groups that need special care. Their "extra wants" result from their fight for survival—the necessity of adapting to extreme conditions in their natural environment over a long evolutionary period. At this point, we will only comment on some general peculiarities. Further information, and departures from the rule, can be found in the plant portraits.

Bromeliads

Bromeliads are plants from the tropical and subtropical regions of Latin America. They are divided into epiphytes and ground bromeliads. All bromeliads have poorly developed root balls and therefore need only small, shallow pots. They cannot tolerate calcium and so must be potted in calcium-free potting mix and watered with decalcified, or soft, water. Bromeliads, as a rule, are watered from the top and supplied with liquid fertilizer. Note, however, that they do not tolerate inorganic fertilizers very well; using them easily leads to salinization of the potting mix. Bromeliads with a rosette-like growth should always have water in their funnels.

These plants like a light, warm location. In addition, tree bromeliads need high humidity. Species with soft leaves cannot tolerate full sunshine.

Ferns

Ferns thrive in all climatic zones where things can grow. All of them tolerate only calcium-free water and potting mix with a high organic content. Most ferns from tropical regions do best if given year-round temperatures of 65–75°F (18–24°C), a light location without direct sun, and very high humidity. The root balls should always be moist but not wet. Ferns are sensitive to salt and should therefore only be given organic fertilizer in a weak concentration. Because their roots generally grow horizontally, choose pots that are shallow and wide rather than deep and narrow.

Orchids

Orchids are among the most treasured plants, but they also make up the most numerous plant family. Around 90 percent originate in the hot regions of the tropics; the remainder are from cooler regions. (Local indigenous orchids are not suitable as houseplants.) Among orchids, as among bromeliads and ferns, there is a distinction between earth-dwelling species and those that live on trees. Epiphyte orchids are more often chosen as houseplants.

Orchids need a special soil medium, may only be given decalcified water, and grow in special pots. Dark pots are unsuitable because they heat up too quickly, which doesn't suit the roots. Like all plants with storage organs, orchids need a rest period.

Their location must be light, and have even warmth and high humidity. Watering them requires the famous "green thumb." The medium must feel dry before orchids are given more water.

Palms

Palms live in all the tropical and subtropical zones of the world. They grow in most rain forests, in the higher, cooler regions of the Andes and Himalayas, on sunny beaches, and in oases.

Bromeliad: Neoregelia *hybrid*

Fern: Blechnum brasiliense

Orchid: Paphiopedilum *hybrid*

PLACEMENT AND PURCHASE

All palms have fronds that grow from a single point. They are divided into two groups depending on the shape of their fronds: pinnate or palmate. The species that have thick stems (long or short) or numerous thin stems are those most often cultivated as houseplants.

Palms grow in the greatest variety of soils, and there are no strict guidelines for the potting mixture. Exotic palms thrive on a compost-based mix. The commercial growers also offer special palm mix. The container must be deep. Demand for nutrients and moisture varies; in all cases, the water should be as soft as possible.

Room palms need a light but only partially sunny location. They can take unsatisfactory lighting conditions for a time, but die if permanently placed in a dark corner.

Normal room temperatures are fine. Placing palms on a balcony or patio in the summer, so long as it is sheltered from wind and rain, has a beneficial effect on growth.

Succulents

Hardly any plant group reveals so many varied, sometimes bizarre, types of plant structure, leaves, and flowers as the succulents. Most succulents are at home in the dry regions of Africa and the Americas where the sun is strong—that is, in regions where it rains only a few weeks in the year. To withstand the dry periods as well as possible, the plants have developed several adaptations. They usually have a branched, flat, root system that grows just below the surface of the earth so that every small drop of water is accessible. To reduce evaporation, the leaves are either thickly covered with fine hairs or a web of thin fibers, wrapped in a protective layer, or closely packed together so as to minimize the unprotected surface area. The skin of the leaves is often leathery and thick. As well, these plants can store a great deal of water in their tissues. The potting mix must, above all, be extremely porous and at least one-third sand. Plastic pots and bowls have proved to be very good.

Full sunlight, high temperatures, and dry air create an ideal environment for these plants. Between heavy watering, the soil should become fairly dry. Use specialized fertilizer.

Cacti

Botanists classify cacti among the succulents. All cacti must be given soft water and demand a special potting mix (available commercially). They require few nutrients, but must be provided with special cactus fertilizer. Cacti grow in almost any kind of container. Desert cacti absolutely require a sunny location; epiphytes should be placed in a light spot with only occasional direct sun. Humid air suits none of the cacti. In the summer, normal room temperatures are fine, but during the rest period it must be cooler. The annual rest periods should be respected. Water desert cacti in the summer when the soil feels dry—but then water thoroughly. During their rest period, the plants need hardly any water. Fertilize lightly during the growing season.

The natural environmental conditions of plants cannot really be reproduced in a home. Nevertheless, their surroundings and their care should approach these conditions as closely as possible.

Palm: Chrysalidocarpus lutescens

Succulent: Haworthia baccata

Cactus: Lobivia tiegeliana

WHAT YOU SHOULD

NOW ABOUT PLANTS

Plants from all corners of the world come together on our windowsills, balconies, and patios. Hundreds of years ago, the first specimens were brought to Europe from faraway lands by explorers and adventurers. Studying the life of these plants is fascinating to botanists and, above all, to gardeners who love to experiment.

This chapter—a brief excursion into botany—will introduce you to the different plant habitats, the variety of plant forms, and the structure of plants.

Conditions in their native habitat determine the form of plants. Succulence, here illustrated by ice plant (Delosperma) and Aloe mariothii, is a matter of life and death in their South African homeland. The Christmas cactus has blooms that are particularly adapted for fertilization by hovering hummingbirds.

A Brief History of Plants

Where should treasured tropical and subtropical specimens be placed when introduced to cooler climates? Originally, orangeries were used for this purpose, but these were soon followed by greenhouses built of glass. Nowadays, a terrarium will allow you to keep some exotic jungle plants in your living room.

As often happens, when it is a matter of tracing the origin of anything European, the history of houseplants and container gardening leads us back to ancient Egypt. The desire to decorate the home with plants depends on a well-developed domestic culture. While the tribal peoples north of the Mediterranean were still living in caves and hovels, the rich, the mighty, and the beautiful along the shores of the Nile already inhabited solidly built houses and palaces. In Egyptian works of art dating back about 3000 years, we can see small trees and shrubs planted in stone vases and troughs. We may assume that for many thousands of years BCE, sophisticated, ancient societies in other parts of the world also hit on this notion of displaying plants in containers.

In continental Europe, it was the societies of ancient Greece and Rome that first set a high value on a civilized lifestyle. The Greeks and Romans decorated their houses, built around a central atrium, with tub plants, using plants from their own surroundings. These were brought into their central courtyards and used to decorate their rooms. It was not until the fifteenth century, when daring explorers in the pay of southern European kings and merchants sailed the world's oceans in tall ships and discovered new continents, that the first botanical treasures from distant parts reached the Old World along with other kinds of rarities. Of the few plants that survived the journey, some adapted well to the mild climate of Southern Europe.

Even then, however, European botanists recognized that most plants from tropical regions would need special protection, and so brought them indoors. How long these very first "houseplants" survived is not known.

Over the next centuries, the exotic flora of Asia, Africa, and South America (and, no doubt, other booty as well) lured more and more men, hungry for adventure, on uncomfortable and often dangerous journeys through distant lands. Courageous explorers and curious botanists, God-fearing missionaries and fearless soldiers of fortune sallied forth as "plant hunters." Whereas the conquistadors of earlier centuries generally came from Italy, Spain, and Portugal, the plant hunters and collectors were mostly English, French, and German.

Houses for exotic plants

But where, in cool central Europe, could the tender imported plants be kept? Initially, the problem was solved by building them their own houses. In the late sixteenth century, and increasingly in the seventeenth century, European potentates had "plant houses" constructed for reasons of interest or prestige. The first, called "orangeries," sheltered mostly orange trees and other citrus trees, palms, and fig trees. Many botanical gardens, too, gradually acquired plant houses. Before long, wealthy private citizens also wanted to surround themselves with beautiful plants. The solidly built orangeries gave way to more lightly constructed greenhouses and conservatories.

Plant container with an epiphyte branch

WHAT YOU SHOULD KNOW ABOUT PLANTS

The gardens of Versailles are world famous.

Many exotic plants can survive in our latitudes only in containers, because they have to spend the winter in a sheltered room. In Versailles, for example, one can admire an entire parade of container plants during the summer months.

The Wardian case

Exotic plants soon became extremely desirable property. Their transport to Europe, however, still presented almost insurmountable difficulties. Plants tended to dry out or rot in their moldy shipping crates during the long months at sea, and only a few specimens reached their destination in relatively undamaged condition. These were guarded like precious treasures, and were priced accordingly.

In the first third of the nineteenth century, an accidental discovery by an English physician, Dr. Nathaniel Ward, led to the ideal "packaging" for transporting plants. Ward cared little about plants; his hobby was butterflies. He usually set his caterpillars to pupate on a layer of soil in closed glass containers. One such enclosed glass container lay in a corner, forgotten, for months.

When it came to light once more, a small fern was growing in the soil. Dr. Ward, interested as he was in natural phenomena, discovered that the moisture from the soil had evaporated, condensed on the inside of the glass, and, when cooled, trickled down once more into the soil. As a result, the tiny fern always had enough moisture to develop. Using this principle, not only were containers for the transport of plants constructed in artful designs, but large "Wardian cases," as big as tallboys, soon graced the salons of European high society. Because they were usually planted with ferns, they became known as "ferneries."

Nowadays, we use closed glass containers, called "terrariums," that operate on the same principle.

The cultivation of houseplants

Dealing in plants became a lucrative business. Soon imports ceased to be the sole source of supply; these highly prized specimens were cultivated and interbred in large nurseries. The invention of central heating made it possible to maintain the necessary temperatures in greenhouses even during the winter months. Many of the varieties of indoor plants we know today are already 100 or 200 years old. The long winters, without either bright flowers or very much greenery, are probably the reason that the cultivation of houseplants primarily developed in Central and Northern Europe. Particularly in Germany and Holland, houseplants enjoyed ever-greater popularity.

By the first half of the twentieth century, the use of houseplants had come to be taken for granted.

Native Habitat and Plant Types

If properly cared for, the plants presented in this book will live in our homes for many years, or at least for an entire summer.

Almost all of them hail from distant climatic zones. Even if they have been cultivated in temperate climates for a long time, they have remained "exotics." To be able to care for these plants appropriately, it is important to know something about their home environment.

Tropical plants

The belt that encircles the globe between the Tropic of Cancer and the Tropic of Capricorn, and is divided by the equator, is known as the tropics. About 40 percent of the earth's surface lies in this region, which contains great variations in climatic conditions and in vegetation. The tropical regions can be roughly divided into rain forests, mountain forests, savannas, steppes, and deserts. What all tropical climates have in common is the absence of seasonal changes and the equal amounts of day and night—twelve hours of each. Climatic conditions change gradually from one place to another, and plants of any one family or genus will also penetrate these imaginary boundaries.

TROPICAL RAIN FORESTS. These equatorial forests are steaming hot during the day and cool down considerably at night. It rains very often, and the humidity is at least 90 percent. Under the thick canopy created by giant trees, the light gets gradually dimmer as one approaches the forest floor.
• houseplants that stem from tropical forests never go into dormancy, a condition induced in plants from other climatic zones by seasonal fluctuations in light and temperature. Nonetheless, rain-forest plants do reduce their metabolic activity during our winters, when the duration of daylight is short. These plants do not like direct sun, and need high humidity.

TROPICAL MOUNTAIN FORESTS. The climate of the tropical mountains is characterized by lots of rain and mist, the cooler temperatures that go with higher altitudes, and powerful sun rays.
• Plants from these regions need plenty of light, high humidity, and a cool location.

SAVANNAH AND STEPPES. Typical for these parts of the tropics are alternating rainy and dry seasons, poor, porous soil, high temperatures, and strong sun.
• Many succulents come from savannas or steppes. To care for them in our window boxes we must first of all ensure that they have the dry periods and low level of nutrients to which they are accustomed.

DESERTS. Relatively few plants have adapted to the extreme conditions offered by the desert environment. The temperature between day and night can vary by as much as 90° F (50° C). There is hardly any rain. A little dew in the morning is often the only moisture available for months on end.
• Desert plants need very little water, but a great deal of sun and heat. In addition, we must offer the plants definite rest periods during which they should be kept dry and, usually, cooler.

Subtropical plants

The regions between the tropics and the temperate zones are known as the subtropics. These areas extend to about the thirty-fifth or fortieth parallel (North and South). The length of days and the amount of precipitation vary from season to season, but the difference in temperatures between summer and winter is not as extreme in the subtropics as in the temperate zones. The rainy season comes either in the summer (as in New Zealand or Chile) or in the winter months (as in the Mediterranean regions and California). Subtropical regions, too, include a number of climatic variants: forests, cooler mountain areas, and desert-like plains.

In horticultural parlance, plants may be classified into two major categories according to their temperature requirements: "coldhouse" plants and "hothouse" plants. In the coldhouse, it is warm in summer, and cool, but above freezing, in winter. In the hothouse it is around 68°F (20°C) all year, and humid.

Hardy or not?

The concept of hardiness must be seen in the context of native habitat. It goes without saying that many plants from warm regions would not be able to survive the cold season in the temperate zones, and so would be "not hardy" there. Some convergence is possible, however. In regions with especially mild winters—for example, the wine-growing regions—more robust denizens of the Mediterranean and other subtropical areas of the world can survive outdoors if their roots are covered with an insulating layer of mulch in winter. But there are limits to this winter hardiness in the case of container plants. Their root area is much less protected. Frost can penetrate from all directions. It is therefore essential to wrap the entire container with some insulating material. "Hardy" is the term applied both to indigenous plants and to those that have become completely acclimatized.

What You Should Know about Plants

From the forests of Asia we get such plants as the cast iron plant (*Aspidistra*); from the East African Usambara mountains comes the common African violet (*Saintpaulia*), while the yucca is at home in the deserts of Mexico and the southern United States.

• Plants from the subtropics need their rest periods and—according to the rainfall in their native habitat—more or less water. They are used to variation between daytime and nighttime temperatures.

Plant types

The plant kingdom is immeasurably rich in the variety of its forms. True, relative to the extensive offerings of nature, only a few plant species have found their way into our living rooms; but they are enough to demonstrate the wealth of available forms, growth patterns, and lifestyles.

WOODY PLANTS. These are defined as those whose shoots harden in their first year. Woody plants become older than any other plants. Some specimens, true giants, have witnessed several hundred or even several thousand years. Among the woody plants, we also count the shrubs, which are equally capable of attaining a venerable old age. These plants are perennials. Some woody plants drop their leaves every year (deciduous plants) whereas others do not (evergreens). In the latter category we find some of the most beloved houseplants, such as Norfolk Island pine (*Araucaria*), coralberry (*Ardisia*), bougainvillea, camellia, citrus trees, figs (*Ficus*), silk oak (*Grevillea robusta*), schefflera, and indoor linden (*Sparmannia*). These plants never

Plants need rest periods

Many plants cease to grow for a few weeks every year and enter a sort of hibernation. The technical term for this is "dormancy." Plants native to the cooler parts in the northern hemisphere will enter dormancy in the period when there is little sun and it is cold—i.e., between November and the beginning of March.

Plants indigenous to other climates will often choose the dry season to put their economy on the back burner. Their rest period does not necessarily coincide with the northern winter: winter in the southern hemisphere comes during the northern summer. During dormancy, plants want to stay cool, are watered little, and are never fertilized. Many herbaceous perennials, bulbs, and tubers reduce their foliage, and some drop all their leaves. This is a totally natural process.

If plants are not allowed to rest, this will have a negative effect on the quantity of flowers, on growth in the following spring, and on their general development.

Plants without a clear-cut dormant period also pass through several different metabolic phases in the course of a year. The growth phase usually begins in the spring and is easily identified by the formation of new shoots and leaves. These signal that a more intensive program of care is called for—that is, more frquent watering and fertilizing— because the plant now needs many more nutrients to give it strength to grow.

reach their full size in containers, but, with good care, they can last for decades.

SUBSHRUBS. The new shoots of the so-called subshrubs remain soft and, in temperate latitudes, generally die back in the winter. Older parts of the plant will turn woody and continue to produce new shoots. These plants, too, are classified as perennials. Many subshrubs are found on our windowsills—for example, the flowering maple (*Abutilon*), copperleaf (*Acalypha*), ti-plant (*Cordyline*), shrimp plant (*Beloperone*), and leadwort (*Plumbago*).

HERBACEOUS PERENNIALS. In the temperate zones, all above-ground parts of perennials die back every fall, and the rootstock generates a new plant in the spring.

Perennial houseplants come from warmer regions of the world and remain green all year long—for example, elephant's ears (*Caladium*), umbrella sedge (*Cyperus*), and wandering Jew or spiderwort (*Tradescantia*). The perennials on the window ledge also include bulbs such as amaryllis (*Hippeastrum*), and "tuberous plants" such as cyclamen, which eventually lose their above-ground parts and then grow fresh ones within a few months. All these perennials can grow quite old, even as pot plants.

ANNUALS AND BIENNIALS. Many of our summer flowers are annuals. They germinate, grow, flower, and form finished seeds in a single year, then die. Biennials are plants that germinate and grow in the first year, and bloom, bear fruit, and die in the second. Many flowering container plants belong in this category.

The Structure of a Plant

No matter how different our various houseplants may look, they still share certain basic structural features. All consist of a part that is above ground—the stem on which leaves and flowers grow—and a part that is below ground—the root.

Habit (growth form)

Plants can be classified into large categories based on their "habit" or growth form. Many succulents develop rosette-like structures—for example, the African violet (*Saintpaulia*) and the *Siderasis*. Their grassy growth form characterizes both sedge (*Carex*) and sweet flag (*Acorus*). Cupid's bower (*Achimenes*) and diverse ferns share a bushy form. *Calathea* and many cacti share an upright growth form. A tree-like habit is demonstrated by most species of *Ficus* and by Norfolk Island pine (*Araucaria*). Devil's ivy (*Epipremnum*), varieties of grape ivy (*Cissus*), hanging fuchsias (*Fuchsia*), and Swedish ivy (*Plectranthus*) are all climbers.

Stem axis (stem)

The stem axis or stem of plants is usually cylindrical and is divided into internodes and, at points where the leaves emerge, nodes. The stem can be branched or single, thick or thin, soft or woody. Within it run the vessels that carry water and nutrients from the roots to the leaves and flowers. Stems are flexible, can twist and turn. This enables them to ensure that the leaves are always in an advantageous position with respect to the available light.

Leaves

Leaves, or more accurately, foliage leaves, are usually flat, green plant parts in which the life-sustaining functions of photosynthesis and respiration (→ page 37) take place. A leaf consists of the blade, with its network of veins, and the leafstalk, or petiole. Leaves come in the most varied shapes, colors, and sizes. Some houseplants are kept solely for the sake of their leaves and, if correctly grouped, create a colorful and interesting picture on the windowsill. If a plant loses its leaves for reasons other than natural ones, it is unable to build up its reserve of nutrients and dies.

Flowers

Flowers serve as agents of reproduction. They carry the plant's reproductive organs: the female egg cells and the male pollen. Whether they are gorgeous, showy, and huge or tiny and modest, whether their colors are garish or the most tender pastels, whether they give off an intoxicating fragrance or smell rank, flowers have only one thing in mind: sex. For fertilization, flowers often need insects, which they attract with their colors and perfumes. Wasps, bees, and other insects carry pollen from flower to flower and "lose" it on the stigma. Sometimes the wind helps out as well, carrying the desired pollen to the flowers.

A flower will typically consist of sepals, petals, stamens, and pistils, in which the ovules reside. Where several blossoms are united, we speak of an inflorescence. Flowering is the third stage, after germination and growth, leading to the ultimate goal of the plant, the ripening of seeds. Plants will produce as many flowers as they need to guarantee their reproduction. Once enough flowers have been fertilized, the plant stops blooming. All its energy is now used to develop fruit and seeds. House and balcony gardeners shamelessly exploit this purposeful design of nature. By removing wilted blooms, and usually fertilized ones as well, the gardener forces the plant to continue to set new buds. During this period, flowering plants need a lot of fertilizer to be able to take the stress.

Seeds and fruit

The seed is that part of the plant formed after its ovules have been fertilized. It consists of a rough shell, the seed coat, the embryo, and some stored nutrients for the embryo's initial needs. Seeds can be as big as a head or as tiny as a dust particle, and can appear singly or in large numbers. Some are scattered by the wind; others need animals to disseminate them. Those carried by the wind are generally light and equipped with some form of extension, such as fine hairs or wings. Seeds distributed by animals are often wrapped in a brilliant, juicy covering to stimulate the animal's appetite.

Houseplants seldom have a chance to form seeds. For one thing, insects are missing; for another, special weather conditions are required to ripen fruits.

Roots

Roots serve to anchor the plant in the soil, to channel water and nutrients into the plant, and to store nutrient reserves. For the latter purpose, certain root parts develop into specialized storage organs, such as tubers, bulbs, and fleshy root swellings called rootstocks or rhizomes.

WHAT YOU SHOULD KNOW ABOUT PLANTS

This imaginary plant combines many flower, leaf, and root forms. Naturally, it only shows a fraction of the manifold ways plants can shape their leaves, flowers, subterranean organs, and fruits. This great variety of forms evolved because plants, tied to a single location, had to adapt as best they could to their native habitat and its prevailing conditions (climate, light, pollinating agents, and so forth).

Plants are limitlessly inventive.

AND PROPAGATION

All plants with which we surround ourselves in our home are forced to grow artificially in pots, boxes, and tubs, far from their natural locations. They can only survive with our help.

In this chapter you will learn about the needs of house, balcony, and container plants, how to fertilize and water them correctly, when they need repotting, how they are propagated, how to get them through your vacation, what to do when pests or diseases strike, and much else.

After each major topic there is an illustrated how-to section, showing the various tasks, pests, or diseases.

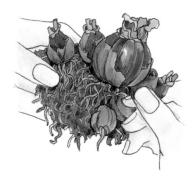

Whether it's a matter of planting, repotting, or propagation—when you know how to do it, success is virtually assured.

Tools and Growth Factors

When houseplants have an appropriate location, good light, and optimal care, they will grow as tall as their internal growth program permits. These magnificent *Dracaenas* have nearly reached the ceiling.

Tools

Like all work, the care of plants demands good tools. The basic tool kit for the house and balcony gardener consists of:
- hand-held rake
- trowel
- hand-held cultivator
- hand-held digging fork
- small watering can (0.25–0.5 gal. (1–2 L)) with a long, narrow spout for bushy plants
- watering can with a measuring scale (makes it easier to give correct doses when fertilizing)
- pump can with a long, bent spout, to reach hanging plants
- watering can with a filter, to prepare water
- spray gun
- all-purpose gardening scissors
- sharp knife
- household scissors
- gardening gloves
- florist wire
- raffia
- string
- wood and bamboo stakes in various lengths
- charcoal powder for disinfecting cuts
- various fertilizers for different plant species
- various potting mixtures and supplements for different plant species
- various plant containers
- large plastic bucket for mixing soils
- water softener, if required
- plant lights, if the locations are too dark
- systems for vacation and long-term watering
- platform with wheels for large plants
- transport aids (wheelbarrows) for container plants
- connector for a garden hose near the terrace

- Tools must be cleaned thoroughly after every use.
- Old pots that are reused must be washed thoroughly for hygienic and aesthetic reasons.
- Cleaning agents that add a shine to leaves are not advised. It is enough to dust the plants and wash them off carefully with a soft, damp cloth.

Growth and care factors

Four factors determine the well-being of our houseplants:

LIGHT is the source of energy for the complicated process of photo-synthesis. Every plant has its own light requirements, which must be taken into account when choosing a location. Too much light is as harmful as too little.

WARMTH is another important growth factor. It stimulates the intake of nutrients and growth itself, and promotes soil fertility. Plants from the tropical rain forests love round-the-clock warmth. Tropical mountain-dwellers, including many orchids, are used to night temperatures that fall a few degrees, and therefore are happy if we turn the heat down on winter nights. Mediterranean species, too, must be given a cooler placement when the shorter days begin. One thing is important for all plants: warm earth. The ground heat should never fall below room temperature. "Cold feet" are as damaging to the health of our green guests as to our own. Those with under-floor heating will discover how their tropical plants, in particular, thrive mightily. Because more heat (and light) means that more water is used, it is important to water often in light locations with high temperatures,

and to water more sparingly in cool areas.

AIR, in conjunction with humidity and air temperature, is an important growth factor. Plants breathe through tiny pores in the leaves, taking in carbon dioxide, splitting it, and releasing oxygen. Plant roots, too, need air, which is contained in the small cavities in loose soil.

WATER is the means of transport that moves the nutrients through the vascular system of a plant. Water requirements are very different from one plant to the next and also depend on the time of year, the temperature, and the illumination. Here, too, it is important to determine the right quantity—but it is always better to keep plants a bit on the dry side, rather than to drown them. Plants with big, soft leaves evaporate a great deal of moisture from their surfaces and are therefore pretty thirsty.

NUTRIENTS are taken in through the root organs of plants. The needs and "appetites" of species are very different. Some require more nitrogen, others more phosphorus. Here, too, it is a matter of the right quantity at the right time. Too much feeding is often as damaging as too little.

Picture to the right: Dracaena *as a container plant*

Light: Growth Factor Number One

Plants experience light intensity quite differently from humans. Only close to a window is it light enough for them. Even 6 or 7 feet (2 m) away from the light source, it is already too dark. However, this deficiency can be overcome with plant lights.

Without light there would be no plants. Light is the energy source that, with the help of chlorophyll in the leaves and stems, turns carbon dioxide into carbohydrates (sugar, starch). This process is called photosynthesis (→ page 37). The amount of light that houseplants need for this work varies considerably, depending on the species and the living conditions to which their native location has accustomed them.

Light intensity

Plants immediately next to a window receive the full measure of light—that is, 100 percent. But even 3 feet (1 m) from the window, the light intensity is only 50–80 percent, depending on window size. At a distance of six to seven feet (2 m) the light intensity falls to about 25 percent, at 10 feet (3 m) to about 10 percent. Expressed mathematically, this means that the amount of light diminishes as a square of the distance from its source.

Light intensity is measured in lux.

To measure it we use a "lux" or light meter. At values between 700 and 1000 lux, plants can only just survive (for a while, at least) and, accordingly, they look pathetic. From 2500 lux, growth normalizes, and from 10,000 lux, no more damage is to be feared.

Light requirements

It is impossible to indicate the light requirements for every plant at all times of the year. The symbols in the plant portraits can serve as a guide: sunny, light, part-shade, shade.

The leaves of plants also serve as a clue. Plants with white- or yellow-variegated leaves and reddish or very dark leaves usually need more light (not direct sun) than do species with green foliage, because their leaves contain less chlorophyll. The smaller quantity of chlorophyll must do the same job as the larger amount in totally green leaves; to do this, more energy (i.e., light) is needed. If a plant with variegated leaves is placed in a dark location, it will

eventually turn green: that is, the leaves will produce more chlorophyll—a self-defense mechanism—because the greater amount of chlorophyll will enable it to do the necessary work with the smaller amount of light. Soft leaves usually indicate that the plants prefer a partially shady location. Plants that grow in hot, sunny areas and receive much light have, over time, evolved protection against both light and evaporation. Such plants include cacti that have no leaves at all; succulents with thick, fleshy leaves; and plants with leathery leaves (rubber tree), very small leaves (*Euphorbia milii*), gray-green leaves (*Ceropegia*), or very hairy leaves (*Kalanchoe* species).

Long- and short-day plants

In many species, the duration of daylight in their native habitat at particular times of the year has a great influence on their flowering. It is customary to distinguish between long-day and short-day plants.

The long-day plants only develop flowers if they receive more than twelve hours of daylight for a period of several weeks. Short-day plants can only tolerate twelve or fewer hours of daylight in their bud-forming time. The bud formation of the so-called day-neutral plants is not influenced by the duration of light.

In the greenhouse or at home, it is possible to fix the duration of light yourself with the help of special lamps that are commercially available. These lamps create good lighting conditions in unpromising places, or can brighten dark days.

The lighting conditions in a room are very uneven.

SUCCESSFUL CARE AND PROPAGATION

Light incidence and direction of growth

Plants have a very intimate relationship with light. Thus, several species are accustomed to a particular incidence of light. If their light requirements are not met, the plants shed buds and blooms. For plants that need a certain incidence of light to flower, one can put a light marker on the pot to ensure that they always face the same way in the period of bud formation. In contrast, other plants must be turned periodically, lest they grow lopsided by seeking the light.

Changes of lighting conditions should not be sudden. If you want to treat your houseplants to a time outdoors in the summer, do not put them into direct sun right away. Even on a windowsill the sunshine is sometimes too much for plants. Particularly around noon, sensitive species must be given shade.

Photosynthesis

Photosynthesis, primarily carried out by plants, is the basis for all life in this world. Simply put, this works in the following manner. Through tiny pores in the undersides of their leaves, plants absorb carbon dioxide and moisture from the air during daylight hours. Through their roots, they absorb water-soluble minerals. With these inorganic materials, however, plants cannot do anything. So, through a chemical process with several steps (referred to as fixation) they transform the carbon dioxide and minerals into organic materials (sugar and starch) with the help of chlorophyll. However, this "chemical factory" must be driven by energy, and the plant draws its energy from light (photosynthesis).

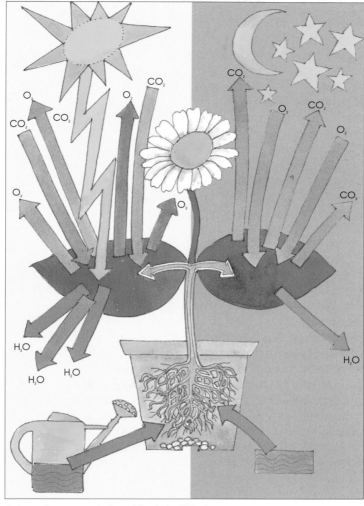

Schematic representation of the "plant" factory

Respiration

Carbon dioxide is continuously produced in large quantities. Humans and animals are constantly breathing it out, and every fire releases this gas. Just as large is the consumption of oxygen, which living beings breathe in, and without which no fire burns. The supply would soon be used up, were it not for plants.

The fixation of carbon dioxide taken from the air produces oxygen in the leaves—as a by-product.

At night, when the photo-synthesis factory is not working because light is absent, part of the accumulated materials are released. The plant now produces carbon dioxide and consumes oxygen (respiration).

Undoubtedly, plants enrich the room air with oxygen throughout the day, while lowering its carbon dioxide content. Yet photosynthesis is not nearly as strong indoors as it is outside.

The chemical processes in plants are uninterrupted. The most important are photosynthesis, respiration, and transpiration: During the day, carbon dioxide (CO_2) splits into carbon (C) and oxygen (O_2) and the latter is released. At night, on the other hand, plants breathe in oxygen and release carbon dioxide. Water (H_2O) is also taken in and partly evaporated, through the leaves—more during the day, under the influence of light and warmth, than at night when it is dark and cooler.

Light markers (see the picture, below) guarantee a constant incidence of light.

Light marker

Air and Temperature as Growth Factors

Relative humidity is very important for the well-being of plants. Higher humidity can be achieved by spraying or by increasing the evaporation surface.

The quality of the air, the percentage of moisture it contains, and temperature are additional important growth factors for plants.

Air quality

Plants need air to live, just as do all other living beings. Because leaves work continuously as large filters, one might assume that plants are indifferent to air quality. But this is false. Most growing things intensely dislike sticky, stuffy air (caused when they are placed too close together), drafts, and air polluted by exhaust fumes, smoke, or the vapor of wood preservatives or other chemicals.

Of course, there are exceptions. It has been determined that certain green plants, such as spider plants (*Chlorophytum comosum*), take in and transmute the poisonous fumes of formaldehyde. Formaldehyde is, among other things, the source of synthetic resin and various materials that bind, disinfect, and preserve, but it is also produced by incineration and can be found in automobile exhaust and cigarette smoke. The quantity processed by plants is so small, however, that polluted rooms cannot be purified properly by leaf mass alone.

Other plants, particularly trees and shrubs, are to some extent resistant to exhaust gases of all kinds. The nursery specialist speaks, in this connection, of industrial resistance. If the balcony or terrace opens onto a street with heavy traffic, it is advisable to ask for suitable plants when buying container plants.

Unsurpassed for toughness is the cast iron plant (*Aspidistra elatior*). It not only tolerates a dark, cool location, but also drafts and smoke. Aspidistras are, therefore,

Spraying: direct humidity

Evaporation: indirect humidity

often placed in gas stations, stores, and workshops.

Not only the leaves, but also the roots need air, or more precisely, oxygen. Often plants suffer because the soil becomes so dense in the course of time that only a little oxygen can reach the roots. You should loosen the top surface of the soil occasionally, but without damaging the roots.

Humidity

Relative humidity, closely linked with air, can be measured with a hygrometer. Depending on their origin, plants need very different amounts of humidity. A relative humidity that is comfortable for humans, animals, and plants lies between 60 and 70 percent.

From spring to fall these values

are easily reached in the temperate zone, for when rooms are unheated, less water is needed to achieve the required humidity than when they are very warm. Heated air is dry and often contains only between 40 and 50 percent relative humidity. At such values, it is absolutely necessary to raise the humidity artificially.

Humidifiers are available in a variety of forms, from electric models and room fountains to simple containers placed near radiators.

In order to give plants on a windowsill a better climate, one can arrange to have water evaporate near them. For this purpose, the plant containers may be placed in bowls or tubs filled with water and pebbles or clay granular. Another possibility is to put the flowerpots inside bigger pots, and fill the space between them with absorbent material that is kept moist constantly. The trade also offers special evaporating dishes that allow plants to rest on a grid above the water. The plant container itself must never touch the surface of the water, as roots that are constantly moist rot quickly. Most houseplants appreciate being showered with a fine spray, especially epiphytes, which take in a lot of water through their above-ground portions.

SUCCESSFUL CARE AND PROPAGATION

Temperature

Our room and balcony plants come from all climatic zones of the world. Some species are accustomed to high, constant, temperatures throughout the year, whereas others need the day and night temperatures to be different. It is obvious that you cannot simulate every desired climate zone in a single living room, but you can group plants with the same needs together, and influence their climate artificially.

AIR TEMPERATURE. Many plants adapt surprisingly well to different air temperatures. Plants can survive departures from the norm without damage if you allow for the fact that leaves evaporate more water on warm days than on cool ones, and continuously adjust the quantity of water to the temperature—that is, water more in warm weather and spray the leaves more often. Most plants are satisfied with temperatures of 68-75°F (18-24°C).

SOIL TEMPERATURE. The temperature of the soil has a great significance—something that is often overlooked. Warmth stimulates the microorganisms in the soil, encourages the roots to take up more nutrients and water, and initiates the process of growth. During the growing season the soil must never be allowed to cool down markedly, otherwise the activities necessary to life will be arrested.

Behind a pane of glass, sunshine can generate a lot of heat, causing plant leaves to evaporate a lot of moisture. However, the planting mix in the plant pot stays relatively cool because it is usually shaded by leaves. Indeed, the

Heating mat for potted plants

plant may get "cold feet," which causes the roots to reduce their activity and transport less water to the leaves than they require because of the high degree of evaporation. The result is that plants will droop even if the mix is moist.

No plant can tolerate cold in the root area. Electric heating mats provide the necessary soil heat. They are available in various sizes.

Many house plants are very glad to be outside in the summertime.

A summer break on the balcony or patio is like a vacation for many houseplants. However, you should only put the plants outside in late spring, and bring them indoors again when night temperatures fall to 50-54°F (10-12°C). Ensure that the wind cannot overturn them and that plants with water-sensitive leaves and limited thirst do not stand in the rain.

Life-Giving Water

Plants consist largely of water. Water serves them as a means of transport of nutrients and also keeps them upright.

Water as a means of transport

"Raw materials" are carried up through the roots to the "leaf factory"; the finished "products" are carried on up to the tips of the shoots so that new cells can form, and then either back to the roots (tuber, bulb, rhizome), as reserves for bad times, or to the flowers if fruits are developing there.

Plants that get too little water become limp, but too much water also makes the leaves hang. Their drooping appearance causes many plant lovers to reach for the watering can once more, thereby involuntarily increasing the damage. Too much water in the soil forces almost all the air out of the root area; but air is needed for the fine rootlets to absorb water. Thus, overwatering prevents the roots from delivering the necessary quantity of water to the leaves. One might almost say that the roots are drowning and the leaves are drying out.

How much water?

"... and how often must I water this plant?" are perhaps the questions most often asked at the time of purchase. There are no exact answers. Usually the instructions are confined to "generously," "moderately," and "sparingly," terms that describe only the most basic requirements.

Water "generously" means: The soil must always be moist. Only the surface may feel dry.

In cases where water requirements are "moderate," the top 0.8–1.2 in. (2–3 cm) should be allowed to dry before you reach for the watering can again. Water "sparingly" means that two-thirds of the soil may be allowed to dry. In this case, test the soil by carefully inserting a wooden shish-kebab skewer—damp earth will cling to it.

For every plant, the quantity of water depends on the time of year, the material and size of the plant container, the composition of the planting mix, and the local temperature, which may change from day to day. Watering requires sensitivity and some knowledge about the meaning and function of water in the life of plants.

Water temperature

Water temperature also plays an important role. Water should be at about the same temperature as the soil: room temperature, or around 68°F (20°C). This temperature is usually reached if you leave the watering can standing in the room for a day. On a drafty windowsill made of marble or tile, however, the water will never warm to room temperature.

Water quality

In their natural habitat, plants are always "watered" with rainwater, and some also demand soft water under cultivation. But many plants are quite content with normal tap water. Very hard water must definitely be decalcified, however. There are various water softeners. If the water is known to be hard, it is enough to boil it for five minutes. The calcium separates out and remains behind in the pot as scale. For harder water, the trade offers chemicals and filter systems for softening the water. CAUTION: plants cannot tolerate distilled water.

The right way to water

Some plants have water-sensitive leaves, hearts, or tubers. These species should generally be watered through their saucers. But if they always get their rations "from below," the water will travel in only one direction through the soil, namely from bottom to top. Water is absorbed by the soil, but also rises upward through its own efforts, only to evaporate on the surface. The result is that the nutritive salts also only move in this direction and collect in the upper portion of the soil where they do the plant little good. This is because they are absorbed by the fine rootlets in the lower region of the root ball. Every four weeks, you should water these plants carefully from above, so that

House plants that require softened water
Anthurium
Aphelandra
Begonia
Camellia
Citrus
Dieffenbachia
Dipladenia
Dizgotheca
Fittonia
Gardenia
Hydrangea
Ixora
Jasminum
Leptospermum
Maranta
Medinilla
Myrtus
Orchids
Pentas
Rhododendron
Room ferns
Room palms

TIP

What to do when the root ball of a plant is completely dried out? Place the pot in a pail filled with water. So that the dry earth doesn't swim to the top, weight the soil down with large pebbles. Let the pot remain in the water until no more tiny bubbles rise up. After this procedure, part of the water that has been sucked in will run off into the saucer through the pot's drainage hole. Don't forget to pour off this surplus.

SUCCESSFUL CARE AND PROPAGATION

the nutrients are once more swept into the lower part of the pot.

There is no general rule for watering, only a fundamental recommendation: It is better to water too little than too much! If you also obey the following tips, your plants will neither drown nor dry out.

- Water according to the needs of the plants, not according to a schedule.
- Increase the water quantity slowly after the rest period and reduce the quantity gradually at the end of the growth period.
- Always use water at room temperature, so as not to "shock" the roots.
- Water in the morning, never while the midday sun is shining (there is danger of scorching), and at night only in emergencies.
- When watering, be thorough. Frequent small doses of water do more harm than good, because they only moisten the surface and little moisture reaches down to the rootlets.
- Don't always water in the same place. In time, this will form channels in the substratum so that the water will not distribute itself evenly throughout the soil.
- Excess water must be tipped out of the saucers or outer pots half an hour after watering.
- Water drops that dry on the leaves leave behind gray spots. In sunlight, these drops act like magnifying glasses and cause brown blotches.
- Soften water containing a lot of calcium. (Your water company can tell you how hard your water is.)
- Plants need more water in the growing period, in a light location, at high temperatures, when humidity is low, if they have

Platycerium *grows well in wooden plant baskets.*

soft, large leaves, if their pots are too small or made of clay, if the planting mix contains a lot of peat or loam, and if the plants are exposed to wind and heat out-of-doors.

- Plants need less water during their rest period, in a dark location, at low temperatures, at higher humidity, if they stand in the rain, if the mix is mulched or closely covered with growth, if they have leathery leaves, if the foliage is covered with a layer of wax, and if their pots are too large or made of plastic or glazed clay.

Watering is difficult in the case of plants that grow in a particularly porous substratum and in a container that is not completely enclosed—such as orchids or ferns in plant baskets. Dip the basket in a pail of water for a short time. Before hanging it up again, drain thoroughly.

Watering during Vacation Times

The automatic vacation watering apparatus in the picture cares for up to 36 pot plants. The system consists of a transformer with a timer, a 14V low-voltage pump, a distribution hose and a drip hose, three drip distributors, each with 12 connectors and caps to seal unused connectors. The drip distributors give out varying quantities of water once a day (0.5, 1, or 2 oz. (15, 30, or 60 mL)), so that you can meet the needs of each plant by connecting it to the appropriate distributor.

For the plant lover, the annual vacation is the best time of the year, but for plants these weeks often mean a period of thirst. This is especially so if they are expected to manage on their own in the summertime. The best vacation watering "systems" are reliable neighbors and friends, but these are not always available—or at least not as often as the plants would like. The solution: long-term watering arrangements that can manage ten to fourteen days without attention and only need to have their water reservoir refilled occasionally in case of an extended vacation. The methods range from self-devised clever tricks to ingenious commercial systems. How long the reserve lasts, depends on the capacity of the

water tank. Before the start of your trip, water the plants thoroughly and put them in a shady, cool place, to minimize water demand and evaporation. Do this as well with boxes on the balcony and patio containers. Here are a few tips for vacation watering.

Plants under a hood

Some plants can survive a long weekend very well under transparent plastic bags. The bags must be put on so that they nowhere touch the plants. Thin rods can be used to maintain the distance. Hoods work only with plants that can tolerate high humidity for a short time. Covering the substratum with plastic film provides a certain protection against evaporation.

Watering with bottles

Bottles filled with water and upended over plant pots and boxes can also help for a limited period. But to prevent the water from flowing out too quickly, you should close the bottle with a cork that has had a hole drilled into it.

Capillary matting

The best place for this system is the kitchen sink. One part of an extremely absorbent capillary mat, well dampened, is placed on the draining board and the other part hangs into the filled sink. Through the drainage hole of the plant container, you then insert a well-dampened special wick into the soil; the other end lies on the damp mat and is covered and weighted down by the vessel—nothing must

Automatic vacation watering for pot plants

be allowed to show. Capillary mats and special wicks can be obtained from appropriate suppliers.

Wicks

This system draws water from a pail into the plant containers with the help of special wicks or bands. The wicks are well dampened. One end is pulled through the drainage hole and to the surface with the help of a sack needle. The strands are then separated and covered with a sprinkling of potting mix. The other end lies at the bottom of a pail of water, weighted down with a stone. The pot stands on a wooden grid above the pail.

Another method has the wick, ribbon, or absorbent tape plunged into the soil from above. The other end is weighted down at the bottom of a water container that stands higher than the plants.

The thicker the wick, band, or tape, the more water is transported.

Drip method

Plastic spouts that are connected to the water reservoir by a hose are economical and durable. The tips of the spouts are stopped up with cotton. This creates a suction system operated by atmospheric pressure. The cotton serves as a filter and must be renewed sooner or later, depending on the hardness of the water, or the suction system will stop working.

Clay cones

Well-dampened clay cones are filled with water, sealed, and inserted into the soil. They are then linked to a reservoir by thin connector hoses.
CAUTION: Because clay attracts calcium from the water, the cone's pores eventually get clogged up.

Once it has lost its porosity, the cone becomes unusable.

Double-bottomed containers

For the windowsill or balcony, you can buy plant containers whose lower parts are water reservoirs. In principle, these work according to the wick method. Thick bands or strings connect the water reservoir and the potting mix. Such containers also simplify watering in non-vacation times, as they give plants water only when they need it.

Automatic watering

Those who have to look after many plants on the balcony or patio will find their work made easier throughout the season by the installation of an automatic watering system. Accessibility of

water and power connections is a prerequisite. A hose system connects the plant containers with the water supply, and each plant is provided with its own "water source." The installation is regulated by switches that are programmed to open at certain times. They work better in conjunction with moisture sensors, which are inserted into the soil and connected to the system. The valves then open in response to need, which is signaled by the sensors.

The watering system described on page 42 also works on the balcony or patio. To meet the greater water requirements of the plants, however, two, three, or more drip hoses, along with their supports, must be attached to the soil. A friendly neighbor only has to refill the water reservoir now and then.

An "automatic watering can" for container plants

Watering at a Glance

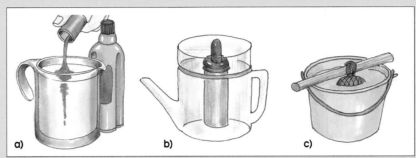

Measuring humidity. Water gauges offer the beginner some help in watering, but they cannot replace sensitivity and experience. A variety of types of instruments is available.

Softening water. To soften water for room plants, there are several possibilities:
a) Add liquid or powdered softening agents to the plant water.
b) Use a watering can with a filter containing an ion-exchange cartridge. This must be replaced periodically (and the used cartridge disposed of as hazardous waste!).
c) During the night, suspend a cloth sack filled with about 1 lb. (500 g) of peat moss in 2.5 gal. (10 L) of water. The peat moss draws the calcium out of the water. After three uses, the peat moss must be replaced.

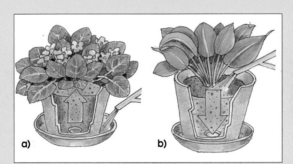

Watering from above or below?
a) Plants with water-sensitive leaves and tubers should be watered from below, by filling the saucer with water. After thirty minutes, tip out any excess water.
b) When watering from above, do not apply all the water to a single spot or water in the same spot every time. Doing so creates craters and channels in the soil, and prevents the water from distributing itself evenly.

Watering bromeliads. In the case of bromeliads, which live on trees in their native habitat and thus receive water from above, one must always be sure that there is water in the reservoir. The growing medium must also be watered.

Watering cacti. So that the body of the plant won't get wet, cacti are watered with a can that has a long spout. Cacti should be watered infrequently, but thoroughly. In between, allow the soil to dry out.

TIP

If you are not absolutely sure that a plant needs water, it is better to leave it be. More plants die from too much water than from too little.

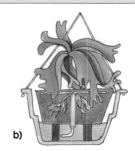

Immersing in water. Parched plants may be left in a container of water until no more air bubbles rise to the surface. The soil may need to be weighted down to prevent it from floating away.

Watering hanging plants. Hanging plants are not easy to water. Because one usually cannot see into the pot, the water tends to overflow.
a) and b): It is a good idea to use plant containers with an integrated water reservoir. In these containers, the plant rests on supports and a wick sucks the water from the reservoir into the soil.

Watering cans with very long spouts also make it easier to water hanging plants and render unnecessary risky gymnastic exercises on chairs and stools.

SUCCESSFUL CARE AND PROPAGATION

Plants under hoods. Plants that can tolerate high humidity may be covered with a transparent plastic bag for a long weekend. The bag must not come into contact with the leaves.

Clay cones. These are filled with water and inserted into the soil. The clay constantly gives off water to the soil; it receives the water from a hose that hangs into a storage reservoir.

Wicks. A thick, damp wick is drawn through the drainage hole to the top of the plant, wrapped around the plant, and covered with soil. The other end hangs into a container of water.

Bottle watering. On the balcony, plants can survive for several days if corked bottles filled with water are stuck into the soil. A sizable hole must first be drilled into the cork.

Newspapers as reservoirs. If you need to leave your plants for three or four days, set them in a cool area in a plastic tub on top of a thick layer of damp newspaper; also, be sure to stop up the gaps between the pots with damp paper. The water in the paper will evaporate and provide high humidity for the plants. As a result, they will lose less water. Water plants thoroughly beforehand.

Capillary mats on the draining board. A special matting material makes it possible for you to preserve your plants from drought for extended periods during your vacation. One end of the matting hangs into a sink full of water; the rest lies on the draining board, under the plant containers. With a heavy-duty needle, a thick wick is inserted into the soil of each plant through the drainage hole of the container. The external end of the wick rests under the plant pot.

Automatic watering. An automatic watering arrangement saves a great deal of labor. Small ceramic spikes, pushed into the containers, are linked with one another and with the water main. Whenever the spikes dry out, this produces a pressure differential that opens the valves, so that water can flow. The water from the main goes through a pressure-reducer.

Root balls in clay granular. An ideal way of watering evenly is to put the plants in large hydroculture containers and fill them with clay granular. On the bottom of the container, place a layer of clay granular about 1 in. (3 cm) thick, set the root ball on this, and fill the container with clay granular until the root ball is covered to about 1 in. (2-3 cm).

All vacation watering systems, even the most perfect, can let you down. It is important, therefore, to test your arrangement over a long weekend before beginning your vacation.

Planting Media

Planting media give plants support and provide them with the necessary nutrients. Their composition differs according to location. In nature, billions of microorganisms and microscopic life forms can be found in healthy soil. These continuously transform natural waste (fallen leaves, dead wood, plants, and animal remains) into new soil and nutrients.

In the planter, this cycle does not take place. People must provide the right soil mix, replenish it, and supply the appropriate nutrients.

Types of potting mix

Most houseplants grow and thrive in good commercial soil, in mixes based on bark, and in peat-free or peat-poor mixes. Certain plant groups have special needs, for which special mixes have been developed (→ pages 48–49). The concept "plant substratum" is equivalent to "culture medium" or "base" and also includes all synthetic soils or soil amendments frequently used by nurseries to cultivate plants, such as clay aggregates, clay granulars (Turface), perlite, vermiculite, pumice, rice husks, and chips of cork, wood, and Styrofoam. Commercial potting soils also generally contain a long-lasting fertilizer that supplies plants with essential nutrients for two to three months.

Ordinary potting mixes

Ordinary potting mix for houseplants is primarily made up of peat moss, compost, bark, clay, loam, tree leaves, and sand, in different proportions. To ensure that plants on the windowsill or balcony do not die, their normal mix should fulfill certain conditions:

- A good soil must be able to store water, but be sufficiently porous and loose to let enough air reach the roots.
- The loose soil structure should remain stable for a long time. That means that the organic elements must not rot too quickly, lest the soil become hard and impermeable.
- The soil must be able to bind and release nutrients so that they are available to the plants. Water and nutrients run off in sand, while clay can bind them too tightly.
- All mixes should be free of disease, weed seeds, and traces of pesticide.
- For most houseplants, the ideal pH value lies between 5 and 6.5. Potting soils have become articles of mass consumption, and no one really knows what is hidden in the bags. Evaluation is costly and demands extensive chemical analysis. Sadly, it is not impossible that flower soils also contain residues of plant sprays and heavy metals from general air and soil pollution.
- Do not reach for the cheapest products, and make sure that details of the soil composition are printed on the packaging.
- One can also learn something from the product names. Planting media offered as "flower soil" are not subject to regulation and can differ a great deal in quality. "Milled Peat" consists entirely of peat, whereas ordinary potting mixes have a large peat component.

Peat belongs in the bog

Undoubtedly, much too much expensive peat is being used. Some peat-based mixes contain 100 percent peat moss, enriched with lime to raise the low pH value of peat. In addition, these products contain nutrients, in lesser concentration for salt-sensitive plants and promoting growth, or in greater concentration for all-purpose use. In other products there is also a great deal of peat (60–80 percent), especially in the ordinary potting mixes.

Considering how much peat is used in potting mixes, and the kind of natural environment out of which peat comes, one might think there were nothing but bog plants on earth. Producers defend the large peat component on the following basis: high storage capacity for water; crumbly, loose texture; good structural stability; and—thanks to lime amendment—a favorable pH value in the range of "lightly acidic" (5–6.5), which most houseplants prefer.

Peat moss holds more water than any other substratum component (approximately 2 lb. (1 kg) per quart of peat moss), but this does not mean that the water is totally available to the plants. Peat moss can suck in a great deal of water, but the roots can only absorb about 45 percent of the available water. So peat-rich mixes still feel damp when the plants are already dry. And, of course, water also evaporates from the surface of the substratum. Once peat moss is dried out, it can seldom be used again: water simply runs off the dried-out peat fibers.

Although ordinary potting mix does not consist of pure peat, even a soaking can only help a little then, if at all. You can contribute to the protection of the environment by using a mix with a low proportion of peat, or one that is entirely peat-free.

TIP

Increasingly, so-called eco- or bio-soil is available. It contains much less peat moss than most other media. The new mix is very good for house and balcony plants. Eco-soil is unsuitable only for those plants that need decidedly acidic soil.

SUCCESSFUL CARE AND PROPAGATION

Tree-bark humus

The alternative to peat moss is tree-bark humus. There are several excellent products that are 30–50 percent tree bark and a small part peat moss and clay. These are good for house, balcony, and container plants.

To loosen and stabilize the soil's structure, environ-mentally conscious producers today also mix in cocoa chips, wood chips, and rice husks or—not quite so environmentally friendly—bits of Styrofoam.

Garden soil and compost

Garden soil and compost are suitable for houseplant cultivation only with reservations, and they should always compose only part of the mix. Both may include weed seeds and, possibly, disease pathogens or pests. Garden soil may contain too much lime or too much sand; well-rotted compost is full of nutrients. Use only sterilized garden soil and compost (thirty minutes in the oven at 250°F (120°C)) and sieve it. For many container plants on the balcony or patio, humus-rich and lime-rich garden soil may be used. As well, such soil has the advantage of being heavier than industrial soil, and so makes the containers more stable. Compost is also good for large plants. But be sure the garden soil you use is sieved and makes up only part of the mix.

Bark mulch

Bark mulch is of little use to house-plant gardeners, but a great aid to lovers of container plants and to those with a large roof garden. Soil covered with mulch stays moist and weed-free longer. In addition to the usual mulches made of the bark of evergreens, there is also rose mulch, made from rose cuttings. In the fall or winter, try to get a forestry school or nursery to give you scraps of deciduous wood cuttings—preferably from fruit trees. Bark mulch from fruit trees or other deciduous trees rots more slowly and makes the soil less acidic than does mulch made from the chipped bark of evergreens.

Recipes for Mixing Your Own Media

Many plant lovers swear by their own potting mixes. Of the many variations, here is a small selection:

Soil for container plants
3 parts lime- and humus-rich garden soil, sieved
3 parts aged compost (sieved)
2 parts bark
2 parts sand

Mixtures for epiphytic bromeliads, ferns, and orchids
1 part cork scraps
1 part pine bark
1 part Styrofoam chips
1/2 part sieved compost
1/2 part charcoal

Mixtures for terrestrial orchids
2 parts evergreen bark
1 part peat moss
1 part aged compost
a little lime

Mixtures for terrestrial ferns and bromeliads
3 parts leaf mold
3 parts coarse peat moss
2 parts coarse sand (large-grained river sand, from which the lime has been washed out)

Soil for cacti and succulents
1 part coarse sand or perlite
2 parts compost

Soil for azaleas, hydrangeas, Erica, and camellias
1 part garden soil
1 part leaf mold or tree bark
2 parts synthetic scraps or wood chips

Soil for palms and similar plants
1 part ripe compost
1 part wood chips
1 part sand
1/2 part synthetic chips
1/2 part lime

Special Mixtures

Many lovers of specific plant groups also mix their media according to their own recipes and prefer them. The effort is only worthwhile, however, if you need to provide for large numbers of specimens of a single group.

The trade does offer perfectly adequate ready-made substratum mixes for plants with special needs.

Orchid mixes

Planting mixes for orchids must be extremely porous and contain few nutrients, as befits their lifestyle as epiphytes (→ pages 22–23).

The main component of orchid mix used to be the root fiber of ferns and mosses of indigenous species of *Osmunda regalis*, *Polypodium vulgare*, and sphagnum (*Sphagnum*). However, in a number of countries, these plants are now protected and may no longer be gathered. Today's media are composed of coarse peat fiber, bark media of European pine and cork, or the bark of American evergreens (Redwood bark, Vitabark). There is also one mix (Meranti) that is made from the shavings of a South Asian tree. These basic substances are mixed with inorganic additives such as perlite, tile shards, lava, pumice, mica granulate, and clay aggregate, or with Styrofoam chips to maintain structural stability. The mixes for terrestrial orchids include sand or gravel. To prevent rot and diseases, a bit of charcoal should be added to the mix. There is a fully synthetic substratum called Orchid Chips. The chips, like those of Styrofoam, are composed of synthetic polystyrene, but have a specially roughened surface so that they can store water and nutrients. For these mixes, there are special fertilizers such as Orchid Quick.

Mixes for cacti and other succulents

Cacti soil is nutrient-poor and porous. The main component (around 50 percent) of any mix is peat moss, compost, or leaf mold—the plants don't notice the difference. What is important is to enrich the mix to ensure good drainage by adding coarse sand, lava rubble, pumice, or a similar synthetic product. Leaf cacti and many succulents also grow in good potting soil, however.

Palm mixes

Palms, in their early years, need particularly loose soil; as they mature, the substratum may contain a little lime. Palm mixes, therefore, are largely made up of leaf mold or compost, and, always, a little sand.

Fern mixes

The natural soil of terrestrial ferns is loose and rich in organic material. The mix for these houseplants must correspond. No such substratum is commercially available, but the mixture is easy to make:
3 parts coarse peat moss
3 parts leaf mold or compost (sterilized)
2 parts coarse sand or perlite
Epiphytic ferns also grow in this substratum. If you cannot mix it yourself, you can use lightly fertilized ordinary potting mix.

CAUTION: Ferns can't stand lime!

Bromeliad mixes

The media available for bromeliads usually consist of equal parts of peat moss and leaf mold or compost, with Styrofoam chips mixed in.

CAUTION: Bromeliads can't tolerate lime!

Azalea mixes

Azaleas need especially acidic soil, as do the various species of rhododendron. The available mixes contain a lot of peat moss (at least 50 percent). The other components are compost and sand.

Potting mix for flowering balcony plants

Ideally, this soil would have a different combination of nutrients from ordinary potting mix. So that balcony plants will flower luxuriantly, it should contain more phosphorus, to stimulate the formation of buds.

Clay aggregate for hydroculture

In the past few decades, hydroculture has developed as an alternative to soil cultivation.

Clay aggregate in a variety of sizes gives support to the roots and absorbs a lot of moisture. The plants are nourished by water-soluble nutrients. This system is recommended to those who do not have much time to care for their plants and who must leave them alone for a few days at a time. The water supply often lasts for weeks, and the fertilizer reserve for months.

The transition from soil culture to hydroculture does not always succeed, however, nor is it advisable for every plant. The soil must be removed from the root balls before the plants are placed in their new substratum. Older and weak specimens should be spared this procedure.

In general, leafy plants do better in this soil-free system than flowering plants. Species with thick roots survive the transition more easily than plants with fine roots.

The essential implements and precise instructions for care are often available as a complete package from specialist stores.

TIP

Potting soil should not be reused, not even when mixed with new soil or compost. It could contain hitherto undetected pest eggs or fungal spores.

SUCCESSFUL CARE AND PROPAGATION

Clay granular for storage of water and nutrients

A mix of half soil, half clay granular is another alternative that can be recommended for neglected plant friends. It is not necessary to free the roots from soil in the transition; instead, the entire root ball is transferred to a bigger pot and surrounded with specially prepared clay chips. This granulate can store water to 130 percent of its own weight. A moisture sensor indicates when watering is required. Special slow-release fertilizer serves as nourishment. This system, together with explanations, is also available as a package.

Clay aggregate and clay granular as a drainage layer

The porous material absorbs water very well, even when there has been overwatering. In boxes on the balcony and in large planters, these clay products, used as a drainage layer, have the added advantage of reducing the weight of the containers.

In hydroculture, the root ball of the plant is surrounded by clay aggregate in a pot with many slits. This plant pot is then placed in a larger outer pot, and the gap between the two is filled with a nutrient solution. Some plant pots also have special arrangements for accommodating nutrients in tablet form. A water gauge with the markings "Minimum," "Optimum," and "Maximum" is inserted into a holder designed for this purpose. A red level recorder indicates the water quantity.

Leafy plants do well in hydroculture

It's simple: the insertion of a water gauge into a hydroculture receptacle.

Nutrients and Fertilizing

In the wild, nature assures the regular supply of nutrients, but in pot culture humans must take over this task. The need for fertilizer varies just as much as the demand for water. Some species are hungry and others undemanding; some expect equal rations all year long, whereas others need to be nourished only at certain times. As well, many plants like a "menu" designed according to their particular preferences, rather than a "standard mush."

Plant nutrition

Plant nutrition consists of six primary nutrients (nitrogen, phosphorus, potassium, calcium, magnesium, sulfur) and a number of trace elements (e.g., iron, copper, manganese, molybdenum, zinc, chlorine, boron). These nutrients influence certain life functions and are present in various quantities in the available products, depending on the plant species. Giving the incorrect dose of a nutrient—too much or too little—harms the plants and often prevents the intake of other nutrients.

The function of trace elements in plant nutrition is roughly similar to the role of vitamins in human nutrition.

Fertilizers

Several fertilizers have their contents clearly marked on the packaging, but other producers—not exactly to the joy of the consumer—have chosen an obscure form of labeling, involving a series of three numbers, e.g., 8/6/12 or 8:6:12. This means, always in the same order, the percentage of nitrogen, phosphorus, and potassium. In this context, one speaks of a standard fertilizer designation, and occasionally of NPK fertilizer. Sometimes the series has four numbers, the last referring to the percentage of magnesium. Calcium content and the presence of trace elements must also be marked on the packaging.

STANDARD FERTILIZERS are synthetic fertilizers, either organic or mixed organic and inorganic, which are adapted in their composition to the needs of certain plant groups. The products are either derived from natural materials of vegetable or animal origin, or are produced synthetically.

NATURAL FERTILIZERS (i.e., organic fertilizers) work more slowly because they contain nutrients in a form that is inaccessible to plants. The living organisms in the soil must break these materials down before plants can use them. In ordinary commercial soils, there are usually not enough of these living organisms, so, when repotting, it is necessary to use a natural fertilizer that has been enriched with microorganisms in powder form.

The Most Important Minerals and Their Tasks

Nitrogen (N)

Nitrogen is essential for development, furthers new growth, and leads to the formation of chlorophyll. Too much nitrogen stimulates excessive green growth, swells the tissues, and renders the leaves soft and susceptible to diseases. A lack of nitrogen stunts growth and turns the leaves yellow.

Phosphoric Acid (P_2O_5)

Phosphoric acid makes for healthy roots, the formation of buds, and the ripening of fruits and seeds. Flowering plants benefit from fertilizer with a high phosphate content.

Too much phosphoric acid impairs the metabolism and hampers root formation. A shortage of phosphoric acid hampers the development of blooms, and makes the leaves discolor to a reddish-brown.

Potassium (K_2O)

Potassium plays an important role in photosynthesis and in the management of water, strengthens the entire tissue structure, and boosts the ability of plants to defend themselves against pests and diseases.

Too much potassium disturbs growth and leads to chlorosis, especially of the older leaves.

Magnesium (Mg)

Magnesium is essential in the formation of chlorophyll.

When there is not enough magnesium, the leaves turn yellow while their veins remain green.

Calcium (lime) (Ca)

Calcium works indirectly on the nourishment and health of plants.

Sulfur (S)

Sulfur is a building block of important plant components. A shortage produces chlorosis, especially in young leaves. Too much sulfur does relatively little harm.

SUCCESSFUL CARE AND PROPAGATION

The powder should be mixed into the soil at planting, and later occasionally sprinkled over the soil and lightly worked into the surface. Those who give their plants natural fertilizer practically ensure against over- or under-feeding and excessive salting of the soil. Organic fertilizers generally contain less potassium. This lack can be made up by adding compost to the mix or by putting a small amount of potassium magnesium sulfate into the fertilizer.

SYNTHETIC FERTILIZERS (inorganic fertilizers) contain nutrients such as mineral salts that are easily soluble in water and are taken up by the roots immediately. That means that they act quickly, but also that incorrect doses are just as quick to damage the plants. In addition, there is a danger that the salts will settle in the mix and thereby kill every living organism in the soil.

ORGANIC–INORGANIC FERTILIZERS are products that contain mineral salts as well as organic components. Their aim is to produce speedy results while limiting the potential for damage. This category also includes organic fertilizers with a low potassium content to which potassium has been added in a form adapted to plants.

PLANT FERTILIZERS are available in liquid and powder form, as tablets, spikes, or granules. They are dissolved in the water, sprayed on the leaves (foliar fertilizer), or added to, or mixed into, the soil as time-release fertilizer. Depending on their nutrient makeup, they are suited to different plant groups. Fertilizer for leafy plants is high in nitrogen, and that for plants in flower is high in phosphorus. Fertilizers for cacti and succulents contain little nitrogen and calcium, but relatively more phosphorus and potassium. Orchid fertilizer is notably less concentrated. Fertilizers for azaleas or rhododendron are calcium-free and contain few salts. They are also good for hydrangeas and ericas. Foliar fertilizer works quickly and is used especially for epiphytes (orchids, bromeliads) and as emergency aid for neglected plants. Don't spray it on hairy leaves! As well, one can get special fertilizers for balcony plants and individual plant species.

How much fertilizer?

A plant's nutrient requirements depend on several factors: the plant's species, its age, and the time of year. Demanding plants are called "heavy feeders." They are given fertilizer more frequently, and in a more concentrated form, than those with lesser appetites, the "weak feeders." Neither very young nor aging plants should be fertilized too much.

Commercial potting soils generally contain enough slow-release fertilizer to last for two to three months. Very peat-rich mixes hold the supply for less time than compost-based mixes, or those with a large clay component.

It is hard to tell how much fertilizer is available to a newly acquired plant. You never know how long it has been living in its soil. It is a good idea to start fertilizing after about eight weeks.

Plants are individualistic with respect to the quantity and frequency of their nutrient intake. The plant portraits give further details. Nevertheless, there are several basic rules:

- Never fertilize onto a dry substratum. Doing so burns the fine hair roots.
- Plants do better if they are given weak doses of fertilizer often rather than high concentrations less frequently.
- After the winter rest period, increase fertilizing gradually; reduce it slowly in late summer.
- Fertilize only during the growing period, never during the rest period.
- Sick plants should not be fertilized.
- For plants that tend to get overlooked, slow-release fertilizer spikes are the ideal solution.

There are special fertilizers for hydroculture. In addition to a granular, which is simply scattered over the bottom of the outer pot, nutrient batteries and pills are on the market.

Fertilizer battery for hydroculture

Fertilizer pill for hydroculture

Repotting

All pot plants must be repotted periodically, as the soil eventually loses its loose texture and becomes overloaded with deposits from the water and fertilizer, as well as debris from the plant itself. As well, the roots eventually need more space. Normally, the roots develop in relation to the growth of the entire plant: They must spread out ever farther to meet the plant's increasing need for nutrients and for stability. The roots often grow in a circle or push themselves out of the pot at the top or bottom, displacing the soil.

When to repot?

Repotting is always done in the spring, when the first new tips or leaves show themselves. Never repot during the rest period or while the plant is in bloom.

Not all plants must be repotted in new soil annually, although this suits most of them. The need to repot is signaled by the plants themselves.

- If possible, take the plant out of the soil. If the ball consists entirely of roots, it is high time to repot.
- If you notice blackish, weak roots with an unpleasant odor when making this check, repotting into fresh substratum will probably save the plant's life.
- If the roots emerge from the drainage hole or lie naked on the surface, it is absolutely essential to repot.
- If the leaves remain small, the blooms scanty, and the new growth minimal, it is a sign that the plant is unhappy about its living quarters.
- Green algae on the surface of the pot and moss on the substratum indicate waterlogging within. Change the soil at once.

Plant containers

New clay plant pots should be soaked in water for at least two hours, otherwise they will draw too much moisture out of the substratum. Old pots must be cleaned thoroughly, inside and out. Any whitish calcium deposits can be brushed off using diluted vinegar. If the pots are already very old, it is best to part with them.

Practical advice

- Take your time when repotting.
- For repotting bigger plants, you need a helper.
- Water the plants thoroughly a few hours before repotting.
- It is best to do the job out-of-doors on a warm day, or in the kitchen.
- Do not rinse off the old soil into drains. It is better to add it to your compost.
- All utensils needed for repotting should be close at hand, because it is hard to lay aside plants that are out of their pots.

For repotting you need:
- fresh soil
- new pots (0.75–1.5 in. (2–4 cm) larger than the old ones)
- appropriate saucers to place under the pots
- trowel, watering can, scissors, possibly a hammer
- supports, and twine for attaching the plants to them
- charcoal powder for disinfecting cuts
- material for drainage (clay aggregate, clay granular, gravel, Styrofoam chips)
- larger clay fragments for covering the drainage hole

To prepare the pots, cover the drainage holes with clay fragments and fill in the drainage layer. This must be 0.4–0.75 in. (1–2 cm) thick in small pots, 2–4 in. (5–10 cm) in larger ones.

Removal from the pot

To remove a smallish plant from its container, hold your hand over the surface and support the plant between two fingers, then overturn the pot. In case this doesn't do the trick, tap the rim or bottom of the pot against the edge of a table so that the root ball releases itself from the wall of the container.

With bigger plants, separate the root ball from the side of the pot using a long knife and lift it out gently, while a second person holds on to the pot. Too strongly rooted plants can only be freed without damage to the roots by smashing their clay containers, or cutting off their plastic pots.

Handling the roots

When repotting, it is extremely important to damage the plant's roots as little as possible!

The root fibers should be loosened somewhat with a wooden stick, and the soil carefully removed on the sides, bottom, and upper surface.

Only damaged and blackish roots should be cut off! Any resulting cuts on thicker roots should be sprinkled thoroughly with charcoal powder to disinfect them.

SUCCESSFUL CARE AND PROPAGATION

For repotting, you need time, new pots and corresponding saucers, fresh soil, a watering can, a pair of scissors, and many other things. The job is best done out-of-doors.

Only begin the repotting process when all utensils are at hand.

Potting

The plants should never stand deeper in the new pot than in their previous one. Put planting mix into the pot until the plant is level with the lower edge of the watering rim. Fill with soil all around and press down lightly from time to time. In between, shake the pot repeatedly, so that the soil reaches all the gaps.

If the plant needs a support, it should be inserted at this time. Do not stick it into the substratum afterward, or the roots may be damaged.

Additional care

Water the plants lightly at first so that new, fine roots can develop, spread in search of water, and anchor themselves in the fresh

What do you do when plants get too big?

Sometimes plants threaten to burst the bounds of their home environment. You can stem the tendency to grow too big by repotting less often. Do not give such plants a larger container when re-potting, and lightly trim their root balls. Dust the cuts with charcoal powder to disinfect them. As the reduced roots cannot nourish the big plant properly any more because its leaves and branches with-draw most of the water, you should also prune the above-ground portion of the plant correspondingly.

potting mix. As some roots are always damaged during repotting, too much water may produce rot.

Once new shoots appear, water in the customary fashion. The plants will need fertilizer in about eight weeks.

Alternatives to repotting

After a time, very large room or container plants can't be repotted even by two people. Regularly, in spring, remove the top layer of soil as deeply as possible without damage to the roots. Carefully loosen the soil that remains with a blunt wooden stick. To replace the soil you just removed, top-dress with a particularly nutrient-rich potting mix.

Repotting at a Glance

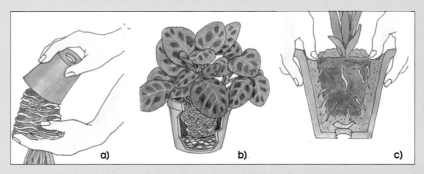

Repotting leafy and flowering plants. Water the plants several hours before repotting.
a) Hold back the earth and plant with the palm of your hand, then turn the pot over.
b) To protect the roots from waterlogging, place a thick drainage layer (consisting of clay aggregate, gravel, or clay fragments) on the bottom of the new container, before you set the plant in it.
c) Place the plant in the center of the container, but not lower than before. Fill the pot with fresh soil and press the soil around the stem down firmly . Keep the rim high enough for watering!

Reducing the root ball.
Extremely matted root balls, or those that are too big, can be cut back by a third in the spring. Cut all around with a sharp, clean knife.

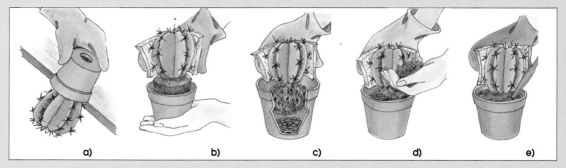

Repotting cacti. To repot cacti it is absolutely essential to work with strong gardening gloves.
a) Before repotting, let the soil dry out. Tap the upturned pot lightly on the edge of a table.
b) A piece of Styrofoam or fleece, or a thick layer of newspaper, will keep the thorns of the cactus from piercing your gloves.
c) Carefully shake the old soil from the root balls and remove damaged roots. Place a drainage layer in the new container. It is also advisable to put thin fleece between the drainage layer and the soil before setting the plant in its new pot.
d) Start by carefully putting in only a little soil mix, and make sure that the cactus stays in the middle of the container.
e) Make sure to leave a watering rim of about 0.4–0.75 in. (1–2 cm).

Occasionally, specialist stores carry fern or moss roots, or sphagnum moss, as orchid planting mix. One hopes this is old stock, for nowadays these plants are protected species in a number of countries.

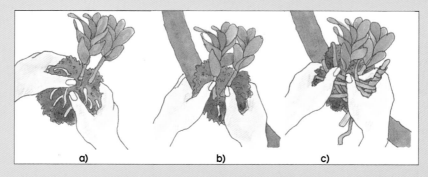

Tying up orchids. Many orchids grow on trees in their native habitat. You can also give them this opportunity on your windowsill:
a) Surround all aerial roots with moistened potting mix.
b) On a piece of wood designed for epiphytes (available commercially), attach the orchid in such a way that no water can remain standing in the heart of the plant.
c) For tying up, discarded women's stockings, cut into strips, are excellent, but so is plastic-coated wire or raffia. Don't tie the roots too tight!

Repotting in Clay Granular.
When you use this method, the new pot must be substantially larger. The plant, with its root ball, is placed upright in the center of the container and surrounded with clay granular.

SUCCESSFUL CARE AND PROPAGATION

Shifting to hydroculture. Hydroculture has many advantages, especially for those plant lovers who are not confident about watering and fertilizing. Leafy plants, especially, make the transition to hydroculture relatively easily.
a) First of all, carefully rinse all the soil from the roots—remaining soil mix can cause rot!
b) Cut off damaged roots with sharp, clean scissors.
c) The pot in which the plant will grow is one-quarter filled with moistened clay aggregate. The plant gets put on top of this and the gaps and the pot are filled with the remaining clay aggregate.
d) Place the pot into an outer container, insert a water gauge, and water the plant with lukewarm water until the indicator stands at "Optimum." The plant should be fertilized for the first time after four weeks.

Repotting hydroculture plants. These plants do not need to be repotted each spring. It is time to repot only when the roots stick out of the granular and emerge from the openings of the container.
a) On the bottom of the new, larger plant container, place about 0.75 in. (2 cm) of well-moistened clay aggregate.
b) Take the plant out of its old pot and, having cut off dead roots, set it in the new pot.
c) The plant should not rest deeper in the granular than before. Fill gaps and pot with granular.
d) Insert the water gauge, fill it with water at room temperature to the "Maximum" mark, and add fertilizer.

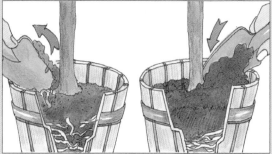

Rinsing the medium. If you have ever overfertilized, it is important to rinse out the soil before real damage is done to the plant. If the size of the pot permits, allow lukewarm water to run through the soil for around fifteen minutes in the sink or bathtub. It may be necessary to weight down the top layer of the soil mix so that it doesn't drain away.

Renewing the top layer of mix. Big container plants are often hard even to move, let alone to repot. In order to renew the potting mix at least in part, carefully remove the top layer with a small shovel or your hands. If possible, loosen the remaining substratum. Don't damage the roots or stem of the plant! Fill up with new potting mix.

Pruning, Training, and Overwintering

To cultivate house and balcony plants successfully, more is needed than correct placement, watering, fertilizing, and repotting. You also need to know about pruning, training, and overwintering.

Pruning

Houseplants do not need to be pruned regularly. Only on particular occasions does the plant lover reach for a clean, sharp knife or, in the case of woody branches, for pruning shears. More often, it is a matter of breaking off, pinching out, or trimming new growth so that the plant will branch better. The best time to prune is before sprouting or after flowering. Larger pruning cuts should be disinfected with charcoal powder or, if the plants are in flower, with water.

THINNING. If branches are too crowded or tangled, the excess parts are removed. Always cut 0.2 in. (0.5 cm) above an outward-turning bud (dormant bud).

CUTTING BACK. Older or rangy plants are stimulated to forceful new growth by cutting back severely, by up to two-thirds.

COSMETIC CUT. Some foliage plants or shrubs develop unnaturally long shoots. These can be cut off at their base at any time.

TRIMMING. To keep bushy plants or the crowns of single-stemmed plants in shape, trim off any stray shoots right away.

BREAKING OFF OR PINCHING OUT. In order to make newly rooted, strong cuttings or young plants

---

Container plants that must be brought indoors before the first frost:
Bougainvillea, Cyperus papyrus, Datura, Ensete, Erythrina cristagalli, Hibiscus, Lantana camara hybrids, Tibouchina urvilleana.

Container plants that can survive temperatures to 23°F (–5°C):
Abutilon, Acacia, Callistemon, Cas-sia didymobotrya, Cera-tonia siliqua, Citrus limin, Lampran-thus, Leonotis leonurus, Lepto-spermum, Passflor, Plumbago auriculata.

Container plants that can survive temperatures to 10°F (–12°C):
Albizia julibrissin, Araucaria aroucna, Aucuba japonica, Cupressus semper-virens, Eriobotrya japonica, Ficus carica, Lagerstroemia indica, Laurus nobilis, Mag-nolia grandiflora, Nandina domes-tica, Phyllostachys, Punica gran-atum, Trachycarpus fortunei, Viburnum tinus.

---

branch better, remove the growing tip immediately above the uppermost pair of leaves.

Training

A plant that is expected to develop in a particular direction must be pruned regularly. To achieve a tall single-stemmed plant, every stem except the main one, and all the side shoots except in the crown area, are removed from a young shrub or flowering plant. Once the main stem has reached the desired height, it is capped. Trim the crown frequently, so that it gets bushy.

Overwintering

Very few plants are winter hardy, not even the indigenous species, once they are growing in a container. How much frost a plant can tolerate will depend on its most sensitive part: the root ball. In a container, the roots are protected by much less soil than they are in their natural location, and so are more frost-sensitive. Some of them can manage in protected corners if given a warm blanket made of burlap, Styrofoam, reed matting, or twigs. More delicate species, however, must be taken to a frost-free room in winter. All plants that can overwinter in the dark should go into the basement, because they shed their foliage. The same goes for tubers and bulbs—provided that the basement is not too warm or dry. For evergreens, a cool stairwell is suitable. The best winter quarters are glassed-in balconies, unheated garden rooms, or greenhouses with heating for especially cold days.

All rooms should be aired now and then. Once a week, a tour of inspection is called for. Cut off any sick or wilted parts right away. Most plants cannot go through the winter entirely without water. The darker their location, the less they require watering. Evergreen plants are thirstier than deciduous ones. In no case allow the root balls to dry out completely! Tubers and bulbs, on the other hand, must be kept absolutely dry.

SUCCESSFUL CARE AND PROPAGATION

Botanical name	English name	Pruning	Overwintering temperature	Can stand the dark—(x) only at low temp	Must have light	Keep dry	Water every four weeks
Abutilon	Flowering maple	When potting	32/68°F (0/20°C)		x		x
Aeonium	Aeonium		41/77°F (5/25°C)		x		x
Agapanthus	Agapanthus		32/68°F (0/20°C)		x		x
Agave	Agave		32/77°F (0/25°C)	x		x	
Aucuba	Aucuba	Possible	23/68°F (–5/20°C)	(x)	x		x
Bougainvillea	Bougainvillea	Possible	50/77°F (10/25°C)		x		x
Callistemon	Callistemon	Possible	41/68°F (5/20°C)		x		x
Camellia	Camellia	Possible	23/60°F (–5/15°C)		x		x
Chamaerops	Mediterranean palm	Remove old leaves	23/77°F (–5/25°C)	(x)	x		x
Chrysanthemum	Chrysanthemum	When potting	41/60°F (5/15°C)		x		x
Citrus	Citrus plant	Possible	41/68°F (5/20°C)		x		x
Cordyline	Dracaena	Remove old leaves	32/68°F (0/20°C)		x		x
Cycas	Sago palm	Remove old leaves	32/68°F (0/20°C)		x		x
Datura	Datura	When potting	41/60°F (5/15°C)	x		x	
Dracaena	Dragon tree	Remove old leaves	41/77°F (5/25°C)		x		x
Ensete	Ensete	Remove old leaves	50/77°F (10/25°C)		x		x
Ficus	Fig	Possible	23/50°F (–5/10°C)	x		x	
Fuchsia	Fuchsia	When potting	41/60°F (5/15°C)	(x)	x		x
Gardenia	Gardenia	Possible	41/68°F (5/20°C)		x		x
Heliotropium	Heliotrope	When potting	41/60°F (5/15°C)		x		x
Hibiscus	Hibiscus	Possible	50/77°F (10/25°C)		x		x
Impatiens	Impatiens	Possible	39/68°F (5/20°C)		x		x
Jasminum	Jasmine	Possible	32/68°F (0/20°C)	(x)	x		x
Nerium	Oleander	Possible	32/60°F (0/15°C)	(x)	x		x
Passiflora	Passion flower	Possible	41/68°F (5/20°C)		x		x
Phoenix	Date palm	Remove old leaves	32/68°F (0/20°C)	(x)	x		x
Trachycarpus	Windmill palm	Remove old leaves	23/68°F (–5/20°C)	(x)	x		x
Washingtonia	Washington palm	Remove old leaves	41/68°F (5/20°C)		x		x
Yucca	Yucca	Remove old leaves	32/77°F (0/25°C)	(x)	x		x

The adjoining table includes the most important container plants and indicates how they should be cared for in the wintertime. The four-week watering interval applies only to the stated minimum temperatures. If overwintering in warmer or brighter locations, check the moisture content of the root balls regularly, even in the winter.

Pruning and Overwintering at a Glance

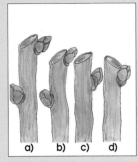

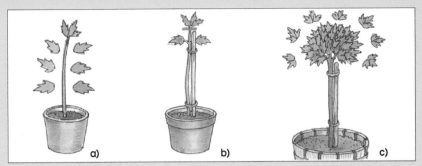

Correct pruning
a) The cut must be just above a bud and away from it.
b)–d) Too big or too small intervals, or a cut at the bud, are wrong.

Training to create a standard plant
Almost all young woody plants and subshrubs can be trained as standards. However, it takes several years to achieve the desired goal.
a) Remove the side shoots regularly.
b) Once the plant has reached the desired height, cut off the tip. Give the plant a support, without fail!
c) Trim the shoots often, so that the crown becomes full and bushy.

Pinching out. In order to make cuttings or young plants branch properly instead of just shooting up, you need to guide their long-term development by carefully nipping off the tips of the shoots with your fingernails.

Trimming. When older plants get too rangy or too big, they may be trimmed all around. The right time for this step is either before new growth begins in spring, or after flowering in the late summer.

Overwintering cut. Container plants that overwinter in dark basements should be cut back drastically in fall. Also remove the remaining leaves. Do not allow the root balls to dry out!

Spring pruning. Many container plants are cut back sharply after wintering, before they are put outside once more. Geraniums (see drawing) should be cut back to 8 in. (20 cm). This makes the new growth much bushier.

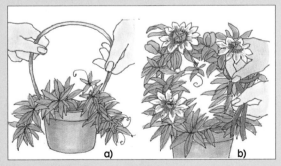 

Training plants around a curved support. Twining plants and climbers often grow 3 ft.- (1m-) long shoots. Instead of letting these hang down or climb straight up, train them around a wire arch.
a) Carefully insert the support into the pot.
b) Twist the shoots gently around the wire and attach them loosely at several points.

Creating a pyramidal plant. Many plants also allow themselves to be shaped into pyramids.
a) Fuchsias, ivy, geraniums, and other plants grow on pyramid-shaped supports with only a little help.
b) A tent of scarlet runner beans makes an attractive summer decoration. Strings are led down from the top of a stake in the center of a large plant container and fastened to the rim of the pot.

SUCCESSFUL CARE AND PROPAGATION

How to prevent injuries. It is very easy to hurt yourself on the sharp leaf ends of the agave. An effective countermeasure is to stick corks, used tennis balls, or pieces of Styrofoam on the points of the leaves.

Overwintering outdoors. If there is no room in the house, it is possible to use covers of burlap stretched over a strong wire support.

Earth shelters. If several pots need to overwinter out-of-doors (e.g., fuchsias), it is best to build an earth shelter for them. Leave the plants in their pots and place them in a previously dug trench. Fill the gaps with a scattering of leaves, and cover the trench with a fine mesh and a layer of twigs and leaves.

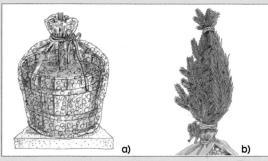

Winter protection for container plants. Many container plants can withstand the winter outdoors if well protected. Place them on a thick Styrofoam mat or on planks so that they can be shielded against cold and wet from below.
a) Cover the container and the surface of the soil completely with a layer of bubblewrap.
b) Cover the above-ground parts of the plant with pine branches.

Protection against frost and winter sun. Hardy container and climbing plants can be protected against heavy frost and drying winter sun with mats made of reeds or straw. These should be removed on frost-free days.

Protection against snow. In snowy regions try giving plants that are already protected with transparent foil and/or twigs an additional shelter made of boards so that they don't break under the weight of the snow.

Plant care in winter quarters. Even in their winter quarters, plants need a little attention. Quite apart from the fact that they must not be allowed to dry out and so must be watered occasionally, it is even more important to look out for their health.
a) Wilted parts must be removed at once so that they do not begin to rot or get moldy.
b) Fallen leaves must be brushed off the substratum and removed. Otherwise, they will harbor fungi or bacteria.
c) On frost-free days, air the area well, to prevent fungal growth. But keep the windows shut at night and when it is very cold.
d) Should disease or pests attack in spite of all this, the plant must be isolated at once and treated with a fungicide or an insecticide. Remove all affected plant parts carefully!

TIP

In hardy evergreens and conifers, what is often regarded as frost damage is actually due to drying out. The warmth of the winter sun evaporates a great deal of water from the leaves and needles, but the roots in the frozen soil cannot resupply their needs. This is what makes winter protection against the sun so important.

Why Plants Fall Ill

An arrangement of diverse container plants is an eye-catcher on any patio. Where many plants are placed together, however, diseases and pests spread quickly. For this reason, regular checks are important.

They arrive by flight or crawling, hide in the soil, and damage our houseplants: biting and sucking insects and fungi, along with viruses and bacteria. If plants are in good condition, they survive many plagues with only light scars. Specimens weakened by errors in care, however, make ideal fodder for pests and provide fertile soil for carriers of disease.

Most common mistakes

Most plants succumb not from neglect, but from too much attention: they are drowned, overfed, or given too much sun.

WATERING ERRORS

Too much, too cold, or too hard water has killed many a plant. If the drainage hole is plugged up, dangerous excess moisture will build up in the pot—the precondition for root rot.

Not all plants can stand having drops of water on their leaves. Moreover, wet leaves are prone to fungal attack.

WRONG LOCATION

Light and temperature are largely determined by location. If the plants are poorly placed, sun-hungry species will get too little light, lovers of warmth will be too cold, and vice versa. Plants are also upset by temperature fluctuations, or by heat buildup from the sun and, in winter, cold shock if they stand between the curtain and the windowpane. In addition to the right air, ground temperatures are important. "Cold feet" can make plants sick. Also, do not underestimate the strength of the spring sun. Sensitive plants on the windowsill should be given shade.

AIR IS ESSENTIAL FOR LIFE

The quality of the air also plays a major role. Dry heated air, stale air, or air fouled by smoke or other pollutants (fumes from furniture or textiles) is harmful to most houseplants. Also, plants should be well spaced so that the air can circulate—poor ventilation encourages fungal growths. Many plants are sensitive to drafts.

CORRECT CONTAINERS, RIGHT POTTING MIX

The size of the pot and the nature of the potting mix influence root development. Excessively dense, musty, or improper mix, and pots that are too small—or too large, in the case of weak rooters—hamper growth. Occasionally, you should loosen the soil with a fork, and remove any deposits (algae, moss, mold) from the surface.

TOO MANY OR TOO FEW NUTRIENTS

Both are equally damaging. Also, the composition of the fertilizer must be correct. Too much nitrogen, for example, makes the plant tissue soft and spongy.

Most plants do not require the same amount of fertilizer throughout the year. Woody plants should only receive fertilizer until August, so that the wood ripens and hardens. If fertilizing continues, the wood remains soft and prone to attack by pests and diseases. Use fertilizer specifically designed for particular plant groups.

PLANTS ALSO NEED REST

Many houseplants need a rest period, at times of year when they would be resting in their native habitat. During the rest period, they should be placed in a cooler location, watered very little, and hardly fertilized at all. If plants miss this phase in their annual growth cycle, they weaken and become subject to diseases.

ENSURE CLEANLINESS

Withered flowers and leaves serve as hotbeds for many disease-causing agents, so you should regularly cut off any dead plant parts with a sharp knife. Every cut is a wound and should ideally be dusted with charcoal powder. Many plant diseases are carried by tools and hands that have come into contact with sick plants. Shears and knives should be disinfected at once, and hands washed thoroughly. Brush off old pots hard and scrub with soapy water, inside and out, before reusing them.

REGULAR CHECKUPS

If you discover pests or fungal growth early on, it is often possible to save the plant. Once a week, inspect your green room decorations thoroughly, especially on the underside of the leaves. Pay attention to every small thing! Changes in development and growth can be signs of damage. If no outer symptoms are visible, it may be that the root balls are sick. Isolate sick plants at once! In the case of bargain plants and short-lived plants, it is better to throw them out right away, before they can infect their neighbors. And don't forget overwintering plants!

Picture facing: Container plants from southern regions create a holiday atmosphere on the terrace

What to Do When Pests Attack

Not even optimal care gives absolute protection from pests or fungi. Nevertheless, there are many ways to help sick plants. If only a few pests have appeared, or if the disease has been recognized at an early stage, mechanical methods and gentle medicines have a good chance of success. More drastic chemical preparations should only be used as a last resort!

Mechanical and biotechnical methods

Should the weekly inspection reveal pests or damaged areas, go into action at once!

- If the infestation is minimal, the lice or other pests can be removed, scratched off, or brushed off relatively easily.
- A lukewarm shower—cold water may give the plants a shock—washes many things away. Don't forget the undersides of the leaves! So that the plant doesn't fall out of its pot when you turn it upside down, place the pot in a plastic bag and tie it together tightly above the soil. Plants prepared in this way can also be plunged, head down, into water to which a few squirts of dish-washing liquid have been added. Unfortunately, this method only works with smaller plants.
- Diseased or damaged plant parts should be removed at once. Immediately thereafter, wash your tools and hands thoroughly.
- Whiteflies, humus flies, and other nuisances can be caught on the windowsill by inserting small yellow tags coated with non-drying glue into the flowerpot.
- Bothersome spider mites can be bumped off with very humid air—provided that the affected plants can stand high humidity. After the plant has been thoroughly watered, the above-ground portion is stuck for 10–14 days into a transparent plastic bag tied together above the soil. The moisture that evaporates from the leaves is captured in this cover.

Tested home remedies

You can't expect wonders from home remedies, but they are worth trying.

AGAINST A LIMITED INCIDENCE OF APHID USE:
Stinging-nettle and cold-water extract
Rhubarb-leaf tea
Wormwood tea

EFFECTIVE AGAINST POWDERY MILDEW FUNGUS:
Horsetail broth
Garlic tea

AGAINST FUNGI GENERALLY:
Stick peeled cloves of garlic into the soil.

AGAINST SCALE INSECTS AND MEALYBUGS, IT HELPS TO:
Spray or wipe with alcohol and soap solution

Natural methods

Insects have enemies that can be introduced selectively.

On the balcony and patio many of these useful creatures appear by themselves or can be attracted

---

Recipes for Home Remedies

Stinging-nettle and cold-water extract
Steep 1 lb. (500 g) of fresh, not-yet-blooming stinging nettles for 12–24 hours in 1.3 gal. (5 L) of water, sieve, and spray plant repeatedly at full strength. Stinging-nettle extract or powder can be obtained commercially.

Rhubarb-leaf tea
Cover 8 oz. (250 g) of cut-up rhubarb leaves with 0.4 gal. (1.5 L) of boiling water, let steep 15 minutes, drain, and spray undiluted.

Wormwood tea
Cover 5 oz. (150 g) of the fresh leaves of flowering stalks, or 0.5 oz. (15 g) dried leaves with 1.3 gal. (5 L) of boiling water. Let steep 15 minutes, drain, and spray undiluted.

Horsetail broth
Steep 10 oz. (300 g) of the fresh herb for 24 hours in 0.8 gal. (3 L) of cold water, bring to a boil, and let simmer for 30 minutes. The cooled liquid is then sieved, thinned with water in a proportion of 1:5, and sprayed on the plants once a week.

Garlic tea
Chop 2.5 oz. (70 g) of garlic cloves and cover with 0.25 gal. (1 L) of boiling water. Steep for 6 hours. Sieve and spray undiluted.

Alcohol and soap solution
Dissolve 0.75 oz. (20 g) soft soap in 0.25 gal. (1 L) of hot water, let cool, and add 3 tsp. (20 mL) alcohol. Brush this solution repeatedly on the scales or webs of lice.

SUCCESSFUL CARE AND PROPAGATION

Damaging flying insects are caught with sticky yellow tags.

A successful battle against whiteflies, humus flies, and other flying insects can be won using bright yellow, sticky plastic strips or tags. The plant pests stick to the panels, which are coated with a gluey substance.

by certain plants. These include, hoverflies, which especially like marigolds, calendula, and petunias. When fully developed, the hoverfly will nourish itself on the nectar and pollen, while its larvae devour aphids. There are also plants that chase away certain insects. Here's a tip for the patio and balcony gardener: nasturtium and garden cress planted in the earth around the tree trunks keep woolly apple aphids away from small fruit trees. The following useful protectors can also be introduced into enclosed rooms.

AGAINST APHIDS:
Lacewings (*Chrisopa carnea*) in the garden room, greenhouse, or plant window. Predator gall gnats (*Aphidoletes aphidimiza*) in the

garden room or greenhouse.
AGAINST WHITEFLIES:
Ichneumon wasps (*Encarsia formasa*) in the garden room or greenhouse.

AGAINST RED SPIDER MITES:
Predator mites (*Phytoseiulus persimillis*) in the garden room, greenhouse, plant window, and office.

AGAINST THE LARVAE OF THE BROAD-NOSED WEEVIL:
Parasitic nematodes (*Heterorhabditis sp.*) in all potting soils.

AGAINST THE LARVAE OF HUMUS FLIES:
Parasitic nematodes (*Steinernema bibionis*) in enclosed rooms.
AGAINST MEALYBUGS:
Australian ladybugs (*Cryptolaemus*

montroizier) in the garden room, greenhouse, plant window, and office. (They need high temperatures!)

Biological remedies
It would be wrong to assert that biological remedies are never poisonous. Many "harmless" herbs are harmful in high concentrations, but even a minimal quantity of certain materials can be deadly—nature does create extremely potent poisons. Many biological remedies for protecting plants are indeed truly harmless. Nevertheless, it is important always to follow the instructions of the manufacturer.

On the balcony and patio, plant lovers can call on a great number of eager helpers when it is a matter of keeping their plants healthy: ichneumon wasps, lacewings, hoverflies, ladybugs, earwigs, spiders, and others. All of them destroy pests.

What to Do When Pests Attack

Hoverflies love *Ipomoea*. Those who have these flowers on their balcony or patio get useful insects, whose larvae eat aphids "on the house."

The following materials of natural origin are included, among other things, in protective plant remedies:

PYRETHRUM is fairly poisonous. It acts on the nerve system of warm-blooded and cold-blooded creatures when it enters the bloodstream. Use caution if you are injured! Pyrethrum is an ingredient of sprays, powders, and liquid pesticides. It helps against biting and sucking insects, but bees are not endangered. Also available are preparations with synthetically manufactured pyrethroides. If the pesticide is made from genuine flower extract, the packaging says "Natural Pyrethrum."

PARAFFIN OIL, WHITE OIL gums up the breathing organs of scale insects, mealybugs, and spider mites. Only plants with hard foliage can stand this active substance. It is sprayed directly onto the plants.

POTASH SOAPS are available as sprays. They act on the breathing organs of sucking insects, but spare bees, lacewings, ladybugs, and other useful creatures. Soap-like mixtures are good for plants with soft foliage.

LECITHIN acts against powdery mildew and is available as a spray.

Protection through strengthening
In addition to protective agents, there are also plant-strengthening agents. These contain natural ingredients that latch on to the plant's cell tissue and heighten its defense mechanisms. They are used as a preventive against particular pests or diseases. The following substances fall in this category:

CHALKY ALGAE is dusted on the leaves to increase their defenses against fungal diseases and insects. It also dries up the insect larvae.

EXTRACT OF ALGAE contains many growth agents that are important to plants. It is offered as a liquid or a powder. Both are applied to the leaves. Algae extract heightens the plant's defenses against pests.

SILICIC ACID is a constituent of many plant-strengthening agents. It reinforces the tissue and heightens the resistance to fungi.

ETHEREAL OILS are marketed for plants under the label "Aromatic Plant Care." Sprays are available for house, balcony, and container plants—or for massed plants. There is a concentrate that should be thinned before use.

The effectiveness of this product, which won an ecological prize in 1993, has been demonstrated. It encourages plant growth and protects against diseases and pests.

Flower essences
These essences, which act directly on the energy systems of humans by way of small energetic oscillations, have also demonstrated extensive therapeutic effects when used on animals.

Their advocates also insist that they have a beneficial effect on plants. Against fungal attacks, they use "Crab Apple," for preventive strengthening, "Walnut," and for sickly plants, "Rescue," the so-called First Aid Drops. Put ten drops in a 2.5-gal. (10-L) watering can.

The essences are also available from drugstores on prescription.

Chemical remedies
Chemical plant-protection prepar-ations are also not a universal panacea; besides, they are not environmentally friendly. In the case of particularly valuable or rare plants, their use is justified if more gentle methods have not brought results.

- Always follow the manufacturer's directions exactly, and never use preparations designed for the outdoors in a closed space.
- Store the preparations so that children and pests are not endangered. Leftovers should be disposed of as hazardous waste.
- Protect yourself by wearing gloves. Take care not to get the preparations into your eyes, and do not inhale them.

TIP

Essences from plants help other plants. Flower-essence sprays and aromatic flower preparations for the care of roots can increase the plants' resistance. The principle comes from nature, where plant communities protect one another with their exhalations.

Trailing petunias and morning glories attract useful hoverlies.

The Most Common Pests

Together with houseplants, a whole series of insects has made itself at home on our windowsills. They often like it better there than outside, and propagate explosively because they can't be reached by their natural enemies. Among the most common and most dangerous plant pests are:

Spider mites, red spiders

The house and balcony gardener has most contact with the ordinary spider mite (*Tetranychus urticae*) or with the greenhouse spider mite (*Brevipalpus obovatus*). These tiny pests are greenish yellow or red, multiply very quickly, and scramble from one plant to the next. Both their larvae and the mature animals are extraordinarily greedy and not particularly choosy. Their incidence and spread are increased by high temperatures, low levels of humidity, and overfertilizing. Spider mites sit on the undersides of leaves next to the leaf veins, pierce the leaves, and suck out their sap.

Aphids, greenflies

This family is enormous, but he houseplant gardener mostly has to deal with the green peach aphid (*Myzus persicae*), which hardly spares a single pot plant. The animals multiply with amazing speed. Their development is enhanced by dry room air. They prefer weak plants, whose soft cell tissue they can penetrate more easily with their piercing organs; they also like the tender tips of shoots. The pests cause triple damage: they pierce the veins of the leaves and suck out the sap. In the process, they manage to inject a poison into the plant. Finally, they leave behind, with their feces, a sticky, sweet liquid (honeydew) on

Hibiscus with aphids

Whiteflies (enlarged)

which sooty mold, among other things, makes itself at home.

Scale insects

Of this large group of insects, the ones that bother houseplants most are the armored scale lice and the hemispherical scale lice; the remainder tend to prefer outdoor plants. To fight against these pests is particularly difficult because one usually discovers their presence only when the larvae have already been sheltered under their shields. The young larvae, extremely mobile and sensitive, are hard to detect with the naked eye. In a dry, warm environment, typical in winter when the central heating is on, scale insects feel particularly happy and multiply rapidly. They, like other pests, prefer weak hosts. The animals construct their scales

Scale insects adhere strongly

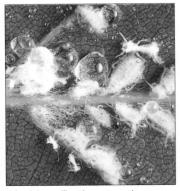

Mealybugs like dry, warm air

out of a waxy mass that they produce themselves, and under it, they lay their eggs. The shell of an armored scale louse is whitish yellow to brown, rather flat, and not connected to the larva below. The brownish, hemispheric "shield" of the hemispherical scale louse is the hardened skin of its back. Like the aphids, the scale insects harm leaves in three ways: by piercing and sucking them dry, by injecting poison with their saliva, and by emitting honeydew.

SUCCESSFUL CARE AND PROPAGATION

Mealybugs

These minute pests, which also belong to the scale insect family, are pink to light brown. Constantly in motion, they develop no firm scales. Their feces form whitish, woolly flakes, under which the animals often hide. They like to sit in large colonies on the root crown, the undersides of leaves, or in the leaf axils of plants. They cause the same sort of damage that scale insects do, and, like them, are happiest in a dry, warm environment.

Whiteflies

This insect also belongs to the scale insect family. It mostly appears in greenhouses, as it requires a temperature of 60–77°F (15–25°C) and 80 percent humidity. The whiteflies usually appear on the undersides of leaves. The microscopic larvae are mobile only in the youthful stage of their development; thereafter, they adhere firmly to the plant. In addition to the harm caused by their sucking, whiteflies endanger plants by emitting honeydew.

Thrips

These small insects become a major nuisance, especially when the room's air is warm and dry. Under these circumstances, they proliferate explosively. Mostly they are only noticed, however, when the .04 in.–.08 in.- (1–2 mm-) long slender, dark-winged creatures whiz about in large numbers. Thrips fly from one plant to the next and also get swept in by the wind. The mature insects lay their eggs in the tissue on the undersides of a plant's leaves. There, after a few days, the larvae are hatched. Often remaining close together, they pierce the leaves and flowers, and suck out the juice.

Stem and leaf nematodes

These tiny, colorless, transparent worms are everywhere, in the soil and in the water. They belong to the host of earth-dwelling creatures that account for soil fertility. Several species live as parasites, either of the roots (root-knot nematodes, root-gall nematodes) or of the above-ground parts of plants (leaf nematodes) and do much damage.

Nematodes must have enough moisture to be active and mobile. They "swim" or snake about like little eels—hence the name "eelworm"—through the moisture in the earth and, among other things, are carried from plant to plant through the water. They penetrate particularly easily through pores in leaves or into damaged plant parts.

The nematodes pierce into the plant tissue with their spikelike mouth parts, suck the juice, and inject poisons with their saliva. The affected plant parts begin to rot and are welcome nourishment for bacteria and fungi.

Additional pests, symptoms, and remedies can be found on pages 72–73.

Springtails (picture below, enlargement) are really only 1/16 in.–3/16 in. (1–4 mm) long. They appear in large swarms, usually in response to a mistake in caring for the plants. Wet soil and poor composition of the potting mix encourage their proliferation. However, they do no harm.

How Dangerous Are Springtails and Algae Gnats?

Even when they appear in great numbers, springtails do hardly any damage to plants. They feed on fungi, algae, and rotted organic matter; very seldom do they gnaw on living plants. The white or black, extraordinarily mobile creatures can live only in very high humidity. They rest in and on the soil, or on the underside of flower pots that stand in outer pots. Their incidence can be kept to a minimum by keeping the soil dryer. It may be necessary to repot the plant and do without the outer pot. Plunging the root balls in water for several hours drives the springtails out of the soil, so that they can simply be drained away. Humus flies, too, although a nuisance, are harmless. Only the larvae do damage to the fine hair roots, if they cannot find enough dead plant parts in the potting mix, or if the soil is too dry. Fully mature plants survive their attacks without difficulty, but seedlings and young plants may succumb. The small creatures stick to yellow tags. However, humus flies cannot be exterminated; they always come flying back.

Springtails, enlarged

The Most Common Diseases

Many problems are caused by fungi or by mistakes in caring for plants. Yellow leaves (chlorosis) often signal poor nourishment (lack of iron); burnt tips are an indication of dry air. Powdery mildew and gray mold are common fungal diseases.

Improper handling is the reason that many plants perform poorly—but poor care is not necessarily synonymous with carelessness. Poor care does, however, result in physiological damage. Other causes of problems are pests and fungal, bacterial, or viral infections.

It is not always evident what has made a plant sick, for many symptoms can have multiple causes. The selection of diseases and illustrations of problems provided here is limited to the most common ones; further symptoms and conditions are described on pages 70–71.

Physiological Damage

Mistakes in caring for houseplants and balcony plants cause a variety of problems. Here are a few examples:

YELLOW LEAVES (CHLOROSIS) often signal that the plant lacks iron or magnesium. This can occur when the plant water contains too much calcium. Calcium binds iron in the soil in a form that plants cannot take up.

DRIED-UP leaf spots are often caused by "sunscorch," e.g., when the plant is exposed, unshielded, to the full midday sun.

CORKY GROWTHS on the stems or leaves often develop because a plant is watered too often and excessive humidity is combined with insufficient light.

FAILURE TO THRIVE may have a number of causes, among them root damage (pot too small, too much moisture), sharply fluctuating temperature and humidity, inadequate light, and over-fertilization.

Citrus fruit with chlorosis

Palms with burnt tips

Begonia with powdery mildew

Poinsettia with gray mold

BLOOM ROT can be caused, among other things, by fertilizing with nitrogen, bad placement, or failure to provide a resting period.

TIP BURN is usually a sign that the air has been dry for too long.

Fungal diseases

Fungi are another kingdom of organisms, separate from plants and animals. Fungi multiply by way of spores that are broadly distributed by wind, water, and living things. Some are useful and harmless; others cause diseases in humans, animals, and plants. Soil fungi can occur anywhere, even in potting soil. Several kinds invade the tissue of roots, often by way of damaged areas, and plug the nutritive pathways with mycelia.

ROOT ROT is caused primarily by fungi of the genus *Pythium* or *Phytophthora*. Favorable conditions for the growth of these harmful fungi are excessive humidity, too much salt in the substratum (overfertilization), too cold a location, and watering with excessively cold water.

DAMPING OFF AND BLACKLEG, caused by the fungi *Phoma lingard* and *Pythium debaryanum*, are the bane of every gardener. They most often attack seedlings and rooted cuttings. Often the spores of the fungus are first brought home in the soil mix.

BASAL ROT is caused by, among others, the fungus *Fusarium*, whereas *wilt* is caused by the fungus *Verticillium*.

Successful Care and Propagation

BASAL ROT OR CROWN ROT IN AZALEAS is due to *Cylindrocladium* fungi. These fungi grow inside the plants and block up the nutritive pathways. Make sure, when buying azaleas, that the leaves look fresh and healthy.

ROOT ROT AND TUBER ROT IN CYCLAMEN signal an invasion of *Thielaviopsis basicola* or *Cylindrocarpon radicicola*, which penetrate the tubers with an internal netting of mycelia. If you identify this disease, throw the plants out immediately.

POWDERY MILDEW is a term that covers several fungi, all of which cause the same symptoms and damage, but each of which specializes in infecting a different plant genus. Transmission from one genus to another is not possible. The spores are brought in by the wind, rest on leaves and stems, and find their nourishment in the tissue of the plant. Poor location, excess nitrogen fertilizer, placing the plants too close to each other, poor air circulation, and warm humid weather hasten the spread of the fungi.

DOWNY MILDEW is also caused by a variety of fungi, which generally specialize in infecting certain plants. The spores survive the winter in the soil, then find their way to the underside of the leaves, penetrating any cracks, and there develop their mycelia. These become apparent as a thin, white coating. The spores prefer a damp environment.

GRAY MOLD only occurs in damaged plant tissue. The fungus (*Botrytis cinerea*) lives both on plants and in the soil. Its spread is assisted by a cold, damp environment, poor air circulation, and inadequate light.

RUST can be caused by many thousands of kinds of rust fungi. The houseplant gardener is mostly plagued by pelargonium rust (*Puccinia pelargonii-zonalis*) and by fuchsia rust (*Pucciniastrum epilobii*).

SOOTY MOLD FUNGI settle on the sugary droppings deposited on the leaves by mealybugs, scale insects, and aphids, and there develop their mycelia. Wherever this occurs, light can no longer reach the leaf, thereby disturbing the process of photosynthesis.

LEAF SPOT can be caused by a great number of different fungi. Especially at risk are weak plants, as well as leaves that have been damaged by other causes. The spread of the fungi is speeded by significant changes in temperature.

Bacteria and viruses

Houseplants are not prone to many bacterial diseases, nor do these occur very often. Bacteria are usually introduced via watering, and actively penetrate the plants through wounds or cracks. There is no effective way to fight bacteria. The affected plants should be destroyed.

Viruses are spread by aphids, whiteflies, and other damaging insects, or are transmitted by dirty scissors and knives. Viral diseases, too, are incurable, so the infected plants should likewise be destroyed.

OLEANDER CANCER is caused by the bacterium *Pseudomonas tonelliana*, which has specialized in infecting the oleander (*Nerium oleander*).

BACTERIAL LEAF-SPOTTING DISEASES are caused by bacteria whose species have specialized in invading certain plants. Pelargonium (geranium) blight is caused by the bacterium *Xanthomonas pelargonii*, the oily leaf-spot disease of begonias by *Xanthomonas begoniae* and the fatty leaf-spot disease of ivy by *Xanthomonas hederae*. These bacteria are encouraged by high humidity, high temperature, poor air circulation, and too much fertilizer.

BACTERIAL SOFT-ROT in houseplants is caused by different species of bacteria, which cause similar damage. Their spread is encouraged by a warm and damp environment.

MOSAIC DISEASES are due to a number of viruses, each specializing in a group of (usually) related plants. They cause the foliage or petals of plants to change color. In some cases, these "problems" are deliberately selected and are described as "variegated leaves." Examples are the spotted mosaic leaves of the flowering maple (*Abutilon*), variety 'Thompsonii,' or the Rembrandt tulip (*Tulipa*), which has striped or flame-streaked petals. In most other cases, however, it is proper to speak of mosaic diseases. Certain viruses may cause such damage that the leaves drop off, and the plant stops growing, or the leaves may remain but are permanently discolored.

Bacterial leaf-spot disease (see picture, below) first appears as individual, small, round spots that look like fat spots, but these soon grow and eventually blend into one another.

Begonias with oily leaf-spot disease

Problems and Diseases at a Glance

Pale leaves (mineral chlorosis)
SYMPTOMS: The leaves turn pale and become yellowish, while the veins remain green.
CAUSE: Lack of iron or magnesium. Both elements are needed for the development of chlorophyll. Water that contains too much calcium also causes this problem, because it binds iron in the soil.
REMEDY: The acute deficiency can be treated with iron chelate or brown algae extract. Water with softened water.

Cold damage
SYMPTOMS: Pale spots form on the leaves.
CAUSE: Rapid drop in temperature on the windowsill between the panes and the curtains, or using water that is too cold when watering.
REMEDY: In the cold season, move the plants or put thick layers of newspaper in front of the windowpanes and do not close the curtains so that the circulating room temperature reaches the plants.

Nitrogen deficiency
SYMPTOMS: Leaves fewer, sometimes almost transparent.
CAUSE: Insufficient nitrogen. Among other things, nitrogen is essential for the development of chlorophyll.
REMEDY: Immediate improvement can be brought about by application of a nitrogen-rich fertilizer added to the water. For the longer term, mix a small amount of bone meal carefully into the top layer of soil. Possibly repot in fresh soil.

Sunscorch
SYMPTOMS: Reddish, silvery-white, or brown spots form on the leaves.
CAUSE: The plant was suddenly exposed to full sunlight in the spring.
REMEDY: Move the plants into the shade. In the spring, do not move plants into direct sun right away, and above all make sure to shield them from the midday sun.

Yellow leaves
SYMPTOMS: The leaves turn yellow and eventually fall off.
CAUSE: Excessive watering, nitrogen deficiency, or a location that is too dark. With some plants it is normal for older leaves to yellow and drop off.
REMEDY: Water only when the soil is dry. When sufficiently recovered, exchange the soil, and water less thereafter. Fertilize regularly with an appropriate fertilizer. Move the plant to a brighter position.

Rolled-up leaves
SYMPTOMS: The edges of the leaves roll up, sometimes becoming dry. The rolling is a defense mechanism of the plant, which enables it to shrink its surface area and thus lose less water through evaporation.
CAUSE: Either the plant is too warm or it is getting too little water.
REMEDY: Water the plant thoroughly, possibly even soaking it in water for a short time, and choose a cooler location.

Black leaf spots
SYMPTOMS: Brownish black spots form on the leaves, or the edges of the leaves discolor and become dark.
CAUSE: Conditions that are too dry or too moist, overfertilizing, exhausted soil, or lack of humidity in the air.
REMEDY: Increase humidity, check fertilizing and watering, possibly repot with new soil.

Corky growths
SYMPTOMS: Corky growths develop on the plant's shoots and won't go away.
CAUSE: In leaf cacti, the result of great changes in temperature, a too-dark location combined with excessive damp, and irregular watering.
REMEDY: Move the plant to a brighter location, avoid the above mistakes in caring for it, and carefully remove the damaged parts.

TIP

Sick parts of plants should always be cut off immediately, before any other measures are taken, because bacteria, and especially fungi, multiply quickly.

70

SUCCESSFUL CARE AND PROPAGATION

Powdery mildew
SYMPTOMS: A white, floury film develops on the surface; this later turns brownish.
CAUSE: Wind-borne spores of fungi. The infection is made worse by overfertilization, a warm and damp location, and too-close placement of plants.
REMEDY: Drastically cut out damaged portions of the plant and destroy them. Rinse off the plants with horsetail broth or a fungicide that contains lecithin.

Downy mildew
SYMPTOMS: A whitish film develops on the underside of the leaves, and later turns brownish. Yellowish or brownish spots appear on the surface of the leaf.
CAUSE: Wind-borne fungal spores. A damp and warm environment encourages the infection to spread.
REMEDY: Affected plant parts must be cut out and destroyed. Select a cooler, drier location, and apply the appropriate plant fungicide.

Gray mold
SYMPTOMS: Soft rotting patches, which are later covered by a gray fungal network.
CAUSE: Airborne fungal spores settling on damaged tissue. Excessive humidity and moisture, especially on the leaves, encourage this condition.
REMEDY: Remove and destroy the affected plant parts. In serious cases, throw away the entire plant. Lower the humidity, improve air circulation, or move the plants to a more airy location.

Rusts
SYMPTOMS: Light patches on the surface and brownish patches on the underside of the leaf.
CAUSE: Wind-borne fungal spores, which penetrate the undersides of the leaves. Especially endangered are zonal pelargoniums and fuchsias.
REMEDY: Remove and destroy the affected plant parts. Spray with a suitable fungicide.

Leaf spots
SYMPTOMS: Yellowish and brownish spots on the leaves, which also frequently disintegrate.
CAUSE: Wind-borne fungal spores, which attack weak plants in particular.
REMEDY: Remove and destroy damaged plant parts. Improve the general health of the plants through better care, and treat with the appropriate fungicide as required.

Amaryllis rust
SYMPTOMS: Red, cracked parts of the bulb and shoots of an amaryllis. The plant develops crookedly.
CAUSE: Wind-borne fungal spores, which are often already present at the time of purchase.
REMEDY: In less serious cases, control the disease by cutting out the affected parts and dust the bulb with charcoal powder. Place the plant in a cool location and do not soak the bulb when watering. A cure is impossible.

Root rot
SYMPTOMS: Wilting and gradual death, because the damaged roots are not able to absorb nutrients and water. The roots are discolored, red or brown.
CAUSE: A destructive fungal mycelium that has penetrated and clogged the roots. Overmoist conditions help it to multiply.
REMEDY: Virtually none, once the plant wilts. Badly affected plants must be destroyed, together with the soil and pot!

Basal stem rot
SYMPTOMS: Discolored, semi-transparent, rotten patches on the base of the stems, that develop and enlarge quickly.
CAUSE: Fungal mycelia, which usually appear in the soil. Too much moisture makes them spread faster.
REMEDY: Virtually none. Destroy the plant, soil, and pot immediately!

TIP

It is better to throw out a sick plant than to treat it for a longer period of time with more or less poisonous remedies. As well, this prevents spread of the infection to healthy plants.

71

Pests, Bacteria, and Viruses

Aphids, greenflies
SYMPTOMS: Leaves are sticky, frequently shriveled. Tips of shoots and flowers wilt.
CAUSE: Green, brown, orange-yellow, or black lice that attack the leaves and suck the sap.
REMEDY: Regularly monitor for an attack of aphids and, at the first sign, spray with a soap solution or a broth of stinging nettle. Cut off and destroy badly affected parts. Treat plant with a protective spray. Introduce ladybugs or lacewing larvae.

Scale insects
SYMPTOMS: Sticky leaves with many irregular yellowish spots; when strongly affected, the leaves become dry and drop off. The hard, brownish scale is easy to recognize.
CAUSE: Scale insects prick the leaves and suck the sap. Warm, dry air encourages their multiplication.
REMEDY: Very carefully pick off the scale insects or brush them off with a solution of soap and alcohol. Move the plant to a cooler location and increase the humidity.

Spider mites
SYMPTOMS: Fine white web between the leaves.
CAUSE: Tiny spinning insects that have been either brought in with the plant or introduced after you bought it. Both the larvae and the adults suck sap. Dry air stimulates this infestation.
REMEDY: Raise the humidity and spray or rinse the plant several times with lukewarm water. If the plant will tolerate it, place it for a few days in a transparent plastic bag.

Whiteflies
SYMPTOMS: White spots on the leaves, especially the undersides, followed by falling leaves. Small, white flies, which fly off at the lightest touch.
CAUSE: Whiteflies enter through open windows, or are brought in with other plants. Their development is encouraged by a damp, warm environment.
REMEDY: Lower the temperature. Place the plants in a dry location. Place bright yellow sticky tags in the pots. Most insecticides do not provide effective control.

Stem and leaf nematodes
SYMPTOMS: The leaves at first turn yellow between the veins, but later become brownish or black and eventually fall off.
CAUSE: Tiny threadlike worms that are brought in with the potting soil penetrate the stem, leaves, and flowers, and inhibit the flow of sap. Damp encourages them to multiply.
REMEDY: Remove and destroy the affected plant parts. Change the substratum and lower the humidity.

Root nematodes
SYMPTOMS: The plants wilt, and brownish swellings appear on the roots.
CAUSE: Tiny, wormlike nematodes living in the soil penetrate the roots, causing tissue swelling in which they lay their eggs; the swelling inhibits the absorption of water. Depending on the species of nematode, these swellings can measure from a few thousandths of an inch (a few millimeters) to one-third of an inch (a centimeter).
REMEDY: There is no reliable cure. Destroy the plant, together with its soil and pot.

Broad-nosed weevils
SYMPTOMS: Semicircular notches on the edges of the leaves. Plants wilt quickly. The bug is easy to recognize, but only emerges from its hiding place at night.
CAUSE: The larvae of the bug feed off the roots, while the adults feed on the leaves and stem.
REMEDY: Change the soil. At night, cover the plant, then use a flashlight to illuminate the plant, shake it, and remove the bugs.

Slugs
SYMPTOMS: Leaves that have been eaten, and slimy tracks.
CAUSE: Slugs that prefer to eat at night and shelter during the day in dark, damp hiding places.
REMEDY: Pick off the slugs after dark. Place the plants in upended flowerpots that rest in a bowl filled with water, to isolate them.

Some visible pests can easily be picked off, or wiped off, by hand. This perhaps requires a little willpower, but at least it doesn't cost money.

SUCCESSFUL CARE AND PROPAGATION

Thrips
SYMPTOMS: The leaves and petals first develop yellow spots, then glow silvery-white. Brown feeding spots appear on the undersides of the leaves, and small, black, winged insects are visible
CAUSE: Insects and their larvae infesting the leaves and sucking the sap out of them. They prefer dry, warm conditions.
REMEDY: Increase the humidity, rinse the plants repeatedly with lukewarm water, and place an insect trap in the soil.

Soft-skinned mites
SYMPTOMS: Deformed, rolled-up leaves and flowers, stunted growth.
CAUSE: Tiny web-spinning insects infesting the plants and sucking their sap. The mites prefer a damp, warm environment.
REMEDY: Destroy affected plant parts immediately; if the attack is massive, it is best to destroy the entire plant right away, as there is great danger of infecting others. The most effective insecticides are extremely poisonous and must be used carefully!

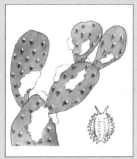

Mealybugs
SYMPTOMS: Cottonlike growth on the plants.
CAUSE: Mobile, pink or light brown bugs damaging the plants by sucking. Dry, warm air favors their spread.
REMEDY: Raise the humidity and place the plants in a cooler spot; spray with soap or alcohol, and wipe off the "cotton" with a damp cloth. (In severe cases, throw out the plant, soil, and pot.)

Leaf miners
SYMPTOMS: Silver-white, random feeding paths in the leaves.
CAUSE: The larvae of miners eat paths through the tissues directly under the epidermis of the leaves and store the uptake of nourishment. Miners usually only appear outdoors.
REMEDY: Destroy affected leaves. Appropriate insecticides are very poisonous!

Oleander cancer
SYMPTOMS: On the leaves, tiny, light speckles that grow rapidly, becoming dark at the center. These also develop where the leaves join onto the stem. Portions of the plant above the damaged area die off.
CAUSE: Bacteria, specific to oleander, are distributed by rain.
REMEDY: Cut off and destroy the affected leaves. Do not place oleander in locations where rainfall is frequent.

Stem rot
SYMPTOMS: The lower part of the stem takes on a brownish tinge and becomes rotten in places; usually, the root is also affected and the plant dies off.
CAUSE: A fungus that lives in the soil. Excessively dense earth, too much water, and too much fertilizer all promote its spread.
REMEDY: Virtually none. One can only seek to prevent the condition by strengthening the plant and ensuring ideal growing conditions.

Mosaic virus
SYMPTOMS: Light or dark green spots on the leaves. Cellular growth and development come to a halt.
CAUSE: A number of viruses, each specializing in particular plants.
REMEDY: None. Do not propagate the plant!

Pelargonium wilt
SYMPTOMS: Transparent spots on the undersides of the leaves. Spots enlarge rapidly and become brown in the center. Leaves and stems wilt progressively, and the plant dies.
CAUSE: Bacteria specific to pelargoniums.
REMEDY: None. Destroy affected plants at once, to prevent the spread of the disease. Do not take any cuttings from infected plants. If outdoor plants are to be overwintered indoors, check them carefully first.

In some European countries, no sprays against bacterial diseases are permitted. Sick plants must be destroyed at once, preferably burned. Under no circumstances should they be thrown on the compost heap or in the garbage can. In some jurisdictions in North America, antibiotics are available for licensed use only, chiefly in agriculture. The bacteria that cause this wilt, and other plant diseases, can survive in the general environment, especially in soil. So it is not a good idea to spread the disease through compost, etc.

Propagation from Seed

Enthusiastic lovers of houseplants do not limit their hobby to the care of their plants: they also consider breeding and propagation as part of their domain. Nor is it even very important that the these processes pay off. It is simply a matter of getting joy from observing how tiny seed kernels or small cuttings turn into beautiful plants. Anyone who loves exotic plants and enjoys experimenting can turn a windowsill into a cabinet of rarities.

There are two preconditions, however: a lot of time and a lot of space.

Plants can be propagated in two ways: from seeds (sexually), and by rooting plant parts (vegetatively or asexually).

Sexual propagation

Most houseplants can be propagated from seeds. However, sowing seeds usually yields many more plants than one has room for. The process gets interesting only if one is given seeds of rare plants or if one enjoys experimenting. In the case of annuals for the balcony, growing from seed is also economical.

WHEN SHOULD ONE SOW?

In most continental climates, one can begin with summer flowers by late winter; other plants are best started in the spring. (In regions where it is warmer earlier, sowing can begin about two months before the usual date of outdoor planting.)

CONTAINERS FOR SOWING

Any pot, bowl, or small box is suitable, so long as it has a drainage hole. However, anyone who wants to end up with a lot of plants should consider getting special seed trays or heated mini-hothouses with a temperature control. Useful, though not beautiful, are the thick Styrofoam flats used by nurseries, which have been stamped with depressions for small pots. The foamy synthetic material is always warm, which prevents problems caused by a seeding mix that is too cold.

Preparing for propagation

- soil for seeding and germinating
- peat pots, if nothing else will do
- seed containers (small pots made of plastic, clay, pressed peat, or recycled paper)
- seed trays or boxes, with or without lids
- possibly heated mini-hothouses with thermostats
- electric heating coils or Styrofoam underlays
- transplanting tool
- rooting powder
- charcoal powder
- sharp knife or razor blade
- labels
- waterproof marker
- transparent plastic bags
- pane of glass for covering
- wood stakes in different lengths
- wire
- water atomizer
- watering can with fine spray head
- gardening gloves

ROOTING MIXTURE

Seeds are usually sown in commercial rooting mix; for the drainage layer, use either 0.4 in. (1 cm) gravel or many layers of absorbent paper that can soak up excess moisture, and that gives up moisture slowly. Before sowing, the soil is dampened thoroughly and smoothed out.

THE SEEDS THEMSELVES

The seeds you use must be fresh. Buy them from seed specialists or other specialist suppliers (→ see the list of suppliers, pages 376–77). The seed packets should give a best-before date, and an indication of whether the seeds germinate in light or darkness—that is, whether the seeds should be covered with soil or only pressed into it. Good products will also tell you whether the seeds should be put into lukewarm water before sowing, if large; whether those with hard coats must be nicked; and how high the germinating temperature of the soil should be.

SOWING

Seeds can be placed in rows or strewn on the mix—but do not forget to indicate where they are with a tag. Finer seeds should be at a distance of about 0.2 in. (0.5 cm) from one another, and larger ones, 0.8–1.2 in. (2–3 cm) apart. Very big seeds are given their own pot. Seeds that germinate in the dark are usually covered with earth to a depth of double the seed's thickness. Before sowing dust-fine seeds, sieve a layer of soil over the surface of the seed tray so that the tiny kernels don't sink too deep into the coarse soil. It is hard not to sow fine seeds too thickly. Make a hole in the seed packet and tap lightly with your index finger. The seed containers are covered with a pane of glass or with a transparent plastic film. Although you should not allow the soil to dry out, you should always spray the surface carefully, using a water atomizer, so that the seeds

SUCCESSFUL CARE AND PROPAGATION

Various seedlings

Seedlings that have been given their own small pots soon develop a good root ball.

Peanut plants (*Arachis hypopaea*) possess a unique quality. The nuts grow in the soil. You can try this out on the windowsill: plant fresh, undamaged peanut kernels (without their shell) in a moist mix of earth and sand, and place in a warm spot (68°F (20°C)). Three months later, the kernels begin to bloom. The flower shoots bend back, grow right into the soil, and there form the fruit.

don't get washed into the soil. The germinating temperature differs with the species.

PROPER CARE FOR SEEDLINGS

As soon as the first seed-leaves appear, the seedlings need light and fresh air, so the cover should be lifted for a few seconds from time to time. The temperature for most species may now be lowered by 7–9°F (4–5°C). The soil must still be kept moist, but seedlings cannot tolerate standing water.

POTTING UP

All plants have very similar seed-leaves, but the first pair of leaves particular to the species soon appears. If the seedlings are too close to one another, the weakest should be pricked out. Potting up should be done when two or three new leaf pairs have developed. Using a potting mix appropriate to the species, transplant into individual pots or larger containers. To transplant, take hold of the seedling by its leaves—not by its stem—lift it out of the soil with the thin end of a transplanting tool, drill a hole in the new soil, and insert the seedling fairly deep down, yet without allowing the leaves to touch the soil. To keep the little plants from becoming etiolated, they must be put into a bright spot, but they cannot tolerate direct sun. Gradually accustom the seedling to lower temperatures. Fertilize for the first time after four to six weeks. Thereafter, the young plants can be cared for like mature plants.

Gallery of rarities

Plant lovers continually try to germinate the pits of exotic fruits, such as leechee, mango, guava, papaya, or star fruit, in order to acquire plants that are out of the ordinary. The good thing is it usually works. The propagating method is the same as with other seeds. To succeed, it is important to keep plants that are used to warmth in a heated propagating case. One should also make sure that the fruits from which seeds are taken are ripe and have not been exposed to frost. As well, be sure that all fruit has been cleaned off the seeds, and that they are dry.

Peanut seedling

Propagation from Cuttings

Hydroculture aficionados can start their next generation of plants hydroponically. For this purpose, special rooting pots and fine rooting granulate are commercially available.

Vegetative propagation means growing new plants from parts of old ones. The "offspring" are exact replicas of the mother plant and exhibit the same characteristics. In comparison to growing from seed, this method produces new plants more quickly, but in smaller numbers.

For your propagating material, select healthy, generously blooming specimens. Propagation can be done using adventitious plants, offsets or offshoots, cuttings, tip or root cuttings, by division of rhizomes or rootstocks, and by air layering.

Some general rules:
- Always use very clean tools.
- Do not touch the surfaces of cuts.
- Make sure the cuts are smooth; otherwise, they will rot easily.
- Before planting offsets in rooting mix, dip their cut surfaces in a rooting solution.

When to propagate

Cuttings, leaves, and leaf cuttings are usually taken in spring or early summer. Herbaceous perennials and rhizomes are also divided in the spring, after the end of the rest pause. Woody cuttings are taken in fall, buried in sand during the winter, and stored in a cool but frost-free location. In the spring they are planted in normal soil. Adventitious plants and offsets can be rooted at any time of year.

Rooting

Plants are able to grow roots out of the layer of tissue (cambium), which lies directly under the epidermis. If the plant is damaged, as when a shoot or leaf is cut off, scar tissue (callus) forms at the wound site to close the wound. From it, small roots grow. This occurs either in rooting mix, water, or, in the case of hydroculture, in fine-grained clay aggregate.

- Do not forget to give pots a drainage layer!
- The cuts of succulents and cacti should be allowed to dry before the cuttings are placed in rooting mix.
- Dust the cuts with a rooting powder, to encourage root formation.
- Bore a hole in the mix beforehand so as not to damage the epidermis of the stem when planting.
- Keep an eye out for the direction of growth of part or stem cuttings: they must be placed growing upward!

Rooting pot for hydroculture plants

- When rooting is done in water, charcoal chips in the glass can prevent rot.
- If several leaf cuttings are to share a container, cover it with plastic film and make a small hole for each stem.
- As soon as a number of roots have formed in the water, pot the plants in loose rooting mix.

Care of new cuttings

Place the saucers or pots in a bright, warm, but not sunny location. Keep an eye on the temperature of the mix: cuttings, too, dislike "cold feet." Styrofoam insulation, available in any builders' supply store, acts almost like a heater when used as an underlay on the windowsill. The soil must be kept uniformly moist, but must not be allowed to store water.

Spray the cuttings and their rooting medium regularly, but not with a powerful jet. The leaves will evaporate moisture in a normal way, but they are not yet able to store water because the roots are still lacking. Improper watering is stressful for cuttings.

Placing the pot in a transparent plastic bag and closing the bag tightly increases the humidity considerably (saturated air). The plastic film must not be allowed to touch the plant, however. Air occasionally! If the cuttings have large leaves, simply cut them in half to reduce the evaporating surfaces.

As soon as new shoots or leaves appear, the cuttings have formed roots. This is the time to remove the plastic.

From then on, the plants may be given a little weak fertilizer every week or two.

If bushy plants are desired, remove the tip of the main stem and, later, also the tips of side shoots.

As soon as the infant plants have become adolescents, repot them in normal soil and a larger pot.

TIP

Plants that "bleed" after they are cut should be held under running water.

Water stops bleeding

Successful Care and Propagation

Various cuttings in a rooting tray

In the rooting tray, several cuttings from a variety of plants can be rooted at the same time. For example, the umbrellas of umbrella sedge can be planted directly in the soil; leaf cuttings of the rubber tree can be rolled together to reduce the evaporating surfaces. A rubber band keeps the bundle tight.

Rooting begonias is relatively quick and easy. If you want to stay on the safe side, dust the cuts with a rooting hormone before planting. Ideally, place a transparent plastic bag over the pot and thereby create saturated air and minimal evaporation. So that they will not rot, make sure leaves do not touch the bag, as the inside becomes covered with condensation.

Dipping cuts in rooting hormone

Providing saturated air

Propagation from Cuttings

Umbrella sedge (*Cyperus*) roots in water, no matter which way round one puts the leaf umbrellas (umbrella rooting).

Making two out of one: the fronds of yucca and dracaenas are cut or sawed off. Planted in sandy soil and covered with transparent film, the "cuttings" often root in 3–4 weeks.

All plant parts, above-ground or subterranean, can potentially generate new plants.

Adventitious plants

Miniature replicas of the mother plant grow on the leaves or leaf edges of certain houseplants. In the case of piggy-back plant (*Tolmiea menziesii*), simply cut off a leaf that contains a well-developed daughter plant and has a stem about 1.2 in. (3 cm) long. Plant into moist rooting soil so that the leaf lies on the surface. In the case of kalanchoe species, e.g., *Kalanchoe daugrenibtuaba*, the new plant grows between the little teeth along the edge of the leaf and there develops aerial roots.

Runners

Complete tiny plants with aerial roots grow at the ends of long shoots or runners on, e.g., the spider plant (*Chlorophytum comosum*) and the mother-of-thousands (*Saxifraga stolonifera*). These can be cut off and potted.

Offsets (offshoots)

New, small, side plants, with their own roots, grow immediately adjacent to the mother plants of, e.g., many bromeliads and of clivia. If the offsets are strong enough (in bromeliads they should already have a vase), they are cut off close to the main stem with a sharp knife and stuck in moist rooting soil.

Bulblets

Small bulbs grow at the base of the main bulb in, e.g., amaryllis (*Hippeastrum*) and veltheimias. Remove the largest side bulbs when repotting and plant them in their customary soil mix.

Tip layering

This method involves stimulating root development in the shoots by bringing them into contact with the soil. The leaf nodes are pressed into the surface of the soil of a small pot with a paper clip. If one slits the stem at the point where it touches the soil, roots develop more quickly. Plants with many creeping shoots propagate in this way naturally, e.g., mosaic plant (*Fittonia verschaffeltii*).

Tip or shoot cuttings

The tips of shoots are most often used for propagation. Cut a piece with two to four pairs of leaves a short distance below another pair. In the case of woody plants, the stem should be half-hardened. To root, place the cutting in rooting soil to a depth of about 0.8 in. (2 cm), or put it in a glass of water.

Semi-hardwood cuttings

Particularly suited for this method are leafy sections of shoots that have not yet hardened but are also not too soft. They are cut

Division of plants that have grown too tall

about 3/8 in. (5 mm) under a leaf node. Each section should be 2–4 in. (5–10 cm) long and have two to four pairs of leaves. Remove the lower leaves and let root in water or potting soil.

Stem cuttings

From stems that have not hardened too much, cut off pieces about 2 in. (5 cm) long. Each piece should have at least one bud. Lay the pieces on top of the substratum, or stick them in. The soil temperature must be 75–79°F (24–26°C) and the humidity very high. This kind of propagation is suitable for philodendron, yucca, and dieffenbachia.

Heel cuttings

From plants with woody stems, pull downward to remove a side shoot. A small piece of bark from the main stem, the heel, must remain attached to it. The cut is smoothed off. This method works with indoor linden (*Sparmannia*).

Leaf cuttings

New plants can also be propagated from the leaves of several species, e.g., the African violet (*Saintpaulia*), propeller plant (*Crassula aborescens*), and echeveria. They root well in water or rooting mix. In the case of begonias, the main veins on the backs of the leaves should be slit with a knife, and this side of the leaf laid on moist rooting mix. So that all parts of the leaf are in contact with the soil, weight it down with little pebbles. Roots develop on the cut side, and small plants on the upper side.

Leaf-section cuttings

In some species, e.g., *Sanseveria*, even small pieces of leaves will

SUCCESSFUL CARE AND PROPAGATION

Leaf cuttings from a variety of plants

Some plants are easily propagated from leaves. These include the African violet (*Saintpaulia*), ivy (*Hedera*), kalanchoe (*Kalanchoe blossfediana*), and various species of sedum.

root. Cut the leaves diagonally and plant in moist rooting soil.

Root cuttings

Both herbaceous perennials with fleshy roots and woody plants can be propagated using pieces of root. In fall, the root is cut close to its crown and divided into pieces about 2 in. (5 cm) long. The bottom end is cut on a diagonal, while the upper remains straight. The cuttings can be planted vertically until spring in a lime-rich soil; or you may put them into a pot so that the cut end coincides with the surface. Spread a little more soil over the top and keep the cuttings frost-free. Don't let the soil mix dry out. Once several pairs of leaves have formed, pot up.

Shoot cuttings

This is how woody plants are propagated. In fall, take off an entire shoot and remove all the leaves. Each shoot may be 4–10 in. (10–25 cm) in length. The lower, diagonally cut end should be just below the bud and the other end just above the bud. Until spring, place the cuttings into soil at an angle, to a depth of one-half to three-quarters of their length. In spring, they are then potted up individually.

Root division

Herbaceous perennials can easily be propagated by dividing their roots. In spring, pull the root balls apart and pot the sections into fresh soil mix.

Air layering

This is a method for rejuvenating old plants. Two rings of about 0.4 in. (1 cm) are cut in the stem about 4 in. (10 cm) under the last leaf, and the bark between them is cut away. Dust the wound with rooting powder. Under the cut section, tie transparent plastic film to form a bag, fill it with moist peat, and close it up on top. As soon as the peat ball is well filled with roots, it is cut from the stem, the covering is removed, and the "offset" is planted in its customary soil mix.

Special Methods of Propagation

Propagation of ferns is very hard and lengthy. The fine spores on the undersides of the fronds often need several months to germinate.

The hobby gardener must pay attention to particular characteristics or take special measures when cultivating and propagating certain plant groups. In this category belong orchids, bromeliads, and palms, as well as cacti and other succulents. Several species belonging to these groups can only be propagated by specialists under carefully controlled conditions. The first commandment, in any event, is extreme cleanliness!

Propagating ferns

In addition to the simple methods—dividing the rhizome or using offshoots—ferns can be propagated from their spores, but this needs a great deal of patience.

PROPAGATION USING SPORES
The spores sit in capsules on the undersides of the fronds. When these capsules turn brown, the spores are ripe. This is the time to cut off the entire frond and place it in a bag that lets in air. Close the bag well and hang it in a warm location. After a week, the dust-fine spores fall off.
- The soil medium, a mix of predominantly peat, must be germ-free. Assure this by placing it in a sieve and dousing with boiling water. Drain and pour at once into small germinating containers. Freezer containers with transparent lids are good for this purpose.
- Scatter the spores on the cooled germinating medium. Try not to touch the spores with your fingers, so as not to transmit germs.
- Close the containers well and put in a warm, bright place.
If you failed to be sufficiently clean in your work, fungi will develop rapidly and endanger germination.

After two to three months, a mossy coating will appear on top of the medium. These are the so-called prothalli, on which sit both female and male organs. Given enough humidity and warmth, propagation ensues.

Several months often pass before tiny fronds are

Tiny fern plants

recognizable. At this point, it is time to prick out the mini-ferns and start cultivating them in small pots. The small fern plants still need the same planting mix, a warm, bright location, and high humidity under a plastic bag or in a mini-hothouse. When the plants are about 1.5 in. (4 cm) high, they can be fertilized. Once the root balls are well developed, transplant the fern to a bigger pot with the customary substratum.

Propagating orchids

With orchids, too, it is extremely important to be clean when you work. Only strong, vigorous plants several years old withstand having their roots divided or their tips removed as cuttings. The best time to propagate is when sprouting starts. Certain rules are generally applicable, among them:
- Always work with disinfected cutting implements and containers.
- Handle roots and aerial roots carefully, as they break easily.
- Dust all cuts with charcoal powder.
- Dampen fresh substratum with soft water before potting.
- Keep the plants in a warm but never sunny place for the first three to four weeks (not even the most sun-hungry of them).
- Do not water, but spray once a day.
- Do not fertilize.

PROPAGATING MONOPODIAL ORCHIDS
Monopodial orchids, which grow vertically upward without significant branching, can be propagated by taking tip or shoot cuttings. The cut-off parts must have at least two aerial roots. Several species develop offshoots (called keikes in the case of orchids), e.g., *Phalaenopsis.* The offshoots, together with a small section of stem at each end, may be detached as soon as enough aerial roots have developed, The new plants often find it difficult to stay upright in loose orchid potting mix, and may have to be supported by a stake or attached to the surface with fine wire.

PROPAGATING SYMPODIAL ORCHIDS
Sympodial orchids with a horizontal shoot axis (rhizome) and pseudobulbs can only be propagated by dividing the rhizome: however, every section must have two or three leafy side shoots or pseudobulbs. The new growth is at the front, and the oldest pseudobulb (called "backbulb" by specialists)

Ripe fern spores

SUCCESSFUL CARE AND PROPAGATION

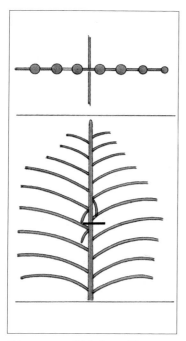

Rhizomes are divided or cuttings are taken, depending on the type of growing form.

at the far end. The cut ends must be dried before the sections are planted. A gentle method is to do the dividing in the old plant container. Cut through the roots and let the plant stand for another four to six weeks. The cut ends have healed by then, and often have begun to develop new shoots.

TISSUE OR MERISTEM CULTURE
For the sake of completeness, we should mention another method of vegetative propagation, the meristem culture. Meristem is the name given to growth tissue that is composed of dividing meriste-matic cells. These growth-tissue explants are detached from the plants and stimulated to cell division by immersion in test-tubes filled with a liquid rooting solution, where they are kept in continuous motion. The cell clumps (callus) thus developed are divided and

further cultivated on a firm culture medium until new plants appear. This method guarantees the creation of young plants identical to the mother plant, but it is only carried out in laboratories.

GROWING FROM SEED
Equally cumbersome is growing from seed; it, too, is usually done by specialized firms on a large scale and under laboratory conditions. Apart from propagation, this process seeks to develop new varieties through crossing. Here is a simplified account of the method:

First of all, the orchids must be pollinated artificially. Germination takes from three to twenty months, depending on the species. Unlike most seeds, those of orchids have no nutritive tissue of their own; instead, in the wild, the nutrients they need in order to germinate are provided by soil fungi. The roots of the orchids live symbiotically with these fungi (called mycorrhiza), but mature plants are not totally reliant on the fungi any longer. The seeds, by contrast, are completely dependent on them. With their hyphae, the fungi penetrate the seed capsules and nourish the embryo with carbohydrates until the

Divided orchid

Offshoots of a bromeliad

germinating sprout has developed roots and leaves, and so is able to take in and transform its own nutrients. The nutrients produced by the fungi are developed synthetically in laboratories and mixed into special rooting soil.

Propagating bromeliads
In addition to propagation from offshoots (→ page 78), bromeliads can be raised from seed.
- Sow the seeds on a mixture of peat and coarse sand (2:1), push them down, but do not cover them.
- If the seeds are well moistened, given a bright location, and covered with a plastic hood at 75–80°F (24–27°C), the first green sprouts may appear in as little as ten days.
- Once three or four leaves have developed, the plants are gradually accustomed to normal air, and the covering is removed entirely after about a week.
- Do not overwater; allow the top layer of soil to dry out before watering again.
- Set the plants in normal bromeliad potting mix when they have six leaves.

Bromeliads can easily be propagated using the offshoots that grow next to the mother plant.

Several species of orchid are divided, but take care when you do this that the sections have sufficient aerial roots.

Special Methods of Propagation

A great deal of patience is needed to grow palms from seed yourself. The most important factor is an even temperature of both air and soil.

Propagating palms

Several species of palms develop offshoots, which are cut off and set in a mix of equal parts of peat and coarse sand or perlite. Although a plastic cover stimulates development, roots still need up to twelve weeks to form. Water very little during this period. When a new shoot appears, air several times a day and eventually remove the hood entirely. From then on, you can water a little more, and fertilize once a month. Do not transplant in a normal potting mix until the plant's first spring. Palms that develop offshoots include the fishtail palm (*Caryota mitis*), the Mediterranean palm (*Chamaerops humilis*), and the butterfly palm (*Chrysalidocarpus lutescens*).

GROWING
FROM SEED
Growing from seed needs much patience (see Table). Palms from the tropics need an even temperature of 77–86°F (25–30°C) for both air and soil. Palms from subtropical regions need 68–77°F (20–25°C). Use any ordinary seeding mix. After sowing, dampen the earth and cover with a pane of glass. Air briefly once a day. The soil must never dry out!

Once the seedlings appear, set the seed tray in a bright but not sunny location. If the palms are strong enough, transplant them to small single pots, also in special rooting soil. Do not remove all the seeds from the plant, as they contain much-needed nutrient tissue (endosperm). Young coconut palms, for example, nourish themselves for three years on the coconut. Transplant the young palm into normal soil only when all the seeds have fallen off.

Young palms on the windowsill

Table of germinating periods

Genus	Germinating period in months	Genus	Germinating period in months
Acanthophoenix	24–26	Latania	1–2
Alphanes	1	Licuala	1–6
Archontophoenix	2–4	Linospadix	1–4
Areca	1–3	Livistona	1–4
Arenga	1–12	Lodoicea	6
Attalea	3–4	Metroxylon	1–3
Bactris	2–3	Microcoelum	2–3
Bentinckia	1	Normanbya	1
Borassus	2–12	Nypa	1
Brahea	2–4	Orbignya	2–4
Butia	6–8	Phoenix	2–4
Calamus	1–4	Pinanga	2–4
Carpentaria	1–2	Polyandroccos	5
Caryota	1–3	Pritchardia	1–3
Chamaedorea	1–6	Ptychosperma	1–2
Chamaerops	2–4	Raphia	1–4
Chrysalidocarpus	1–3	Reinhardtia	1–2
Cocos	1–6	Rhapis	2–4
Copernica	2–4	Rhopolostylis	1–2
Corypha	1–4	Roystonea	1–2
Cyrtostachys	1–3	Sabal	2–4
Dictyosperma	2–4	Salacca	1–3
Elaeis	2–5	Syagrus	2–4
Euterpe	1–3	Thrinax	2–4
Geonoma	2–3	Trachycarpus	1–4
Gronophyllum	1–2	Trithrinax	2–4
Howeia	2–10	Veitchia	1
Hyophorbe	2–4	Verschaffeltia	1
Hyphaene	2–4	Wallichia	3–5
Jubaea	2–6	Washingtonia	1
Laccospadix	2–4		

Credit: *Palms* by Frank O. Steeb, Mosaik Verlag

SUCCESSFUL CARE AND PROPAGATION

Mammillarias in a nursery

Propagating cacti and other succulents

Vegetative reproduction of these is relatively simple. Many form offshoots, e.g., *Gymnocalcium*, *Echinopsis*, and *Lobivia*. Stem cuttings can be taken from *Opuntia*, among others. In the case of leaf cacti, every two to three segments form a cutting—for example, on the Christmas cactus (*Schlumbergera*); or entire shoots can be detached from the main stem, as in *Epiphyllum*. Tip cuttings can be taken from columnar species; and columnar shoots can, in turn, be divided into several cuttings of around 5 in. (10 cm) in length. From branched succulents, you can simply separate off a shoot.

- All cut parts should be dusted with charcoal powder and allowed to dry for at least three days.
- Plant in a mixture of peat and coarse sand, in equal parts.
- The cuttings should be stuck only 0.2 in. (0.5 cm) into the substratum. Exceptions are the cuttings of leaf cacti, which are planted to a depth of 0.8–1.2 in. (2–3 cm).
- Keep the soil lightly moistened. At a soil temperature of 65–73°F (18–23°C), roots will form after several weeks.
- At this time, transplant the rooted cuttings to their usual potting mix and care for them like adult plants.

GROWING FROM SEED

If the seed is fresh, and the pot and your hands have been washed thoroughly with soap, growing from seed successfully is relatively easy.

- Use a mixture of peat and sand that has been sterilized in an oven at 176°F (80°C). For very fine seeds, the seeding mix must first be sieved.
- The seed tray should have several bottom holes.
- First, create a drainage layer of around 0.4 in. (1 cm) of sterilized gravel or perlite; then add the mix to 0.4 in. (1 cm) under the rim. Smooth the surface. If you wish to sow several species at the same time, use plastic strips to subdivide the seed tray.
- Fine seeds can be sown on the surface fairly evenly with the help of a paper vase. Press them in firmly. Bigger seeds can be separated and planted individually.
- To moisten the seed bed, place it into a bigger bowl of boiled water until the soil is completely drenched. After draining it well, cover with a glass top. Tip the seed tray slightly so that any condensed water drains off rather than dripping directly onto the seeds.
- The temperature should be 68–86°F (20–30°C) in daytime, and slightly lower at night. Light is not necessary at this stage. Be sure to protect the seed trays against direct sun.
- Depending on the species, the seeds will germinate in two to three weeks. The seedlings often look like small green balls. They need light—but not sun—and air. To air the plants, lift the cover slightly by inserting a small piece of wood. The substratum should not be allowed to dry out, but should also not be damp.
- Separate the plants only after six to twelve weeks, as they like to grow close together.

Grafting cacti

This is a method for improving cacti, rather than propagating them. Cacti with sensitive roots, and species that are slow growing or whose flowers tend to rot, are grafted onto robust, fast-growing ones. Some of the species suitable as understocks are *Trichocereius*, *Echinopsis*, *Selenicereus*, or *Eriocereus jusbertii*.

Grafting is easy (→ page 87).

Mammillaria are not hard to care for and are reliable bloomers. They are cultivated on a large scale by specialists, but amateurs also propagate them successfully.

Citrus plants grown from seed are usually vigorous and grow well, but they bloom only after several years, or not at all. Those who want to have plants that flower and fruit quickly can use a strong seedling as the understock, cut a scion from a citrus specimen that is known to flower, and tie the two together. The professional calls this "improving." Exactly how it works is explained on page 87.

Propagation at a Glance

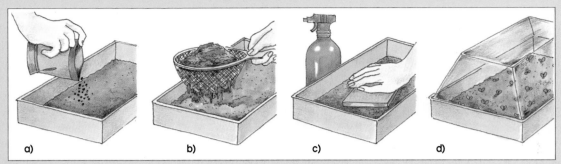

a) b) c) d)

Seeding in trays or flats. Many plants can be sown easily on the windowsill.
a) Place the seeding mix on a drainage layer and smooth it. Divide the seeds as equally as possible over the surface.
b) Dark-dependent seeds must be covered with a thin layer of seeding mix. Light-sensitive seeds are not covered.
c) Using a board, press the soil and seeds down lightly.
d) Cover, and place the seed tray in a warm but not sunny location. Don't forget to label the seed tray with the name of the seeded plant, or put the seed packet itself on the edge of the seed tray, possibly with an annotation of the seeding date.

a) b) c) d)

Potting up. Seedlings are potted up when they have two or three real leaves and look vigorous. The new potting mix must contain nutrients. Do not forget the drainage layer!
a) With a pointed tool, make holes at intervals of about 1.2 in. (3 cm) in the moistened and smoothed-out potting mix.
b) Carefully loosen the little plants
c) Handling the seedlings only by their seed-leaves, carefully separate them from each other. Shorten the root tip somewhat.
d) Place the plants into the prepared holes up to the seed-leaves, and carefully press soil around them. Water using a fine nozzle and place in a warm spot, sheltered from direct sun. Do not keep the mix too damp, but do not let it dry out, either.

Rooting in water. The cuttings of many houseplants root quickly and reliably in water. Take single leaves from begonias or African violets, and put both the leaf and the leaf stem in water. In the case of most other plants, use non-flowering tip cuttings from one-year-old shoots. Remove the lower leaves and stick the stem in water.

Adventitious plants. Several plants form small adventitious plants, or replicas of themselves, on their leaves. These may be detached carefully and stuck into soil.

Tip layering. Long runners can simply be pressed into the surface of the soil with a bent wire or a paperclip. Roots will form at the leaf nodes.

SUCCESSFUL CARE AND PROPAGATION

Dividing orchids. Many roots form on the long, horizontal side shoots of orchids. Cut off sprouting pieces of these shoots, dust the cut ends with charcoal powder, and set into the soil.

Dividing herbaceous perennials. Perennials that have grown too big (here, a *Soleirolia solerolii*) can be divided easily in the spring with a sharp knife. The pieces are stuck in new soil and cared for in the normal way.

Bulblets. The bulbs of many flowering plants develop small daughter bulbs. When repotting in the spring, carefully detach these little bulbs and plant in their own pots with appropriate soil.

Dividing tubers. Dahlia tubers can be cut into several parts with a sharp, disinfected knife. Each part, however, must have a bud. Dust the cuts with charcoal powder.

The proper cut. Tip cuttings should be cut from the ends of the shoots of non-flowering, strong, one-year-old shoots. Cut just below the third or fourth pair of leaves. Remove the lowest pair.

Rooting hormone. Rooting succeeds better if the tip cutting is first dipped in a rooting hormone.

Proximity to the pot wall. Never put cuttings in pots that are too big. If several are to share a pot, put the cuttings as near the sides of the cultivating container as possible. Roots form more quickly in the shelter of the pot wall.

Mini-hothouse. Next to saturated air (created by an overturned, transparent plastic bag), soil warmth (achieved here by using a heat coil) is the fourth guarantor of successful root development.

TIP

Little new plants should never be put into pots that are too big. To form good root balls, they need to be hemmed in. Even on the patio one can observe that seeds that are blown in by the wind always grow around the edges of plant tubs.

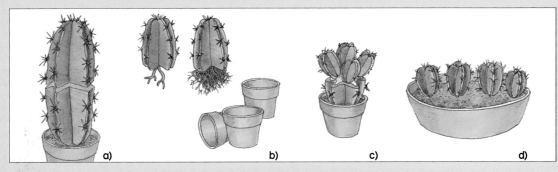

Propagating cacti by division. A single cactus can yield many specimens if it is divided.
a) Cut the upper half off a healthy, non-flowering plant with a sharp, disinfected knife.
b) Dust the cut ends with charcoal power. Then hang them up vertically for ten to fourteen days and let them dry out. Once they have formed enough roots, the new cactus is placed in cactus soil.
c) Small cacti will eventually form on the remaining stumps.
d) If you don't like the stump that way, cut off the small cacti carefully and place them in a bowl of cactus soil. The new plants are then cared for like their parent.

Propagation at a Glance

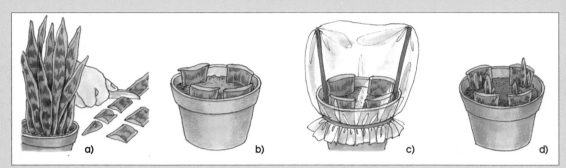

Propagation using parts of leaves. In some plants—for example, begonias, Cape primrose, and snake plants—new plants can be formed from leaf sections. To propagate, select a strong, healthy plant.
a) Cut the leaf diagonally into sections 2–3 in. (5–8 cm) long. Let the cut edges dry for several hours.
b) Stick the leaf sections 0.8–1.2 in. (2–3 cm) into a suitable mix, in the direction of growth. The pieces must not touch.
c) Cover the propagating case with a transparent plastic bag and place in a warm but not sunny location. A soil temperature of 68–71°F (20–22°C) is important.
d) When the leaf parts have developed roots, a new side shoot develops. At this stage, remove the plastic bag. Caution: Variegated leaf parts will produce green-leafed plants only.

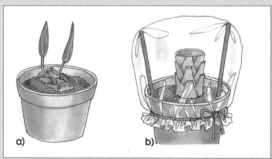

Leaf cuttings. Several plants can be propagated from leaf cuttings. Cut off strong leaves with a sharp, disinfected knife. Place cuttings in the substratum and press lightly.

Leafy crowns. When a pineapple, for example, still has a fresh, green crown, you may cut it off and plant it. Remove the flesh of the fruit. The soil temperature should be 82–86°F (28–30°C).

Propagation using stem cuttings. If such plants as dracaena, dieffenbachia, snake plant, philodendron, or yucca get too tall, you can cut off and plant the crown like a cutting. Cut the stem in pieces, with at least four buds each. Dust the cut ends with charcoal powder. Simply place the stem pieces on the mix, **(a)** flat or **(b)** vertically, in the direction of growth.

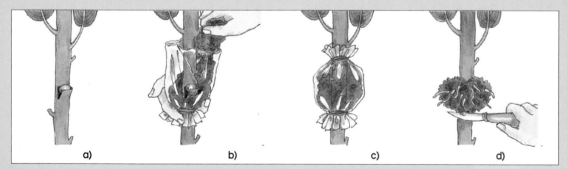

Air layering. This process allows you to transform green giants into reasonably sized houseplants once more.
a) Slit the stem near a bud at the desired height. Cutting from below, slit at most to the center of the stem. Keep the cut open with a matchstick.
b) Below the slit, tie transparent plastic film to the stem like a bag.
c) Fill the "bag" with damp peat and tie it shut above the cut.
d) When the peat ball is full of roots, cut through the stem and plant the upper portion in the customary potting mix. Cut back the remaining plant part to 8–12 in. (20–30 cm) and continue to care for it as usual. Generally, it will grow once again.

Successful Care and Propagation

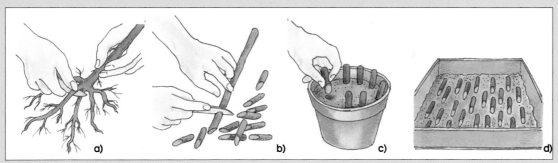

Propagation using root cuttings. Both herbaceous perennials with fleshy roots and woody plants can be propagated easily from root cuttings, in either spring (woody plants) or fall (herbaceous perennials).
a) Cut off the roots close to the root crown.
b) Divide them into pieces about 1.5 in. (4 cm) long. The top cut of each should be straight, the lower one slanted.
c) Plant the cuttings, slanted end down, into a mix of sand and peat. The top, straight end should be level with the soil. Cover entirely with some sand.
d) The cuttings can also be placed vertically in a box and lightly covered with soil. The soil should not be too moist, but not dried out, either. It often takes six months for the cuttings to show new growth.

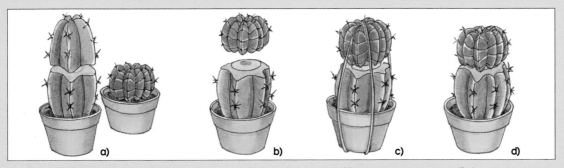

Grafting cacti. Many species of cacti grow faster and better, or bloom earlier, if they are grown on a specific base or understock. Cacti with weak roots receive a stable foundation using this method.
a) With a sharp, disinfected knife, cut through a healthy, single-stemmed cactus. The cut end of the understock must be as large as that of the specimen that is to be grafted on to it.
b) The cut edges of the understock are trimmed to slope outward. After shaving another thin layer from the cut ends, put the parts together in such a way that the rings of their vascular bundles lie directly against one another.
c) Hold the understock and scion together with rubber bands, which should be neither too tight nor too loose.
d) The two parts will have grown together in two or three weeks.

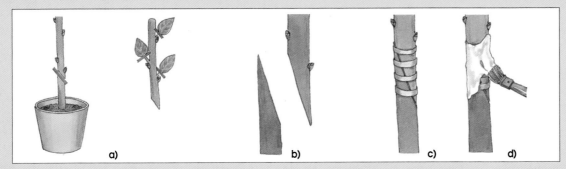

Improving citrus seedlings. Citrus plants grown from seed are vigorous and grow well, but they flower only after many years, if at all. If you want plants that flower and fruit quickly, use a strong seedling as an understock, cut off a scion from a citrus specimen that is known to flower, and graft the two together.
a) Shorten the understock with a long sloping cut. The cut end of the scion must fit on it. Remove all leaves.
b) Place the two pieces together in such a way that the rings between the outer bark and the inner wood of scion and understock come into contact with one another.
c) Tie together with raffia or a special rubber band that is commercially available.
d) Seal the graft union with grafting wax.

TIP

Anyone who has fun cultivating exotic plants from seed should acquire a heated propagating case. Success depends on a high, even soil temperature.

Glossary

A

Adhesive disks: Plant organs (modified leaves) that help a climbing plant to hold on.

Adhesive roots: Short aerial roots along the stem of a climbing plant that attach themselves to supporting structures.

Adventitious plant: Young plant that develops in an asexual manner on the leaves or stems of the mother plant.

Adventitious roots: Roots that grow out of any part of a plant other than the main root.

Aerial roots: Roots that develop on the stem above ground.

Air layering: Vegetative propagation by way of artificially induced root development on the stem of, usually, a woody plant.

Alkaline-intolerant plants: Plants that do not tolerate alkaline soil conditions.

Alkaline: Basic, having a pH value of 7.1 or higher.

Alkaloids: Nitrogen-rich compounds that are often deadly poisons, even in small doses.

Alternate leaf arrangement: Staggered arrangement of leaves on a stem, with only a single leaf on each node.

Annual: Plant that undergoes its complete life cycle in one year.

Anther: The pollen-bearing part of the stamen.

Areola: In cacti, hair-cushions from which spines, flowers, and offsets may grow.

B

Basal leaf loss: Loss of the lower leaves.

Biennial: Plants that develop only leaves in their first year, and flower, bear fruit, and then die in their second year.

Bleeding: The discharge of liquid from wounded plant tissue.

Bonsai: A Japanese gardening art that involves artificially dwarfing and shaping broad-leaf plants and conifers, usually in very shallow plant containers.

Bottom heating: The provision of heat by some means (pad, coil, or forced air) from below to speed the development of roots in cuttings.

Bract: Modified leaf, usually within an inflorescence, adapted to other functions, e.g., that of a petal.

Bud: The embryonic shoot on a stem, branch, or tuber.

Bulb: An underground storage organ composed of a shortened stem covered with modified leaves called scales.

Bulbil: Small bulb, formed from a bud in a leaf axil, which serves for vegetative reproduction when it falls off.

Bulblet: Small side bulb formed from a parent bulb below ground; used for vegetative propagation.

C

Callus: Scar tissue that forms at the places where plants are damaged or cut, in order to close the wound.

Calyx: Collective term for all the sepals considered together.
(→ **Sepal**)

Cambium: a cylinder, one cell layer thick, between the inner bark and the wood of a stem, the cells of which are capable of division, thereby increasing the diameter of the stem.

Capitulum: An inflorescence in which many flower petals sit on the perimeter of a flat flower base.

Carnivorous plants: Plants that kill and digest insects.

Chelate: Compound consisting of iron, zinc, magnesium, or other metals, in a stable, organic form available to plants.

Chlorophyll: The organic catalyst that enables photosynthesis.

Chlorosis: The yellowing of the leaf, primarily the result of a deficiency of iron or magnesium.

Clay aggregate: A granular material derived from fired clay and used to change the soil structure.

Clay granular: Potting mixture that can absorb a great deal of water.

Cluster: Bunch or clump of equally strong shoots, leaves, or flowers arising from the same general point (e.g., chives).

Cockscomb: An abnormal proliferation of tissue at the tip of a stem, resulting in a flattening of the shoot.

Coldhouse: Structure for growing plants at winter temperatures between 35 and 54°F (2–12°C).

Conifers: Trees that usually have needles and bear cones.

Corking: The formation of corky material on the surface of plants, caused by excessive humidity.

Corolla: Collective term for all the petals of a flower considered together.

Cotyledons: → **Seed-leaves**

Creepers: Plants that spread by means of horizontal shoots or runners.

Cultivar: A plant form within a species that has arisen through cultivation. Abbreviated internationally as cv.

Cuttings: General term for portions of plants that are separated from the mother plant and rooted for the purpose of vegetative propagation.

D

Dark-dependent seeds: Seeds that germinate only in darkness and so must be covered with soil.

Deciduous: A plant that drops its leaves in the fall and replaces them the following spring.

Die-back: Dying off of the above-ground parts of a plant.

Dicotyledon: Plant that produces two seed-leaves.

Dioecious: Producing male and female flowers on separate plants.

Dormancy: → **Rest period**

Double: Flowers with many additional petals.

E

Efflorescence: Deposits of calcium and fertilizer salts on the outer surfaces of clay pots.

Epidermis: The outermost, usually single-celled, layer of plant parts.

Epiphyte support: Artificial "tree" that replaces a tree trunk in the domestic cultivation of epiphytes.

Epiphyte: Plant that grows on other woody, treelike plants without damaging them.

Etiolate: Development of long, thin, pale shoots due to insufficient light and other unfavorable conditions.

Evergreen: Plant whose leaves last over several active growing seasons and are not all shed at the same time.

F

F1-hybrid: The offspring that results from crossing two purebred parent plants.

Fertilization: The successful impregnation of an ovule by a pollen nucleus.

Fibrous root: A thin, threadlike, randomly developing root.

Forcing: Causing a plant to bloom out of season by increasing light, warmth, and water.

Frost-hardiness: A plant's tolerance for temperatures below 32°F (0°C).

Fungicide: A remedy for controlling fungi.

G

Genus: A group of related species that share similar features.

Glochids: Tiny, stiff hairs with barbs found in cacti.

Granular substratum: Gritty, well-drained potting mixture.

Growing point: The extreme tip of a shoot where the formation of new plant parts occurs.

H

Habit: Appearance, form, and development pattern of a plant.

Hardness: The degree of mineral salt, usually calcium, dissolved in water.

Hardiness: The ability of plants to survive winters in the open without protection.

Hardwood: Stems of woody plants that have become hard as the result of the depositing of lignin into the cell walls of specialized tissues.

Hardwood cuttings: Year-old woody shoots used for propagation.

Heel cutting: A short side branch, taken as a cutting with a small piece of main stem.

Herbaceous perennial: A plant that dies to the ground in the fall, regenerates in the spring, and lives for three or more years.

Honeydew: Sticky, sweet excretion of aphids or scale insects.

Hothouse: A growing house for plants in which the year-round temperature ranges between 68–77°F (20°–25°C).

Humus: Water-absorptive constituent of soil (usually nutrient-rich) formed by the rotting of organic material.

Hybrid (bastard): A plant resulting from a cross between plants of different species (occasionally between plants of different genera).

I

Inflorescence: The flowering part of a plant, or an aggregation of individual flowers.

Insecticide: Preparation for killing insects.

Internodes: The leaf-free sections of a stalk or stem that lie between two nodes.

K

Keike: An offshoot found along the flowering stem of an orchid.

L

Latex: A milky sap exuded by some plants when wounded.

Leaf axil: The angle between the leaf, or leaf stalk, and the stem on which the leaf is carried.

Leaf veins: The network of vessels that transports water and nutrients to and from the leaf.

Leaf: The principal organ of photosynthesis in higher plants.

Light marking: Mark on a plant container to ensure that the plant is always turned in the same position relative to the light.

Light-sensitive seed: Seed that needs light in order to germinate and so must not be covered with potting mixture.

Lithophytes: Plants that live on stones or rocks.

Long-day plants: Plants that require more than fourteen hours of light in order to flower.

M

Micro-climate: Climate in the immediate environment of the plants.

Miniatures: Genetically dwarf plants.

Miticide: Remedy for controlling mites.

Monocotyledon: Flowering plant that develops only a single seed-leaf, e.g., grasses.

Monoecious: Having both male and female flowers on the same plant.

Monopodial: With the branches or appendages arising from a single axis.

Mutation: A random change in genetic makeup.

Glossary

Mycelium: A fungal network consisting of thin fibers or filaments.

N

Necrosis: Dying off of damaged or diseased plant tissue.

Node: A place on a stem where a leaf is (or has been) attached.

O

Offsets: Young plants that have grown and rooted while still attached to the mother plant.

Offshoots: Young plants growing out of the mother plant on side shoots at ground level.

Opposite: Having leaves, stems, or flowerings growing opposite one another at a stem node.

Orchid Chips: Synthetic potting mixture for orchids, consisting of foamy polystyrene.

Ordinary potting mix: Standard prepared potting soil.

Ovary: The part of the pistil containing the egg cell (ovule) that when fertilized becomes the embryo and then the seed.

P

Panicle: A branching inflorescence, usually broader near the base.

Perlite: A coarse granular aggregate prepared from expanded volcanic ash.

Petal: A member of the second set of floral leaves (corolla) just internal to the sepals, usually colored or white.

Petiole: The stem of a leaf.

pH: A measure of the concentration of hydrogen ions in water and soil. It indicates whether a material is acid (pH 1–6), alkaline (pH 8–14), or neutral (pH 7).

Photoperiodism: The effect of the daily dark/light ratio on the growth and flowering of plants.

Photosynthesis: Chemical process in the leaves of plants that transforms water and carbon dioxide into sugar and oxygen, with the aid of chlorophyll and sunlight.

Phototropism: The hormone-induced leaning of a plant toward light.

Pinching out: Removing the soft ends of shoots in order to stimulate growth in the lower lateral buds and encourage bushier development.

Pinnate leaf: Compound leaf composed of many leaflets growing to either side of a main axis.

Pinnule: Single leaflet of a pinnate (compound) leaf.

Pistil: The female reproductive component of a flower consisting of an ovary and stigma, connected by a more or less elongated style.

Pollen: The mass of young male reproductive cells at the stage when they are released from the anther.

Pollination: Transfer of pollen to a receptive stigma.

Potting up: Transplanting seedlings from the propagating bed to individual pots.

Prickle: Sharp protuberance on the epidermis.

Pseudobulbs: In orchids, above-ground thickened stems that look like bulbs and serve as storage organs.

Pumice: Large-pored mineral of volcanic origin.

R

Raceme: Inflorescence that consists of numerous stemmed single flowers on a long, branchless stalk.

Respiration: The chemical reactions from which an organism derives energy.

Rest period: Period of slowed or stopped growth.

Rhizome: Fleshy stem of a plant that generally grows horizontally just below the soil surface.

Root ball: The root of a plant, together with associated soil.

Root crown: Place where root adjoins the above-ground portion of a plant.

Root cutting: Portion of a root used in vegetative propagation.

Rootstock: → Rhizome

Rooting compound: Hormonal preparation designed to encourage cuttings to root.

Rosette: An extremely short stem axis with very close-set leaves.

Runner: A stolon that roots at the tip, forming a new plant.

S

Saturated air: Air that is so humid that plants cease to give off moisture to it (100 percent humidity).

Scape: Leafless, unbranched, flowering stem that arises from ground level.

Scion: A suitable piece (usually a small shoot) of a desirable specimen of a woody plant, used in grafting.

Seed-leaves: The first leaves of a seedling to appear after germination.

Seed: Fertilized ovule, consisting of an embryo enclosed by a protective seed coat.

Seedling: The first stage of a plant after it emerges from the seed.

Self-cleaning: Plants that naturally shed their dead blooms.

Self-pollination: Pollination of the stigma with pollen from the same flower.

Sepal: A member of the outermost set of floral parts, typically green and more or less leafy.

Sexual propagation: Propagation from seed.

Shallow-rooted plant: Plant with an extended, multi-branched root system.

Shoot: A young, generally slender branch.

Short-day plants: Plants that need

only eight to ten hours of daylight in order to flower.

Shrub: Plant with several woody shoots, springing from the ground up to approximately 20 feet (6 m).

Sinking: Planting a potted plant in the garden, together with its container.

Slow-release fertilizer: Fertilizer that releases its nutrients to plants over a period of time.

Sori (s. sorus): Collections of spore-bearing structures, generally on the undersides of fern leaves.

Spadix: A spike with small, crowded flowers on a thickened, fleshy axis.

Spathe: Large, usually solitary, often colored bract, subtending and often enclosing an inflorescence, usually a spadix.

Species: The smallest grouping of plants that is consistently and persistently distinct, and distinguishable to the unaided eye.

Spike: An inflorescence in which individual stemless flowers sit directly on an unbranched, erect stem.

Sporangium (pl. sporangia): A spore-bearing structure.

Spores: Generally microscopic reproductive bodies that become detached from the parent and give rise directly or indirectly to new individuals.

Standard: A training form of certain plants, in which the crown rests high on a single stem.

Stem cutting: Portion of the stem used in vegetative propagation.

Stigma: The highest, most extended, sticky part of the pistil, which receives the pollen during fertilization.

Stolon: Horizontally growing stem that roots at the nodes.

Stoma (pl. stomata): Pore in the epidermis of plants through which gases (oxygen, carbon dioxide, water vapor) are exchanged.

Stratification: Process by which seeds are exposed to temperatures of 28–39°F (–2 + 4°C) for a period of time, in order to germinate.

Style: Part of the pistil that usually links the stalklike stigma with the ovary.

Styrofoam chips: Flakes of synthetic foam material that are mixed into potting soil.

Subshrub: Plant whose lower portion lignifies or becomes woody, while the upper portion remains soft and dies off at the end of the growing season.

Substratum: Soil or other potting mixture.

Succulent: Plant with thickened leaves or stem adapted for retaining water.

Sucker: A vigorous, vertically growing shoot produced at the base of a plant.

Suction cups: Tiny cuplike formations, usually on epiphytes, which can take up water and nutrients.

Sunscorch: Spots on the leaves caused by exposure to strong sunlight.

Sympodial: With a composite axis produced and increased in length by successive development of lateral buds just behind the tip.

T

Taproot: Single root that grows vertically into the soil.

Tendrils: Long, threadlike append-ages that are sensitive to touch and help vines to climb by twining around supporting structures.

Terminal: Blooms or buds that appear at the tip or end of a shoot.

Thinning: Removal of weak seedlings after germination so that the stronger ones have more room to grow.

Thorn: Stiff, sharp, pointed projection on a plant, that has evolved by transformation out of a leaf, branch, or side-shoot.

Tip cutting: Cutting from the top end of a shoot.

Tip layering: The rooting of young plants at the tip of last year's drooping side stems.

Tuber: Storage organ; the fleshy, thickened portion of either a root (dahlias) or a stem (potatoes).

Umbel: Inflorescence of many single blooms radiating from a common point.

U

Understock: A rooted stem of a vigorous plant to which a scion is grafted.

V

Variegation: Striping, spotting, or mottling of leaves with white, due to an absence of chlorophyll.

Variety: A plant that differs in appearance from its original species type and has developed in the wild.

Vase: Leaf cup found in bromeliads, consisting of bowl-shaped leaves that lie on top of each other, and between which water or humus accumulates.

Vegetative propagation: Asexual reproduction by detachment of some part of the plant body and its subsequent development into a complete plant.

W

Whorl: Three or more blooms, leaves, or stems arising at the same node.

X

Xerophyte: Plant adapted to life in dry places.

Plants bring life into a home. In any location—in a dwelling, hallway, office, balcony, patio, or garden room—plants can create an oasis of contentment. Often, they add the finishing touch to your decorative scheme.

Plants come in a great variety of colors, forms, and perfumes. They are a feast for the eyes and allow much room for individual creativity.

In this chapter you will discover how to display your green and flowering guests most effectively. The chapter also contains numerous planting recommendations for boxes and tubs, which will inspire you to turn your surroundings into a Garden of Eden.

Chinese lantern (Abutilon *hybrid*), *spider plant* (Chlorophytum comosum), *and white marguerite* (Chrysanthemum frutescens) *in a garden room; petunias* (Petunia hybrids) *and lobelias* (Lobelia erinus) *in a plant container*

Fundamental Concepts

Trichloroethelene is a colorless liquid that smells like chloroform. Contained in lacquer and glue, it is thought to cause cancers. Formaldehyde is, among other things, the basic material of synthetic resin, used to glue chipboard. It, too, may cause cancer. Highly toxic, cancer-inducing benzol is the basis of many synthetics.

Outer pots should not compete with the plants themselves. White ones always look elegant. A stronger effect is achieved by using containers of the same color as the flowers in them.

Living greenery brings verve and movement to every room. But a pleasing whole is achieved only if there is harmony in the arrangement and colors of the plants and the relative proportions of the plants and the room. Once these general concerns have been taken into account, your taste and imagination will determine which species you should use in any particular case.

Plants in large rooms

The larger the room, the bigger and more numerous the plants may be. A single, small green plant looks lost in a large space. Several small flowering plants in a basket or arranged on a small table, on the other hand, can serve as a colorful accent. Treelike plants have great decorative importance. Large-leafed species such as dracaena, philodendron, or banyan tree (*Ficus benghalensis*) make their mark in a sparsely furnished room or entrance hall.

Plants in small rooms

Large plants are oppressive in small rooms. To get the best effect, choose mid-size or small plants with large or delicate leaves, and place them where they are highly visible. Don't put too many plants in such a space; if you do, the individual plants cannot make their full impact.

Decorating with plants

Plants look their best against a simple background. Plants with large foliage should be placed in front of wallpaper with a small pattern. Large-patterned wall coverings call out for the filigreed leaves of ferns or umbrella sedge (*Cyperus*). Wood-paneled walls soften the effect of color. Climbing

Plants that improve room climate

Plant name	Particular merits
Abutilon hybrids	increase humidity
Aglaonema	reduce benzol
Aloe barbadensis	reduce formaldehyde
Aphelandra	increase humidity
Asplenium nidus	increase humidity
Chamaedorea	reduce formaldehyde and TCE[*]
Chlorophytum elatum	reduce benzol and formaldehyde
Chrysanthemum morifolum	reduce formaldehyde, benzol, and TCE
Cissus rhombifolia	increase humidity
Cyperus papyrus	increase humidity
Dracaena	reduce formaldehyde, benzol, and TCE
Epipremnum pinnatum	reduce formaldehyde, benzol, and TCE
Fatsia japonica	increase humidity
Ficus benjamina	reduce TCE
Gerbera jamesonii	reduce formaldehyde, benzol, and TCE
Hedera helix	reduce benzol and TCE
Hibiscus rosa-sinensis	increase humidity
Musa oriana	increase humidity, reduce formaldehyde
Nephrolepis exaltata	increase humidity
Pandanus veitchii	increase humidity
Philodendron	reduce formaldehyde
Rhododenron-simsii hybrids	increase humidity
Sanseveria trifasciata	reduce benzol and TCE
Spathiphyllum	reduce benzol and TCE
Schefflera	increase humidity
Sparmannia africana	increase humidity

[*]TCE = Trichloroethelene

plants arranged on an attractive wood or bamboo support and placed in front of a bright wall touched by the sun can be an eye-catching sight.

Also, make sure your decorative scheme takes into account the way light falls into the room. If the plants are placed in front of a bright, sunny wall, their shadows will create an interesting, unusual pattern on the wall or on a plain carpet. Background lighting on the windowsill silhouettes the contours of plants. In the case of soft, thin leaves, the light will make the leaf veins visible and give the foliage a filigreed look. Be careful that the colors of the flowers don't clash with the colors of the room decor. It is clever to have the shades of the curtains, rugs, slipcovers, or pillows echo the colors of the flowers. If the decor is restricted to black and white, strong-colored flowers can add a note of cheer.

Group arrangements

Plants, when correctly placed to complement one another, make a much greater impact on the viewer. This is true whether they are part of a small grouping in bowls and boxes or of a large arrangement of individual pot plants. One only becomes conscious of the diversity of forms among non-flowering plants when several stand close together. For example, grasses next to large-leafed species, or strong shapes next to dainty ones, make for delightful contrasts. You can give an arrangement the finishing touch by adding a spot of color to a group of foliage plants. Large plants should be in the background, smaller ones in front. The groupings do not have to be symmetrical. A smart little ivy (*Hedera helix*) growing over the edge of a bowl looks charmingly casual.

Is living with plants healthier?

For years, the papers have been telling us that plants absorb harmful elements in room air or even render them harmless. Some also say that microorganisms in the soil counter-act the poisons that plants take up through their leaves and give off through their roots.

Although this has been corroborated by science, it makes little practical difference in the domestic arena. To clean polluted air, a room would have to be full of plants, leaving no room for people or furniture. On the other hand, you can actually raise a room's humidity level by introducing plants that need high humidity and give off a great deal of moisture

Spider plants reach a ripe old age and can become enormous.

through their leaves.

Some plants that improve the room climate, increase humidity, and reduce benzol, formaldehyde, and Trichloroethelene are listed in the Table on page 94.

Quite apart from the measurable advantages of houseplants, the psychological aspects are significant. Plants undoubtedly have a positive effect on humans. Business enterprises don't spend a great deal of money for green plants in their offices only because of their looks!

Spider plants (*Chlorophytum comosum*) are said to be an excellent air filter. They particularly like "eating" formaldehyde.

Plants grouped in a single container should have the same requirements for soil, fertilizer, heat, and moisture.

Different Furnishing Styles

Homes are often decorated in an entirely personal, unified style. Plants that fit in with the general decor serve to complete the picture.

Swedish modern

Individual plants like yucca, schefflera, and rubber trees (*Ficus*) fit in well with wooden furniture. Cheerful accents can be added using flowering plants like kalanchoes (*Kalanchoe blossfeldiana*), Calceolaria hybrids, or Achimenes hybrids. Foliage plants with variegated leaves, e.g., *Pisonia umbellifera* or hanging plants like the ivy variety 'Ingrid,' go especially well with light-colored woods. A cactus collection also suits this furnishing style.

Country style

Here color is appropriate. Flowering plants can be used to accent the seasons, e.g., bulbs and primulas in the spring, special geraniums (*Pelargonium* grandiflorum hybrids), impatiens, potted roses, and campanulas in the summer, asters and chrysanthemums in the fall, Christmas cacti and leafy cacti in winter.

But, as in grandmother's day, the rustic style is also complemented by foliage plants.

Modern designer furniture

The straight or gently curved forms of steel, glass, marble, and varnished wood furnishings can be echoed by using equally stark plant shapes such as snake plant (*Sansevieria trifasciata*), Swiss cheese plant (*Monstera deliciosa*), Dracaena, and *Guzmania*; or, by way of contrast, you can introduce plants with a loose, playful aspect: ferns with pinnate fronds, indoor linden (*Sparmannia africana*), grape ivy (*Cissus*), or asparagus fern. But be sure to include flowering highlights appropriate to the season: a bright red amaryllis (*Hippeastrum*), pink azalea (*Rhododendron*), or violet browallia.

Art nouveau and art deco

Plants with simple, gently curving lines fit best into these decorative styles. They include flamingo flower (*Anthurium*), peace lily (*Spathphyllum*), calla lilies (*Zantedeschia*), and palms.

Oriental style

Furniture made of bamboo or rattan, small chests and shelving with plaited sides, and low tables and sitting areas can accommodate bromeliads and orchids, exotic hanging plants like string of pearls (*Senecio royleyanus*) or wax plant (*Hoya*), and climbers like jasmine (*Jasminum*), passion flower (*Passiflora*), and wax flower (*Stephanotis floribunda*). A Japanese atmosphere is created by bamboo, azaleas (*Rhododendron*), grasses, and indoor bonsai.

Classic style

Traditional English or French styles and German Biedermeier furniture harmonize with bushy, vigorously flowering plants with soft contours, e.g., cyclamen, camellias, gloxinias (*Sinningia* hybrids), or begonias, as well as palms and tree-shaped container plants.

Plants and architecture

Anyone who knows how to play around creatively with plants can enhance the style and atmosphere of a house effectively, whether it is a farmhouse, a chalet, an old or super-modern villa, a stately mansion or a simple urban dwelling, an apartment, or an old, modern, or postmodern single-family home. In this process, containers play a major role.

THE RURAL, COUNTRY STYLE emphasizes pots, boxes, and tubs made of wood, clay, majolica, stoneware, and glazed or unglazed pottery, as well as baskets, sandstone tubs, or animal watering troughs made of wood. The plants to use are the classic balcony and tub plants, preferably in a colorful medley.

MODERN HOMES, because of their neutral character, are compatible with all types of containers and plants, provided that one doesn't mix container styles.

SUPER-MODERN ARCHITECTURE calls for a few impressive, green, individual specimens, such as bamboo, palms, or bananas. Flowering plants should be large and, if possible, all one color.

APPROPRIATE FOR VILLAS AND UP-SCALE CITY HOMES, but also for POSTMODERN SINGLE- OR MULTIPLE-FAMILY HOMES, are so-called Florentine containers made of green or white varnished wooden slats, richly decorated and glazed china containers, and terra-cotta pots, either simple or generously ornate. There are no set rules for the selection of plants. Elegance and good taste are underscored by evergreen classics such as laurel and box, or timeless plants like fuchsia and hydrangeas. When decorating with plants, explore how effective a tone-on-tone combination can be.

LIVING GREENER, LIVING BETTER

Pot plants suited to a country-style home

Country-style inside and out. It looks so cheerful in the rustic living room. The blue-and-white outer pots suit cyclamen (*Cyclamen persicum*), African violets (*Saintpaulia*), and indoor linden (*Sparmannia africana*).

Terra-cotta pots, boxes, and containers bring a southern flair to balconies and patios and harmonize beautifully with all plants. Here they are uniting flowering maple (*Abutilon*), white and yellow marguerite chrysanthemums (*Chrysanthemum frutescens*), marigold (*Tagetes*), exacum (*Exacum*), and bell flower (*Campanula*).

In terra-cotta containers, plants look natural and thrive naturally.

Plant Containers and Outer Pots

Pots, boxes, and tubs can be just as important decorative elements as the plants themselves. Things to consider when selecting the appropriate plant container and outer pot include the shape and size of the plant, the color of its flowers, the furnishing style, and personal taste. There are a few guidelines, however:

- Small plants look lost in outer pots that are too large.
- Round containers are more effective than square ones.
- The pot must not be taller than the plant.
- Do not place flowering plants in patterned containers.
- It looks good if the decoration of the outer pot echoes the flowers it contains.
- The effect is enhanced if the pot is the same color as the flowers or leaves.
- Baskets as outer pots go well with a youthful furnishing style, wicker furniture, or a rustic setting.
- Terra-cotta plant containers evoke a feeling of Mediterranean romanticism on a balcony or patio.
- Wooden tubs are durable and have a rural character.
- Outer pots made of copper or brass look classy.
- Old-fashioned porcelain pots look charming with traditional furniture in the English, French, or Biedermeier style.
- Bushy, circular plants look their best in curvilinear containers.
- Use uniform outer pots for grouped plants, though perhaps in different sizes and colors.
- It is hard to go wrong with white pots, baskets in natural colors, and terra-cotta containers.

Plant containers

In addition to ordinary, simple plant containers made of clay and plastic, the trade offers a rich choice of decorative models.

GLAZED CLAY POTS with matching saucers come in all sizes and many colors. They are economical and practical. Do not choose the cheapest on offer, however, because their color will flake off quickly. Be brave and select unusual plant containers shaped like animals or heads.

PLANT CONTAINERS WITH WATER RESERVOIRS are very practical. The material is synthetic, the colors usually white, cream, or brown, the form either round or square.

WOODEN TUBS are available in all sizes, from small ones for the window ledge to barrel-shaped ones for the patio. They should be treated with something that is tolerated by plants and friendly to the environment. (Ask about this when buying!)

For large plants, use four-legged WOODEN PLANT CONTAINERS with a synthetic liner. These are frequently offered in furniture stores. To improve handling, some plant containers have wheels so that they can be moved easily.

Always classic are TERRA-COTTA CONTAINERS. These are available in many sizes and shapes, richly decorated or plain. They have just one disadvantage: their weight. Now there is an alternative from England, Terracast. These plant containers look amazingly like terra-cotta ones, but are made of much lighter, synthetic polymers.

In addition to these "official" plant containers, you can use any OTHER POTS, AS ALONG AS THEY ARE PROVIDED WITH DRAINAGE HOLES. (A drill makes this possible. Only use a thin drill bit at first, so that the pot doesn't crack. You can then follow up with a larger drill bit—but always with restraint.)

Outer pots

Here, there are no limits to the imagination. You can use containers made of ceramic, porcelain, wood, metal, a synthetic, and any kind of basket. Our examples are only meant to stimulate your creativity.

Commercially available OUTER POTS are usually made of CERAMIC and come in an enormous range of forms and colors. Several bushy flowering plants look quite magical in an old washbasin. If you have an old soup tureen, fill it with a spreading plant: a fern or a bromeliad.

In the case of unglazed clay or ceramic pots, an unattractive calcium ring will develop after a time. Unfortunately, simple brushing won't remove this. The most environmentally friendly remedy is to place the pot overnight in a pail of bark compost filled with water. Next day, the calcium ring will have disappeared.

Practical tips

- Don't forget to pour away any excess from the outer pot after watering!
- Plants in synthetic or glazed pots need less water than those in porous clay containers.
- A thick layer of gravel or clay aggregate in the outer pot, beneath the plant pot, prevents rot in the root area. The same effect can be achieved by placing an upturned saucer under the plant.
- There must be a good half-inch (1 cm) of air between the outer pot and the plant container.
- Heavy plants are more easily transported in a basket or tub with side handles.
- Outer pots of wood or plastic store heat.
- Baskets are not watertight. Use plastic wrap and a saucer to prevent damage to the furniture.

LIVING GREENER, LIVING BETTER

For a balcony, ZINC-COATED TIN PAILS and BATHTUBS can be useful. Plant containers should be sunk in clay granular to prevent water buildup.

Indoor plants can be placed in CAST-IRON BUCKETS WITH HANDLES, HEXAGONAL OUTER POTS MADE OF BRAIDED ALUMINUM STRIPS, or SPHERICAL COPPER POTS. Several plants at a time can occupy long copper JARDINIERES or shiny brass containers.

In the case of BASKETS, the choice is virtually unlimited. Some are made of bamboo cane or finely braided bamboo, often with attractive designs worked in, in a variety of depths, round or square, varnished or natural. Other basket materials are willow shoots, straw, cane, and palm leaves.

Rare and costly are FLOWER BOXES made of CHIPBOARD WITH A BAMBOO VENEER, and RATTAN CUBES.

For large, heavy plants, OUTER POTS ON WHEELS are recommended. These can be made of a synthetic, wood, or cane. Just as practical are saucers with wheels, which come in various sizes.

Ornamental peppers, artfully arranged

A magical combination in yellow and red, with a little green: Yellow and red ornamental peppers, painted pots with a matte finish, and yellowish red ceramic apples.

The same color scheme outdoors: Dwarf conifers and ericas, Japanese maple (*Acer palmatum*), and acebia (*Akebia*) in baskets of willow give the look of fall. The yellow-gold melons are a decorative touch.

Willow baskets make robust and economical plant containers.

Accessories

These modern flower stands with integrated plant bowls are available in many colors and different heights. They are excellent for hanging plants.

Picture, right: The brilliantly red amaryllis in colorful decorative outer pots harmonize beautifully with the bunch of sun-yellow forsythia and the cane table.

Flower stands with integrated plant containers

It is often small things that really enable our houseplants to come into their own. After a time, many a plant grows too large for the windowsill, darkens the room, and blocks the view. Yet it remains too small for the floor. There, you look down on it and see little of its beauty. Place it just a few centimeters higher, however, and it will make a completely different impression.

Small-plant furniture

Plants that stand on low tables or stools are particularly attractive. This applies especially to group plantings. By using stools or tables of different heights, you can greatly improve the total picture.

Many furniture stores sell small furniture made of wood (varnished or natural) or synthetic materials as cash-and-carry items. Especially decorative are large animal figurines made of cane or porcelain. On these, spreading plants such as indoor asparagus or fern become showpieces. Also available are special flower tables, of bamboo, rattan, or cane, in various heights. On occasion, such tables are also made of high-quality materials such as rosewood, glass, and steel.

Plants on columns

Plant columns and high tables with a single leg that has been artfully worked have existed since the beginning of houseplant culture. The columns, made of porcelain or wood, chrome, smoked glass, mirror glass, or Plexiglas, can be round, square, or hexagonal. The tables are often made of wrought iron with a marble top. In former times, precious pieces made of hardwood were also available. Now and again one can find such high-class pieces in antique stores. Such an individual antique object will also fit well into a modern decorative scheme. Columns and high tables need separate locations where, come evening, they can be properly illuminated by individual spotlights.

Dividers

Dividers may also be useful in decorating with houseplants. Shelves of Plexiglas or wood can be used to separate a seating area from the rest of the room. Light conditions permitting, these are ideal places for trailing plants or for small-growing species.

A series of large, treelike tub plants, set on stools of different heights, can even take the place of a room divider.

Placing accents

Plant containers, outer pots, and small furniture for plants, available in a wide choice of materials and shapes, allow accents to be created in every room.

Outer pots and stools of bamboo and rattan with straight, even severe lines create an oriental look. Weeping figs (*Ficus benjamina*), indoor bamboo, and palms (even if these do not come from Asia) fit in well with this decor.

Containers and circular baskets with handles, when filled with flowering plants, have a rustic character. White Italian ceramics look cool; ceramics with a rustic pattern, like those from Alsace, look comfortable and cozy. When brightly colored, porcelain looks playful; when it is classically simple, it adds a touch of elegance.

Plants and accessories

Some refer to them as knickknacks, but others see them as lovable accessories. Using small objects that look as if they just happen to lie near plants, you can create a special atmosphere. Make yourself a nostalgic arrangement of pink flowering plants in front of an antique piece of furniture and place a doll from your grandmother's era next to it. Candlesticks, beautiful animal figurines of wood, a picture on the wall that matches the color of the plant, or a table lamp complete the effect. Give your creative decorating talent free rein.

Picture, right: The spirit of spring, with amaryllis and forsythia

Plants in Hanging Planters

Hanging plants can be used in many ways on walls, trellises, ceilings, and balcony railings. Special mountings are available for hanging baskets or planters, but often meat hooks, cords, or strong chains will serve to fasten them.

Hanging planters are frequently used outdoors, on balconies and patios, but are seen much less often indoors. Yet hanging plants, both climbing and creeping species, cannot be accommodated nearly as effectively in any other type of container. Hanging planters allow them to spread all around, and so to develop as nature intended. When you use hanging plants, however, there are some things you should take into account:

- Make sure that you have a stable hook anchored into the ceiling, and a strong chain or heavy cord—wet soil and plants are heavy.
- Make sure the planters you hang on your balcony or patio cannot hit the wall or the window when the wind blows.
- Wire baskets, even when lined with plastic wrap, should only be used outdoors or over a tiled floor. Often, they are not completely watertight.
- For indoors, use only containers from which excess water cannot escape.
- Hanging planters with integrated saucers are not all that attractive, but they are practical. They are often completely covered by trailing plants in a very short time.
- Baskets and clay containers attached to a wall are an alternative to hanging planters.

Watering hanging plants
Watering requires instinctive feeling, as hanging plants have somewhat different needs than pot plants. There are several reasons for this: often the species involved have dense foliage, and thus lose much moisture through evaporation. In the upper regions

Plant container for a wall

Hanging basket on wire fencing

Large bowl for shallow-rooting plants

Mounting device for the banister

Wire basket with moss, foil, or plastic lining

of a room, moreover, temperatures are higher, as heat rises. Outdoors, hanging plants are more exposed to wind than are flowers in boxes or on the ground, so they dry out more quickly. Nevertheless, take care when watering, to avoid a buildup of water. Most hanging planters lack drainage holes, and it is a nuisance to have to take them

down after every watering in order to pour away excess water.

- A drainage layer of light clay granular or Styrofoam chips (so that the planter doesn't become still heavier) spread on the bottom of the hanging planter guards against the danger of water buildup.

LIVING GREENER, LIVING BETTER

- A watering can with a long spout saves you having to climb on a stool every time.
- In very warm summer weather it is a good idea to take down any hanging plants on your balcony and patio twice a week, in order to immerse them in water.

Hanging plants, indoors and out

Not only specifically hanging plants but also creepers or plants that spread as they grow can be used in hanging planters. Here is a small selection:

FOR SHADY LOCATIONS:
Hanging philodendron (*Philodendron scandens*), staghorn fern (*Platycerium bifurcatum*).

FOR BRIGHT TO PARTIALLY SHADY LOCATIONS:
Golden pathos (*Epipremnum pinnatum*), English ivy (*Hedera helix*), strawberry begonia (*Saxifraga stolonifera*), spider plant (*Chlorophytum comosum*), piggyback plant (*Tolmiea menziesii*), grape ivy (*Cissus*), porcelain berry vine (*Ampelopsis brevipedunculata*), Christmas cactus (*Schlumbergera*).

FOR BRIGHT LOCATIONS WITH HIGH HUMIDITY:
Columnea (*Columnea*), lipstick vine (*Aeschynanthus radicans*), pouch plant or guppy fish plant (*Hypocyrta*), dipladenia (*Dipladenia*), *Ficus sagittata*.

FOR BRIGHT LOCATIONS:
Wandering Jew (*Zebrina pendula*), Cape primrose (*Streptocarpus saxorum*), bulrush (*Scirpus cernuus*), burro's tail (*Sedum morganianum*), *Codonanthe crassifolia*, spiderwort (*Tradescantia*), asparagus fern

Peperomia *in terra-cotta cones*

Terra-cotta cones, a new type of decorative hanging planters, are ideal for smaller plants. They hang on thick cords.

(*Asparagus*), angel's tears (*Billbergia*), creeping fig (*Ficus pumila*).

FOR SUNNY LOCATIONS:
Lotus berthelotii, wax plant (*Hoya*), kalanchoe (*Kalanchoe manginii*), hearts entangled (*Ceropegia woodii*), string of pearls (*Senecio rowleyanus*).

FOR THE OUT-OF-DOORS:
Star-of-Bethlehem (*Campanula isophylla*), hanging geranium (*Pelargonium*), fuchsia (*Fuchsia*), Centradenia, morning glory (*Convolvulus sabatius*), petunia (*Petunia*), creeping zinnia (*Sanvitalia procumbens,*), canary vine (*Tropaeolum peregrinum*).

Decorating with Climbing Plants

Climbing supports can look very different, and they can often serve as screens or as decorative elements. To the right, six possible designs for climbing supports.

Many climbing plants do not reveal their aesthetic possibilities when they are young. At first, their growth is bushy, and they only develop long shoots as they get older. Others need a climbing support right from the start. In their native location, they wind their way up and along tree branches.

Don't be surprised that certain species are listed here as both hanging and climbing plants. They are suitable for both.

Indoor climbing supports

Supports for climbing houseplants are made of wood, wire, plastic, rattan, and bamboo. The trade offers them in many shapes, such as trellis, spindle, and round arch (see the drawings, right).

Skilled do-it-yourselfers build their climbing supports as they need them, using wire coated with plastic or nonrusting wire, and bamboo or wood stakes. The weak points of trellises are the places where two stakes intersect. Drill a hole in both stakes near the intersection, draw a wire through, and twist it tightly.

The material for round arches must not be soft or the weight of the plants will press the arch down to a flat oval. The material for spindles, too, must not be too flexible.

The climbing supports should be inserted into the pot at the time of planting. Thick stakes poked into the planting mix later pose a threat to the roots.

Outdoor climbing supports

On the balcony and patio, climbing plants can also grow up the walls. Trellises and concertina barriers are commercially available in several makes, but skilled hobbyists can easily construct them for themselves. For many plants, vertically stretched wires or strings will be adequate. Stable trellises on fixed flower boxes do good service as protection against wind, and as screens.

Fastening the plants

The soft shoots of climbing plants can easily be bent around the supports. Depending on the structure of the support, it is possible to make globes, ovals, or pyramids. To give the shoots a better hold, fasten them loosely to the support at irregular intervals.

You can borrow materials from the kitchen to fasten the shoots: the green ties of freezer bags are excellent for this purpose. *Caution:* Don't crush the plant stems when you tie them up!

Pot grid for small climbing plants

Mossy stake for epiphytes

Wall trellis for large climbers

Column made of wire mesh

Ladder with wire mesh

Plant box with a built-in screen structure

LIVING GREENER, LIVING BETTER

Climbing plants for indoors

Depending on the type of support, climbing and twining plants can be divided into:

PLANTS FOR ROUND ARCHES: Passion flower (*Passiflora,*), wax flower (*Stephanotis floribunda*), wax plant (*Hoya*), jasmine (*Jasminum officinale*), climbing lily (*Gloriosa rothschildiana*), *Dipladenia*.

PLANTS FOR TRELLISES OR SPINDLES: English ivy (*Hedera helix*), Canary Island ivy (*Hedera canariensis*), *Tetrastigma voinierianum*, grape ivy (*Cissus rhombifolia*), *Micania ternata*.

PLANTS FOR MOSS STAKES (commercially available): Philodendron (*Philodendron*), schefflera (*Schefflera*), and arrowhead (*Syngonium*). The tendrils are tied up with wire bent in the shape of hairpins.

Climbing plants for the out-of-doors

Climbers "climb" in very different ways. The usual distinctions are between adhesive climbers, nonsupporting climbers, twining climbers, and tendril climbers.

ADHESIVE CLIMBERS such as English ivy (*Hedera helix*), Boston ivy (*Parthenocissus tricuspidata*), trumpet vine (*Campsis radicans*), or climbing hydrangea (*Hydrangea anormale* ssp. *petiolaris*) do not need any help in climbing. They make their way up any surface, using their adhesive roots or disks.

NONSUPPORTING CLIMBERS, such as jasmine (*Jasminum nudiflorum*) and climbing roses (*Rosa*), need a trellis and must be tied to it.

TWINING CLIMBERS, such as morning glory (*Ipomoea*), black-

A unique room divider: white plaster columns with a white lattice

eyed Susan vine (*Thunbergia alata*), honeysuckle (*Lonicera*), and Dutchman's pipe (*Arostolochia macrophylla*), spiral around string and wire with their shoots. A rough surface makes it easier for them; but the shoots may also be fastened here and there. TENDRIL CLIMBERS, such as sweet pea (*Lathyrus odoratus*), clematis (*Clematis*), nasturtium (*Tropaeolum majus*), and cup and saucer vine (*Cobeaea scandens*), climb up wires or similar supports using thin, wirelike tendrils.

Shade-loving English ivy (*Hedera*) and grape ivy (*Cissus*) grow up this elegant room divider.

Plant Windows

A closed plant window with tropical plants is for the most discriminating. A variety of orchids, tillandsias, and bromeliads live in wooden baskets, pots, and on an epiphyte branch.

Most houseplants stand on a windowsill, but this is far from making the window a plant window in the classical sense. With more or less expense, you can make life more comfortable for the plants that live on your windowsill, while giving yourself a great deal of pleasure. But you should bear in mind that you will no longer be able to open that window.

Plant window with shelves
Shelves built into the window frame are an astonishingly simple and decorative solution. Given a sunny location, such a flower shelf is an ideal spot, e.g., for a small collection of cacti. On the upper shelf, hanging plants do well, and there can always be something in bloom at eye level.

Open plant window
An open plant window can be created easily on a windowsill that is about 20 in. (50 cm) wide (if necessary, widen yours before-hand). It is called "open" because no glass separates the plants from the living room. In order to protect the root system of the plants from cold and drafts, place strips of Styrofoam vertically in front of the window, and cover the windowsill with a Styrofoam mat. If there is a radiator under the window, the Styrofoam will prevent the dry heated air from rising and damaging the plants. Even better are plant boxes with built-in heating or heating pads. But for this, you need an electrical outlet nearby.

Plant tubs are placed on the windowsill and filled with clay granular, which is kept continually moist. The plants are put into the tubs together with their pots.

Experience has shown that it is not really practical to fill the tubs themselves with potting mix. It is easier to care for individual pots, and diseases are less likely to spread quickly.

Because the clay granular constantly evaporates water over a large area, this location suits many plants that would have trouble in dry room air.

Closed plant window
A closed plant window is not so easy to arrange on a windowsill. Considerable construction is involved (→ page 13).

Epiphyte branches
The focal point of a closed plant window is the epiphyte branch

---

Plants suited for the epiphyte branch

Aechmea
Asplenium
Davallia
Guzmania
epiphytic orchids
Platycerium bifurcatum
Rhipsalis
epiphytic tillandsias
Vriesea

---

that supports tree-dwelling plants (epiphytes).

Most of our domestic woods, however, are not suitable for this purpose because they rot too quickly in a humid atmosphere. Only an oak branch or a mature vine might prove sufficiently durable. On the other hand, it is easy to create an epiphyte branch using plastic pipes, the bark of a cork tree, and various other things.

Think about shape and size before you go out to buy any of the components in a builders' yard or hobby shop. You will need:
- Plastic pipes in different strengths and shapes, from the plumbing section (make sure the connectors fit together)
- Branch-shaped cork strips in various diameters, cut open at one side
- A large bowl
- Several stones and contact cement for the "foot," needed to stabilize the branch
- Copper wire or some other nonrusting wire
- Nonrusting screws
- Glue
- Fine, flexible, nonrusting wire mesh
- Smallish clay pots
- Small plant boxes made of wood (available from stores specializing in orchids, specialty stores)
- Reindeer moss, orchid mix, or fibrous peat

Fastening plants to an epiphyte branch
There are several ways to attach the plants:
- Make small baskets out of wire mesh and fasten them to the forks of the branch.
- Fill a bent piece of bark that has been fastened to the stem with dampened mix.
- Wind the roots around the stem and tie them with damp moss.

The planting mix must never be allowed to dry out, but the nutrient requirement is very low. Occasional spraying with a liquid fertilizer solution is enough for these undemanding plants.

For tying plants to an epiphyte branch, used nylons cut into strips are very good. They are remarkably elastic and relatively unobtrusive.

Picture, right: View into an extended plant window

Miniature gardens

This miniature landscape, created by French potter Claude Michael (*La Garde Adhémor*) out of fired clay, is a masterpiece. It has been planted with euonymus (*Euonymus*), myrtle (*Myrtus*), and English ivy (*Hedera helix*).

A complete small garden in a room, or on a balcony or patio? This is no jest. Magical miniature gardens can be created in large plant containers, with all the features that belong to a normal garden: trees, shrubs, and flowers.

A miniature garden can be created using either plants that are genetic dwarfs or young plants, but one can also use normal plants whose growth has been thwarted.

Young plants will serve for only a limited period. When they grow too big, they will have to move to separate quarters.

• In miniature gardens, as in other group plantings, the needs of all the assembled plant species must coincide.

Controlling growth
If the roots don't have room, the above-ground portion of a plant will remain small. To inhibit growth, the plants are set in tiny plant baskets only a few inches (cm) across, made of noncorrosive stainless steel weave. In these, the roots cannot spread out, but water and nutrients can find their way to the roots unhindered.

The following plants are examples of those well suited to such a setting: coleus (*Coleus*), English Ivy (*Hedera helix*), many rubber tree species (*Ficus*), Hawaiian schefflera (*Schefflera arboricola*), aucuba (*Aucuba*), ti-plant (*Cordyline fruticosa*), croton (*Codiaeum variegatum var. pictum*) and various species of dracaena (*Dracaena*).

Complete systems for cultivating miniatures, with exact instructions, are commercially available.

Miniature plants for miniature gardens
Mini-plants are in fashion, and the trade has followed the trend.

Would you like a rose garden on the windowsill? The cultivar 'Colibri' will give you red flowers, 'Baby Masquerade' is orange colored, and 'Dwarf Queen' and 'Dwarf King' are pink.

Some plants offered as minis are African violets, cyclamen, begonias, peace lilies (*Spathiphyllum*), poinsettia (*Euphorbia pulcherrima*), impatiens (*Impatiens*), azaleas (*Rhododendron*), and many leafy cacti.

Don't count on dwarf growth lasting forever. In the nursery, the plants were often treated with chemical substances that inhibited growth. Without them, they will grow normally after a while.

Miniature gardens for the balcony and patio
Outdoor miniature gardens have a long tradition. A great variety of winter-hardy dwarf trees and

Decorative plant container made of fired clay

The "tree of a thousand stars" is a magical indoor bonsai.

hebaceous perennials, most from the Alpine regions, will thrive in the limited space of a plant trough.

To create a realistic impression of a garden, you can plant together evergreens, miniature roses, flowering dwarf perennials, and grasses. In between, you can indicate narrow paths across bright sand, and use stones to vary the scene. Unfortunately, this is not the place to go into detail. To do so would exceed the limits of this book. Good forestry schools and perennial nurseries will advise you on the choice of suitable plants.

Bonsai for interiors

Traditional bonsai are outdoor plants from climatic zones that approximate our weather conditions. They cannot survive for long indoors. Indoor bonsai are woody plants from the Mediterranean region, the subtropics, and the tropics. They have long been regarded as normal pot plants and do quite well in our homes. Where

temperature, light requirements, humidity, and rest periods are concerned, these miniature trees do not differ from their bigger relatives. Nevertheless, a few peculiarities must be taken into account when caring for indoor bonsai:

- Use special potting mix, bonsai fertilizer, and a watering can with a fine nozzle.
- Bonsai grow in shallow bowls with little soil, often slightly mounded. So that the dry soil isn't swept off when you water, first give it a good spraying.
- In the limited space, nutrients are consumed more quickly than in a normal pot. Fertilize more often, but always in weak doses and never on dry soil. Never fertilize shortly before and after blooming, after repotting or trimming the roots, or when the plant looks sick.

Species suitable as indoor bonsai

In order to avoid acquiring a bonsai plant for your home that is only suitable for growing outdoors, here is a list of popular interior bonsai species:

Acacia baileyana
Adenium obesum
Albizia julibrissin
Araucaria heterophylla
Ardisia crenata
Bambusa vulgaris
Bougainvillea glabra
Calliandra tweedii
Camellia japonica
Carissa macrocarpa
Cassia hebecarpa
Chrysanthemum frutescens
Cissus microphylla
Coffea arabica
Cuphea hyssopifolia
Cupressus macrocarpa
Cytisus racemosus
Eugenia brasiliensis
Ficus species
Fuchsia magellanica
Hedera helix
Hibiscus rosa-sinensis
Ixora javanica
Leptospermum scoparium
Myrtys communis
Nicodemia diversifolia
Pelargonium rhodanthum
Pistacia lentiscus
Pittosporum tobira
Polyscias fruticosa
Psidium cattleianum
Rhapis excelsa
Rhododendron species
Rosmarinus officinalis
Serissa foetida
Trachelospermum jasminoides

Serissa foetida, ("tree of a thousand stars," also called "snow in June"), is one of the most beautiful indoor bonsai, and relatively easy to grow. This evergreen woody plant, from southeast Asia—here an unusual miniature with variegated leaves, photographed at the Bonsai Center in Heidelberg—is a generous bloomer.

The plant-portrait section indicates, for every species, whether it is suitable as a bonsai. Bonsai suppliers are listed on page 376.

Desert and Tropical Mini-Gardens

Miniature cacti gardens are easy to make. Arrange the plants, still in their pots, on a drainage layer of clay aggregate to establish their position. Then remove the cacti from their pots with the help of a paper sleeve, set them in the bowl, and fill the gaps with cactus mix, clay aggregate, or gravel.

Plant collecting can become an obsession. Those who have once lost their hearts to cacti and succulents can never get enough of them—literally. There are about 3000 species divided into more than 600 plant families. The variety of form is incredible, bizarre, and exhilarating.

A colorful mélange is the best way to convey the marvelous wealth of forms offered by cacti and other succulents. Start small, with a few plants in pretty dishes. The more varied the growing forms, the better. Make the surface of the soil part of the design. You can conjure up a "landscape" with little stones, gravel, and sand.

Caution: Plants in a container must have similar needs with respect to potting mix, summer and winter temperatures, water, and nutrients.

Drainage layer of clay aggregate

Arranging the plants

Removing the cacti from their pots

Finished desert garden

Desert gardens

Cacti are the plants best suited to the mini-garden. Most of them require the same treatment, and most grow very slowly.

If you want the cacti garden to look like a landscape, the plants must have different shapes. For the background, use the tall-growing *Cleistocactus* species and also the venerable old man cactus (*Cephalocereus senilis*). Next to these, the lower *Opuntia* species look very decorative. In the foreground, let globular *Mammillaria* or *Parodia* species spread out. Pay attention, too, to the colors of the cacti and the shapes of their ribs and thorns.

The colors of the dishes or troughs must not compete with the plants. It looks best if the color of the container echoes one of the colors of the planting. Pay particular attention to this when using

flowering cacti. The proportions, too, must be in accord. For example, small globular cacti should be placed in plant bowls that are as shallow as possible.

The surface of the potting mix must be part of the design scheme of every desert garden. You can cover it with all sorts of materials: rounded pebbles, rough-edged stone chips, clay granular in a variety of grain sizes, pumice, coal slag, sand in a variety of shades. To create interest, put in lumps of "rock" a few inches/centimeters high, or gnarled roots.

Bottle gardens

Plants that need very humid air find it hard to thrive in normal rooms, but can enjoy optimal living conditions in, e.g., bulbous bottles of untinted glass. There, they can create their own climate, as in a

"Wardian case" (→ page 27). The basic principles for a bottle garden are as follows:

- Do not use flowering plants. They only look good for a short time and always have to be removed as soon as they have finished blooming, which is not so easy. Moreover, opening the container frequently is bad for the system, which only works properly if it remains sealed for a reasonable length of time.

- The neck of the container must be narrow enough to be tightly sealed, and wide enough so you can work inside it.

- To prevent rot, mix small pieces of charcoal into the drainage layer composed of pebbles, clay granular, or clay aggregate. Depending on the size of the bottle, this layer should have a thickness of 1.2–2.4 in. (3–6 cm).

PLACEMENT AND PURCHASE

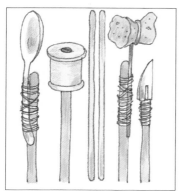
Home-made tools

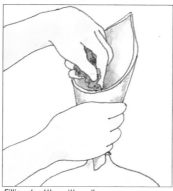
Filling bottle with soil

Distributing and smoothing the soil

To create a bottle garden you require several homemade implements: a spoon tied to a handle, for shoveling **(a)**, a spool of thread to press the plants firmly into the soil **(b)**, chopsticks to hold the plants **(c)**, a small sponge tied to a handle to clean the inside glass surfaces **(d)**, and a sharp razor blade for cutting and trimming **(e)**. Remove the plants from their pots with the help of a paper clip, place them into the prepared holes using two chopsticks, and tamp the soil down firmly.

Unpotting the plants

Inserting the plants

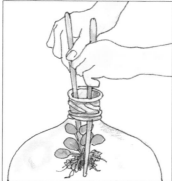

Tamping down the soil

- This should be topped with 2–4 in. (5–10 cm) of previously moistened potting mix, consisting of equal parts of flower soil and peat. To keep the plants from growing quickly, the soil should contain few nutrients.
- Experiment with the arrangement of the plants on a piece of paper the size of the planting surface. Higher growers should be set behind smaller ones.
- Trim rampant root balls to make the plants grow more slowly.
- Set in the plants that will grow around the circumference of the bottle first, then those in the center.
- Using a teaspoon attached to a handle, dig and plant one hole at a time. Once you have stowed away all the small tropical plants, press down the

soil firmly and spray the small rain-forest plants, using a fine nozzle. The interior surface of the bottle can be kept clean with a small sponge attached to a stable but flexible wire.

If the decorative bottle garden is well sealed and placed in a bright but not sunny location, it will give you many months of pleasure. Occasionally, you will have to air it and also trim any plant that has become too big with a razor blade attached to a rod.

It is best to buy young plants with attractive patterned or colored leaves, and ones that will remain small and grow slowly. Herewith, a selection of such plants:
Acorus gramineus, Adiantum raddianum, Callisia elegans, Didymochlaena truncatula, Ficus pumila, Fittonia verschaffeltii 'Minima,' Hatiora salicornioides,

Pellaea rotundifolia, Pellionia pulcher, Peperomia, Pilea, Pteris ensiformis 'Victoriae,' Rhipsalis mesembryanthemoides, Selaginella uncinata, Tradescantia albiflora, Zebrina pendula.

111

Four Seasons on the Balcony

At every time of year, the balcony looks different: In spring, tulips (*Tulipa*), ranunculus, and hydrangeas grow among dwarf conifers or deciduous trees.

Summer on the balcony can combine summer flowers like lantana (*Lantana*), marigolds (*Tagetes*), and busy Lizzies (*Impatiens* New Guinea hybrids) with house plants like grape ivy (*Cissus rhombifolia*) and Boston fern (*Nephrolepsis exaltata*).

Spring

It needn't always be pansies. Many lovely spring flowers can be planted in boxes and bowl-shaped planters. Try planting a variety of bulbs and tubers in fresh soil: crocus, winter aconite (*Eranthis hiemalis*), snowdrops, early narcissus and tulips, hyacinths, and daffodils. Protect the containers well if they are outdoors, or overwinter them in a cool part of the house.

These spring bloomers also look pretty between permanent plantings of evergreens. Or, in spring, you can buy and plant your containers with some of the many forced bulbs that are available. But be sure not to begin the balcony season too early, lest your spring display succumb to frost.

Summer

Try to get away from the usual geraniums, petunias, and begonias. A huge variety of summer flowers is on offer. For sunny locations there are slipper flowers, liverwort, blue daisies, marigolds, heliotrope, low summer asters and bushy marguerites, nasturtiums, and lobelias; for shady locations use fuchsias and busy Lizzies (*Impatiens*).

People with a good sense of smell enjoy roses and lavender, sage and marjoram, fragrant geraniums and rosemary.

Attractive grasses between the flowering plants make the design less formal and create the impression of a natural garden.

Fall

It is not necessary to have an entirely new planting in your balcony boxes for the fall. Many summer flowers bloom until the first frost, and it would be a shame to throw them away prematurely.

A spring balcony with flowers from bulbs and tubers

A summer balcony with summer flowers and houseplants

LIVING GREENER, LIVING BETTER

Fall balcony with beautiful foliage colors

Winter balcony with a birdhouse

In late summer or early fall, replace those that have finished blooming with asters or chrysanthemums, which will continue to give you new color until the first frost. Summer asters and dahlias also bloom until the first frost.

Small trees and bushes for boxes and tubs should be planted in the spring rather than in fall, as they would be in the garden.

Winter

Only one plant flowers in the winter: the snow heath. The other species of heath (*Erica*), which you can buy everywhere in the fall, turn brown after frost. A winter balcony need not be monotonous, however. Grasses in the balcony boxes can be left as decoration. In between, you can insert branches of fir, pine, spruce, juniper, arbor-vitae or other evergreens, branches with berries from the garden, or the attractive seed pods of herbaceous perennials. Those who want to introduce color can do so using branches of corkscrew hazel or other shrubs, painted red and white.

In fall, heath (*Erica*), milkwort (*Senecio*), and late-blooming pansies look very attractive in balcony boxes and bowl-shaped planters alongside small conifers and deciduous shrubs with colorful foliage.

Snow and frost transform a balcony with permanent planting, wilted plants, and branches with red berries, into a winter fairy tale.

Balcony Plantings

You can create a particular mood on your balcony or patio by drawing its architectural features into the design. A wrought-iron railing creates a different atmosphere than does a concrete parapet, and the effect of a balustrade or floor made of wood differs from that of brick walls and terra-cotta floor tiles. A careful choice of plants, colors, and combinations can highlight and enhance such elements.

Our suggestions for balconies apply also to roof gardens and patios. Caution: When combining plants, be sure to take the light conditions into account.

The recommendations made here are limited in the first instance to species described in the plant-portrait section.

The romantic balcony

The balconies of older apartment houses often have especially beautiful decorative railings made of artfully curved cast-iron poles decorated with ornaments and rosettes. A dainty bistro table with a marble top and matching chairs completes the romantic impression. An old metal washbowl stand, transformed into a flower holder, is the final touch. If you paint everything, including the boxes, white, the plants will stand out especially well.

Choose annuals with many small buds and smallish leaves. In no case should the planting make a heavy impression. A combination of blue and white flowers looks delightful, and a totally pink balcony is magical, while lilac and yellow flowers create stronger accents.

The country balcony

The classic country balcony is long, decked, has a thin wooden balustrade made of decorated planks, and overflows with geraniums. Wooden washtubs and animal drinking troughs serve as

> **Plant specimens for the romantic balcony:**
> *Begonia semperflorens* hybrids, *Bellis perennis, Brachycome iberidifolia, Campanula carpatica, Chrysanthemum paludosom, Felicia amelloides* 'Blue Daisy,' *Gomphrena globosa, Impatiens walleriana, Lathyrus odoratus, Lobelia erinus, Primula, Rosa, Viola wittrockiana* hybrids.

plant containers.

The right plants can create a rural atmosphere even in less "classic" surroundings, however. Naturally, geraniums belong in the picture. It is up to you to determine whether the planting should have one, two, or a multitude of colors. The main thing is that the colors should be strong and the flowering vigorous. If possible, leave no corner unplanted. You should not only decorate the upper edge of the railing, but also suspend hanging plants outside and from the roof. A country balcony is beautiful only if it is on the sunny side of the building. Only there can the flowers suited to a country balcony develop their full splendor.

The elegant balcony

In modern buildings, balcony balustrades are often made of transparent plastic and metal, or of straight, white poles. These are materials that create a cool, elegant atmosphere. Suited to it are balcony furniture with simple lines and plant containers made of

> **Plant specimens for the country balcony:**
> *Ageratum houstonianum, Calceolaria integrifolia, Callistephus chinensis, Chrysanthemum* species, *Felicia amelloides, Dahlia* hybrids, *Helianthus, Pelargonium, Petunia* hybrids, *Salvia splendens, Tagetes* hybrids, *Tropaeolum* hybrids.

earthenware or porcelain. Avoid too much color and vigor on the elegant balcony. We recommend a great deal of green, colorful leaves, creamy white and lilac flowers next to each other, or some fuchsias in a variety of colors. The elegant balcony may be sunny or partly shady.

Many vacationing houseplants do well in this picture, e.g. *Aloe, Billbergia nutans, Catharanthus roseus, Chamaedorea elegans, Clivia, Corynocarpus laevigatus, Crassula arborescens, Cycas revoluta, Cyrtomium falcatum, Yucca, Washingtonia.*

> **Plant specimens for the elegant balcony:**
> *Agapanthus praecox, Celosia argentea, Coleus blumei* hybrids, *Cuphea ignea, Fuchsia, Gazania, Heliotropium arborescens, Nicotiana x sanderae, Schizanthus wisetonensis* hybrids.

LIVING GREENER, LIVING BETTER

A spring balcony with many plants in beautiful containers

The freshness of spring is captured by these plants in lovely terra-cotta containers and glazed ceramic pots. Here are assembled tulips (*Tulipa*), hydrangeas (*Hydrangea*), and myrtle (*Myrtus communis*) trained as a standard.

This cheerful mix of various balcony flowers, houseplants, and container plants, together with a ceramic ball topped by a flute player, points to an owner who most probably regards summer as a poem. Cheerfully combined are a standard daisy or marguerite (*Chrysanthemum frutescens*), blue scaevola (*Scaevola*), felicia (*Felicia*), Cape primrose (*Streptocarpus*), gloxinia (*Sinningia*), petunia (*Petunia*), campanula (*Campanula*), and ageratum (*Ageratum*).

Summer cheerfulness and poetry rule on this balcony.

Planting Suggestions at a Glance

Spring. Tulips (*Tulipa*), hyacinths (*Hycinthus orientalis*), common primrose (*Primula* vulgaris hybrids), and auricula primrose (*Primula auricula*) are typical spring flowers. The lovely blooms are a treat for the eye, and hyacinths give off a pleasing perfume as well. The auricula primroses are somewhat frost-sensitive. After blooming, the plants may be put out in the garden. With luck, they will come back the following year.

Summer. A long-lived and very attractive arrangement for summer consists of petunias (*Petunia*) in a number of shades of pink, framed by blue lobelia (*Lobelia erinus*). Petunias don't tolerate rain very well. To be able to enjoy them all summer long, cut off wilted blooms regularly, and shorten excessively long shoots. If you cut lobelias back by one-third after their first flowering, they will form new blooms.

Fall. A flower box with English ivy (*Hedera helix*), creeping juniper (*Juniperus*), heath (*Erica*), or other small-growing evergreens gives the effect of great variety because of the plants' contrasting foliage. Heath is available in various colors in the fall. This planting can withstand cool days, but if there is strong frost, place the plant in a protected corner of the balcony and cover well. The soil in the box is not sufficient protection.

Winter. Between dwarf columnar conifers, snow heath (*Erica herbacea*), and English ivy (*Hedera helix*), add some strawflowers. This winter-proof arrangement creates a lively impression because of the colors and the variety of the plants. Plants need water in the winter, too, although not as much as in the summer. Water only during frost-free periods; otherwise, the soil will turn into a lump of ice, and even winter-hardy species can't tolerate that very well.

Aromatic box. It is enormously satisfying to be surrounded by a cloud of fragrance on the balcony. Scented-leaf geraniums are available in a variety of types. The plants may smell like lemon, pine, peppermint, cinnamon, or apple. Heliotrope smells like vanilla, the spurflower (*Plectranthus*) like camphor. Marjoram, rosemary, or thyme are not only a joy for self-indulgent noses; they also flavor food.

For nibbling and seasoning
a) It is fun to be able to pick some of your own ever-bearing strawberries now and again. Together with pansies (*Viola wittrockiana* hybrids) in a big pot, they make a charming corner-piece on the balcony.
b) Both attractive and useful is a planter filled with ornamental pepper (*Capsicum*), oregano (*Origanum vulgare*), and thyme (*Thymus vulgaris*).

116

Cheerful company. Nasturtium (*Tropaeolum* hybrids), a double-flowered cultivar of pot marigold (*Calendula*), and geraniums with variegated leaves (*Pelargonium* zonal hybrids) are easy to care for and bloom all summer long. All you need to do is cut off the wilted flowers regularly. Nasturtiums can be nurtured on the windowsill from early spring. They should be put outdoors only in late spring.

Hanging plants. The morning glory 'blue Mauritius' (*Convolvulus sabatius*) really comes into its own in a hanging planter. Black-eyed Susan vine (*Thunbergia alata*) twists around the supports. Nasturtium (*Tropaeolum* hybrids) is also available as a trailing or climbing plant. The center consists of Cape asters or felicia (*Felicia amelloides*).

There are endless possibilities for planting balcony boxes. In these pages you will find ten attractive suggestions, along with two tasteful ideas for large containers, and a charming arrangement for a hanging planter.

Colorful variety. Yellow pansies and low marigolds (*Tagetes patula* hybrids), lilac Johnny jump-ups (*Viola cornuta* hybrids), pansies (*Viola wittrockiana* hybrids), pinks (*Dianthus*), blue bell flowers (*Campanula*), and small English ivy plants (*Hedera helix*) create an arrangement of joyful color.

Romantic box. Blue Mauritius morning glory or another morning glory (*Convolvulus sabatius*) and pink petunias completely cover the sides of the container after only a few weeks. To go with them, red impatiens and, as an amusing spot of color, yellow gazania (*Gazania*). Such a closely packed box must be watered and fertilized more often. Also, watch out for pests and diseases, which spread quickly.

Elegant arrangement. This example shows how different begonia species are from one another. The rex begonia (*Begonia rex* hybrid) decorates with its lovely foliage, the elatior hybrid begonia (*Begonia* elatior hybrid) with its delicate array of flowers. The creeping fig (*Ficus pumila*) provides a green framework. This box also fits perfectly on a windowsill. The plants do equally well indoors and outside.

Harmony in pink. The flower colors of primroses (*Primula vulgaris* hybrids), English daisy (*Bellis perennis*), and dwarf azaleas (*Rhododendron* species) are perfectly attuned to one another. All three plants have cultivars of different colors of flowers. You can put together a colorful arrangement using the same plants—just as you please.

117

Plantings for the Patio

Patios are movable gardens. Until a short time ago, tub plants were something out of the ordinary. Only a few Mediterranean plants and exotics were cultivated in plant containers, because they needed to be taken into the house during the winter. Nowadays, everything is planted in tubs, troughs, pots, and boxes: annuals, perennials, small trees, and shrubs. The tree nurseries offer nearly all the popular trees, from apple trees to zebrina arbor-vitae (*Thuja plicata 'zebrina'*) in "patio format." Skillfully arranged, they enable us to conjure up small gardens in a variety of styles on our patios and balconies.

The Oriental patio
Shaded, subdued light mixed with a few spots of sunshine, such as is provided by a large foliage tree on the patio, are the ideal conditions for an oriental ambiance. Wooden flooring, straw mats as demarcation, ceramic containers with Asiatic ornamentation, a Japanese stone lantern, bamboo furniture, and predominantly non-flowering plants (including permanently planted evergreens) create a certain serenity that the hectic pace of everyday life tends to erase. Patios in the oriental style are oases of peace.

In the small traditional home gardens of Asia, which are often only a few feet square, every plant is regarded as an individual. A profusion of plants is never set on the small surfaces. Flowers are given less prominence. Behind this is the thought that one experiences the beauty of the blooms much more intensely if one can admire them for only a few weeks every year instead of being surrounded by them from spring to fall.

On an oriental patio, too, houseplants are heartily welcome as summer guests, e.g., umbrella sedge (*Cyperus*) and the rapsis (*Rapsis*). As flower accents, use hydrangeas (*Hydrangea*) with their pale colors, and azaleas with their short but intense ecstasy of bloom.

The Mediterranean patio
Mediterranean dreams can become reality on the patio or roof garden. The main role is

> **Plant specimens for the Oriental patio**
> *Aucuba japonica, Bambusa, Buxus, Cupressus cashmeriana, Cyperus, Hedera helix, Polystichum, Rhododendron*, ferns, and grasses.

played by many magnificent tub plants, most of them from southern Europe. The motto should be "Lively and light-hearted." Cheerful colors are called for—also in the furnishings. A floor of terra-cotta or marble tiles and white walls provide the appropriate frame, and the picture is completed by brown clay amphorae, pots, and boxes in various sizes.

A little wildness and unrest do not go amiss on an "Italian" patio. Fanatical lovers of order should decide on a different style. The more pots and tubs you collect, the better. Always move flowering specimens into full view so they can give maximum pleasure.

The rustic patio
A colorful multiplicity of domestic annuals and perennials lends a rustic character to a patio. The picture is completed by a columnar ballerina apple tree or a

> **Flowering container plants for the Mediterranean patio**
> *Abutilon, Bougainvillea, Campsis radicans, Canna indica* hybrids, *Capparis spinosa, Caryopteris x cladonensis, Cassia, Cestrum, Citrus* species, *Cytisus, Datura, Hibiscus rosa-sinensis, Lagerstroemia indica, Lavandula angustifolia, Nerium oleander, Plumbago auriculata, Punica granatum.*

pear espalier in a large box, a few vegetables on the wall—cucumbers, beans, and peas climb willingly and quickly—and colorful summer flowers, interspersed with herbs. Naturally, geraniums mustn't be omitted! Everything can be cultivated in plant containers without difficulty. To go with this, use rustic wooden furniture, baskets, and cans.

> **Plant specimens for the rustic patio**
> *Chrysanthemum fructescens, Helianthus annuus,* and other summer flowers, *Ipomoea tricolor* and other climbers, tuberous begonia hybrids, *Lantana camara* hybrids, *Lilium* hybrids, *Pelargonium peltatum* hybrids, *Petunia*, potted roses, herbs, and small fruit trees.

Caution: Don't forget to take weight into account on a roof terrace: large container plants are very heavy.

LIVING GREENER, LIVING BETTER

Tone-on-tone: patio planting with violet scaevola (*Scaevola aemula*), petunias (*Petunia*), and clematis (*Clematis*), pink geraniums (*Pelargonium* zonal hybrids), English ivy (*Hedera helix*) and myrtle (*Myrtus*) standards, asparagus, spindle tree (*Euonymus*), and opuntia.

Patio planting in pink and violet

Aromatic Gardens and Herb Gardens

Compose a bouquet of fragrances for yourself, using a variety of scented geraniums. Also, the leaves last for a long time in a vase. Herbs may be grown in balcony boxes, tubs, and bowls just as well as in the garden. Assembled on this patio (picture, right) are tricolor sage (*Salvia officinalis* 'Tricolor'), nasturtiums (*Tropaeolum* hybrids), lavender (*Lavandula angustifolia*), parsley (*Petroselinum crispum* ssp. *crispum*), peppermint (*Mentha x piperita*), thyme (*Thymus vulgaris*), *Sempervivum* species, and scented geraniums (*Pelargonium* species).

Scented houseplants were treasured much more in earlier times than they are today. Perhaps this is because "bad smells" were more widespread in the nineteenth century. As well, the custom of wearing a gardenia on a lady's evening dress or sticking one in a gentleman's buttonhole had more than a visual purpose. About 150 years ago, England had nurseries devoted solely to cultivating gardenias for this use.

- Odors are a matter of taste, and individuals react to them differently. Some people get headaches from heavy, sweet scents, and find them unpleasant. What one nose greets with eagerness, another can't stand. Sniff around the florists to try things out before you decide.
- Also, do not place too many different fragrant plants on the windowsill. One or two specimens of an intensely fragrant species is often enough.

Aromatic plants for every season

Most plants have their aromatic materials in their flowers, so one can only enjoy their fragrance during the flowering period. That means that your pleasure will be circumscribed unless you arrange things so that flowering scented plants stand on your windowsill at every season. Here are a few examples: Already in early winter, you can find forced hyacinths (*Hyacinthus orientalis*), followed by ismenes (*Hymenocallis narcissiflora*) and lily of the valley (*Convallaria*). From early spring to fall, the peace lily (*Spathiphyllum*) is in bloom; from late spring to early fall, the wax plant (*Hoya*); from midsummer to fall, the gardenia (*Gardenia jasminoides*); and from midsummer to early fall, the blue exacum (*Exacum affine*).

In winter, jasmine (*Jasminum officinalis*) blooms and gives off its perfume. Among the orchids, too, there are treats for the nose, such as *Cattleya velutina* and *C. labiata*, *Coelogyne cristata* and *C. pandurata*, and *Lycaste aromatica*.

All year long, you can enjoy the fragrant leaves of myrtle (*Myrtus communis*) and many wonderful scented geraniums.

Container plants and smaller species in the flower box can provide wonderful aromas on the balcony and patio, but herbal plants and spice plants also have fragrances—as well as catering to your love of variety in the kitchen.

Aromatic plants for outdoors:
Aloysia triphylla, Carissa grandiflora, Cistus, Citrus, Datura, Eucalyptus citriodora, Heliotropium, Ipomoea, Lathyrus odoratus, Lobularia maritima, Nerium oleander, Nicotiana, Osmanthus, Petunia, Pittosporum, Skimmia, Tropae-olum, Yucca.

Herbs for the balcony, patio, and windowsill:
Anise, balm, basil, borage, caraway, celery, chervil, chives, coriander, cress, dill, garlic, hyssop, juniper, laurel, lovage, marjoram, mugwort, nasturtium, oregano, parsley, peppermint, rosemary, sage, savory, sorrel, tarragon, thyme, wormwood.

A scented-leaf geranium in a bowl.

Picture right: Herb garden on the balcony, in terra-cotta containers

PLANTS FROM A TO Z

The following section gives you portraits of some of the most beautiful plants for the house, the conservatory, the patio, and the balcony. You will encounter more than 500 genera and over 1000 species and learn about their care.

All the better-known and easily available plants are listed in the first part, pp. 122–347. The second section, pp. 348–375, introduces rare and specialized plants that are less commonly encountered.

Some of the plants are also shown as they grow in their native habitats. It will surprise you how different some plants look on their home ground from the way they appear in our living rooms.

This is a true eye-catcher: a colorful planter bearing a neat horticultural product, a standard-trained shrub.

How to Use the Encyclopedia of Plants

For easy reference, a standard format has been applied in compiling the portraits of the plants in this book. Each plant's ID includes at least one color photograph. In the case of important genera, significant species and varieties are also depicted. Plants are arranged alphabetically by their botanical names. Botanical nomenclature is a constantly evolving international enterprise. Changes, especially where the family names are concerned, are currently being introduced: for example, the aster family will be changed from *Compositae* to *Asteraceae,* All names in this North American edition are based on *An Integrated System of Classification of Flowering Plants* by Arthur Cronquist (New York: Columbia University Press, 1981) and on *Standardized Plant Names* by Harlan P. Kelsey and William A. Dayton (Harrisburg, Pa.: J. Horace MacFarland Company, 1942).

Components of Each Plant Portrait
The Botanical Name of a plant is internationally valid and the only scientific name by which it can be recognized anywhere in the world. It consists of two parts, the generic name (e.g., *Begonia*) and the specific epithet (e.g., *corallina*), which produces *Begonia corallina,* the name of this species. If a plant's main listing is only its generic name, for example, *Begonia, Ficus,* or *Pelargonium,* this means that more than one species will be introduced. If the name of a genus is followed by another name in parentheses, as it does for *Datura (Brugmansia)* or for *Dizygotheca (Schefflera),* it indicates that the genus name is being changed. The old name, in parentheses, may still be in use, but the new one is the only valid one.

The English name is printed directly below the botanical name. Often, a plant is commonly referred to by the botanical name of its genus, but in some cases other names are given.

The Symbols are for the benefit of those readers who are looking for a quick way to determine a plant's needs with respect to location and care. A special symbol will also warn those who need to know that a plant or its parts are poisonous.

Location Requirements:

☼ Full sun. The plant can stand day-long and year-round exposure to sunlight.

○ Bright location, not full sun. The plant needs the lightest possible location, but cannot bear the sunlight, especially not at noon.

◑ A location in partial shade. The plant needs some shade and will grow better if shade is provided.

● Shady location. The plant is used to full shade in its native habitat or is able to grow in the shade.

Watering Needs:

 The plant must always be kept moist, though not wet; the root ball should never be allowed to dry out.

On hot days, plants in containers and planters require a complete soaking once or twice a day. Plants kept indoors where the air and the floor are warmed by heating vents have to be watered once or twice a week.

 The watering needs of the plant are average. Water

it moderately; though the root ball should never dry out completely. In summer, water plants in containers and on balconies thoroughly at one- or two-day intervals. Indoor plants should be watered about once a week.

 The plant has low watering needs and should be watered only rarely.

The Need for Nutrients:

🔔 This plant requires heavy fertilizing. During the period of growth, feed it frequently, as often as once a week if a diluted mixture is used.

🔔 This plant is average in its need for nutrients. Feed it every two weeks, though some species could require feeding less often.

🔔 The plant needs little fertilizing and should be fed only very rarely. Alternatively, the fertilizer it is offered can be reduced to one-half or one-third of the manufacturer's recommended amount per litre of water.

Atmospheric Humidity Requirements:

The plant requires high humidity and should either be placed in a humid environment or be frequently misted with lukewarm, nonalkaline water.

☠ This plant is poisonous or contains substances irritating to mucous membranes or skin.

The Most Important Points covered concerning each plant are printed in bold letters so the reader can quickly select the information needed.

THE MOST BEAUTIFUL PLANTS FROM A TO Z

Family: Here you will find the botanical provenance of the plant. The English name of the Family is listed first, followed by its botanical one, as in Arum, Araceae.

Native Habitat: Here you can see where the plant originally came from or the place where it is thoroughly established. For cultivars, whose pedigree is too complex or untraceable, as for example for Fatshedera, you will find: "Cultivated in France."

Flowering Time: Here you will find the time of year when the plant usually is in full flower; since the North American edition will serve readers in several climate zones, a general indication of the flowering season is more useful than trying to state the exact month. Still, we buy the majority of the plants for our homes for their wealth of flowers, and we would like to know when we will be able to enjoy them at their best. In the case of some plants, you will find either "Not a flowering plant," as for the ferns, or "Seldom blooms under cultivation," which applies to many subtropical plants that in cultivation hardly ever mature beyond the youthful stage.

Directions for Care
This section always begins with a description of the plant. Growth habit, size, structure and color of leaves and flowers, typical characteristics, and idiosyncrasies are covered.

Where several species and subspecies are worthy of mention, each is separately described. This section will also mention if a plant is poisonous or is in some other way a threat to your health.

The most important aspects of care are listed in point form:

Location: This is important and will inform you as to the plant's needs for light, atmospheric humidity, and temperature throughout the year.

Care: Here you will learn all about watering, providing humidity, fertilizing, spraying, transplanting, pruning, and any other required care measures.

Propagation: This section gives you the appropriate methods of propagation, including whether the plant germinates in the dark or the light, whether it needs warm soil and how warm, and how long germination takes.

Pests and Diseases: This is where you will find what pests, insects, mildews, bacteria, viruses, or other physiologically damaging factors have been known to endanger the plant in question.

Uses: Here you will be introduced to various ways of displaying the plant.

TIP: Here, the author shares her own experiences with one or the other of the plants in question.

Special Information
Starting on page 348, this section provides botanical descriptions or other interesting details concerning the plant that is being presented.

How to Find a Plant
Ideally, you have bought a plant that is tagged and labeled with its proper botanical name. In that case, you simply leaf through. "The Most Beautiful Plants from A to Z" to locate your plant. If you know the English name, look it up in the index.

If the plant you want to identify is unknown to you, compare it to the

pictures in the book till you find it. By the way, should your experience differ from the recommendations of the author, continue your own successful care techniques. We must remember that the affection we have for a plant is an important factor in the success of the care we give.

Understanding Plant Names
A plant's botanical name is its official ID. Within the text it is always printed in italics. A plant's official name is usually made up of two parts: the name of the genus, e.g., *Dieffenbachia* and the name of the species, its specific epithet, e.g., *bowmannii*.
Plants that are the result of interbreeding may have an additional name (given in normal print and in single quotation marks), which indicates the cultivated variety or cultivar, e.g., *Dieffenbachia bowmannii* 'Camilla.' Some plants have additional labels, for example, var. (variety), which indicates a plant that varies from the species, but is not the result of deliberate breeding. Similarly, ssp. refers to a subspecies, a naturally occurring variation of botanical significance. X: This multiplication symbol points to horticultural hybrids. An example: *Caryopteris x clandonensis.* When a species is defined entirely in terms of horticultural breeding, its name indicates this fact: *Cymbidium* hybrid, or *Coleus-Blumei* hybrid.

Abutilon – Acalypha

The yellow-blooming *Abutilon* hybrids grow ample in a container and, with good care, can reach 6.5 ft. (2 m) in height.

Abutilon megapotamicum is an altogether more graceful plant; its thin, slightly arching branches look good cascading from a hanging basket.

Yellow-blooming Abutilon *hybrid*

ABUTILON
Flowering maple

○ ◑

Family: Mallow, *Malvaceae*
Native Habitat: Tropics and subtropics
Flowering time: Late spring to fall

The well-known *Abutilon* hybrids are the result of the crossing of various species. Varieties with variegation are available; these are the result of a virus infection. The hallmark of the hybrids, which can grow up to 10 ft. (3 m) in height and breadth, is the charming, bell-shaped flower in white, yellow, red, and pink.

Pretty varieties are, among others, 'Ashford Red' (salmon), 'Boule de Neige' (white), and 'Canary Bird' (yellow). *A. megapotamicum* blooms from spring till late summer; its thin, drooping stems make it an ideal hanging plant. The variety 'variegatum' is popular for its lightly flecked leaves. Its blossoms are not as large as those of the hybrids, but they offer a vivid color contrast between the lemon-yellow corolla and the deep red of the sepals and the violet stamens. *A. pictum*, a Guatemalan species that blooms from late summer to late fall, is commercially represented by the variety 'Thomsonii,' with yellow-spotted leaves and salmon-colored flowers.

Also attractive is *A. megapotamicum* grafted onto a stock of *A. pictum*.
Location: Light to partial shade. In the summer outdoors, in a warm location, protected from wind and rain; during the winter at 50–54°F (10–12°C), free of drafts.
Care: Protect from strong summer sun and water generously, but avoid waterlogging the roots. Fertilize every 14 days. Cut back on watering in the winter. Since the shrub grows unevenly, pruning it back by half is recommended in late winter.
Propagation: In spring, from tip cuttings with soil temperature held at 68–72°F (20–22°C). For hybrids, seeds are available. Sown in winter, the plants will bloom in the same year.
Pests and Diseases: Aphids, spider mites, scale insects. Drafts and changes in location may cause leaves and blooms to fall. Keeping the plant too cool in the winter may also result in loss of leaves.
Uses: A very attractive container plant for a cool, light location. It will bloom in the conservatory almost all year and can be transferred outdoors in the summer.

Abutilon megapotamicum

Acacia armata

ACACI
Acacia

Family: Legume, *Fabaceae*
Native Habitat: Tropics and subtropics; above all, Australia
Flowering Time: Spring and summer

Shrubs and treelike plants, their flowers are usually yellow. For a low-growing species, *A. armata*, the kangaroo thorn, is recommended. *A. baileyana* (usually offered as mimosa) is a richly blooming, small tree.
Location: Light to full sun. In summer warm, in winter 39–43°F (4–6°C).
Care: In summer, water very generously, and till the beginning of fall, feed every 14 days, using nonalkaline fertilizer. In winter, cut back watering drastically.
 Always use softened water.
Propagation: Cuttings, under plastic in summer, but without heating the soil. Transplant to peat-rich acid loam (rhododendron mixture).
Pests and Diseases: Seldom.
Uses: Container plant. Since florescence takes place for several weeks in the winter or early spring, acacias are particularly suitable for sun rooms and conservatories.

ACALYPHA
Acalypha

Family: Spurge, *Euphorbiaceae*
Native Habitat: Tropics and subtropics
Flowering Time: Late winter to autumn

A. hispida is a very attractive flowering plant. Its flowers resemble red, hanging bottle brushes that often reach 20 in. (50 cm) in length. The variety 'alba' has white flowers.
 By comparison, *A. hispaniolae* grows only to a height of 4–6 in. (10–15 cm) and has a more spreading habit. Its leaves are more heart-shaped. It makes a very pretty hanging plant, which will bloom from spring to fall.
Acalypha wilkensiana hybrids sport spectacular leaves, which vary in coloring and shape. Beautiful varieties are: 'marginata' (leaves are olive-green with pink edges), 'musaica' (bronze-red, patterned leaves), 'goldsefiana' (light green with a white-toothed margin).
 Every species of acalypha is poisonous in all its parts!

Acalypha wilkensiana hybrids

Acalypha hispaniolae

Location: Light, but not full sun. Warm all year long; even in winter never under 61°F (16°C).
Care: For well-developed "cats' tails" it is necessary to supply lots of light without any direct sun as well as very high humidity, which implies frequent misting with softened water. Keep the root ball moderately moist. Between late winter and the end of summer, feed every two weeks.
Propagation: By tip cuttings in spring, with bottom heating and very high atmospheric humidity.
Pests and Diseases: Whiteflies, aphids, and spider mites, if kept in too dry a location.
Uses: A beautiful flowering plant for a light, not-too-dry location.

Since acacias tend to lose their leaves starting at the roots, an underplanting is recommended, using some low-growing ground cover, for example *Epipremnum*. To avoid disturbing the dense network of rootlets, it is best to plant both the acacia and the ground cover at the same time.

Acanthocalycium – Acorus

The lilac-colored flowers of *Acanthocalycium violaceum* can be up to 3 in. (8 cm) across. *Acanthorhipsalis monacantha* blooms orange and its fruits are violet.
The Brazilian guava, *Acca sellowiana*, displays its characteristic bright red stamens.

Acanthocalycium violaceum

Acanthorhipsalis monacantha

Acca sellowiana

ACANTHOCALYCIUM VIOLACEUM
Acanthocalycium

Family: Cactus, *Cactaceae*
Native Habitat: Argentina
Flowering Time: Late spring to summer

This densely barbed cactus can grow spherical or form a column about 8 in. (20 cm) high. It carries strong yellow thorns and opens lilac-colored blossoms up to 3 in. (8 cm) at the ribs.
Location: In summer, a light and sunny spot outside is possible as long it is protected from wind. Winter location must be light and almost completely dry, with temperatures between 41–50°F (5–10°C).
Care: Even during the period of growth, the summer months, watering has to be cautious so the plant is never wet. It is best to allow the soil to dry out completely between waterings. As soon as buds are visible, begin light feeding with cactus food or hydroponics fertilizer.
Propagation: By sowing in soil kept at 68°F (20°C). Mature plants will produce offsets.
Uses: A beautiful cactus for the windowsill or for a cactus house.

ACANTHORHIPSALIS MONACANTHA
Acanthorhipsalis

Family: Cactus, *Cactaceae*
Native Habitat: Argentina, Bolivia
Flowering Time: Winter

An epiphytically growing cactus with flat or sharply edged pendant branches and orange blossoms about 0.6 in. (1.5 cm) wide.
Location: Very light but no direct sunlight. Year-round temperature of 64–68°F (18–20°C). It can summer outdoors if it is protected from both sun and rain.
Care: The plant needs an acidic loam that contains perlite and peat and will hold moisture. It thrives only on calcium-free water. Never allow the planting medium to dry out completely between waterings. Mist frequently with softened, lukewarm water. Starting in the spring, feed it every four weeks with cactus food, till early fall, then reduce watering.
Propagation: By separating off some stems, letting them dry somewhat, and planting them into a peat-sand mixture.
Pests and Diseases: Mealybugs.
Uses: Suitable for hanging baskets.

ACCA SELLOWIANA
Brazilian guava

Family: Myrtle, *Myrtaceae*
Native Habitat: South America
Flowering Time: Late spring to winter, depending on culture

A. sellowiana, formerly *Feijoa*, has dark green leaves. Their underside is covered by a dense mat of fine white hairs. This bushy shrub is grown as a fruit tree in its native habitat. A burst of brilliant red stamens fans out from the attractive white flowers. The fruit resembles the kiwi and requires five to seven months to ripen.
Varieties: `Triumph' and `Mammoth.' `Crolidge' is a self-fertilizing variety.
Location: Sunlight year-round, warm in the summer, outdoors if protected. Keep cool in winter, at 46–50°F (8–10°C).
Care: Water very generously and feed every two weeks. In the winter, cut back on the watering.
Propagation: By head cuttings in soil kept at 77°F (25°C).
Pests and Diseases: Occasionally scale insects and mealybugs.
Uses: Container plant for a light spot in the sun room.

TIP

Regular pruning can counteract *Acca sellowiana*'s tendency to leaf loss. `Triumph' and `Mammoth' are varieties that are not pollinated easily: either help them out with a small paintbrush or choose self-fertilizing varieties.

THE MOST BEAUTIFUL PLANTS FROM A TO Z

Achimenes longiflora

ACHIMENES
Achimenes

Family: Gesneriad, *Gesneriaceae*
Native Habitat: Central and South America
Flowering Time: Summer to early fall

Nowadays, only richly blooming hybrids are available. Flowers come in white, pink, and purple, plain and with a contrasting eye. Pretty varieties include 'Ambroise Verschaffelt' (white with violet veins), 'Camille Brozoni' (mauve with a white eye), 'Little Beauty' (small blue-red flowers). *A. erecta* only grows to 18 in. (45 cm); its green leaves are veined in red, its blossoms scarlet.

A. grandiflora reaches 24 in. (60 cm), with reddish shoots and purplish red flowers; the variety 'Liebmanii' is slightly smaller.

A. longiflora is 12 in. (30 cm) high and bears green leaves that may be reddish underneath; it blooms bluish-violet.
Location: Light and warm; avoid direct sun.
Care: Keep the plant evenly moist, avoiding cold water while it is growing and in bloom; soon afterwards its shoots will die off and its scaly rhizomes can be over-wintered in peat moss at 50°F (10°C). Starting in winter, plant in fresh, nonalkaline soil and keep warm and moist. After sprouting, feed every 14 days.
Propagation: Either by cuttings at a soil temperature of 68°F (20°C) or by dividing the rhizomes in the spring.
Pests and Diseases: Aphids, thrips, and soft-skinned mites.
Uses: Flowering plant for a light, warm location at a window; some varieties make good hanging plants.

ACORUS GRAMINEUS
Sweet flag

Family: Arum, *Araceae*
Native Habitat: China, India, Japan
Flowering Time: Hardly ever blooms as a houseplant

A bog plant with creeping roots and grasslike, upright leaves. Leaves of 'Argentostriatus' are striped white, those of 'Aureovariegatus,' yellow. 'Pusillus' reaches only 4 in. (10 cm) in height.
Location: Light, cool, and preferably very airy. Green-leafed cultivars need less light. Keep very cool in winter (as low as 32°F (0°C)) and outside in summer.
Care: Water generously, keeping water in the saucer. The root ball should never be dry. The soil should contain sand and peat. Feed every 14 days in summer, every 6–8 weeks in winter.
Propagation: Divide the root ball in the spring.
Pests and Diseases: Heat or atmospheric dryness can favor spider mites and thrips or impede growth.
Uses: Green plant for light, cool rooms.

Achimenes longiflora is one of the parents of our current hybrids, which were developed during the past century. Today we have, in addition to the plain colors, whites, pinks, and purples with contrasting eyes or pretty veining.

Acorus gramineus is a great plant for the poolside in the summer months.

Acorus gramineus

Adenium obesum is related to the oleander, on which it can be grafted. In its native habitat, *Adenium obesum* can assume some startling shapes (see the illustration below).

The very delicacy of its leaves proclaims the sensitivity of the maidenhair fern.

Adenium obesum

ADENIUM OBESUM
Adenium obesum

Family: Dogbane, *Apocynaceae*
Native Habitat: Arabia, Africa
Flowering Time: Twice: spring to summer and again in fall

Partial succulent plant with a thick stem, leathery leaves, and marvelous flowers. To speed growth and secure flowers, the plant is usually grafted on

Adenium obesum *in nature*

oleander. The white, red-rimmed flowers often appear twice a year. All parts of the plant are poisonous.
Location: Full sun and warm. Can summer outdoors. Never keep it below 50°F (10°C).
Care: Early spring to fall: feed every three weeks with cactus food. Let the soil dry out, then soak well. In winter reduce watering. On the windowsill, turn the plant occasionally to ensure even growth. Between the two flowerings, the plant may need repotting in standard potting soil. Cut off any shoots of the graft stock (oleander) below.
Propagation: By cutting or by seed in the spring.
Pests and Diseases: Occasionally scale insects or mealybugs.
Uses: Flowering plant for sunny, warm spots.

ADIANTUM
Maidenhair fern

Family: Polypody (Fern) *Polypodiaceae*
Native Habitat: Tropical and subtropical rain forests of Central and South America
Flowering Time: No flowers

A fern with wiry, black stems and delicate leaves. Well-known species include: *A. raddianum* and its cultivars, 'Goldelse,' 'Brillant,' 'Fragrantissimum,' 'Gracillimum' (with the smallest fronds); *A.*

Adiantum tenerum

tenerum with the varieties 'Fritz Lüthi,' 'Scutum,' and 'Scutum roseum' (young leaflets are reddish).
Location: Partial or complete shade; warm, 68–77°F (20–25°C); high humidity.
Care: Water the plant with soft water at room temperature, spray indirectly, and place over water on a bed of pebbles. Feed biweekly with diluted plant food (I use hydroponic fertilizer). Repot in standard soil mix with high peat content.
Propagation: By spores, with bottom heat, 75–79°F (24–26°C) or by division.
Pests and Diseases: If mishandled, aphids, scale insects, and mealy bugs.
Uses: Green plant for a warm, shaded, humid location, maybe a glassed-in solarium

Aechmea fasciata

AECHMEA
Aechmea

Family: Bromeliad, *Bromeliaceae*
Native Habitat: Tropics and subtropics of Central and South America
Flowering Time: Late spring to fall

A tough epiphytic bromeliad, whose hard, spiky-edged leaves form a water-tight funnel. The best known species is *A. fasciata*, its best cultivars are 'Silver King' and 'Super Auslese.' Its marbled leaves are banded in white, about 20–22 in. (50–55 cm) long, and enclose the pink flower. *A. chantinii*'s green leaves carry white cross-stripes. *A. fulgens* rivets attention with scarlet flowers; its cultivar "discolor" sports leaves olive above and purple below.

The rosette of *A. marmorata* (now called *Quesnelia marmorata*) consists of brown-mottled olive-green leaves, smoky violet beneath. Although these plants will die back after blooming, they form offsets to propagate themselves.
Location: Light, but not full sun; keep room over 65°F (18°C).

Care: Spring to fall, keep evenly moist. Nonalkaline water, free of fertilizer, may stand in the cup. Reduce watering late fall to early spring. Feed every two weeks. Transplant every two years in standard potting soil. Remove dead rosettes.
Propagation: Choose good-sized offsets and plant.
Pests and Diseases: Scale insects. A cold position will result in brown leaves.
Uses: Flowering plant for a light, warm place in a room or window.

AEONIUM
Aeonium

Family: Stonecrop, *Crassulaceae*
Native Habitat: Canary Islands
Flowering Time: Spring to summer; seldom blooms in cultivation

Most species of this genus carry their leaf rosettes on their stems. The greenish yellow or red flowers issue from the center of the rosettes. One of the best species is *A. arboreum*, about 3 ft. (1 m) high. Its bare, intricately branched upper stems bear dark green rosettes. On 'Atropupureum' these turn dark red in summer. The habit of *A. tabuliforme* differs: its 20 in.-(50 cm)-wide rosettes form a dense ground cover.
Location: Sunny, warm; in summer in a protected spot outdoors. Cooler in winter, but not below 50°F (10°C).

Aeonium arboreum
'Atropurpureum'

Care: Every two weeks feed with cactus food and water moderately. Hardly any water in winter. Repot in cactus mix as needed in spring.
Propagation: Root rosettes or single leaves in sandy soil kept at 68-77°F (20-25°C), allowing cut surfaces to dry first. *A. tabuliforme* can only be raised from seed.
Pests and Diseases: Chiefly in winter, mealybugs and spider mites. If kept too dark, the leaf rosettes will turn green.
Uses: Succulent green plant for light, warm location, or container plant for a succulent collection.

TIP

When an *Aechmea* is growing well but will not bloom, I use the "apple trick": wrap the plant along with two or three apples in plastic for at least 14 days. The ethylene the apples give off promotes flowering.

Aeschynanthus – Ageratum

Aeschynanthus radicans

Cultivation has lessened *Aeschynanthus's* craving for the jungle climate and has made it more able to adapt to our living rooms.

Agapanthus is counted among our most beautiful container plants.

AESCHYNANTHUS
Basket vine

Family: Gesneriad, *Gesneriaceae*
Native Habitat: Southeast Asia
Flowering Time: Early summer to early fall

The hallmarks of this basket plant are fleshy, leathery leaves and red to orange flowers, usually in terminal clusters. *A. parasiticus* is best adapted to the home. All others require high temperatures to set flowers. For the hothouse, try *A. radicans* with red and *A. speciosus* with spectacular yellow-orange blooms.

Location: Light, but not full sun, at 68–77°F (20–25°C). A cool rest period at 60–65°F (15–18°C) in winter will promote efflorescence.

Care: Lukewarm, nonalkaline water given in moderation and reduced in winter. Early spring to late summer, administer a low dose of plant food every 14 days. Frequent spraying and putting the pot on a bed of wet pebbles does wonders. Do not spray when in bloom.

Propagation: By tip cuttings in early summer at a soil temperature of 68–77°F (20–25°C). Cuttings placed on damp, warm soil will root at the nodes.

Pests and Diseases: Aphids and thrips in dry air. Any shifts in temperature and moisture will cause blooms to fall.

Uses: Hanging plant for the window or a humid and warm greenhouse.

Aeschynanthus speciosus

A magnificent Agapanthus

AGAPANTHUS
Agapanthus

Family: Lily, *Liliaceae*
Native Habitat: South Africa
Flowering Time: Summer

Herbaceous perennial, up to 3 ft. (1 m) in height, with straplike evergreen leaves and blue or white flowers in umbels on long stems. The Headbourne hybrids, of more compact habit, are hardy in milder regions. Their flowers are smaller but more numerous.

Location: In summer, full sun in a protected spot outdoors; in winter, quarter light and cool at 46–50°F (8–10°C).

Care: Water well but without soaking in summer; keep almost dry in the winter. From spring to efflorescence, feed weekly, then reduce to once a month. Since *Agapanthus* blooms more profusely when its roots are crowded, there is no need for frequent repotting.

Propagation: By division.

Pests and Diseases: When waterlogged, the plant can attract rot-causing fungi.

Uses: Marvelous display plant for a light location.

The Most Beautiful Plants from A to Z

Agave americana 'Marginata'

Ageratum houstonianum

Even in a container, *Agave americana* can be considered a heavyweight, and it grows more and more difficult to move into its winter quarters.

Dark pink *Ageratum* varieties look good with blue balcony flowers.

AGAVE
Agave

Family: Century Plant, *Agavaceae*
Native Habitat: Mexico, India, tropical and subtropical Central and South America
Flowering Time: Summer, but in temperate zones very rarely

A succulent that forms leaf-rosettes with a high flower stem bearing pale yellow to violet-tinged green bells at the tip. *A. americana* is the best known of the 300 or so species. It grows large even in a con-tainer. The long, sword-shaped leaves end in a sharp thorn. The yellow-leafed variety, 'Marginata,' is well liked; 'Aureavariegata' and 'Argenteo-variegata,' also varie-gated, are rarer. The plant has become established along the shores of the Mediterranean, where it can reach 16–26 ft. (5–8 m). In temperate regions it seldom blooms.

More delicate agaves include *A. filifera* with dark green leaves that bear white threads along the edges and *A. victoriae-reginae*, with com-pact, semi-spherical rosettes.
Location: Full sun all year; outdoors in summer. Winter: airy and cool but free of frost.

Care: In summer keep moderately moist, in winter, dry. Spring to fall apply cactus food every few weeks. The rule is that less feeding and water is better than too much. Use a clay and humus soil mix that will drain well.
Propagation: By offsets is simplest, as starting from seeds is difficult.
Pests and Diseases: Rarely; excessive dampness in winter can cause root rot.
Uses: *A. americana* is an impressive display plant for a sunny balcony or terrace. The smaller species make good leafy plants for windows or, in shallow dishes, for the cactus house.

AGERATUM HOUSTONIANUM
Ageratum

Family: Aster, *Asteraceae*
Native Habitat: Mexico, Guatemala, Belize
Flowering Time: Late spring to fall

A small annual with dense habit, 6–25 in. (15–60 cm) in height. *Ageratum* bears blue, pink, or violet flowers in compact umbels. Well-known varieties: 'Blaue Donau' (medium blue), 'Pacific' (purple-violet), and 'Blue Blazer' (light blue).

Ageratum contains cumarin, which can irritate mucous mem-branes and cause hay fever.
Location: Sun or partial shade.
Care: Place young plants 8 in. (20 cm) apart in standard flower mix-ture; water generously and feed every two weeks. Remove wilted flowers.
Propagation: From seeds in late winter or early spring with soil temperatures at 65–68°F (18–20°C).
Pests and Diseases: Spider mites.
Uses: Flowering annuals for the garden, for planters on balconies and terraces; popular as a border plant. *Ageratum* looks good with low-growing marigolds.

TIP

It is safest to "disarm" large agaves before they are moved for the winter; this can be done by fitting pieces of cork over their thorns.

Aglaonema – Alocasia

Aglaonema commutatum, here shown in the variety 'Albovariegatum,' is one of the best-loved foliage plants, though it is not easy to take care of.

The pretty fruits of *Aglaonema crispum*, (formerly *A. Roebelinii*) are poisonous. See illustration below.

In a cool but very light sun room, *Albizia lophantha* blooms from fall to spring.

Aglaonema commutatum

AGLAONEMA
Aglaonema

Family: Arum, *Araceae*
Native Habitat: Southeast Asia
Flowering Time: Seldom blooms in cultivation

These bushy plants, about 20 in. (50 cm) high, have beautifully marked or mottled leaves. If fertilized, the typical, bract-enclosed spadix may produce small red, poisonous fruits. Various leaf colorations, ranging from white patterns to a silvery sheen, occur among *A. commutatum var. robustum's* cultivars, 'Treubii,' 'Pseudo-bracteatum,' 'Fransher,' 'Tricolor,' and 'Silverking.' *A. pictum* is smaller

The red berries of Aglaonema

and daintier; *A. crispum* can grow up to 3 ft. (1 m) high.

Location: Variegated cultivars need lots of light, though no sun; others prefer part shade. Keep at room temperature all year, never under 65°F (18°C).

Care: Keep moderately moist with nonalkaline water and feed lightly, every two weeks, reducing both in the winter. *Aglaonema* cannot tolerate dry air; best kept on a wet bed of pebbles. Plant in standard potting mix containing Styrofoam bits.

Propagation: By division or by tip cutting with bottom heat. (Not easy.)

Pests and Diseases: Spider mites, scale insects, mealybugs, aphids, if air is too dry in winter. Brown leaves due to hard water or if water or air are too cold. Leaf spot, if sprayed.

Uses: A pretty foliage plant that thrives best in a light, enclosed sun room; an excellent hydroculture plant.

Albizia lophantha

ALBIZIA
Albizia

Family: Bean, *Fabaceae*
Native Habitat: Tropical and subtropical Africa, Asia, and Australia
Flowering Time: *A. julibrissin* summer to fall; *A. lophantha* in the winter.

A. julibrissin is a slow-growing tree that may reach 6–10 ft. (2–3 m). Its leaves are feathery, and older specimens bring forth pink, spherical flowers.

A. lophantha grows 6–10 ft. (2–3 m) high, and its flowers range from creamy white to yellow.

Location: Full sun and warm, even outdoors in summer; in winter, cool and light at 37–46°F (3–8°C).

Care: Water frequently and feed every two weeks in summer. Prune if it grows unevenly or too high. Remove all leaves before its winter rest.

Propagation: From seed.

Pests and Diseases: Scale insects.

Uses: Smaller exemplars in light but cool rooms; larger ones in containers or set out in the conservatory. Suitable for bonsai.

ALLAMANDA CATHARTICA
Allamanda

Family: Dogbane, *Apocynaceae*
Native Habitat: Brazil
Flowering Time: Spring to late fall

Of the fifteen species of alla-manda, only *A. cathartica* is widely known. The long arms of this fast-growing climber carry attractive yellow flowers and dark green, shiny leaves. Nurseries treat young plants with growth retardants, so that they do not reveal their spreading habit till maturity. 'Grandiflora' blooms lemon yellow; 'Hendersonii' has large orange flowers. All plant parts are poisonous.
Location: Warm and light all year; even in winter never under 65°F (18°C). Plant prefers warm soil.

Allamanda cathartica

Care: From spring to fall, water evenly, spray regularly. Reduce moisture in winter. Feed weekly in summer; in winter only if in a very light location, then every 4 weeks. Repot in spring in standard potting soil. Pruning down to one-third of the stems in early spring promotes budding. This climber requires no support.
Propagation: By tip cutting with bottom heat.
Pests and Diseases: Spider mites, scale insects; yellow leaves if not fed enough; stem and root rot if kept too cool or wet in winter.
Uses: For the greenhouse, conservatory, or poolside. Suitable for hydroponics.

Alocasia sanderiana

ALOCASIA
Alocasia

Family: Arum, *Araceae*
Native Habitat: Tropical Asia
Flowering Time: Seldom blooms under cultivation

Beautiful leaf plant with impressively colored shield or arrow-shaped leaves, 12–16 in. (30–40 cm) long. *A. cuprea*, syn. *A. metallica* has olive-green, metallic leaves; *A. lowii* is dark green and *A. sanderiana* is blue: all have white veins. The plant can irritate mucous membranes.
Location: Partial shade, humid and warm. Not under 65°F (18°C) in winter.
Care: During the growth period, keep evenly moist with lukewarm, nonalkaline water and feed lightly every 14 days. Water very sparingly in winter.
Propagation: Let runners or rhizomes root in a heated propagating bed.
Pests and Diseases: Spider mites, scale insects, mealybugs, and aphids if air is too dry; brown leaves if soil is too cold.
Uses: Best in an enclosed sun room or hothouse.

Because of its spreading habit, *A. cathartica* is best kept in a large, light room; it is even better suited to a conservatory.

Alocasia looks very attractive beside a garden pool, where the plant can profit from the higher atmospheric humidity—always assuming that it is a warm summer.

TIP

In warm summers, my own alocasia stands beside the garden pond, in a partially shaded spot, protected from the rain.

Aloe – Amaryllis

Aloe variegata

Aloe variegata as well as A. arborescens give you problem-free enjoyment.

The leaves of aloysia can be dried and used to make a tea; in France it enjoys great popularity under the name "Verveine."

ALOE
Aloe

Family: Lily, *Liliaceae*
Native Habitat: South Africa, Madagascar
Flowering Time: Spring to summer, but seldom blooms as a houseplant

The most popular species of this member of the lily family are rosette-forming, low-growing forms. The following can be found in most succulent collections: *A. aristata*, with thick, toothed leaves, and *A. variegata* (the tiger aloe), with irregularly speckled, yellow-green leaves. Other low-growing species include *A. humilis*, a ground cover with leaves in various shapes and colors, and *A. striata*, whose leaves are bluish white with red edges. *A. arborescens* can be quite tall, and forms a bare trunk that branches higher up. The juices of this species help heal burns. Several aloes,

chiefly *Aloe vera*, are used commercially for cosmetics, as their juice is supposed to benefit the skin.
Location: In summer full sun, protected from rain; in winter, light and cool, at 40–50°F (5–10°C).
Care: Only moderate watering required, and in winter hardly any. Avoid wetting the rosette or waterlogging. Feed lightly, rarely, and only in summer, with cactus food. If necessary, repot in spring.
Propagation: By careful division of the root stock.
Pests and Diseases: Rarely.
Uses: Since Alpinias require extremely high atmospheric humidity, they cannot be kept in normal living areas for any length of time. They will, however, thrive in a warm and humid greenhouse or conservatory without major problems.

Aloe arborescens

Aloysia triphylla

ALOYSIA TRIPHYLLA
Aloysia

Family: Verbena, *Verbenaceae*
Native Habitat: South America, West Indies
Flowering Time: Summer to fall

Fragrant shrub, 3–6 ft. (1–2 m) high. The white to pale mauve flowers appear during the summer, either in axial spikes or in terminal panicles. Lancetlike, fresh green leaves unfold along the stem, in opposition or in whorls. When rubbed, they give off an intense lemony smell.
Location: Sunny and warm in summer, possibly outdoors; cool in winter 37–50°F (3–10°C), light or shade.
Care: During the growth period, till late summer, water generously and feed biweekly. Since the plant drops its leaves in the winter, just water it enough to prevent the root ball from drying out. Spring pruning ensures fullness.
Propagation: By tip cutting.
Pests and Diseases: Rarely.
Uses: Container plant for light, warm spots; in summer out of doors.

THE MOST BEAUTIFUL PLANTS FROM A TO Z

Alpinia purpurata, 'Red Ginger'

ALPINIA
Galangal

Family: Ginger, *Zingiberaceae*
Native Habitat: Tropical Asia, Pacific islands
Flowering Time: Spring to summer, but seldom blooms in cultivation

Galangal is a large plant with strong rhizomes and powerful, leafy stems. The efflorescence, often very large, occurs in terminal panicles or racemes. *A. purpurata* is valuable for its cut flowers; *A. vittata, syn. A. sanderae*, grows up to 18 in. (45 cm) and has elongated leaves banded in white. Under favorable conditions, *A. Zerumbet* will grow as high as 10 ft. (3 m) and may bloom.
Location: Light, warm, and humid; During winter keep at only 60°F (15°C).
Care: During growth, water to keep the root ball evenly moist and provide high humidity. Dry roots immediately result in leaf damage. Feed every two weeks from spring to fall. To ensure flowering, observe a rest period from late fall to early spring, while cutting down on watering.
Propagation: By careful division of

the root stock.
Pests and Diseases: Rarely.
Uses: Galangal cannot survive in a room for any length of time: it needs high humidity. On the other hand, in a hothouse or a humid conservatory the plant thrives.

Inflorescence of Alpinia purpurata

Amaryllis bella-donna

AMARYLLIS BELLA-DONNA
Belladonna Lily

Family: Lily, *Liliaceae*
Native Habitat: South Africa
Flowering Time: Fall

The belladonna lily's flower rises 20–28 in. (50–70 cm) out of a brown, fist-sized bulb. The trumpet-shaped blossoms are 3–5 in. (8–12 cm) across, pink or white, and have a light fragrance. The leaves emerge, depending on location, in late winter or spring. The plant is poisonous. The belladonna lily (true amaryllis) is often confused with *Hippeastrum*, which is sold commercially as "amaryllis."
Location: Sunny and warm; in summer in containers outdoors; in winter, light and not below 50°F (10°C).
Care: In summer, keep evenly moist and feed every 14 days; in winter reduce watering. Repot only every five or six years.
Propagation: By bulbs or seeds.
Pests and Diseases: Scale insects, spider mites.
Uses: A beautiful bulb plant for a pot or container.

Galangal is an attractive flowering or leafy plant. As it requires very high atmospheric humidity, however, it cannot survive long in a living room. In a greenhouse or conservatory and with good care, galangal can produce magnificent inflorescences. See illustration below.

Amaryllis bella-donna is a good cut flower. If you own more than one plant, try sacrificing a few blooms for display in a vase.

If you add some rotted cattle manure to the standard soil mix of your galangal, it will grow very well.

Ampelopsis – Anisodontea

Since ampelopsis has no adhesive disks, this member of the grape family needs support for its climbing shoots.

Luckily, *Ananas comosus* can tolerate dry room air; it can be grown on a windowsill over a radiator.

Ampelopsis brevipedunculata

AMPELOPSIS BREVIPEDUNCULATA
Ampelopsis, porcelain berry vine

Family: Grape, *Vitaceae*
Native Habitat: Southeastern United States
Flowering Time: Winter

A vigorous climbing plant with three-lobed leaves and small, insignificant flowers. The variety 'Elegans' has small leaves, marbled in pink, white, and green.
Location: Light and moderately warm, no direct sun. In summer outdoors; in winter, cool, just above freezing.
Care: In summer water generously and feed every 14 days. In winter keep cool. Reduce watering till leaves fall, then keep almost dry. Prune in the spring.
Propagation: In summer, by 2 in.- (5 cm-) long tip or stem cuttings.
Pests and Diseases: Spider mites, thrips; leaf loss is natural in winter.
Uses: Hanging or climbing plant for the house or for greening the conservatory. Suited to hydroponics.

Ananas comosus 'Aureovariegatus'

ANANAS
Pineapple

Family: Bromeliad, *Bromeliaceae*
Native Habitat: Tropical Central and South America
Flowering Time: Depends on cultivation

For indoor gardening, the best varieties are *Ananas comosus* 'Variegatus,' with white-striped leaves, and 'Aureovariegatus.' Its deeply toothed leaves are reddish and can grow up to 3 ft. (1 m) long. For the windowsill, *A. nanus* is suitable, with its 8–12 in.- (20–30 cm-) wide leaf rosette. The leaves of *A. bracteatus* are edged in creamy yellow; it sports vivid red bracts.

None of the pineapple species bloom easily in the house. After they bloom, their leaves die off. Note that their leaf edges are very sharp.

Location: Very light, but no noon sun and warm year-round.
Care: In summer soak regularly with nonalkaline water and feed weekly with diluted fertilizer. Reduce both in the winter to give the plant a rest. The plant needs a lot of fresh air, especially where it is hot.
Propagation: By offsets that are half as large as the mother plant. The plume of leaves can also be peeled off the fruit and rooted in sandy seeding soil, but this only works when both soil and air are warm and moist.
Pests and Diseases: Occasionally, scale insects.
Uses: Leaf plant for a light, warm location; it needs a lot of space.

THE MOST BEAUTIFUL PLANTS FROM A TO Z

Anigozanthos flavidus

ANIGOZANTHOS
Kangaroo paw

Family: Bloodwort, *Haemodoraceae*
Native Habitat: Australia
Flowering time: May to July

This herbaceous perennial has only recently become available as a houseplant. It has strong rhizomes and long, lance-shaped leaves. The flowers resemble the hairy paw of a kangaroo; those of *A. flavidus* are yellow green, those of the species *A. manglesii* are pink. *A. pulcherrimus* bears yellow blossoms in panicles whiskered in red.
Location: Light and warm, but not sunny; can be outdoors in summer. In winter at a cool 50–54°F (10–12°C).
Care: Water generously through the summer, using nonalkaline water.

Every 14 days apply a low concentrate of nonalkaline fertilizer, such as azalea food. Winter watering should be light. A soil mixture high in peat or other organic materials and some sand is recommended.
Propagation: By seed or by careful division of older plants.
Pests and Diseases: Spider mites.
Uses: Houseplant for a light location; outdoors in summer.

Anigozanthos manglesii

Anisodontea capensis

ANISODONTEA CAPENSIS
Cape Anisodontea

Family: Mallow, *Malvaceae*
Native Habitat: South Africa
Flowering time: Summer

A richly blooming shrub with somewhat tacky, elongated leaves; its habit is about 3 ft. (1 m) in height. The flowers are red or dark red. The plant is often standard trained or trained to a small pyramid-shape.
Location: Sunny; in summer, outdoors. In winter, at 50–54°F (10–12°C).
Care: Keep evenly moist in summer and feed every 14 days. Snip dead shoots to encourage further flowering. Keep almost dry in winter, when occasional dryness is less harmful than waterlogging. Prune and repot in the spring.
Propagation: By tip cuttings or seeds.
Pests and Diseases: Seldom.
Uses: House and container plant for a sunny location; in summer out-of-doors.

The kangaroo paw thrives out-of-doors in the summer months, forming a good-looking container plant.

This close-up picture below clearly shows the resemblance to a kangaroo's paw.

Of the twenty or so species, only *Anisodontea capensis* is well known outside of South Africa.

In rainy, dark summers, the kangaroo paw may not bloom, but this does not mean it will not bear flowers the following year.

Anthurium – Araucaria

The genus *Anthurium* offers spectacular flowering and foliage plants.

The somewhat stiff spikes of *Aphelandra squarrosa* are reminiscent of candles, very different from those of *A. tetragona*.

Anthurium crystallinum

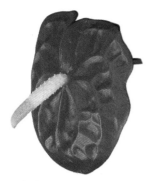
Anthurium andraeanum

ANTHURIUM
Anthurium

Family: Arum, *Araceae*
Native Habitat: Tropical rain forests of Central and South America
Flowering time: Any time of year, depending on species and cultivation

The chief attraction of anthurium is its red, white, or spotted spathe that sets off the long spike of tiny flowers in white, orange red, or yellow. The spike is straight and yellow on the larger *A. andraeanum* hybrids, curved and orange on the smaller *A. scherzerianum* hybrids. *A. crystallinum*, is sought for its spectacularly veined leaves. *A. veitchii* has leaves 3 ft. (1 m) long.
Location: Light or partial shade, never sunny; warm. Temperatures of 60–65°F (15–18°C) for winter rest period. *A. crystallinum* and *A. veitchii* never under 65°F (18°C). Provide warm soil and protect from drafts.
Care: Water evenly and spray with lukewarm, nonalkaline water to provide humidity. Feed every 14 days, reducing water somewhat in winter. Repot every 2–3 years in

spring, using loose, humus-rich soil.
Propagation: By division of older plants, tip or stem cuttings, or air layering.
Pests and Diseases: Aphids and scale insects. If kept too moist and cool, grey mold and root rot.
Uses: A decorative house and greenhouse plant. Species with variegated leaves are suitable for enclosed solariums, hothouses, and hydroculture.

Aphelandra squarrosa

APHELANDRA
Aphelandra

Family: Acanthus, *Acanthaceae*
Native Habitat: Central and South America
Flowering time: Depending on species, spring to fall

The flower spikes (which may reach 8 in. (20 cm)) and their bracts can last 6–8 weeks, depending on the species, the smaller ones tending to wilt sooner. Two great species are: *A.*

Aphelandra tetragona

aurantiaca, of a low habit, with longish green leaves limned in silver gray, its flowers orange red, and *A. tetragona*, at 5 ft. (1.5 m) one of the taller species, its flower spikes carrying big, red blossoms, 1–3 in. (4–7 cm) long. Only older exemplars will bloom. Best known of all is *A. squarrosa* with its hybrids. It is routinely treated with growth retardants to keep it compact while young. Its leaves are beautifully veined in white; its flower is yellow. Good varieties: 'Domia,' 'Leopoldi,' 'Louisae,' and especially, 'Fritz Prinsler.'
Location: Light, no sun. In winter not under 60°F (15°C), *A. tetragona*, not under 68°F (20°C).
Care: Except in winter, keep evenly moist. Use only lukewarm soft water, for spraying as well. Feed every 14 days.
Propagation: By tip cuttings in a heated rooting bed.
Pests and Diseases: Aphids, scale insects, and mealybugs if kept too dry; leaves will roll up and fall off due to atmospheric dryness, cold, or drafts.
Uses: Flowering plant for a light, warm spot; likes hydroponics.

TIP

To preserve its bushy habit, *Aphelandra* is pruned back when it is transplanted in the spring.

THE MOST BEAUTIFUL PLANTS FROM A TO Z

Aporocactus flagelliformis

Araucaria heterophylla

APOROCACTUS FLAGELLIFORMIS
Aporocactus

Family: Cactus, *Cactaceae*
Native Habitat: Mexico
Flowering Time: Spring

This cactus grows 5 ft.- (1.5 m-) long stems, up to 1 in. (2 cm) thick. Its flowers are red to purple and about 3 in. (8 cm) wide. Other beautiful species are *A. conzattii* (red flowers), *A. mallisonii* (vivid red) and *A. martianus* (dark pink).
Location: Light and warm, but no noon sun; warm summer, outdoors, out of rain and wind. Winter, light and at least at 54°F (12°C).
Care: In summer water generously, in winter hardly at all, with soft water, and feed every 14 days. Transplant into cactus mixture, high in peat. Do not turn the plant once buds have set, to prevent their falling off.
Propagation: By tip cuttings.

Pests and Diseases: Spider mites and mealybugs.
Uses: House and container plant for light, warm location; can be used as a hanging plant.

ARAUCARIA HETEROPHYLLA
Norfolk Island pine

Family: Araucaria, *Araucariaceae*
Native Habitat: Norfolk Isles

Evergreen conifer with horizontal graceful branches. *A. heterophylla* grows into a 200 ft. (60 m) tree in its native land; as a house plant it is barely 6-7 ft. (2 m). The variety 'Glauca' has blue-green needles; 'Gracilis' is more compact.
Location: In summer light, but no direct sun. Relatively cool: about 65°F (18°C) in summer, 41–50°F (5–10°C) in winter.

Care: Let it summer outdoors in a light but shaded spot. Water regularly with lukewarm, soft water and feed every 14 days with acid fertilizer (e.g., rhododendron food); spraying occasionally also helps. Repot every 2-3 years in rhododendron soil mix. If you place this plant in a corner, it will grow crooked.
Propagation: Treat tip cuttings with rooting compound before planting them in warm (77°F (25°C)) soil. Even if high humidity is maintained, propagation is difficult.
Pests and Diseases: Scale insects. Limp branches indicate either too much water or too much heat.
Uses: Green plant for a light, cool room. Suited to hydroculture.

After flower buds appear, *Aporocactus flagelliformis* should not be turned again, to prevent buds from falling.

In the days before central heating, when apartments used to have cool rooms, *Araucarias* were seen more commonly than now.

The fruit of the strawberry madrone, Arbutus unedo

Arbutus – Asclepias

(–5°C)), it can stay outdoors well into fall.

Care: Water evenly in summer, using soft water, and feed lightly every 14 days. In winter, water just enough to preserve the leaves. I lost my first specimen to incorrect watering. The root ball should neither dry out nor become waterlogged: either might kill the tree. Repot as needed in standard potting soil.

Propagation: By tip cuttings in soil at 68–77°F (20–25°C). Seeding is possible, but it is a long wait till the first flower appears.

Pests and Diseases: Rarely, spider mites.

Uses: Evergreen container plant of shrubby habit for cool garden rooms and, in summer, for outdoors.

ARBUTUS UNEDO
Strawberry madrone

Family: Heath, *Ericaceae*
Native Habitat: Mediterranean region
Flowering Time: Winter, spring

A beautiful evergreen shrub whose shiny green leaves are almost oval. Creamy yellow flowers in hanging panicles resemble those of lily of the valley. The fruit, which gives the plant its name, is red. It is edible but tasteless. Often flowers and fruit appear at the same time.

Location: Very light all year, in summer outdoors if protected from wind. Overwinter in an airy place at 37–46°F (3–8°C). As it will tolerate short spurts of cold (down to 23°F

TIP

To ensure the formation of fruit, ardisia has to be pollinated by hand, using a fine brush. Good air circulation also helps the plant to fruit.

ARDISIA
Ardisia

Family: Myrsine, *Myrsinaceae*
Native Habitat: Tropical Asia
Flowering Time: Spring, summer

A. crenata, the best-known species, is a small tree 24–47 in. (60–120 cm) high, with 4 in.- (10 cm-) long leathery, evergreen leaves. The flowers are about 0.5 in. (1 cm) wide, white to pink, and cluster in terminal inflorescence. Most attractive are the pea-sized scarlet berries that adorn the tree from fall to well into spring. *A. malouiana*'s bladelike, dark green leaves are up to 10 in. (25 cm) long. A white stripe marks the center of the leaf on top; the underside is reddish and, in season, the red berries are in evidence.

Location: Year-round light, no direct sun, in summer out of doors; winter at 54–60°F (12–16°C).

Care: Except during dormancy, the plant needs regular watering, if possible nonalkaline. In heated rooms spray frequently, except during flowering. March to October, feed every 14 days.

Pests and Diseases: Scale insects and mealybugs in dry rooms. Loss of berries due to high temperatures in winter.

Uses: Pot or container plant for house or garden room. A good hydroponic plant.

Ardisia crenata

THE MOST BEAUTIFUL PLANTS FROM A TO Z

Areca catechu

Asclepias curassavica

Asclepias syriaca requires so much care and, above all, such high humidity that it cannot survive long in an ordinary room.

The bulging fruit of the milkweed will open to release its seeds, which the wind can pick up by their silky, silver-white hairs.

ARECA CATECHU
Betelnut palm

Family: Palm, *Arecaceae,*
Native Habitat: Philippines
Flowering Time: Seldom blooms in cultivation

The slender form of this slow-growing palm may reach 100 ft. (30 m) in height in its native setting. The seed contains, among other chemicals, the alkaloid arecalin, a stimulant like nicotine, and a curing agent that accounts for the red mouth and teeth of those who chew the betelnut.
Location: Light or partial shade; high humidity and year-round temperatures around 68°F (20°C).
Care: Keep evenly and amply moist; water in the saucer is tolerated and also serves to keep the air near the plant humid. Spray frequently. Feed biweekly in summer, using diluted plant food.
Propagation: From seed, in soil 68–86°F (20–30°C). Seeds take 2–3 months to sprout.
Pest and Diseases: Rarely.
Uses: Green plant for humid hothouses; young plants suitable for enclosed solariums. Its use as a houseplant is limited.

ASCLEPIAS CURASSAVICA
Blood flower milkweed

Family: Milkweed, *Asclepiadaceae*
Native Habitat: Tropical South America
Flowering Time: Summer into fall

This good-looking subshrub has long, narrow, dark green leaves and orange to scarlet flowers in umbels. Unfortunately, it is quite poisonous and therefore is seldom found in cultivation.

Location: Sunny and warm; in the spring outdoors; in winter, light at 54–60°F (12–15°C).
Care: Keep evenly moist in the summer and feed biweekly. Carrying the plant to another season is not worth your trouble, as it will not grow. Instead, replace it from seeds.
Propagation: By seed in midwinter.
Pest and Diseases: Rarely.
Uses: Flowering plant for a light, warm location; good on a balcony or terrace in the summer.

A bowl planted with Asclepias

The fruit of Asclepias syriaca *is shaped like a spindle*

Asparagus – Asplenium

Asparagus densiflorus

Asparagus asparagoides

A. densiflorus 'Sprengeri' is more than florists' green: it is a pleasant-looking foliage plant.

Asparagus asparagoides is a herbaceous perennial that can grow up to 6–7 ft. (2 m) in height.

The roots of some asparagus species can expand into a tuberous clump.

ASPARAGUS
Asparagus

Family: Lily, *Liliaceae*
Native Habitat: Africa, Asia
Flowering Time: Summer

A shrublike plant, asparagus has a very short trunk and branched, upright or climbing stems. The "leaves" are really modified side shoots (phylloclades) that take needlelike or roundish shapes.

A. asparagoides has ovoid pseudo-leaves, and the scent of its flowers is reminiscent of oranges. *A. densiflorus* 'Sprengen' provides the well-known florists' green. 'Meyeri' is a variety that produces long, upright or slightly curved shoots that are thickly "leafed" all around. Especially useful in a solarium is *A. falcatus*, whose fast-growing shoot will twine and climb. *A. setaceus* used to be a routine addition to cut flowers; its "needles" are very fine and in late summer it may set red berries.

Location: Light to partial shade; warm (about 68°F (20°C). *A. densiflorus* can be outdoors in summer. In winter, light, not much under 54°F (12°C).
Care: Keep evenly moist; do not let the plant dry out. Feed weekly from spring to fall and monthly in winter. Plants in normal room atmosphere will need frequent spraying. In winter adjust watering to the warmth of the room.

My own *A. densiflorus* 'Meyeri' spends the whole summer in the atrium. I hang *A. falcatus* on the fence, where it can climb till late

The enlarged root ball of an ornamental asparagus

summer, when it is cut back so that it takes up little room in winter storage, where both plants are shaded from all but the morning sun.

Propagation: By division or seeds.
Pests and Diseases: If winter treatment is too warm or dry, spider mites can appear. Please note: the plant does not react well to chemical spraying of any kind.
Uses: Green plant for light, warm locations; in summer outdoors. *A. falcatus* is a good solarium plant.

THE MOST BEAUTIFUL PLANTS FROM A TO Z

Aspidistra elatior

ASPIDISTRA ELATIOR
Aspidistra, cast-iron plant

Family: Lily, Liliaceae
Native Habitat: China, Japan
Flowering Time: Rarely blooms in cultivation

The long-stemmed leaves of aspidistra are reminiscent of spears; its insignificant flowers are of a murky violet color. The rarely seen cultivar 'Variegata' is especially handsome; its leaves are striped in white.
Location: Dark or light, as long as it is not in the sun. Prefers an outdoor location at 55–70°F (13–21°C) in the summer. 'Variegata' has to have light to retain its white stripes.
Care: Keep evenly moist in summer, but avoid waterlogging. Feed once a month with a weak solution. Every 2-3 years transplant in the spring, using standard potting soil.
Propagation: By division: each part should have at least two leaves.
Pests and Diseases: Occasionally, scale insects or spider mites.
Uses: This undemanding green plant can be put in rooms, cool stairways, or on a landing. As with chlorophytum and billbergia, it is impossible to kill aspidistra, except by keeping it too wet in cool, dark places. Not even drafts or the dry air in apartments can hurt this most modest of plants. I often forget to look after my own aspidistra, which stands happily all summer on the terrace.

ASPLENIUM
Spleenwort

Family: Polypody, *Polypodiaceae*
Native Habitat: Tropical rain forests of Asia, Africa, and Australia
Flowering Time: Not a flowering plant

As a houseplant, the bird's nest fern (*A. nidus*), has found wide acceptance. Its large, shiny green leaves come together in a funnel-shaped rosette. The leaves have smooth edges, but the variety 'Fimbriatus' is notched.

A. antiquum resembles *A. nidus*. *A. bulbuferum*, the mother spleen-wort, carries small "bulbs" on its fronds. This species has very high care requirements and can thrive only with serious fern collectors.

Asplenium antiquum *growing epiphytically on bark*
Below: Close-ups of Asplenium nidus

Location: Light or partial shade; no sun. Warm all year, in winter partial shade at 60°F (16°C). Please note: bottom heat is a requirement; the plant may have to be placed on a heating pad.
Care: Provide even moisture and always use soft water. Feed it very lightly every 14 days in the summer and raise its humidity by frequent spraying. Its loose soil should contain lots of peat.
Propagation: *A. nidus* by spores; *A. bulbiferum* by removing the small plants along with some roots from the leaf edges.
Pests and Diseases: Scale insects; dryness and cold will cause the leaf edges to turn brown.
Uses: A foliage plant for a not-too-light, warm spot; for terrariums, or perhaps the bathroom or the kitchen.

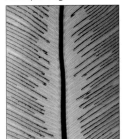

Fiddlehead

Fern sporangium

Asteriscus – Bambusa

Asteriscus maritimus
and its cultivars have
just recently become
commercially
available.

The genus *Astrophytum*
includes both thorned
and thornless species,
among them the
bishopshood.

Asteriscus maritimus

ASTERISCUS MARITIMUS
Astericus

Family: Aster, *Asteraceae*
Native Habitat: Mediterranean region
Flowering Time: Summer

Asteriscus is a hairy perennial of spreading habit, about 10 in. (25 cm) high; its flowers are yellow. Since it was introduced to the European market in 1986, it has become a favorite balcony plant. Unlike those of the species, the flowers of some of its cultivars, e.g., 'Gold Coin' and 'Gold Dollar,' will remain open even when rained on.
Location: Full sun and warm. In winter light, at about 50°F (10°C), and almost dry.
Care: During the growing period, keep evenly dry and avoid waterlogging. Feed regularly to the end of summer and keep removing wilted flowers.
Propagation: By tip cuttings in summer.
Pests and Diseases: Aphids.
Uses: Perennial plant for the balcony; suited as ground cover and for planters, troughs, containers, bowls, and hanging

TIP

One of the bishop's miter varieties is completely green. This has to be provided partial shade, since the absence of the white "flakes" means that it lacks protection against the sun.

Bishop's miter in a cactus collection

ASTROPHYTUM
Astrophytum, star cactus

Family: Cactus, *Cactaceae*
Native Habitat: Mexico, Texas
Flowering Time: Any time of year

To this genus belong such spherical cacti as the sea urchin cactus (*A. asterias*), with its thornless ribs and white-flecked skin, the globular bishop's miter (*A. myriostigma*), its sharp-edged ribs also unarmed, and the star cactus *A. ornatum*, whose rounded youthful habit becomes columnar with maturity. All three species bear yellow flowers.
Location: Sunny and warm; in winter cool, around 50°F (10°C).

Care: In summer, water lightly, letting the soil dry out completely before watering again. Feed with cactus food once a month. Let dry out in winter. Use a cactus mix with a clay granular for planting.
Propagation: From seed at a soil temperature of about 82°F (28°C).
Pests and Diseases: Mealybugs.
Uses: A cactus for a sunny window or a cactus collection.

THE MOST BEAUTIFUL PLANTS FROM A TO Z

Aucuba japonica

Bambusa vulgaris

BAMBUSA
Bamboo

Family: Grass, *Poaceae*
Native Habitat: Tropical Asia
Flowering Time: Hardly blooms in cultivation

Bamboo grows many feet high in its Asian home; in containers it remains considerably shorter, though over the years it can reach 6–10 ft. (2–3 m). The varieties listed are not hardy in temperate areas: *B. glaucescens* 'Alphonse Karr' has yellow or reddish stems striped in green, and green leaves. Varieties 'Wang Tsai' and 'Golden Goddess' are similar. 'Fernleaf' stands out for its frondlike leaves.

The stem of *B. vulgaris* 'Striata' is thick and yellow with green stripes.
Location: Sunny and warm; in summer best outdoors. In winter not under 41°F (5°C).
Care: Keep evenly moist in summer and feed every month.
Propagation: By division.
Pests and Diseases: Spider mites in winter.
Uses: Container plant for a sun room; in summer for outdoors; young specimens for living areas.

Aucubas can tolerate some frost, so there is no rush about moving them indoors in the fall; they can also be put outside quite early in the spring.

Whether in a pot or in a container, bamboo is always an unusual sight in temperate climates, and its lovely leaves have an oriental air.

AUCUBA JAPONICA
Aucuba

Family: Dogwood, *Cornaceae*
Native Habitat: East Asia
Flowering Time: Spring

This dioecious evergreen shrub, 6–10 ft. (2–3 m) in height, is hardy in milder climates, such as the Mediterranean region. The leaves are elliptical, leathery, and green. The flowers, which appear in spikes, are small and modest, but the fruit is scarlet and decorative. They are slightly poisonous, however.

More interesting than the green species are its variegated, yellow-spotted or dotted cultivars, 'Cro-tonia,' 'Picturata,' and 'Variegata.'
Location: In summer outdoors, in partial or full shade, protected from wind and rain; in winter, light and cool at 43–46°F (6–8°C).
Care: Keep moderately moist. In its cool winter position, water only rarely. Repot only if needed in spring, in standard soil mix and not too large a pot. Plants that have grown too large can be pruned.
Propagation: By division.
Pests and Diseases: Spider mites in winter.
Uses: An impressive evergreen container plant for the atrium, balcony, or a cool sun room.

Since aucuba is dioecious, it is best to have two plants, one female, one male. This makes the production of fruit possible.

Beaucarnea – Begonia

Beaucarnea recurvata has become a fashionable houseplant, and is offered in supermarkets for mass consumption.

Leaf begonias stimulate the collector in us. Here is a group of three *Begonia masoniana* 'Iron Cross,' a cultivar of *Begonia boweri*, and a *Begonia rex* hybrid.

Beaucarnea recurvata

BEAUCARNEA RECURVATA
Pony-tail palm

Family: Agave, *Agavaceae*
Native Habitat: Mexico
Flowering Time: Seldom blooms in cultivation

In its native Mexico this agave forms a shrub or treelike plant. At its base, the stem is thickened and at its apex it bears a plume of long, narrow, gray-green, downward-arching leaves. In cultivation, *Beaucarnea* (formerly *Nolina*) grows about 3 ft. (1 m) high, its narrow leaves about 24 in. (60 cm) long.
Location: Sunny, in summer outside but protected from rain. In winter, light, at about 50°F (10°C).
Care: In summer, water moderately, and feed lightly once a week. The plant tolerates hard water. Keep almost dry in winter.
Propagation: From seed or by the occasional offset.
Pests and Diseases: Aphids, spider mites, and scale insects if too warm in winter.
Uses: Green plant for a light location, outdoors in summer. Suitable for hydroculture.

Flowers of Beaucarnea

The three best-known begonias

BEGONIA
Begonia

Family: Begonia, *Begoniaceae*
Native Habitat: Tropical and subtropical Asia, Africa, and North and South America
Flowering Time: Depends on the species

This huge family includes over 1000 species worldwide, with untold hybrids and varieties. Generally, we differentiate the colored leaf, coral, flowering, shrub, and tuberous begonias.
Colored leaf begonias: This group includes the Rex Begonias with their gorgeously colored leaves. *Begonia masoniana*'s cultivar 'Iron Cross' is a great example, with a dark brown cross clearly drawn on its apple-green leaves. Two well-known varieties of *Begonia boweri* are: 'Cleopatra' (brown, crimson amaranth red, and shades of green) and 'Tiger' (reddish yellow leaves spotted in greenish yellow).
Location: Light but not full sun; keep warm, even in winter not under 60°F (16°C) with bottom heating.
Care: Year-round keep moderately moist with soft, lukewarm water. A humid environment is required, but the plant should not be sprayed. During periods of growth, feed

THE MOST BEAUTIFUL PLANTS FROM A TO Z

Colorful Elatior *hybrid begonias*

Eliator hybrid begonias first became available in 1907 and have been bred since to be ever more spectacular.

The exotic, spotted Mexicross hybrid (below) is a descendant of *Begonia boweri*.

every two weeks. When pot-bound, transplant using standard or flower soil mix.

Propagation: By cuttings of tip, leaf, or root. From seed with bottom heating (73°F (23°C)).

Pests and Diseases: Root nematodes, mealybugs, and root rot if kept too wet and cold. Spraying the leaves causes leaf spot.

Uses: Foliage plants for a light, warm location.

Hybrid Mexicross begonia

TIP

To keep the leaves from becoming smaller, flowers should be pinched off colored leaf begonias as they appear.

Begonia

Tuberous begonias charm partly with their flowers, some of which are of very impressive size, and in part by their tolerance for shade.

Their graceful pendant habit makes some tuberous begonias ideal hanging plants.

BEGONIA (CONTINUED)
Begonia

Flowering begonias (*Eliator* hybrids): Mostly annual, horti-culturally produced strains with simple or double flowers, large or small, in red, pink, yellow, or white. They bloom any time of year, but prefer the fall and winter.

Tuberous begonias: These hybrids have earned their prominent place on the balcony and patio by their tolerance for shade, by the fullness and size of their flowers, and by the fine range of their colors, which cover all shades of the rainbow except blue. There are five groups:

Grandifloras have large flowers and grow up to 24 in. (60 cm) high. Both wind and rain endanger their flowers, so outdoors they require support. The 'Memory' series is very popular.

B. grandiflora compacta hybrids also have large flowers, but grow more compact: 'Fortuna' (crimson), 'Gold Crown' (yellow). The Benary-F1 hybrids are tuberous begonias with medium-sized flowers, for example, the red 'Nonstop.' The hybrids of the 'Clips' series come in yellow, orange, white, and mixed. The "small-flowering" begonias of the older 'Bertini' series, were about the same size as the above groups, which now have largely supplanted them.

Cascading begonias, whose shoots tend to bend downward, can bring color to a protected balcony. Varieties come in series: 'Musical,' 'Happy End,' and 'Illumination.'

Colorful assortment of tuberous begonias of the hybrid 'Nonstop Mix'

A cascading tuberous begonia

Begonia limmingheana

Location: Light to partially shaded. Outdoors, protected from wind.

Care: Provide soil rich in humus that drains well. In summer, keep evenly but moderately moist, and feed once a week. Before the first frost—not any earlier, as a short exposure to light frost does no harm—cut the stems about 1 in. (2–3 cm) above the tubers, dig up the tubers, and store them in a dry, cool place, at about 50°F (10°C). Take great care not to injure the tubers, as they can become infected. Starting in early spring, plant in a light, warm place.

Propagation: By division of the tubers, in the spring.

Pests and Diseases: Aphids and powdery mildew.

Uses: Patio and balcony plants for locations that are not too sunny and are screened against the wind.

Two members of the begonia family that are ideally suited to hanging baskets: *Begonia limmingheana*, one of the oldest shrub Begonias, and the modern Benary hybrid 'Illumination,' a tuberous begonia.

Begonia 'Illumination'

Begonia

Pink Perpetual begonia

Red Perpetual begonia

White Perpetual begonia

The coral begonia
(*Begonia corallina*)
hybrids please
especially by their
interestingly speckled
leaves, which have
earned them the
name "trout
begonias."

Begonia metallica
attracts attention by its
burnished foliage and
its downy, vivid pink
flowers.

BEGONIA (CONTINUED)
Begonia

Wax begonias (*Begonia semper-florens* hybrids) bloom as annuals in beds and borders, in planters and in dishes. They are used as fillers in public gardens and formal plantings. There are numerous varieties in white, pink, and all shades of red.

Location: Light; tolerates direct sun.

Care: Keep evenly moist, avoiding both drying out the root ball and waterlogging it. Feed moderately every 2–3 weeks.

Propagation: By seed in early winter at soil temperatures of 74°F (23°C).

Pests and Diseases: Powdery mildew.

Uses: As an annual flowering plant for sunny balconies, patios, and beds.

Coral begonias: Perennial and usually bushy begonias, which can grow to impressive size.

These fast-growing hybrid coral-lina begonias (trout begonias)

Begonia corallina hybrid

Begonia metallica

have pink to red hanging flower clusters and often attractively patterned leaves; they can reach 6–7 ft. (2 m) in height. Well-loved varieties are 'Madame Charrat,' 'Luzerna,' and 'President Carnot.' The variety 'Tamaya' has recently been developed in Italy and is frequently presented trained as a standard.

Begonia limmingheana is a climbing or spreading plant. With its 5 in.- (12 cm-) long oval leaves and pendulant shoots it is suitable for a hanging basket. *Begonia metallica* has leaves that are 3–5 in. (8–12 cm) long; they gleam metallic on top and are colored purple underneath.

Location: Light all year, but not too sunny; warm (68–72°F (20–22°C)). In winter, if possible, not under 60°F (16°C).

Care: Keep evenly moist with soft water. Feed well from spring to late summer. For repotting use a standard soil mix with Styrofoam bits. Should the plant get too large or leggy, prune it back.

Propagation: By tip cuttings rooted in water or soil.

Pests and Diseases: Aphids and thrips, if under- or overwatered; when too wet, powdery mildew.

Uses: Flowering plant for a light, warm room; *B. limmingheana* as a hanging plant.

THE MOST BEAUTIFUL PLANTS FROM A TO Z

The new Italian hybrid of *Begonia corallina*, 'Tamaya,' is very famous; here it is shown trained as a standard with pink azaleas and sword ferns.

Begonia corallina

Bellis – Blechnum

Bellis perennis looks good with low-growing forget-me-not; or try it in planters or in a flat dish with spring bulbs.

Although *Beloperone guttata* will live for many years, the shrublets are generally discarded at the end of their blooming season.

Bellis perennis *'Pomponette'*

BELLIS PERENNIS
English daisy

Family: Aster, *Asteraceae*
Native Habitat: Europe, Africa, Asia
Flowering Time: Spring to early summer.

Biennial compact hybrids of *Bellis perennis*, these 4–8 in.- (10–20 cm-) high plants are used on balconies and in the garden. Many much larger varieties with double or globular flower heads are available, such as 'Medicis,' white, pink, and red. A few other lovely cultivars, among many others, are 'Pomponette,' 'Teppich,' and 'Super Enorma.' Although a perennial, *Bellis perennis* is regarded as a biennial because by the third year it produces very few flowers.
Location: Sun to partial shade.
Care: Water amply during the growth period. Remove wilted blooms and feed weekly. Use standard potting soil.
Propagation: From seed in summer for flowers in the following year.
Pests and Diseases: Powdery mildew.
Uses: Balcony and garden flower; also suitable for borders.

BELOPERONE GUTTATA
Beloperone shrimp plant

Family: Acanthus, *Acanthaceae*
Native Habitat: Mexico
Flowering Time: Almost all year

Of the thirty or so species, only *B. guttata* is in cultivation. Now its botanical name is *Justicia brandegeana*. This densely branched shrub or subshrub can grow to 4 ft. (1.2 m), but in a container it will hardly reach 31 in. (80 cm). Its leaves are about 2 in. (6 cm) long, and ovoid. The insignificant, white blossoms stand along an 8 in.- (20 cm-) long spike, which also carries yellow-brown bracts. This shingled cover of decorative "leaves" remains fresh long after the flowers have fallen.
Location: Very light all year, no mid-day sun. Warm in summer; it thrives outdoors. Not under 54°F (12°C) in winter.
Care: Water amply in summer, less so in winter. Feed every 3–4 weeks from early spring to late summer. To maintain bushiness, I prune back my beloperone when I transplant it in the spring. I cut back mostly older, leggier stems, reducing them to about a third of their size.
Propagation: By seed or tip cuttings, preferably under plastic, in spring, with bottom heating.
Pests and Diseases: Aphids and spider mites. If kept too wet or too dark in winter, leaves will turn yellow; if kept too dry, they will fall.
Uses: Houseplant for a light spot or container plant for a sun room.

Beloperone guttata

Billbergia nutans

BILLBERGIA NUTANS
Queen's Tears

Family: Bromeliad, *Bromeliaceae*
Native Habitat: Tropical South America
Flowering Time: Any time of year, depending on culture, but usually in winter

Billbergia has narrow grasslike leaves about 12 in. (30 cm) long that grow in a rosette. Reddish bracts together with the modest, greenish violet flowers form a cascading inflorescence.
Location: Light to partial shade; humid and warm. In summer possibly outdoors, in winter not under 54°F (12°C).
Care: Keep well watered in summer, less moist in its cool winter position. Dryness prevents blooming, which can, however, be promoted by daily spraying. Feed weekly in summer.
Propagation: By offsets removed in the spring when they have reached 4–6 in. (10–15 cm), or by division.
Pests and Diseases: Scale insects.
Uses: Houseplant for a light, warm spot.

BLECHNUM
Blechnum

Family: Polypody, *Polypodaceae*
Native Habitat: South America, New Caledonia; *Blechnum spicant*, worldwide
Flowering Time: Not a flowering plant

As beautiful houseplants, the following *Blechnum* species are best: *B. brasiliense*, which can grow quite large and develop a 3 ft.- (1 m-) high stem; *B. gibbum*, also a stemmed species; and *B. spicant*, the European ribbed fern, with dark green fronds about 20 in. (50 cm) long.
Location: Partial shade, warm, humid. In winter at least 54°F (12°C). (*B. spicant* can tolerate 37–41°F (3–5°C)).
Care: Water generously with soft water in summer; letting the root ball dry out damages the plant. Feed lightly once a month. To

Blechnum gibbum

create humidity, place the pot inside another one, filling the space with wet sand. Use a loose, humus-rich soil for potting.
Propagation: By spores, with bottom heating.
Pests and Diseases: Aphids, scale insects, spider mites, if air is too dry.
Uses: Green plant for a warm place with open shade and a humid atmosphere. In summer on the balcony or patio, out of the sun.

The many varieties of *Billbergia nutans* are all relatively easy to take care of.

From the center of the ring of its fronds, *Blechnum brasiliense* uncurls its fiddleheads, i.e., its young leaves. (See picture below.)

Older exemplars of *Blechnum gibbum* may grow too large for a room; a solarium or conservatory with temperature control is a better place for them.

Blechnum brasiliense

Bougainvillea – Browallia

In this close-up of the flower of bougainvillea, one can see the visually dominant bracts, against which the small flowers are nearly insignificant.

In this picture you cannot tell that bougainvillea is really a climber with long, thorny shoots.

BOUGAINVILLEA
Bougainvillea

Family: Four o'clock, *Nyctaginaceae*
Native Habitat: South America
Flowering Time: Late spring to summer

This fast-growing, 10–13 ft.- (3–4 m-) high shrubby climber is represented in nurseries mostly by its hybrids. In bloom, the plant is completely covered by the bracts that can be violet, red, pink, white, or yellow orange. Among the bright bracts, the little yellowish white flowers are discernible.
Location: Sunny, warm; in summer outdoors, out of the wind. In winter, cool (at 46–50°F (8–10°C)); protected from drafts.
Care: In summer, the plant needs even moisture and plant food every week. In winter, in a cool place, keep almost dry. Repot young plants every year, older ones every 2–3 years, in pots not too large. Prune as needed. Too much warmth in winter will lessen flowering. The long shoots need the support of a trellis or arch to prevent damage to the delicate flowers.
Propagation: By tip cuttings with bottom heat and growth hormone treatment. Not easy.
Pests and Diseases: Occasional scale insects. Yellow leaves are a sign of overwatering; leaf loss in summer means the plant is too dry; in winter, leaf loss is natural.
Uses: Container plant for the house, best for a conservatory; in summer for out-of-doors.

Bougainvillea blossoms in a close-up

Bougainvillea hybrid blooming profusely

TIP

When my bougainvillea does not want to produce flowers, I prescribe a short rest period, during which I do not water it.

The Most Beautiful Plants from A to Z

Bouvardia hybrid

Brachycome iberidifolia

Browallia speciosa

BOUVARDIA
Bouvardia

Family: Madder, *Rubiaceae*
Native Habitat: Mexico
Flowering Time: Summer to fall

Bouvardia is a shrubby plant with long, narrow leaves. The flowers appear in umbels or umbellate clusters; they are simple or double, white, pink, or red. As houseplants, *B. leiantha* and *B. longiflora* are best.

Location: Light all year, no strong sun. Outdoors in summer; in winter at 41–50°F (5–10°C).
Care: During the growing period keep moderately moist and feed once a week. In winter keep nearly dry, especially *B. longiflora*. Prune often for bushiness. If plants grow too large, divide and plant in standard soil mixture in spring.
Propagation: By tip and root cuttings (the latter are slower) with bottom heating.
Pests and Diseases: Aphids.
Uses: Container plant for sun rooms and for outdoors in summer.

BRACHYCOME IBERIDIFOLIA
Swanriver daisy

Family: Aster, *Asteraceae*
Native Habitat: Australia
Flowering Time: Spring to fall

This is a flowering annual with delicate compound leaves on shoots about 16 in. (40 cm) long. Till late fall the starlike flowers continue to open—blue, white, or pink, depending on the variety. They have a soft fragrance.

Location: Sunny spot outdoors.
Care: Water generously to prevent any dryness of the roots, and feed once a week. Remove dead blooms. For the balcony, plant in standard soil mixture.
Propagation: From seed at 68–71°F (20–22°C) soil temperature or by cuttings.
Pests and Diseases: Whiteflies.
Uses: For dishes, hanging baskets, and balcony planters.

BROWALLIA SPECIOSA
Browallia

Family: Nightshade, *Solanaceae*
Native Habitat: Tropical America
Flowering Time: All year

Browallia is a subshrub, 12–20 in. (30–50 cm) high, with large blue flowers and narrow, dark green leaves. Like all the nightshades, the plant is poisonous. As an annual flower, use the species *B. grandiflora* and *B. viscosa*, placing them on the windowsill in very early spring.

Location: Light, maybe sunny; warm. Shade from the noon sun in the summer. Not under 60°F (15°C) in winter.
Care: Water generously in summer and feed biweekly. Water more moderately in winter. Repotting is not an issue, as browallias age fast and are usually kept only one year.
Propagation: From seed in spring, with bottom heat, or by cuttings.
Pests and Diseases: Spider mites, scale insects. Whiteflies when the air is too dry.
Uses: Houseplant for a light, warm location.

Browallias are seen relatively seldom as house plants, but I predict that in time they will become more familiar as windowsill flowers.

In its Australian habitat, the Swanriver daisy (*Brachycome*) grows among rocks and stones.

Browallia is named after the Finnish bishop Johan Browallius, himself a botanist and friend of Carl von Linne, who was the developer of the binomial system of naming plants generally in use now.

Brunfelsia – Caladium

The somewhat leggy brunfelsia may not sprout side shoots even after heavy pruning.

Buddleja indica deserves to be better known: it can tolerate shade, and its demands for care are modest in other respects as well.

Once again, fashion may be turning to box, which is now planted with some frequency at entryways and in containers.

Brunfelsia pauciflora var. calycina

Buddleja indica

Buxus sempervirens

BRUNFELSIA
Brunfelsia, rain tree

Family: Nightshade, *Solanaceae*
Native Habitat: Tropical Central and South America
Flowering Time: Winter to spring

This is an evergreen shrub with leathery green leaves and large, disk-shaped flowers, ranging from white to blue violet. The species commonly offered is *B. pauciflora var. calycina*. The plant is poisonous.
Location: All year, light, warm and humid. Keep B. pauciflora cool in the winter months (50–54°F (10–12°C)) to promote bud formation.
Care: Keep evenly moist with soft, lukewarm water and feed biweekly in the growing season. Use soil with lots of humus and no calcium.
Propagation: By tip cuttings at 86°F (30°C) soil temperature and using a growth hormone; it is slow and difficult.
Pests and Diseases: Scale insects, spider mites; leaves fall if either waterlogged or dried out.
Uses: Houseplant for a light, warm location or a solarium.

BUDDLEJA INDICA
Buddleja, butterfly bush

Family: Butterfly bush, *Buddlejaceae*
Native Habitat: Madagascar
Flowering Time: Hardly blooms in cultivation

Buddleja, formerly called *Nicodemia diversifolia*, is an enchanting small evergreen, densely branched. Its shiny, dark green foliage is the shape of oak leaves.
Location: Partial or full shade and warm, but the plant can tolerate temperatures between 41–68°F (5–20°C).
Care: Water amply in summer and feed weekly. Cool in winter and reduce watering. Repot annually in standard potting mix and prune as needed, especially young plants; this will ensure bushiness.
Propagation: Any time of year by cuttings; they root well in soil with bottom heating.
Pests and Diseases: Spider mites, if kept too dry and too light.
Uses: Foliage plant for partially shaded spot in a room or greenhouse, or in a hanging basket.

BUXUS SEMPERVIRENS
Box

Family: Boxwood, *Buxaceae*
Native Habitat: Europe, Africa, Asia
Flowering Time: In spring

Box is an evergreen, densely branched shrub or tree. In the wild, it can reach up to 26 ft. (8 m), but there are many much smaller varieties that make good container plants, e.g., 'Suffruticosa,' used for borders, and 'Bullata' or 'Faulkner.' The ovate leaves are, according to the species, dark green or spotted in yellow green. Box is poisonous in all its parts.
Location: Sunny or shaded outdoors. If the plant is in a container, it needs to be sheltered from protracted frosts, perhaps in the garage.
Care: Water regularly during periods of growth and feed monthly.
Propagation: By cuttings in spring or summer. They take a long time to root.
Pests and Diseases: Rarely.
Uses: Hardy container plant for balconies and patios; good for low borders and as a specimen plant.

Caladium bicolor *hybrids*

Caladium bicolor hybrids are peerless foliage plants. What is not generally known is that "caladium" means "plant with edible roots" in the language of its homeland. Thus, in South America, caladium is considered a useful plant.

CALADIUM BICOLOR HYBRIDS
Caladium

Family: Arum, *Araceae*
Native Habitat: Tropical America
Flowering Time: Seldom flowers in cultivation

This is a colorful foliage plant with flat tubers. Many varieties with white, pink, and red markings or marbling are available. 'Candida,' for example, is a luminous white with dark veining; 'John Reed' has leaves marbled in red and green. In late summer or fall, the leaves dry up and fall off.

Location: Light or partial shade; no sun; even warmth (68–77°F (20–25°C)) and humid air are necessary.
Care: During growth, provide even moisture and indirect atmospheric humidity. Reduce watering in fall. After the leaves are gone, keep tubers in sand or in the pot at 65°F (18°C) for the winter. In early spring plant in a good flower mix till they sprout, providing light, warmth, and moisture. As soon as the leaves appear, increase humidity by placing the pot over water that can evaporate, as in an orchid dish with a wire mesh plate. Till the end of summer, feed biweekly.

Propagation: By tuberous offshoots, or by dividing the tuber itself, where each part must have at least one "eye," or bud.
Pests and Diseases: Aphids, when air is too dry.
Uses: Best suited to enclosed sun rooms or conservatories because the plant needs high humidity.

Although the colored leaves need high atmospheric humidity, they cannot be sprayed because water will cause brown spots.

Calathea – Callisia

It is unfortunate that calathea's need for atmospheric humidity means that in most rooms its lifespan is limited.

This picture gives some idea of the range of patterns and shapes calathea's leaves can take. A botanical collection could provide a complete overview.

CALATHEA
Calathea

Family: Prayer plant, *Marantaceae*
Native Habitat: Tropical South America
Flowering Time: Spring to summer

Most of these lovely foliage plants grow about 8–10 in. (20–25 cm) high. They originate in the tropical rain forests of South America, which fact alone indicates that they will have special needs. The leaves of all calathea species—be they short or long, long- or short-stemmed, oval or elongated—share the characteristic stripes and spots, while flowers vary somewhat among the species. *C. lancifolia* has narrow leaves up to 20 in. (50 cm) long, with olive-green spots and fluted edges. *C. makoyana* bears a dark green design on the white field that runs down the central rib. The leaves of *C. ornata* show pink designs on their green top side and are red underneath.

Location: All year, light or partially shaded and warm (daytime over 68°F (20 °C), at night not under 65°F (18°C)). Keep it cooler in winter, in soil at 54–59°F (12–15°C). Protect from drafts.

Care: Water amply in summer and feed biweekly; provide high atmospheric humidity. In winter reduce water. Transplant every 2–3 years into light soil high in peat.

Propagation: By division.

Pests and Diseases: Scale insects and spider mites when air is too dry.

Uses: Foliage plant for an enclosed sun room, hothouse, or conservatory.

Calathea makoyana *with Aglaonema*

Leaves of some calathea cultivars

TIP

When the leaves of calathea begin to roll up, it is time to increase atmospheric humidity.

THE MOST BEAUTIFUL PLANTS FROM A TO Z

Calceolaria *hybrid*

Calliandra tweedii

Callisia elegans

CALCEOLARIA
Calceolaria, pocketbook plant

Family: Figwort, *Scrophulariaceae*
Native Habitat: Central and South America
Flowering Time: Spring to fall

The characteristic feature of this colorful annual is the lower lip of the flower, blown up to resemble a shoe. Offered as a plant for house, balcony, or garden, calceolaria gives pleasure by the variety of its yellow, orange, or red-patterned flowers.
Location: Light, but not sunny; partially shaded. Inside, as cool as possible, around 59°F (15 °C); outside protected from rain and wind.
Care: Water generously and feed weekly. The root ball should always be damp, but never wet.
Propagation: From seed, in winter; hybrids by cuttings, in late summer.
Pests and Diseases: Aphids, white-flies, spider mites; limp leaves indicate insufficient water.
Uses: Wonderful flowering plant for the garden, the balcony, or the home.

CALLIANDRA TWEEDII
Calliandra, fairy duster

Family: Bean, *Fabaceae*
Native Habitat: Brazil
Flowering Time: Early summer

The stems of this evergreen plant are thin and hanging, the compound leaves delicate. The flowers, reminiscent of powder puffs, are densely set with long, flame-red stamens.
Location: Light or sunny, warm and humid. In winter not under 59°F (15°C).
Care: Keep moist all summer and feed every two weeks. Spray frequently to give the plant moist air. When repotting in the spring, prune lightly to prevent legginess.
Propagation: From seed or by tip cuttings.
Pests and Diseases: Aphids, white-flies.
Uses: Evergreen container plant for a warm greenhouse or conservatory. Can be trained as a standard.

CALLISIA
Callisia, variegated wandering Jew

Family: Spiderwort, *Commelinaceae*
Native Habitat: Central and South America
Flowering Time: Early summer

Spreading or upright plant with small white flowers in the leaf axils. *C. elegans* 'Striata' is a creeping variety, its foliage striped in green and white. *C. fragrans* is an upright plant with dark green leaves. *C. repens* grows long shoots set with small round leaves.
Location: Light to partial shade, the colored varieties needing more light than the green ones; warm, at least 59°F (15°C) and humid.
Care: Water generously with soft, lukewarm water and spray often. Feed weekly from spring to fall. Trim long shoots.
Propagation: By cuttings under plastic.
Pests and Diseases: Thrips, spider mites.
Uses: Hanging plant for a light, warm spot in the conservatory or greenhouse.

While calceolarias are still used on balcony railings and in planters, as houseplants they are not in fashion right now.

Calliandra is not by any means a foolproof plant, and even with good care, it does not necessarily bloom each year—no one knows why.

Callisia makes a lovely ground cover and is an excellent hanging plant because of the length of its shoots.

Callistemon – Camellia

To achieve *Callistemon citrinus* plants with a nice, bushy habit, prune them when they are young.

Combining different varieties of *Calluna vulgaris* can produce great effects.

Camellia sasanqua and its cultivars make good house plants.

Callistemon citrinus

Calluna vulgaris 'Jan Dekker'

Camellia sasanqua var. fragrans

CALLISTEMON CITRINUS
Callistemon, bottlebrush

Family: Myrtle, *Myrtaceae*
Native Habitat: Australia
Flowering Time: Summer

This evergreen shrub derives its name from the resemblance of its flower spikes to brushes. The flowers assembled on the stem in a compact mass have no petals: it is their long, vividly scarlet stamens that stick out like bristles.
Location: Light or full sun and warm. In summer outdoors, in winter at 43–46°F (6–8°C).
Care: In summer, water amply with soft water, but avoid waterlogging; feed biweekly. Trim extra-long shoots after the flowers fade. In winter, water only to prevent the roots from drying out.
Propagation: By cuttings in summer, with bottom heating.
Pests and Diseases: Scale insects; yellow leaves result from hard water or too much fertilizer.
Uses: Container plant for a sunny spot or the sun room.

CALLUNA VULGARIS
Scotch heather

Family: Heath, *Ericaceae*
Native Habitat: Europe, Siberia, Asia Minor
Flowering Time: Summer to late fall

Heather is a dwarf shrub, only 8–35 in. (20–90 cm) high, with small, scale-like leaves in green, yellow, or gray-green. Its bell-shaped flowers form terminal racemes in pink, red, or white. Some varieties have double flowers, others bloom at different times of year.
Location: Sun or partial shade outdoors, in sandy, acidic soil.
Care: In summer, water evenly but lightly. Feed in spring and early summer. In winter, water even more lightly without letting it dry out. In spring, prune back.
Propagation: In summer by cuttings or tip layering; in spring from seed outdoors.
Pests and Diseases: Rarely.
Uses: Flowering plant for planters, dishes, borders, and heath gardens.

CAMELLIA
Camellia

Family: Tea, *Theaceae*
Native Habitat: Asia
Flowering Time: Fall to spring

Camellias are evergreen shrubs with hard, shiny, dark green leaves and large flowers that open in winter. The blossoms may—according to species or variety—be simple, semi-double, or fully double, and vary from 2–6 in. (5–16 cm) in width. The cultivars of *C. japonica* and the Williamsii hybrids are significant.

Varieties of *C. japonica* are, among many others, 'Matterhorn' (white, double), 'Yucumi Guruma' (simple white), 'Cheryll Lynn' (double, pink), 'Gloire de Nantes' (semi-double, pink), 'Alexander Hunter' (simple, red), 'Apollo' (semi-double, red), 'Mathotiana' (double, red), 'Daikagura' (semi-double, light pink with white spots), 'Tricolor' (semi-double, striped in white).

Some Williamsii hybrids are 'Boven Bryant' (semi-double, dark pink), 'Donation' (semi-double, pink with darker veining), 'Freedom Bell'(simple, light red), 'Water Lily' (double, light pink). As houseplants, varieties of *C. sasanqua* can also be considered.

Location: Light or partial shade, no sun, cool (not above 65°F (18°C)). In summer outdoors. High humidity required. In full bloom, camellias can be brought into the warm living room for a short span.

Care: Keep moderately moist all year using soft water. Once new shoots appear, feed weekly with flower fertilizer, diluted by half, or with azalea food. With the first buds, stop feeding and decrease watering. Repot, if necessary, after flowering when growth begins, into acidic soil. Pruning is not good for camellias.

Propagation: By tip cuttings in late summer with bottom heating and using growth hormones.

Pests and Diseases: Scale insects, aphids, mealybugs, and broad-nosed weevils. Rust and leaf fall are due to excessively high winter temperatures.

Uses: Magnificent flowering plant for pots, containers, and planters, for the sun room or greenhouse. To use strictly as a houseplant, shop for appropriate varieties.

An exquisite rarity: a camellia as a bonsai

Blossoms of some camellia varieties

A small assortment of the lovely camellia varieties available. Nurseries specializing in camellias will have far more.

TIP

To ensure that camellias do not lose their buds or flowers, protect them from frequent jolts or movements. Hard water and dry air are also damaging to them.

Campanula poscharskyana

Campanula isophylla *'Alba and Mayi'*

CAMPANULA
Bell flower

Family: Bell flower, *Campanulaceae*
Native Habitat: Southern Europe
Flowering Time: *C. fragilis*, spring to summer; *C. isophylla*, spring to fall

Of the many species of bell flower, two are especially suited to being houseplants:

C. fragilis, the delicate bell flower, has creeping or hanging shoots and heart-shaped leaves. The blossoms are white or light blue, often with a lighter center. The plant is usually raised as an annual and is well suited to a hanging basket.

C. isophylla's shoots are longer, its flowers larger. The variety 'Mayi' blooms blue, 'Alba,' white. This species also lends itself to use as a hanging plant.

To plant around the balcony or patio, try *C. carpatica:* its habit is a densely bushy mound, its flowers are blue violet or white. *C. portenschlagiana* also forms pillows of foliage, while *C. poscharskyana* grows long shoots; both bloom dark blue violet.

Location: Light, no strong sun; airy and cool, 44–60°F (7–16°C). In summer outdoors, shady. In winter at 50°F (10°C).

Care: In summer feed weekly and water regularly. After flowering, prune well and keep relatively dry till the spring; repot in flower soil.

Propagation: By tip cuttings or division.

Pests and Diseases: Spider mites, aphids, gray mold if too wet; yellow leaves if too dry.

Uses: Hanging plant for cool, light rooms; in summer for balcony or terrace.

TIP

Bell flowers grow better if they receive soft water.

Campsis x tagliabuana

Canna indica *hybrids*

Campsis x tagliabuana is ideal as a green cover on walls or over pergolas, where its thick foliage also provides shade.

It is possible to grow canna in containers and large dishes, but it can also be planted in beds if the rhizomes are stored to protect them from frost.

CANNA INDICA HYBRIDS
Canna

Family: Lily, *Liliaceae*
Native Habitat: Central and South America
Flowering Time: Early summer to autumn

A magnificent perennial with large, blue-green leaves and large flowers in terminal panicles, flame red, orange, or yellow. The roots are thickened, tuberous, and spreading. There are numerous varieties that differ in the color of leaves and flowers, and in height, which ranges from 1–6 ft. (30–200 cm).
Location: In summer, outdoors, sunny, and protected from wind. The rhizomes at 50–56°F (10–12°C) in winter.
Care: Sprout the rhizomes in standard soil mix in the spring; move them outside in late spring. Till the end of summer, water amply and feed weekly. After the first frost, cut back to 8 in. (20 cm) and store the rhizomes in a cool place.
Propagation: By division or by rhizomes.
Pests and Diseases: Aphids; rhizomes will rot if stored damp.
Uses: Container or bedding plant.

CAMPSIS
Trumpet creeper

Family: Indian Bear, *Bignoniaceae*
Native Habitat: China, United States
Flowering Time: Summer and fall

This deciduous, fast-growing vine bears compound leaves and trumpet-shaped flowers in orange or red. The flowers open in terminal umbellous clusters. *C. grandiflora*, from China, is not hardy in temperate climates. *C. radicans*, a North American species, and the shrubbier cultivar *C. x tagliabuana* can winter outdoors in milder areas.
Location: Full sun, protected from wind. Container plants in winter not below 41–50°F (5–10°C).
Care: Water amply in summer and feed weekly. Trumpet creeper needs a good pruning in the autumn; it regenerates vigorously.
Propagation: By soft cuttings or tip layering.
Pests and Diseases: Aphids, spider mites.
Uses: Climbing and espalier plant for southern walls; container plant for the garden room.

The trumpet creeper blooms on its new shoots, so it is best to prune it in the fall, after the flowers have faded.

Capsicum – Cassia

The dainty fruit of *Capsicum annuum* can be used as a spice, but it is very hot, so be cautious.

Carex brunnea is a proof of the fact that humble grasses can be valuable in decorating a room.

Since the *Caryopteris* hybrid 'Ferndown' begins blooming in mid-fall, it makes a useful complement to the usual summer flowers.

Capsicum annuum

Carex brunnea

Caryopteris x clandonensis

CAPSICUM ANNUUM
Red pepper

Family: Nightshade, *Solanaceae*
Native Habitat: Central and South America
Flowering Time: Spring to summer

The ornamental pepper is closely related to our vegetable peppers. An annual and not hardy in colder regions, this 16 in.- (40 cm-) high plant is intricately branched. After blooming, it produces fruit that can be ovate or pointed and can vary in color from red, orange, and yellow to violet and even white. *Capsicum* is usually offered in autumn in a fertilized state. The green parts of the plant are poisonous.
Location: Light, but not sunny; cool.
Care: Water modestly but regularly and feed weekly. To prevent the premature shriveling of the fruit, place the plant on wet pebbles.
Propagation: From seed in spring.
Pests and Diseases: Aphids, spider mites; gray mold if plant is too wet.
Uses: Ornamental plant for a light, not-too-warm room.

CAREX BRUNNEA
Sedge

Family: Sedge, *Cyperaceae*
Native Habitat: Southern Asia, Australia
Flowering Time: Seldom blooms in cultivation

C. brunnea 'Variegata' has 12 in.- (30 cm-) long, 1/8 in.- (3–4 mm-) wide, grasslike leaves. They are striped, green and white, making this a very good-looking ornamental plant.
Location: Very light, full sun is possible, warm. The plant needs high air humidity and in winter no less than 50–60°F (10–15°C).
Care: The root ball has to be kept moist all year so it never dries out. Spraying is helpful. Feed lightly once a month and repot in spring into standard potting mix.
Propagation: By division.
Pests and Diseases: Aphids and spider mites.
Uses: Foliage plant for a light, warm spot in a room or solarium. *C. morrowii*, the Japanese sedge, is also a suitable houseplant. This plant has to stand cool and shaded, and its root ball has to dry out somewhat between waterings.

CARYOPTERIS X CLANDONENSIS
Beard flower

Family: Verbena, *Verbenaceae*
Native Habitat: East Asia
Flowering Time: Late summer to late fall

This is a small, deciduous shrub with blue flowers that cluster umbel-like at the ends of the year-old shoots. The somewhat compact and very opulently blooming variety 'Kew Blue' is appropriate for a large container. Commercially, the varieties of this hybrid are widely offered.
Location: In summer, outdoors, sunny and out of the wind. In winter, light or shady, at 41–50°F (5–10°C).
Care: Water modestly in summer; keep somewhat dry rather than waterlogged; feed monthly till early fall. In winter, water more rarely, but do not dry out. Prune in spring to ensure bushiness.
Propagation: By cuttings in summer.
Pests and Diseases: Too much water will cause damage.
Uses: Plant for balcony and garden rooms.

Cassia siamea *in its native habitat*

How magnificent a plant *Cassia siamea* really is can be seen in this photograph of a "djohar" tree in tropical Asia.

Typical of *Cassia didymobotrya* are the compound leaves and the yellow, candlelike flowers.

Cassia didymobotrya

CASSIA
Cassia

Family: Bean, *Fabaceae*
Native Habitat: Tropics and subtropics
Flowering Time: Summer to late autumn; *Cassia didymobotrya* all year in an airy garden room

Cassia is a 3–10 ft.- (1–3 m-) high shrub with pinnately compound leaves. Its blooms are yellow. *C. carymbosa*, the most robust species, has golden yellow flowers. *C. didymobotrya*'s remarkable flowers are 12 in.- (30 cm-) high upright candles, also golden yellow. Nowadays, other, more delicate cassia species are available as seeds or at specialty nurseries. Many cassias are poisonous.

Location: Full sun, warm; in summer outdoors. In winter, light and cool; not under 50°F (10°C).
Care: Water generously in summer; in winter just keep the soil from drying out. Spring to early fall, feed weekly. You can prune anytime. Repot if needed in standard soil mix, using a generous-sized pot.
Propagation: By cuttings of still-herbaceous, non-woody shoots or from seed.
Pests and Diseases: Aphids on new shoots, whiteflies if kept too warm, molds if kept too wet in winter.
Uses: Container plant for balcony, patio, or sun room.

Cassia didymobotrya

167

Casuarina – Celosia

Beef wood may not be the most beautiful of container plants, but it is very interesting. In its homeland, the plant is used extensively along the seashore, as it is able to tolerate salt.

Since catharanthus is poisonous, it is a good idea to take extra care when pruning it.

The *Cattleya* hybrid 'Moneymaker' is regarded as a botanical treasure.

Casuarina equisetifolia

Catharanthus roseus

Cattleya *hybrid* 'Moneymaker'

CASUARINA EQUISETIFOLIA
Beef wood casuarina

Family: She oak, *Casuarinaceae*
Native Habitat: Southeast Asia, Australia
Flowering Time: Winter

This tree, which in its habitat will reach 100 ft. (30 m) in height, is only 5–7 ft. (150–200 cm) tall in cultivation. Its habit is reminiscent of enormous, intricately branched horsetails. The stunted scalelike leaves are interesting, as are the diminutive flowers, the female ones red spheres or cones, the male ones yellow-brown spikes.
Location: Full sun; outdoors in summer. Cool and light in winter at 41–50°F (5–10°C).
Care: In summer, water and feed only lightly, in winter just keep the root ball from drying out. Since it grows fast, casurina needs vigorous pruning.
Propagation: By cuttings under plastic or from seed.
Pests and Diseases: Unknown.
Uses: Container or garden room plant.

CATHARANTHUS ROSEUS
Catharanthus

Family: Dogbane, *Apocynaceae*
Native Habitat: Madagascar, tropical regions
Flowering Time: Early spring to fall

The leaves of this shrublike perennial are about 3 in. (8 cm) long and are marked by a white central rib. The flower is more than 1 in. (3 cm) wide; pink or white; it has a dark center. Usually raised as an annual, it is a poisonous plant.
Location: Light, warm, humid; in summer outdoors, protected from rain. Winter at no less than 54°F (12°C).
Care: In summer, water amply and feed biweekly. If kept in a room, spray often. Do not let the root ball dry out in winter. Prune in the spring and repot as needed.
Propagation: By tip cuttings in late summer.
Pests and Diseases: Rarely.
Uses: Flowering plant for a light, warm room, balcony, or patio.

CATTLEYA
Cattleya

Family: Orchid, *Orchidaceae*
Native Habitat: Tropical America
Flowering Time: Depending on species or variety, anytime

Nowadays, you can buy cattleya species, varieties, and even intergeneric hybrids, which are marked by an "x," e.g., x Brassolaeliocattleya or x Potinara. Cattleya grows in its own habitat (epiphytically on trees). Out of the creeping rhizome grow side shoots (pseudobulbs); these can be up to 12 in. (30 cm) long and they carry longish oval leaves and flowers in spikes. We distinguish two groups: the first has only one leaf per pseudobulb and large flowers; the second bears two or three leaves and much smaller, but prettier, flowers. Important members of the first group are *C. labiata*, *C. maxima*, and *C. massiae*. To the second group belong, among others *C. bicolor*, *C. bowringiana*, *C. forbesii*, and *C. granulosa*. Especially suited to home cultivation are the hybrids of cattleya and *Laelia*, the x Laeliocattleya hybrids. If you are

Once the shoots of the cattleya are fully formed, the plant is best placed in a slightly cooler situation; watering can also be slightly reduced. If kept too warm at this stage, the plant will form only leaves and no flowers.

The Most Beautiful Plants from A to Z

Cattleya skinneri

Celosia cristata

Such a luxuriant *Cattleya skinneri* will form the centerpiece of any conservatory.

The cockscomb and the plumed celosias are old-fashioned balcony plants, but they may make a comeback anytime soon.

CELOSIA CRISTATA
Cockscomb

Family: Amaranth, *Amaranthaceae*
Native Habitat: Tropical Africa
Flowering Time: Summer

Celosia is an annual, 6–27 in. (15–70 cm) high, whose curious inflorescence is vividly colored. The palette ranges from crimson through flame red and orange to lemon yellow. Botanically, the cockscomb is now *C. cristata* 'Cristata'; the "feathered" cockscomb is called *C. cristata* 'Plumosa.' The celosias, which grow up to 27 in. (70 cm) high, are distinguished from the low-growing varieties, better suited to planters and dishes.
Location: Sunny and warm outdoors.
Care: Water modestly and feed biweekly. Snip off dead blooms to encourage new ones.
Propagation: From seed; do not bury them, as they need light to germinate.
Pests and Diseases: Aphids.
Uses: Flowering annual for planters, dishes, and for bedding.

willing to make the necessary arrangements, you can host the most beautiful of orchids, e.g., *C. skinneri, C. gaskelliana, C. loddigesii,* or *C. dowiana.*
Location: Very light and airy, but protected from sun. By day 65–68°F (18–20°C); by night somewhat cooler. High atmospheric humidity is a must.
Care: Cattleya requires lots of water to grow. When the roots fill the pot, the plant needs orchid food once a month. Spray the leaves frequently during the summer. Reduce water during their rest period, keeping the root ball barely moist. Repot every 2–3 years in orchid soil. Those that bloom in fall or winter are repotted in spring, the others after they have bloomed.
Propagation: By division of the rhizome, once it has more than four side shoots. Rub the cuts with charcoal powder and plant the pieces in peat moss.
Pests and Diseases: Scale insects, spider mites, thrips. If kept too dark, no flowers form; if the air is too cool or too dry, the plant dies.
Uses: Magnificent flowering plant for light, warm, humid situations, greenhouses, and conservatories.

TIP

The flower of the cockscomb can be dried and will retain its fresh look for years.

Centradenia – Chamaecereus

Centradenia is a relative newcomer on the houseplant market. It makes a good hanging plant and can be used for underplanting; it would look very good under a standard-trained plant.

Cereus peruvianus must surely be the most popular columnar cactus.

The subtle beauty of ceropegia can be fully appreciated only when seen up close. It is enhanced if it is planted in an unusual container, such as this copper can from the Swiss canton Wallis.

Centradenia *'Cascade'*

Cereus peruvianus *'Monstrosus'*

Ceropegia woodii

CENTRADENIA
Centradenia

Family: Melastome, *Melastomataceae*
Native Habitat: Central America
Flowering Time: Spring to fall

Centradenia is a balcony flower with slightly arching branches. Stems are four-sided and densely covered with small, pointed leaves that are dark green, reddish, or red, according to the variety. The very numerous, small pink flowers appear in clusters.
Location: Light or partial shade; warm. In summer, outdoors; in winter, light and cool.
Care: Keep moist while it is growing; feed lightly every two weeks. Prune back in the fall. Keep free of frost in winter, and moist enough to prevent its drying out. Repot in spring.
Propagation: In summer, by cuttings.
Pests and Diseases: Scale insects and mealybugs.
Uses: Hanging plant for balconies, patios, and sun rooms.

CEREUS
Cereus

Family: Cactus, *Cactaceae*
Native Habitat: South America
Flowering Time: Summer and fall

This fast-growing columnar cactus may grow treelike or resemble a shrub. Its flowers open only at night. *C. jamacaru* 'Monstrosus' origin-ated in Brazil, where it reaches 33 ft. (10 m), but dwarf varieties are now available. *C. peruvianus* 'Monstrosus' has denser, red-brown thorns. *C. forbesii* is very beautiful, its thorns a whitish shade.
Location: Sunny; in summer out of doors. In winter cool (46°F (8°C)).
Care: Spring to fall, feed monthly and water sparingly. In winter, keep almost dry. Repot annually to prevent its becoming pot-bound.
Propagation: From seed or by cuttings, which root easily after they have dried a little.
Pests and Diseases: Mealybugs and scale insects.
Uses: Houseplant for a sunny, warm location.

CEROPEGIA WOODII
Ceropegia

Family: Milkweed, *Asclepiadaceae*
Native Habitat: South Africa
Flowering Time: Almost all year

The stems of ceropegia emerge from a 2 in.- (5 cm-) thick tuberous root. They are up to 7 ft. (2 m) long, wire thin, and bare; at intervals there are two fleshy, heart- or kidney-shaped leaves, light green with silver marbling on top, reddish underneath. The flowers appear singly and stand like little violet candles along the stem. The stems will root on the soil and form small tubers.
Location: Sunny; in summer outdoors, protected from wind. In winter not under 54°F (12°C).
Care: Keep moderately moist all year. To avoid waterlogging, ensure good drainage. Spring to fall, feed with cactus food every two weeks.
Propagation: By tuber pieces or by stem section cuttings, allowing cuts to dry out before planting.
Pests and Diseases: Rarely.
Uses: A hanging plant for a sunny situation. Good for hydroculture.

Cestrum elegans

Chamaecereus silvestrii

CESTRUM
Cestrum

Family: Nightshade, *Solanaceae*
Native Habitat: Tropical and subtropical America
Flowering Time: Depending on the species, spring to fall

Cestrum is an attractive evergreen container plant. *C. auranticum* is fairly common; it has yellow flowers that open in the fall. *C. elegans'* red flowers appear in spring; while the creamy white blossoms of 'Newellii' have an intoxicating fragrance, especially at night. Cestrum will bloom at intervals, following periods of rest. All parts of the plant are poisonous.
Location: Sunny and airy; in summer outdoors. In winter light at 41–50°F (5–10°C).
Care: In summer, water frequently and feed weekly. In winter, water just enough to preserve the leaves.

Instead of overwintering the plant in a light place, you can also prune it back and keep it relatively dark. Repot every spring in fresh soil, preferably in a mixture of half garden soil and half compost, or in a standard mix.
Propagation: By tip cuttings in spring.
Pests and Diseases: Aphids, whiteflies, gray mold, if kept too wet in the winter.
Uses: Container plant for a solarium; in summer for the terrace or balcony.

CHAMAECEREUS SILVESTRII
Peanut cactus

Family: Cactus, *Cactaceae*
Native Habitat: Western Argentina
Flowering Time: Spring and summer

Chamaecereus is a dwarf shrub with many eight-ribbed, light green branches as thick as a finger. They bear short thorns. The flowers are like short, 1.5 in.- (4 cm-) wide funnels, hairy and bright red. They open by day and close at night. Numerous hybrids with orange and yellow flowers are available.
Location: Sunny and warm in summer; light and cool in winter.
Care: In spring and summer, as soon as buds appear, water amply and feed every two weeks. Keep cool and light in winter to ensure plenty of flowers.
Propagation: By the offsets that develop on the shoots.
Pests and Diseases: Mealybugs, spider mites if kept in too dry or too stuffy an atmosphere.
Uses: Houseplant for a light location, or outdoors, in summer.

After blooming, cestrum may produce pea-sized, dark red, white, or almost black berries.

Chamaecereus silvestrii has been botanically reclassified as *Echinopsis.*

I plant my cestrum for the summer in a slotted, plastic bushel basket; it blooms much better this way.

Chamaedorea – Chamelaucium

Chamaedorea ernesti-augusti, with its beautiful broad leaves, is not yet generally available.

Chamaedorea elegans produces flowers when still young. They should be removed, because they take strength needed for growth.

Chamaedorea ernesti-augusti

CHAMAEDOREA ELEGANS
Pigmy Palm

Family: Palm, *Arecaceae*
Native Habitat: Central America
Flowering Time: All year

This is one of the best-loved palm trees, cherished for its graceful stem and for its fresh green, slightly arching fronds. Chamaedorea's yellow flowers start opening when it is young. The plant is dioecious; the flowers of the female plant are fragrant, those of the male are not.

Recently, *C. metallica,* a 3 ft.- (1 m-) high species with metallic leaves, has become available. Less common is *C. ernesti-augusti,* with its dense crown of upright to slightly arched fronds on slender stems. Its leaves are whole, wedge shaped, metallic green, serrated at the upper edges, and incised at the tip.

Location: Light or partial shade, warm (around 50°F (20°C)), humid. In summer outdoors. In winter cooler.

Care: In summer, water generously and spray occasionally. Spring to fall, feed with half-diluted plant food every two weeks. Dunking the plant weekly prevents its drying

Chamaedorea elegans

out. *C. metallica* needs less moist soil and less humid air. Repot when the roots grow over the edge of the tub.

Propagation: By offsets or from seeds, which can happen only if you have both a male and female plant. You can ensure pollination by using a little brush. Sprout the seeds in a shady, warm, moist spot. Plant three young seedlings in one pot to enhance the chances of producing plants of both sexes.

Pests and Diseases: Scale insects; spider mites if too dry or warm in winter. Root rot if waterlogged.

Uses: Container plant or for

planting in the conservatory. Good for a northern window or other shaded, cool places.

Chamaerops humilis

Chamelaucium uncinatum

Chamaerops humilis is unusually variable. There are variants with one stem and others that grow several. Previously, some of the plant's varieties were assigned to different species.

Chamelaucium uncinatum is not a well-known myrtle, but we hope it will find wider acceptance.

CHAMAEROPS HUMILIS
Mediterranean palm

Family: Palm, *Arecaceae*
Native Habitat: Southern Europe
Flowering Time: Spring and summer

This is the only palm native to Europe. It tends to grow several trunks and hence appears bushy.

The fan-shaped, blue-green leaves are deeply incised; their stems are armed with strong, sharply pointed thorns.
Location: Light or sunny; in summer outdoors. In winter light and cool (about 50°F (10°C)). The palm requires a lot of room.
Care: In summer, water generously and feed every two weeks; little watering in winter. If needed, repot in standard potting mix.
Propagation: From seeds, which take 2–3 months to sprout.
Pests and Diseases: Aphids if too warm, root rot if too wet in winter.
Uses: House and container plant; bedding plant for a cool conservatory.

CHAMELAUCIUM UNCINATUM
Chamelaucium

Family: Myrtle, Myrtaceae
Native Habitat: Australia
Flowering Time: In spring

Chamelaucium is an evergreen shrub, 3–7 ft. (1–2 m) in height. Its arching branches carry narrow, needle-like leaves and pink or white flowers in terminal clusters.
Location: Full sun; warm; in summer outdoors, but protected from rain. Light and cool in winter at 41–50°F (5–10°C).
Care: In summer keep evenly but moderately moist; feed only once a month with half-diluted fertilizer. Prune after flowering to ensure bushiness. Repot when needed in standard soil mix.
Propagation: By herbaceous cutting with bottom heating or from seed.
Uses: Very lovely flowering plant for a sunny, warm spot outside, in summer; in winter for a room or conservatory.

To prevent injuring yourself while moving the Mediterranean palm, it is best to tie up its thorny crown.

Chlorophytum – Chrysalidocarpus

In an appropriately large container, chlorophytum will produce so many hanging offsets that the plant seems hidden behind a curtain.

Chlorophytum's numerous white flowers are not especially showy.

CHLOROPHYTUM COMOSUM
Chlorophytum

Family: Lily, *Liliaceae*
Native Habitat: South Africa
Flowering Time: All year

This undemanding member of the lily family grows its leaves in dense rosettes. The leaves are 8–16 in. (20–40 cm) long, narrow, crisp, and striped in yellow or yellow green. The small, white, star-shaped flowers appear at the ends of yellow shoots; these later also carry the offset. The long yellow shoots are characteristic of this plant and can grow to 3 ft. (1 m), with many young plants hanging from their tips.

'Variegatum,' with its white or yellow stripes, is the one usually offered, while the green variety is seldom seen.

Location: Light or partial shade; at room temperature all year; it can summer outside, out of direct sun.
Care: Keep evenly moist, not wet, and feed every week in summer. Repot only when the root crown protrudes from the container.
Propagation: By planting the offsets.
Pests and Diseases: Aphids, mealybugs; brown leaves when roots are too wet or too dry. Root rot if waterlogged.
Uses: Green plant for columns or hanging baskets; in summer for balconies or patios.

Chlorophytum comosum

Close-up of the flower of chlorophytum

Choisya ternata

CHOISYA TERNATA
Mexican orange

Family: Rue, *Rutaceae*
Native Habitat: Mexico
Flowering Time: Early summer, spring in the conservatory

The Mexican orange is about 6–7 ft. (2 m) high, an evergreen shrub with leathery, shiny green leaves that spread like fingers. The terminal or axial umbels of the white flower smell like oranges.
Location: Light or sunny, warm; in summer also outside. In winter at 41–50°F (5–10°C).
Care: All summer, water regularly, more amply in a sunny position. Use soft water; feed monthly. Cut watering drastically in winter. Prune vigorously. Repot in late winter. Assure good drainage.
Propagation: By tip cuttings, with bottom heating.
Pests and Diseases: Rarely. If too warm in winter, spider mites.
Uses: Container plant for a light position; use outdoors in summer; plant in the conservatory.

Chrysalidocarpus lutescens

CHRYSALIDOCARPUS LUTESCENS
Areca palm

Family: Palm, *Arecaceae*
Native Habitat: Madagascar
Flowering Time: Rarely blooms under cultivation

This is a low-growing palm, seldom reaching more than 6–7 ft. (2 m) in cultivation. Its fronds are comblike, light green, and slightly arched.
The plant's new branches grow right from the roots, so it becomes quite bushy; it also grows offsets. It may still be found under its old name, *Areca*.
Location: Light, no sun, and warm all year; never under 65°F (18°C).

Care: During growth, keep the root ball evenly moist; in a warm room, there can be water in the saucer. Spring to fall, feed weekly. In winter, spray the fronds frequently. Repot older plants only when the roots completely fill the pot.
Propagation: From seed or by offsets.
Pests and Diseases: Spider mites if air is too dry; yellow leaves and brown leaf spots also indicate that the plant is kept too dry.
Uses: House and container plant for greenhouse or for a conservatory. Excellent for hydroculture.

The Mexican orange has acquired a reputation as an excellent garden plant because, planted in a bed, it can withstand temperatures down to –18°F (–10°C).

The butterfly palm thrives outdoors in summer if kept in a shady spot.

The Mexican orange is a sturdy alternative to the more finicky citrus trees. If you do not have an optimal winter location for your potted *Choisya*, it will survive in a dark place, if it is just above freezing.

Chrysanthemum – Cistus

The shrubby marguerite chrysanthemum is usually treated as an annual because of constant problems with overwintering.

Although the genus of many so-called chrysanthemums has in fact been changed by botanists, gardeners and chrysanthemum collectors will continue to use the old names for a long time to come.

Chrysanthemum frutescens

Chrysanthemum indicum *hybrids*

CHRYSANTHEMUM INDICUM HYBRIDS
Chrysanthemum

Family: Aster, *Asteraceae*
Native Habitat: China
Flowering Time: Midsummer to early winter

This low-growing perennial has deeply incised leaves and, in its original form, small, simple flowers. Among the hybrids, which are now called Dentranthema Grandiflora, however, the flowers are double or semi-double and the colors include white, yellow, pink, red, violet, and all shades in between. These cultivars make good standards.
Location: Light, not too sunny; cool. In winter, let it rest at 37–41°F (3–5°C).
Care: Keep the root ball evenly moist, feed once a week. Remove dead blooms. This plant is usually raised as an annual.
Propagation: By tip cuttings in spring.
Pests and Diseases: Aphids; spider mites if kept too warm.
Uses: Container and balcony plant for fall; grave ornamentation.

CHRYSANTHEMUM FRUTESCENS
Marguerite chrysanthemum

Family: Aster, *Asteraceae*
Native Habitat: Canary Isles
Flowering Time: Summer

This subshrub has green or gray-green leaves that are finely toothed or more roughly serrated. In summer it is covered with white, yellow, or pink flowers. Correctly referred to as *Argyranthemum frutescens*, the new light pink 'Flamingo' is very attractive. These mums are very nice as standards.
Location: Light and sunny; in summer outdoors. In winter at 41–50°F (5–10°C).

Care: Water the plant freely while it is growing and feed it once a week in summer. Promote flowering by pinching off dead blooms. Move it to a light, frost-free spot in late fall. Water moderately in winter. In the spring, repot in standard soil mix. Prune young plants several times to force a bushy form.
Propagation: By tip cuttings in spring.
Pests and Diseases: Aphids, spider mites; if kept too wet in winter, root fungi can result.
Uses: Balcony and container plant; good for the garden room.

A standard-trained chrysanthemum

CISSUS
Grape ivy

Family: Grape, *Vitaceae*
Native Habitat: Tropics and subtropics
Flowering Time: Seldom blooms in cultivation

The grape ivy is an evergreen leaf plant with twining shoots. *C. antarcatica*, the kangaroo vine, has toothed, egg-shaped leaves, while *C. rhombifolias*'s leaves are tripartite, long-stemmed, and matted in red underneath. *C. striata*, the striped cissus, twines less and has smaller, leathery leaves. *C. discolor*, from the tropical forests of Java, has beautiful elongated, heart-shaped leaves that are scarlet with light markings on top and colored dark red underneath

Cissus rhombifolia *'Ellen Danica'*

Location: Light or partial shade, no strong sun; warm (*C. discolor*, humid). In winter somewhat cooler, but not under 54°F (12°C).
Care: Keep moderately moist and feed weekly in summer. In winter, in a cool place, water just to prevent drying out. If not used as hanging plants, cissus require a small trellis.
Propagation: By tip and stem cuttings in spring with bottom heat.
Pests and Diseases: Scale insects, spider mites; leaves fall if too dry or too wet. Brown spots indicate too much water.
Uses: A beautiful hanging or climbing plant for a room or a garden room. *C. discolor* for an enclosed window greenhouse.

Cistus ladanifer

CISTUS
Rock rose

Family: Rock rose, *Cistaceae*
Native Habitat: Southern Europe, North Africa
Flowering Time: Spring to late summer

Cistus is a 3–7 ft.- (1–2 m-) high, profusely blooming evergreen shrub. Some generally available varieties are *C. x aguilari* (blooms white); *C. ladaniferus* (the gum cistus, blooms white with brown spots); *C. laurifolius* (the laurel cistus, has fragrant white flowers with yellow spots); and *C. x purpureus* (blooms pink with brown spots).
Location: Full sun; in summer best outdoors. In winter, light and airy at 41–50°F (5–10°C).
Care: During growth, keep evenly moist and feed weekly till the end of summer. In winter, water just to keep the leaves healthy. Prune after it has bloomed.
Propagation: From seed or by cuttings (hybrids).
Pests and Diseases: Aphids and gray mold.
Uses: Container plant for a sunny spot or the garden room.

Cissus rhombifolia, the Venezuela grape ivy, is a magnificent and undemanding plant, well suited to a hanging basket or to green a lattice or as a room divider.

England is blessed with a maritime climate, which permits the rock rose to establish itself in the garden; there, cistus has many admirers.

Cissus can be used to turn a dark corner green.

Citrus – Clematis

The origin of the word "orangery" goes back several centuries, when special houses were built to protect the precious and imported citrus trees of kings and nobles—no wonder, considering the fruit!

The intense fragrance of the flowers of all the citrus trees is also carried by the leaves. If you rub a leaf between your fingers, its scent may even tell you whether it is an orange or a lemon.

Citrus mitis *loaded with fruit*

CITRUS
Citrus

Family: Rue, *Rutaceae*
Native Habitat: Asia, cultivated worldwide in the tropics and subtropics
Flowering Time: Depending on species and cultivation, anytime

Citrus is an evergreen, richly branched shrub that grows to about 10 ft. (3 m). Its leaves are oval, dark green, and leathery; its flowers are small, white or creamy, and intensely fragrant.

From the wealth of species, varieties, and cultivars, a small selection:

C. deliciosa and *C. reticulata*, both tangerines, are robust, compact, dark green shrubs. Tangerines can be containerized or set out in a cool conservatory. *C. limon*, the lemon tree, adapts well to containers, but tends to grow leggy. 'Meyeri' is a variety that remains compact and is preferable. *Fortunella margarita*, the kumquat, thrives in any sunny

Citrus aurantium

spot. Especially lovely is the variety 'Variegata' with white- or yellow-variegated foliage. *C. x paradisi*, the grapefruit, is a cross between the pomelo and the orange; even young plants produce clusters of fruit. The leaves of *C. sinensis*, the orange tree, are smaller than those of the lemon, but it blooms much more generously. As a standard-trained cultivar, dealers offer the calamondine, *x Citrofortunella microcarpa*, also called *C. mitis*, which needs a heated location. As houseplants, use the dwarf varieties, offered as "orange trees."

Location: In summer, best sunny and protected. In winter, light and airy at 39–46°F (4–8°C). "Orange trees," light all year, at a constant 55–68°F (13–18°C); free of drafts, summer outdoors.

Care: Keep evenly moist with soft water and feed every two weeks. Prevent waterlogging by ensuring good drainage in the container. Prune anytime the plants get too leggy.

Propagation: By tip cuttings with bottom heat (difficult), or by air layering. Seedlings often revert to the wild form and may bloom only after many years, or never.

Pests and Diseases: Scale insects, spider mites; chlorosis indicates lack of iron due to hard water; leaf loss means that the p·· .it is too wet or too dry and warm. Brown leaves are a sign of cold.

Uses: For containers and conservatories; the calamondine also for the windowsill.

TIP

Citrus trees that stand near stone fruit trees, and especially near apples, lose their leaves.

The Most Beautiful Plants from A to Z

Cleistocactus smaragdiflorus

CLEISTOCACTUS
Cleistocactus

Family: Cactus, *Cactaceae*
Native Habitat: South America
Flowering Time: Spring to summer

The slow-growing, densely thorned, or matted cleistocacti can grow up to 6–7 ft. (2 m) high. They tend to branch near the ground.

   C.baumannii blooms in the color range between scarlet and orange. *C. smaragdiflorus*, with dark thorns, develops flowers when it is only 8 in. (20 cm) high: they are light red with an emerald edge. *C. strausii*, bristled in white, has crimson flower spikes.
Location: Sunny; in summer outside, but protected from rain. In winter at 50–54°F (10–12°C).
Care: Keep moderately moist with soft water; spray often in the evening; give cactus food once a week. In winter drier, but not dried out.
Propagation: By cuttings or from seed.
Pests and Diseases: Mealybugs.
Uses: Houseplant for a sunny spot.

The large-flowering clematis 'The President' in a container

CLEMATIS
Clematis

Family: Buttercup, *Ranunculaceae*
Native Habitat: The Alps, China
Flowering Time: Early summer

Clematis climbs using its twining leaf stems. The lower-growing species are best suited for containers, such as *C. alpina*, the Alpine clematis, with wide-spreading flowers in shades of blue, and *C. macropetala*, with flowers in blues and bluish violets as wide as 4 in. (10 cm). Both species grow about 6–10 ft. (2–3 m) high and are available with double and simple flowers in shades of pink and blue as well as in white. The plant is poisonous.

Location: Light or partial shade. The root crown needs dark shade, the leaves need light.
Care: Repot plants you buy 4–6 in. (10–15 cm) deeper than they were, in standard soil mix or in a slightly alkaline humus mix. Water very freely, but avoid waterlogging. From spring to the end of summer, feed monthly. Prune after flowering or in fall. Protect younger container plants from frost. Plants all need a lattice for support.
Propagation: By herbaceous cuttings with bottom heating.
Pests and Diseases: Clematis wilt.
Uses: For patios, balconies, and to shade the garden room.

With good care, cleistocactus blooms willingly, as this example of *Cleistocactus smaragdiflorus* shows: it has developed fruit.

Clematis is hardy in the temperate regions, where it also is a favorite container plant. Gardeners find clematis a bit unpredictable, especially the large-blooming varieties.

The Alpine clematis can be allowed to spread, as, for example, in a wide tub; the flowers will cascade from its rim like a colored waterfall.

Clerodendrum – Clusia

Clerodendrum thomsoniae is a beautiful but demanding potted plant, especially where atmospheric humidity is concerned; the same goes for its larger relative, *C. speciosissimum*, which requires a tub or other large container.

In England's maritime climate, the cleyera is hardy and can reach 10 ft. (3 m) in height.

Two well-known *Clianthus formosus* varieties are 'Flamingo,' which is pink, and 'Red Cardinal.'

Clerodendrum speciosissimum

Clerodendrum thomsoniae

Cleyera japonica

Clianthus formosus

CLERODENDRUM THOMSONIAE
Bleeding heart, glorybower

Family: Verbena, *Verbenaceae*
Native Habitat: West Africa
Flowering Time: Spring to early summer

This is a climbing shrub with dark green leaves. The red corolla of the flower sits above an inflated white calyx.
Location: Light, no strong sun; warm and humid. In winter, light and cool (50–60°F (10–15°C)).
Care: Keep plant fairly dry after the leaves fall. Toward the end of winter, prune back by one-third and repot in standard soil. Move it to a warmer spot and increase watering. Keep evenly moist in summer and feed weekly after flowering; also decrease water at that time.
Propagation: By tip cuttings with bottom heating. Prune young plants several times.
Pests and Diseases: Flowers drop if the air is too dry; leaf spot, if roots are very cold.
Uses: For a light place in a room; for a trellis in the conservatory.

CLEYERA JAPONICA
Cleyera

Family: Tea, *Theaceae*
Native Habitat: Japan, Korea, China
Flowering Time: Early summer

Cleyera is an evergreen shrub or small tree with leaves about 4 in. (10 cm) long and 1.5 in. (4 cm) wide. Its flowers are yellow-white and very fragrant. The variety 'Tricolor' is usually the one sold because of its irregularly colored, yellow-to-gold leaves, with fine touches of green.
Location: Light or partial shade and cool. In summer if possible outside. In winter at 50–54°F (10–12°C).
Care: Keep the plant moderately moist with soft water, and spray often. Every two weeks, administer nonalkaline fertilizer. In winter, water only occasionally.
Propagation: By tip cuttings under plastic. Prune young plants several times to achieve a bushy form.
Pests and Diseases: Aphids.
Uses: A decorative foliage plant for light, cool rooms, staircases, landings, and garden rooms.

CLIANTHUS FORMOSUS
Parrotbeak

Family: Bean, *Fabaceae*
Native Habitat: New Zealand
Flowering Time: During spring

Clianthus formosus is an evergreen shrub with compound leaves, that grows to about 6–7 ft. (2 m) in height. Its scarlet flower is reminiscent of crab claws. The variety 'Alba' blooms white. Despite its exotic flower and its pretty, feathery leaves, *Clianthus formosus* is not yet established as a container plant.
Location: Light and sunny; in summer outdoors, protected from rain. In winter, cool at 50°F (10°C).
Care: In summer, keep evenly moist and feed every week. In winter, water very moderately and repot in spring in standard soil.
Propagation: By tip cuttings with bottom heating and with very high atmospheric humidity.
Pests and Diseases: Clianthus can be killed by waterlogging.
Uses: Tub plant for the conservatory.

THE MOST BEAUTIFUL PLANTS FROM A TO Z

Clivia miniata 'Citrina'

CLIVIA MINIATA
Clivia, scarlet Kafir lily

   ☠

Family: Lily, *Liliaceae*
Native Habitat: South Africa
Flowering Time: Early to late spring

Clivia is about 20 in. (50 cm) high. Out of a thick stem resembling an onion, the shiny, dark green leaves grow in two parallel arching sheaves that bend in opposite directions. Between them, a magnificent flower stem pushes up in the spring, carrying an upright cluster of 12–20 red or orange, funnel-shaped blossoms. 'Citrina' blooms yellowish white, 'Burvenich' and 'Striata' are variegated. *C. nobilis*, the daintier sister of *C. miniata*, has narrower leaves, smaller flowers, and is very hard to find.

The latex of the plant is poisonous.
Location: Light, no intense sun. In summer outdoors in the shade; in winter light and cool (46–54°F (8–12°C)).
Care: In summer keep moist; from spring to late summer feed every two weeks; in winter keep cool and rather dry. The plant rests through fall and winter; after that, watering should increase, but

slowly or the emerging buds will get caught among the leaves. When the flower stem is 4 in. (10 cm) long, move the plant to a warmer place and water more, but beware of waterlogging. Do not turn the pot at all; cut each stem after it has flowered to prevent the plant's energy going into fruit formation. Wipe the leaves now and then with a wet cloth. Repot every 2–3 years in standard soil mix.
Propagation: By offsets with at least four leaves.
Pests and Diseases: Mealybugs, scale insects; brown leaf tips indicate too much water; pale leaves and the absence of offsets mean more fertilizer is needed.
Uses: A beautiful flowering plant for an east or west window. Ideal for hydroculture.

Flower of the scarlet Kafir lily

Clusia rosea

CLUSIA ROSEA
Clusia

Family: Magosteen, *Clusiaceae*
Native Habitat: Southern United States, Mexico
Flowering Time: Seldom blooms in cultivation

This treelike or shrubby plant grows epiphytically on trees or between rocks in the wild; it looks like the rubber plant (*Ficus elastica*). Rough, leathery, shiny, dark green leaves, up to 12 in. (30 cm) long, sit on thick branches. The flowers, like large pink camellias, are seldom seen on cultivated plants. Both 'Marginata' and 'Aurea variegata' are variegated.
Location: Very light, not sunny; warm all year, even in winter not under 68°F (20°C).
Care: Keep moderately moist with lukewarm, soft water; spray frequently and feed biweekly with half-diluted plant food.
Propagation: By tip cuttings with bottom heating (77–86°F (25–30°C)).
Pests and Diseases: Rarely.
Uses: Foliage plant for light, warm rooms; suited to hydroculture.

Over the years, clivia will grow too big and heavy for a windowsill; then it is time to plant it in a container.

Clusia rosea resembles the rubber plant, *Ficus elastica*, in more than its exterior; the two plants require similar care.

Clusia rosea

Cobaea – Codiaeum

Cobaea scandens was first introduced to Europe in 1709.

Coconut palms are mass marketed, and anyone can buy one; if you are able to keep one alive for many years, however, you can consider yourself blessed with a green thumb.

Cobaea scandens

COBAEA SCANDENS
Cobaea, cup and saucer vine

Family: Phlox, *Polemoniaceae*
Native Habitat: Mexico
Flowering Time: Summer and fall

Cobaea is a climbing shrub, raised by nurseries as an annual; in a tub, it grows 10–16 ft. (3–5 m) high. The leaves are doubly or triply compound; the bell flowers greenish, changing to violet. Blue, red, and white cultivars are available.
Location: Sunny; in summer outdoors. In winter in a cool garden room.
Care: In summer, water generously and feed biweekly. Offer some climbing support and snip off dead blooms to encourage more. Kept in a conservatory, the plant will last several years.
Propagation: From seed in early spring with bottom heat of 65°F (18°C).
Pests and Diseases: Aphids.
Uses: A fast-growing climbing plant that offers an attractive screen for balcony or patio or for the conservatory.

By far the best and easiest way to propagate *Cocos nucifera* is to buy a sprouted coconut from a nursery.

Cocos nucifera

COCOS NUCIFERA
Coconut

Family: Palm, *Arecaceae*
Native Habitat: Tropical regions
Flowering Time: Hardly blooms in cultivation

In the tropics, the coconut palm is a 100 ft. (30 m) tree and is cultivated and valued for its fruit. In our living rooms, the plant barely survives for a year because we buy it when it is still in infancy, dependent for nourishment on its seed, the coconut.
Location: Year-round, humid, warm, and very light. In summer protect from strong sun. In winter not under 65°F (18°C), and if possible, under a plant light.
Care: Keep the root ball moist with soft, lukewarm water. In winter, reduce watering, but spray more. During growth, feed biweekly with weak plant-food solution; provide ample fresh air.
Propagation: From nuts, which must lie in moist peat for about six months with bottom heat. Pot only when roots have appeared. Not easy.
Pests and Diseases: Spider mites, thrips; brown leaves mean that the air is too dry.
Uses: A distinguished plant for a light, warm and airy room; best in a conservatory.

Small-leafed variety of Codiaeum variegatum

moist and spray often. Use soft water. Feed lightly once a week. In winter reduce watering. Water in the saucer is poison in all seasons; good drainage is essential.

Propagation: By tip cuttings, with bottom heating of 77–86°F (25–30°C) and with high atmospheric humidity; or by air layering.

Pests and Diseases: Spider mites, aphids, and mealybugs; leaf fall and leaf damage if kept too cool and dry.

Uses: A sumptuous foliage plant for light, warm, and humid environments, such as the greenhouse or planted in the conservatory; suited for hydroculture.

Croton is sometimes called the "miracle shrub," an appellation well deserved, as few other houseplants can offer the spectrum of leaf colors, the range of variegation, the markings, and the many leaf forms. Here are the leaves of 'Geduldig,' 'Goldfinger,' 'Aucubafolia,' 'Norma,' and 'Van Ostensee.'

CODIAEUM VARIEGATUM VAR. PICTUM
Leaf croton

Family: Spurge, *Euphorbiaceae*
Native Habitat: Southeast Asia
Flowering Time: Seldom blooms in cultivation

The leaves of this splendid foliage plant vary in color and shape: wide or narrow, whole, lobed, or even rolled up. The colors adopted by the leathery, shiny leaves range from yellow through green and orange to purple to almost black. Spotted, veined, speckled, and striped leaves are found among the many cultivars. The latex is slightly poisonous and affects skin and mucous membranes.

Location: Year-round, light, warm, and humid; no direct sun. Avoid all drafts. During the winter dormancy, keep cooler (at 60–65°F (16–18°C)).
Care: During growth, keep evenly

Various leaf forms

The "miracle shrub" in its home setting

Codonanthe
crassifolia

Codonanthe – Coleus

Coffea arabica

CODONANTHE CRASSIFOLIA
Codonanthe

Family: Gesneriad, *Gesneriaceae*
Native Habitat: Tropical America
Flowering Time: Spring to summer

Codonanthe is an evergreen shrub with hanging shoots, leathery, elliptical leaves, and white flowers. Their calyx is reddish; the fruit is a red berry.
Location: Light or partial shade, warm and humid. In winter 60°F (15°C).
Care: Water the root ball sparingly and only after it has dried out; feed moderately every two weeks. Spray frequently.
Propagation: By tip cuttings or division with bottom heat.
Pests and Diseases: Aphids.
Uses: A hanging plant for a light, warm, humid position.

COFFEA ARABICA
Coffee

Family: Gesneriad, *Gesneriaceae*
Native Habitat: Tropical Africa
Flowering Time: Summer

The coffee bush, an evergreen shrub with large, shiny leaves, can reach 6–7 ft. (2 m) as a houseplant. The small, fragrant star flowers are pretty and especially so are the red, cherrylike fruit.

Unfortunately, the plant blooms only in its third or fourth year.

The dwarf coffee bush, *C. arabica* 'Nana,' remains smaller, blooms more richly, and grows more slowly.
Location: Year-round light, airy, and out of strong sun; warm (65–68°F (18–20°C)) and humid.
Care: In summer, water generously with soft water and feed biweekly with nonalkaline food. In winter, water moderately. Moist air can be maintained by frequent spraying and by placing on wet pebbles.

Propagation: By tip cuttings and from seed.
Pests and Diseases: Scale insects, spider mites; brown or black leaf tips are due to dry air.
Uses: Smaller cultivars for the living area; larger ones for the conservatory or greenhouse.

Flower of the coffee bush

TIP

I have had fun raising coffee bushes from the seeds of my own plant. With bottom heating to 86°F (30°C), it took about four weeks for the first sprouts to show their green tips.

THE MOST BEAUTIFUL PLANTS FROM A TO Z

Planter with crocus, erica, asters, and grasses

Coleus blumei hybrids and asparagus

COLCHICUM AUTUMNALE
Autumn crocus

Family: Lily, *Liliaceae*
Native Habitat: Europe, Asia Minor, North Africa
Flowering Time: Late summer and fall

Crocus is a bulblike plant; its mauve flowers appear long before the leaves. As houseplants, crocus are made to "bloom dry." Best suited to this process are the large-flowering garden hybrids, such as 'The Giant' (pinkish mauve), 'Lilac Wonder' (lilac), or 'Waterlily' (rosy lilacs and double). Place the bulbs in a flat dish; there, without water and soil, they will sprout and display their pretty flowers.
Location: Sunny.
Care: The bulbs are laid out in late summer, and after they have bloomed they are quickly moved into the garden. Plant them about 4 in. (10 cm) deep and cover them over the winter. Crocus will grow leaves in the spring, which have to turn yellow and die off before being cut. At the end of summer, the bulbs are once again dug up and brought into the house.
Propagation: By bulbs or from seed.
Pests and Diseases: None.
Uses: Dry blooming plant for a room or the balcony; garden plant.

COLEUS BLUMEI HYBRIDS
Coleus

Family: Mint, *Laminaceae*
Native Habitat: Tropical Africa and Asia
Flowering Time: Summer and fall

This foliage plant with square stems and exquisitely colored and marked leaves grows 1-2 ft. (30-60 cm) high. No other houseplant can outdo it in the spectrum of its colors. Its bluish nettle-flowers, however, are quite modest.
Location: All year as light as possible without noon sun. In summer warm; in winter at 50–54°F (10–12°C).
Care: Spring to fall, water freely with soft water; feed monthly. Keep fairly dry in winter. In spring, prune back vigorously and repot. Generally, coleus is raised as an annual.
Propagation: By tip cuttings or seeding, which will produce ever new color variations. Cuttings always resemble the mother plant. Prune young plants for bushiness.
Pests and Diseases: Aphids, spider mites, whiteflies; leaves fall if too cool; legginess is due to a dark position.
Uses: Foliage plant for a light spot in a room; for balcony planters.

Autumn crocus, with its soft violet flowers, can be the centerpiece of a balcony box in the fall.

The leaves of coleus shine more beautifully outdoors because they receive the light they need to develop their colors.

Red-flowering Columnea hybrid

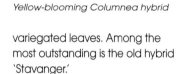

Yellow-blooming Columnea hybrid

COLUMNEA
Columnea

Family: Gesneriad, *Gesneriaceae*
Native Habitat: Tropical Central and South America
Flowering Time: Depending on the species, late summer to spring

Columnea is a lovely flowering evergreen; its creeping or hanging shoots carry small, dark green, fleshy leaves. Among this dense foliage sit the tubular red-to-orange flowers, which are especially spectacular and large in the hybrids. Several species are available: *C. x banksii, C. gloriosa,* with its cultivar 'Purpurea,' *C. hirta,* or *C. microphylla* 'Variegata,' with variegated leaves. Among the most outstanding is the old hybrid 'Stavanger.'

Location: Light or partial shade; no direct sun. Do not move outside; keep warm all year.
Care: Keep evenly but moderately moist with soft water at room temperature. Spray often or place on wet pebbles. Give calcium-free plant food biweekly in summer. A rest period of one month at 54–59°F (12–15°C) in the winter ensures the formation of new buds. Once these are fully formed, move the plant to a warmer location.
Propagation: By tip or stem cuttings with bottom heating.
Pests and Diseases: Spider mites, whiteflies. Dry air and drafts will cause leaf loss. Excessive wetness can lead to gray mold. The plant cannot tolerate calcium in either the water or the fertilizer.
Uses: A very beautiful hanging plant for a warm, humid room; ideal for window greenhouses and for hydroponics.

To stimulate the growth of new flower-bearing shoots, I prune back the branches of my columnea quite vigorously after it has bloomed.

THE MOST BEAUTIFUL PLANTS FROM A TO Z

Convallaria majalis

CONVALLARIA MAJALIS
Lily of the valley

Family: Lily, *Liliaceae*
Native Habitat: Europe, Asia
Flowering Time: Spring; winter, if horticulturally forced

Lily of the valley is not really a houseplant, but a garden and medicinal plant, poisonous in all its parts. Occasionally in the late fall or winter, one can buy *Convallaria* sprouts, young shoots with roots and buds. Sprouts preserved from the previous spring, these young plants were kept in cool storage and are sometimes sold as "chilled" plants.
Location: Partial or full shade; grow at 68–77°F (20–25°C). When grown, move to a cooler location.
Care: Plant the sprouts in peat-rich soil and place the pot in a warm, dark place. Move plants into the light when they reach 4 in. (10 cm) and keep them evenly moist.
Propagation: You can try it with offshoots from your garden, but the commercial sprouts are more reliable.
Pests and Diseases: Gray mold if too wet.
Uses: A flowering gift at Christmas.

Convolvulus sabatius

CONVOLVULUS SABATIUS
Convolvulus glorybind

Family: Morning glory, *Convolvulaceae*
Native Habitat: Southern Europe, North Africa
Flowering Time: Late spring to autumn

This subshrub grows thin shoots as long as 3.2 ft. (1 m); they are set with small, roundish, silvery-green leaves. When in bloom, convolvulus is covered with numberless, blue, violet, or pink funnel-like flowers. They open by day and close toward evening.
Location: In summer full sun. In winter light and cool at 50°F (10°C).
Care: In summer, keep moderately moist; feed once a week. Snip off wilted blooms regularly to promote both more flowers and denser branching. Before moving the plant for the winter, prune back all shoots. Water just enough to prevent the roots from actually drying out. In spring, repot and keep warmer till it is time to move the plant outside.
Propagation: By cuttings in winter, or from seed.
Pests and Diseases: Aphids and spider mites.
Uses: A hanging plant for balcony planters or for a pergola; very good cascading from a column.

After they stop blooming, lilies of the valley can be planted in the garden, where they usually continue to flourish.

The full beauty of the flowers of *Convolvulus sabatius* becomes apparent only when they are looked at up close.

Used as a creeper in the garden, glorybind adapts very well.

Cordyline – Crocus

The family ties between *Cordyline* and dracaena are especially clear in the narrow-leafed species *Cordyline indivisa*.

Cordyline fruticosa and its varieties are so well known that you do not need to search for them long in nurseries.

Cordyline indivisa

Location: Light, no direct sun; warm, not under 64°F (18°C). *C. australis* and *C. indivisa* can summer outside in the sun. In winter, 35–50°F (2–10°C).

Care: Keep evenly moist without overwatering. Administer fertilizer for green plants once a week from spring to fall and once a month in winter. *C. australis* and *C. indivisa* need to be fed only monthly. Repot as needed in loose soil.

Propagation: By stem cuttings placed horizontally in sand or by air layering. *C. australis* and *C. indivisa* by tip cuttings or from seed.

Pests and Diseases: Spider mites, thrips, scale insects.

Uses: A beautiful foliage plant for warm rooms, enclosed window greenhouses, and for heated conservatories. Suited to hydroponics, *C. australis* and *C. indivisa* also make good container plants for cool conservatories, on landings, and in stairways.

CORDYLINE
Dracaena; Ti plant

Family: Agave, *Agavaceae*
Native Habitat: South East Asia, Australia, New Zealand
Flowering Time: Rarely blooms in cultivation

Cordyline is related to the *Dracaena* and is constantly mistaken for it. The difference is in the roots: those of *Dracaena* are yellow, those of *Cordyline* are white and fleshy. The varieties of *C. fruticosa* have magnificently colored leaves: 'Amabilis' (wide, dark green leaves with white or red spots); 'Firebrand' (crimson ovals with light veins); 'Red Edge' (small leaves in red); and 'Tricolor' (green-, yellow-, and red-flecked leaves).

The genus also includes some species that resemble yucca, which make good container or cool garden room plants: the single-stemmed *C. australis* has leaves up to 3.2 ft. (1 m) long; they rise arching from the stem, which branches only after the plant has bloomed— but that hardly ever happens in cultivation. 'Atropurpurea' is a variegated form.

C. indivisa, which also has narrow leaves, never branches at all.

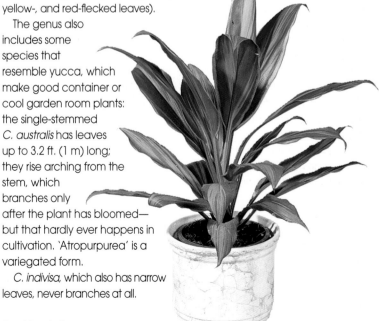

Cordyline fruticosa

Crassula 'Morgan's Beauty'

CRASSULA
Crassula; stonecrop

Family: Stonecrop, *Crassulaceae*
Native Habitat: South Africa
Flowering Time: Spring and summer or in winter

Succulent shrubs with thick, fleshy leaves. *C. arborescens*, jade tree, reaches about 3.2 ft. (1 m) in cultivation. The branched, thick stems carry oval leaves, narrower at the tip; they are whitish gray with red edges. The pink flower spikes appear in summer, but *C. arborescens* seldom blooms as a house plant.

C. exilis ssp. *cooperi* is barely 4 in. (10 cm) high; it grows in massed rosettes of light green leaves with dark dots.

C. perfoliata var. *falcata*, is sold as 'Morgan's Beauty,' a cultivar with white-gray leaves and very beautiful red flowers.

C. muscosa syn. *C. lycopodioides* has square, irregularly branched stems, much like shoelaces, covered with small, green, scalelike leaves in four rows, like roof tiles. The modest, white flowers sit in the leaf axils.
Location: Light and sunny all year;

in summer outdoors, protected from rain. In winter cool at 50-59°F (10-15°C).
Care: Water sparingly in summer; keep almost dry or dry in winter, depending on how cool you keep the plant. During growth, fertilize once a month.
Propagation: By tip or leaf cuttings that should dry out for a few days before being planted; or from seed.
Pests and Diseases: Aphids, mealybugs; root and stem rot if too wet.
Uses: Lovely leaf plant for a windowsill, container, or sun room.

Crassula arborescens

Forced crocus and tulips on a window bench

CROCUS
Crocus

Family: Lily, *Liliaceae*
Native Habitat: Europe, Asia Minor
Flowering Time: Spring

In general, crocus is a garden and balcony plant. As a houseplant, you can use, among others, *C. vernus* for the many colors of its cultivars.
Location: Light but not sunny.
Care: Plant the bulbs in the fall in humus-rich garden soil and place in a cool, dark cellar. When the shoots are 2 in. (5 cm) long, sometime in winter, move the plants to a cool, light room so they form buds. Move them to the windowsill when the buds show about one-third of their length. Water very sparingly and do not feed.
Propagation: By removing the young bulbs and planting them.
Pests and Diseases: Aphids; root rot when too cool and too damp.
Uses: A spring greeting for your living room.

Crassula can summer out-of-doors. Only those species that are covered with a white, frostlike cuticle need some sun protection.

Nothing will kill the popular *Crassula arborescens*, called jade tree, as fast as wet roots.

Crocus can be moved to the garden after it has bloomed. The same bulbs cannot be used again for forcing in the winter.

Crossandra – Cuphea

For the continued growth of young plants of *Crossandra infundibuliformis*, it is important to spray them very frequently.

Small *Cryptanthus* plants look good grouped in flat dishes.

Crossandra infundibuliformis

Cryptanthus bivittatus

CROSSANDRA INFUNDIBULIFORMIS
Crossandra

Family: Acanthus, *Acanthaceae*
Native Habitat: India, Southeast Asia
Flowering Time: Spring to late summer

Crossandra, a subshrub with shiny green leaves and large white, yellow, or orange flowers, is sold in Europe mostly in the form 'Mona Wallhed,' a Swedish creation. This is more compact than the species and blooms brick red; it reaches 16–20 in. (40–50 cm) in height. Other, less attractive species are *C. nilotica*, which blooms orange, and *C. pungens*, which is yellow.
Location: In summer, partial shade; in winter, light, no direct sun; warm; even in winter not under 64° (18°C). Humid.
Care: Water regularly with soft, lukewarm water and spray, more frequently in summer, less so in winter. Feed weekly from midwinter to late summer. Repot in spring in light, humus-rich soil. Remove dead flowers; Prune often for bushiness.
Propagation: By tip cuttings in early summer; prune young plants several times.
Pests and Diseases: Spider mites, whiteflies; rolled-up leaves if air is too dry.
Uses: House plant for a warm, humid location. Good for hydroponics.

CRYPTANTHUS BIVITTATUS
Cryptanthus; earthstar

Family: Bromeliad, *Bromeliaceae*
Native Habitat: South America
Flowering Time: Spring to late summer

Cryptanthus grows as a ground cover in the dry regions of South America. Its flowers are modest, but the leaf rosettes have spectacular colors and markings. After flowering, the rosette dies off, but it ensures its reproduction with the many offsets it leaves behind.
Location: Light, no noon sun; warm all year, 64–68°F (18–20°C).
Care: Keep moderately moist with soft water all year and feed lightly every two weeks. Spray frequently. Repot as needed in soil mix, making sure of good drainage.
Propagation: By offsets.
Pests and Diseases: Spider mites and whiteflies if air is too dry.
Uses: A terrarium plant or ground cover for a window greenhouse. Only with regular spraying can it live as a houseplant.

THE MOST BEAUTIFUL PLANTS FROM A TO Z

Ctenanthe oppenheimiana

Cuphea ignea

CTENANTHE
Ctenanthe

Family: Prayer plant, *Marantaceae*
Native Habitat: Tropical rain forests of South America
Flowering Time: Rarely blooms in cultivation

C. lubbersiana grows 23–32 in. (60–81 cm) high; the leaves are 8 in. (20 cm) long, light green underneath, and marbled in yellow-green on top. The cultivar 'Variegata' is especially lovely in its markings.

  C. oppenheimiana's leaves are 16 in. (40 cm) long on red stems. Underneath they are crimson; on top they are striped green and silver. 'Variegata,' with its impressively colored foliage, is the outstanding cultivar. The leaves of 'Tricolor' are irregularly spotted in white; the petioles are red. These plants will grow to 3.2 ft. (1 m).
Location: Warm year-round (68°F (20°C)) and humid.
Care: Water with soft, lukewarm water and spray frequently. Provide calcium-free, diluted plant food every two weeks during growth. Assure good drainage, as the plant suffers from waterlogging.
Propagation: By division.
Pests and Diseases: If the air is too dry, the leaves roll up.
Uses: A very beautiful foliage plant for a warm, humid room, a window greenhouse, an enclosed glass case, a warm greenhouse, or a heated conservatory.

CUPHEA
Cuphea; cigar plant

Family: Loosestrife, *Lythraceae*
Native Habitat: Central and South America
Flowering Time: Spring to fall

C. hyssopifolia is a bushy plant with 6.5 ft. (2 m) long, pointed leaves and small flowers in red, pink, or white. A pretty variety is 'Rubra.' *C. ignea*, the so-called cigar plant, is about 12 in. (30 cm) high and brings forth strange, vivid red, tubular flowers, whose tips look like glowing cigarettes.
Location: Light, not full sun. In summer outdoors; in winter cool, at 41–54°F (5–12°C).
Care: Spring to fall, keep modestly moist and feed every two weeks. Keep cool in winter and repot in spring in humus-rich soil that drains well. *C. ignea* is usually grown as an annual.
Propagation: From seed or by tip cuttings.
Pests and Diseases: Rarely.
Uses: *C. ignea* for the balcony or garden; *C. hyssopifolia* as a house-plant.

Ctenanthe is a bit difficult to keep and is really best off in an enclosed window greenhouse, or, because of its size, in a heated conservatory.

Of the about 200 species in the genus *Cuphea*, only the two described here have up to now been brought into home cultivation.

TIP

In transplanting ctenanthe, it is best to use acidic soil and to choose a wide pot since ctenanthe's roots like to spread out.

Cupressus – Cycas

Although *Cupressus macrocarpa* is sold as a houseplant, it thrives much better out-of-doors—not that it is hardy in temperate areas.

Cupressus macrocarpa

TIP

Since the Monterey cypress can tolerate temperatures down to 18°F (–8°C), my own plant stays outside till midwinter, when the really hard frosts start, and is back outside in very early spring.

Family: Cypress, *Cupressaceae*
Native Habitat: California
Flowering Time: Seldom blooms in cultivation

This is an evergreen tree with light green scales (needles). The variety 'Goldcrest' has yellow needles and is very sought after.
Location: Spring to fall, light, but no direct sun; best outside. In winter, keep light and cool, at 41–50°F (5–10°C).
Care: Water moderately in summer without allowing the root ball to dry out. In winter, water lightly. Feed only very lightly and that only every three weeks during the summer, to curb its growth. If needed, repot in spring into standard soil. Pruning is well tolerated.
Propagation: By tip cuttings with bottom heat and under plastic.
Pests and Diseases: Spider mites if too warm in winter.
Uses: For short periods on windowsills or in a room; a plant for outdoors in summer or for an unheated conservatory.

CYCAS REVOLUTA
Cycad, "sago palm"

Family: Cycad, *Cycadaceae*
Native Habitat: Southeast Asia
Flowering Time: Hardly blooms in cultivation

This attractive leaf plant grows very slowly, taking one to two years to form one ring of its 6.5 ft.- (2 m-) long fronds.

The cycad appears to be poisonous to humans and animals.
Location: Year-round, light and airy; no direct sun if possible. In summer outdoors, protected from rain. In winter cooler at 50–54°F (10–12°C).
Care: Keep moderately moist in summer; in a dry, warm room spray frequently. As soon as new growth appears in the spring, start feeding lightly once a week, using only organic fertilizer. A layer of well-rotted cattle manure, which can be dry, is effective if applied while the plant is outside. In winter, in its cooler position, cut back watering. Every three to five years, repot into a sandy, humus-rich soil mix.
Propagation: From imported fresh seeds with bottom heating of 86–95°F (30–35°C). It can take one to two months for seeds to sprout.
Pests and Diseases: Scale insects; root rot if too wet.
Uses: A decorative foliage plant for large offices, rooms, or con-servatories. Suitable for hydro-ponics.

Cycas revoluta

This venerable representative of *Cycas revoluta* can be admired in the Munich Botanical Gardens.

The cycad, which originated millions of years before the flowering plants, is dioecious, that is, its male and female reproductive organs are always on separate trees. The closed male cones are on the male trees, the exposed seeds in open ovaries rise like a golden yellow, densely matted mound out of the leaf center of female trees.

Male reproductive organs

Female reproductive organs

Cyclamen – Cymbidium

Cyclamen seems to be a favorite with the creators of ever-more-perfect new hybrids: we have so many to choose from. Especially popular are the Miniature cyclamen; they retain something of the wild flower along with their great delicacy.

CYCLAMEN PERSICUM
Cyclamen

Family: Primrose, *Primulaceae*
Native Habitat: Southern Europe, Mediterranean region
Flowering Time: Usually fall to spring

The heart-shaped, dark green leaves of cyclamen grow out of a corm—a short, thickened, vertical stem. They are marked in lighter green and sit on long, smooth, red petioles. The large flowers sit on similar stems. The varieties fall into many categories: Whole-leaf, large flower, e.g., 'Leuchtfeuer'; varieties with fringed or serrated petals; those with double flowers, e.g., 'Mauve' and 'Vermillion'; Cristata varieties, which show a comblike flower formation; Rococco varieties, with double flowers and fringed edges; and Victoria varieties, whose flowers have a red center and colored petals. The Wellensiek hybrids have small flowers, e.g., 'Sonja,' and the Miniature cyclamen are dainty.

Cyclamen persicum

Location: Year-round, cool and light, in general not over 61°F (16°C). After it has bloomed, the plant can spend the summer in a shady garden bed.

Care: While in bloom, keep the root ball moist and feed every 14 days. Do not wet the corm to prevent rot. Repot every two years in new soil mix, letting the top of the corm protrude somewhat. Remove dead leaves and flowers regularly by twisting them slowly.
Propagation: From seed with bottom heat of 61–68°F (16–20°C); sprouting takes about four weeks.
Pests and Diseases: Spider mites if too warm and dry; root rot if soil is too wet; gray mold if kept too warm and wet. Leaves will fall if the plant is too warm.
Uses: A popular flowering plant for cool rooms.

TIP

Miniature cyclamen, in addition to their charm, have the advantage of being able to tolerate warm room air better than most of the species. Place at least five in a flat dish and fill the spaces in between with wet stones or sand.

Miniature cyclamen

CYMBIDIUM HYBRIDS
Cymbidium

Family: Orchid, *Orchidaceae*
Native Habitat: Asia
Flowering Time: Usually midwinter to early summer

Cymbidium is a terrestrial orchid that seldom grows epiphytically. Its pseudobulbs look like an oval onion, out of which grow three long, straplike, light green leaves. As many as 20 magnificent flowers can stand in the panicle-like clusters. Colors vary from green through white, yellow, pink, and reddish, to brown. The lip is often in a contrasting color and spotted. Both large-blooming hybrids, some of impressive size, and Miniature cymbidium can be found. Well-known cultivars are 'Zuma Beach,' 'Dag Oleste,' 'Excalibur,' 'Mary Pinchess,' and 'Pink Tower.'

Location: Light, warm, airy, and humid. Hybrids and older Miniature hybrids can be outdoors for the summer, well shaded; they profit from the cooler night air in early fall. In winter, light and cool, not under 54°F (12°C).

Care: Early spring to early fall, water freely and spray often. In winter, 59–64°F (15–18°C) by day and 54°F (12°C) by night; reduce watering. During growth, administer orchid food once a month.

Propagation: By division.

Pests and Diseases: Spider mites if air is too dry.

Uses: Large-blooming varieties for conservatories and greenhouses; Miniature cymbidium for light, humid rooms.

Cymbidium hybrids

The large-flowering cymbidium is a marvelous, exotic plant for a cool conservatory. For a room, the Miniature hybrids are more suitable, as they can tolerate higher temperatures. Both types have very long-lasting flowers.

Flower clusters of cymbidium

Cyperus – Cytisus

The older name of *Cyperus involucratus* was *C. alternifolius*; this is the best-known species of *Cyperus*.

Cyperus papyrus is the legendary papyrus plant; photographed in its native Egypt, it is seen below. Very occasionally, we can find the 6.5 ft.- (2 m-) high exotic plant in some nursery in the temperate zone.

Cyperus involucratus

CYPERUS
Umbrella palm, papyrus

Family: Sedge, *Cyperaceae*
Native Habitat: Tropics, subtropics, and temperate zones
Flowering Time: Spring to early fall depending on the species

Cyperus is a marsh plant with long, narrow, bare, three-sided stems; at their tips sit all the grasslike, more-or-less-delicate leaves in umbrella-like formations, or—in the case of *C. papyrus*—more umbellate. Some of the species available are *C. albostriatus*, about 24 in. (60 cm) high; *C. diffusus*, same height with relatively narrow leaves; *C. gracilis*, the dwarf *Cyperus*, 12 in. (30 cm) high; *C. haspan*, like a small papyrus, 12–20 in. (30–50 cm) high; *C. involucratus* syn. *C. alternifolius*, with the cultivar 'variegatus,' 16–60 in. (40–150 cm) high; *C. papyrus*, the papyrus plant proper, with an umbel of threadlike leaves, up to 10 ft. (3 m) in height.

Location: Light, humid, and warm, all year. In winter possibly somewhat cooler. With the exception of *C. albostriatus*, outdoors as of late spring for as long as it is warm in summer.

Care: Except for *C. albostriatus* and *C. haspan*, *Cyperus'* roots can stand in water—as long as it is kept warm. They can spend the summer in the shallow end of the garden pond. Indoors in winter, with the central heating on, spray frequently; give half-diluted plant food every two weeks in summer. Use a nutrient- and humus-rich soil with a clay additive and give the roots room to spread.

Propagation: By division in the spring or by cutting the leaf bundle with 2 in. (5 cm) of stem and burying it upside down in wet sand; you can also float it head down on the surface of water till roots form. *C. papyrus* has to be divided or started from seed. Seeds need light to sprout.

Pests and Diseases: Spider mites; dry air produces brown leaf tips.

Uses: Houseplant; larger exemplars in tubs. *C. papyrus* for warm pools; small plants of any of the species for a small bowl-pond on balcony or patio.

Cyperus papyrus

THE MOST BEAUTIFUL PLANTS FROM A TO Z

Cyphomandra betacea

Cyrtomium falcatum

Cytisus x racemosus

The tamarillo is a poisonous nightshade, but like its relative the tomato, it forms an edible fruit, the tamarillo.

The sickle-shaped leaflets of the holly fern are very decorative.

The cheerful, yellow flowers of broom bring spring into the conservatory.

CYPHOMANDRA BETACEA
Cyphomandra, tamarillo

Family: Nightshade, *Solanaceae*
Native Habitat: Peru
Flowering Time: Depending on culture, late spring to fall

This shrub grows to about 10 ft. (3 m) and produces 10 in.- (25 cm-) long, broadly oval leaves. The flowers remind one of potato blossoms. The decorative part of the plant is the edible fruit, a rounded oval about 3 in. (8 cm) long, in yellow, red, and violet shades. Apart from the fruit, the plant is poisonous.
Location: Sun to partial shade; in summer outdoors, protected from wind. In winter light or darker, at 39–54°F (4–12°C).
Care: In summer, water freely and feed every week. Prune back by one-third before moving it for the winter. Reduce watering. Repot annually in large tubs, using soil that retains moisture well.
Propagation: From seed or by cuttings in summer.
Pests and Diseases: Broad-nosed weevils, whiteflies, aphids.
Uses: Decorative container plant for a balcony or garden or for the conservatory.

CYRTOMIUM FALCATUM
House fern; holly fern

Family: Shield fern, *Polypodiaceae*
Native Habitat: South Africa, Asia
Flowering Time: Not a flowering plant

This undemanding fern has dark green, leathery, shiny leaflets, shaped like sickles. An attractive variety is 'rochfordianum,' its leaflets so deeply incised as to look fringed.
Location: Partial shade; cool and airy. In summer outdoors, in winter at 50°F (10°C).
Care: In spring and summer water freely and give half-diluted plant food once a month. Spray often if kept in a room. In winter reduce water according to temperature.
Propagation: From spores or by division.
Pests and Diseases: Scale insects and mealybugs if too warm in winter.
Uses: For cool, airy rooms; in summer for shady balconies and terraces.

CYTISUS
Cytisus, broom

Family: Bean, *Fabaceae*
Native Habitat: Canary Islands
Flowering Time: Spring to early summer

For pots or containers *C. canariensis* var. *ramoisissimus* and *C. x racemosus* can be used. Both species form shrubs 5–6.5 ft. (1.5–2 m) high, which—come spring or early summer—are covered with racemes of bright yellow flowers.
Location: Year-round, cool and light. Can be sunk into garden soil for the summer.
Care: Water amply in spring and summer, especially while in bloom. It is important to provide good drainage: avoid soggy roots. Adjust winter watering to the temperature. In growth, feed every two weeks; prune lightly after the flowers fade.
Propagation: By soft cuttings after flowering.
Pests and Diseases: Aphids, spider mites.
Uses: Beautiful specimen for a conservatory, or in a container for a room.

Fruit of Cyphomandra betacea

Dahlia – Datura

Dahlias are not just garden flowers; they are used in containers, especially the low-growing hybrids.

Dahlia variabilis 'Gartenfreude'

DAHLIA
Dahlia

Family: Aster, *Asteraceae*
Native Habitat: South America
Flowering Time: Spring to fall

For balconies and for pots, the dahlias generally used are the 8-24 in. (20–60 cm) high Mignon and Top-Mix hybrids, which can be raised from seed. There are other early-blooming varieties suitable for container gardening. The vast majority of the simple, double, or semi-double dahlias, however, are appropriate for garden beds and borders, as their tubers are hardy, making them into the colorful perennials they are.

Location: Sunny, protected from wind, outdoors.
Care: Water freely and feed once a week. Snip dead flowers. In the autumn, take up the tubers, clean them of leaves, and store them dry at 35–50°F (2–10°C) for the winter.
Propagation: From seed or by cuttings from sprouted tubers started in midwinter. Remove the sprouts and plant them in sandy soil. Under plastic they will root in two to three weeks.
Pests and Diseases: Spider mites and aphids; gray mold if too wet.
Uses: A very beautiful flowering plant for flower boxes, dishes, and beds.

DATURA (BRUGMANSIA)
Datura; angel trumpet

Family: Nightshade, *Solanaceae*
Native Habitat: South America
Flowering Time: Early summer to fall; *D. aurea*, fall to winter

Datura, with its trumpet-shaped flowers that can be as long as 20 in. (50 cm), is one of the most impressive tub plants; it can grow quite large at 10 ft. (3 m) high and wide. The leaves are pointed ovals, but will vary in size on the same plant. Some of the species available are *D. aurea* (nodding white or golden yellow flowers); *D. x candida* (8 in.- (20 cm-) long white flowers); *D. sanguinea*, which now also includes *D. rosei* (tubular flowers in yellow-orange with red edges); *D. suaveolens*, angel trumpet (up to 12 in. (30 cm) long, white, yellow, or pink flowers with intoxicating fragrance, especially toward evening); *D. versicolor* (12–20 in.- (30–50 cm-) long flowers that open white and gradually turn apricot).

In addition to these species, there are numerous simple, double, and semi-double cultivars; their classification is difficult and controversial. In addition, one can also buy herbaceous angel trumpet, with white, blue-violet, or blue flowers, e.g., *Datura innoxia*. These herbaceous species include the jimsonweed, *Datura stramonium*. All *Datura* (*Brugmansia*) species are very poisonous.
Location: In summer, sunny or partial shade outdoors; In winter, light or dark and, except for *D. sanguinea*, cool (39–50°F (4–10°C)).

TIP

To avoid shrinking the tubers of your dahlias in winter storage, leave some earth on them or cover them with sand.

The Most Beautiful Plants from A to Z

Datura suaveolens

Whether as *Datura* or as *Brugmansia*, angel trumpet is without a doubt among the most magnificent of tub plants, not to mention its many species and varieties.

Datura stramonium, *seed capsule*

Datura sanguinea

Datura x candida `plena`

Datura aurea

Care: During growth in summer, water very generously and feed once a week. Repot young plants in the spring in much larger containers, using standard soil mix with well-rotted manure added. Snip off dead flowers. Prune plants that have grown too large vigorously in the autumn.

This energetic plant will survive a complete cutback, but as a consequence, flowering will start later the following year.
Propagation: By cuttings, lightly rooted (they will bloom the first year), or from seed (first flowers in two to three years).
Pests and Diseases: Broad-nosed weevils, whiteflies.
Uses: A specimen plant in a tub or lowered into a garden bed; *D. sanguinea* is an attractive flowering shrub for the conservatory.

In long, hot summers, datura will set fruit even in temperate climates. These can be used to propagate the plant.

Davallia – Dianthus

Since davallias grow epiphytically, they can be tied to pieces of bark, where their silvery or brown rhizomes can attach themselves.

In milder regions, *Delosperma cooperi* is hardy and can overwinter outside, but it needs to be protected from being wet.

Davallia mariesii *syn. D. bullata*

Delosperma cooperi

DAVALLIA
Davallia, squirrel's foot fern

Family: Squirrel's foot, *Davalliaceae*
Native Habitat: Tropical Asia, Canary Islands, Southern Europe
Flowering Time: Not a flowering plant

This is an epiphytically growing fern with strong rhizomes, covered with shieldlike brown scales. The fine, compound leaves are triangular. The varieties generally sold are *D. mariesii* syn. *D. bullata* and *D. trichomanoides.*
Location: Year-round light or partial shade; no sun. Warm and humid.
Care: Keep evenly moist with soft,

lukewarm water. Spray often, since davallias require high humidity. Every two weeks administer weak plant food. Use an epiphytic mix or orchid soil for transplanting, always into relatively small pots. Do not cover the rhizomes with soil; let them creep freely.
Propagation: From spores or by rhizome cuttings; placed on top of a mixture of sand and peat, they will sprout under plastic at 68–72°F (20–22°C).
Pests and Diseases: Scale insects; rhizome rot if kept too wet.
Uses: For closed fern cases or window greenhouses. Because of its need for humid air, very hard to keep in living areas.

DELOSPERMA
Ice plant

Family: *Mesembryanthemum, Aizoaceae*
Native Habitat: South Africa
Flowering Time: Summer to fall

The ice plant is a bushy, creeping, or rosette-forming succulent with fleshy roots and daisylike flowers. They are vividly colored, yellow, shocking pink, or white. Two species are somewhat hardy in temperate zones, *D. cooperi* and *D. lineare.* Both species form succulent mounds.
Location: In summer full sun and warm; outdoors if protected from rain. In winter cool (41–50°F (5–10°C)).
Care: Water and feed only rarely; in winter keep almost dry. In spring repot plants in standard soil mix with a clay additive.
Propagation: By tip cuttings, which have dried out somewhat before being planted; or from seed.
Pests and Diseases: Seldom; slugs if outdoors.
Uses: For sunny, warm places, balcony planters, dishes, troughs, and succulent collections.

Dianthus chinensis *hybrid 'raspberry parfait'*

eye); and the novelties, 'Strawberry Parfait' and 'Raspberry Parfait.' A bit difficult to keep is the clove pink *D. caryophyllus*, but with its wealth of long-cascading flowers it is very tempting.

Location: Sunny, airy; protect cascading pinks from rain.

Care: Water moderately; the plant does not tolerate soggy roots. Feed biweekly. *D. caryophyllus* needs lots of clean, fresh air and can stand neither heat nor prolonged rain.

Propagation: *D. chinensis*, from seed in spring with bottom heat of 64–68°F (18–20°C). From *D. caryophyllus*, you can take cuttings in the fall and keep them in winter at 41–43°F (5–6°C).

Pests and Diseases: Aphids, spider mites; carnation rust in wet summers.

Uses: For balcony planters, pots, and dishes.

The annual garden carnation, *Dianthus chinensis*, has innumerable varieties and hybrids. New ones appear all the time.

As beautiful as the clove pink *Dianthus caryophyllus* may be, it is very difficult; best to plant these fresh-air fanatics on a covered patio or balcony.

DIANTHUS
Dianthus, pink, carnation

Family: Pink, *Caryophyllaceae*
Native Habitat: Originally China, Korea
Flowering Time: Summer to autumn

The garden carnation, *D. chinensis*, is nowadays offered mostly in the form of annual hybrids or varieties. It grows 8–12 in. (20–30 cm) high and carries the typical narrow, blue-gray carnation leaves. This group includes the Charm hybrids, ample bloomers in white, salmon, pink, scarlet, and crimson; the Telstar-Crimson series in carmine; the Telstar-Mix group (scarlet, pink, and salmon, with or without an

Dianthus caryophyllus

TIP

Try planting red carnations, say of the Charm series, with blue, cascading lobelias in a balcony planter. The effect from a distance is amazingly strong.

The mantel fern, *Didymochlaena truncatula*, went through a stage of great popularity as a houseplant half a century ago.

Dieffenbachia is the most frequently sold houseplant. It has many species and varieties. All of them have similar needs.

Didymochlaena truncatula

Dieffenbachia bowmannii

DIDYMOCHLAENA TRUNCATULA
Mantle fern

Family: Shield fern, *Aspidiaceae*
Native Habitat: Tropical regions of the world
Flowering Time: Not a flowering plant

This is a terrestrially growing fern; its shiny, dark green fronds are bronzed when young and grow up to 28 in. (70 cm) long on reddish brown petioles. Individual leaflets are oval.

Didymochlaena lunulata is another name this fern is known by.
Location: Light, not sunny; humid. In summer warm; in winter at 54–57°F (12–14°C).
Care: Keep gently moist all year. Water and spray with soft, lukewarm water. If the root ball dries out, the fern loses its leaves. Feed very lightly every two weeks. Provide humid air.
Propagation: By division or from spores.
Pests and Diseases: Scale insects; falling leaves if too dry. Dry air due to central heating is not tolerated.
Uses: For enclosed fern cases and warm conservatories or greenhouses.

DIEFFENBACHIA
Dieffenbachia

Family: Arum, *Araceae*
Native Habitat: Tropical regions of Central and South America
Flowering Time: Seldom blooms under cultivation

Dieffenbachia is one of the best-known ornamental plants. Of the thirty species that grow in South America, only a few play any horticultural role. The first hybrids were created around the middle of the last century in Belgium from *Dieffenbachia maculata* and *D. seguine*. Today there are numerous cultivars. They all carry large, showy leaves on their thick stems. The many varieties and hybrids of dieffenbachia essentially differ in terms of leaf size, shape, and the yellowish- or creamy-white patterns of their variegation.

The most important varieties and cultivars are: *D. amoena* (up to 51 in. (130 cm) high, leaves 24 in. (60 cm) long. Cultivars: 'High Color,' 'Tropic Snow,' 'White Tropic').

D. bowmannii (leaves up to 30 in. (75 cm) long, yellow-green on top, blue-green underneath. Varieties: 'Camilla' and 'Marianne').

D. maculata (up to 3.2 ft. (1 m) high. Varieties: 'Exotica,' 'Jenmannii,' 'Magnifica').

D. seguine (leaves spotted in white. Varieties: 'Irrorata,' 'Lineata,' 'Liturata,' and 'Nobilis').

Dieffenbachia is poisonous in all its parts. The sap can irritate skin and mucous membranes. Wear gloves when you take cuttings.
Location: Light or partial shade all year; no sun; warm and humid.
Care: Water regularly with soft, lukewarm water and feed every two weeks. Repot in spring as needed in standard soil mix or in flower mix. Pruning back a completely bare-stemmed plant will cause it to rejuvenate. Wash leaves occasionally but carefully; remove dead ones.
Propagation: By tip or stem cuttings, with bottom heat.
Pests and Diseases: Spider mites, thrips, and aphids if the air is too dry. Root rot if it is too wet; leaves fall if plant is kept too cold and their edges turn brown if the plant is ever waterlogged.
Uses: A beautiful foliage plant for light, warm rooms, greenhouses, and conservatories. Suited to hydroponics.

Dipladenia boliviensis

DIPLADENIA
Dipladenia

Family: Dogbane, *Apocynaceae*
Native Habitat: Tropical South America
Flowering Time: Spring to late fall

Dipladenia is a subshrub that grows thin, twining stems with rough, dark green leaves and bell-like flowers. The two best-known species are *D. boliviensis* (white flower with yellow throat) and *D. sanderi*, with slightly larger, pink flowers. Now even more beautiful and more amply blooming hybrids are taking their place: 'Amoena' (pink-blooming with dark pink eye, yellow throat); 'Rosacea' (light

Dipladenia splendens

pink with dark edge and yellow throat);

'Rubiniana' (dark pink with wavy edges; large flowering). You may also find *D. eximia* (2–3 in.- (6–8 cm-) wide, bright red flowers) and *D. splendens* (4 in.- (10 cm-) wide, pink flowers, white on the outside with a dark pink throat). The variety 'profusa' has even larger flowers with a yellow-striped throat. Dipladenia is poisonous in all its parts.

Location: Year-round very light, but protected from direct sun; warm and humid.
Care: During dormancy, from fall to early spring, keep moderately dry and cool, at 59-64°F (15-18°C). Then, increase watering. If kept in a room, spray very frequently with lukewarm water. Feed weekly during growth. Repot in spring into standard soil mix with Styrofoam bits. The twining shoots require climbing support.
Propagation: By cuttings with bottom heating.
Pests and Diseases: Scale insects and mealybugs if too warm; root damage if waterlogged.
Uses: For light, humid, warm rooms, or a moist-warm greenhouse.

DIPTERACANTHUS
Dipteracanthus; zebra plant

Family: Acanthus, *Acanthaceae*
Native Habitat: Tropical South America
Flowering Time: Fall to winter, depending on species

This is a bushy, flowering plant with strongly marked, velvety leaves. The flowers are violet, white, red,

Dipteracanthus devosianus

orange, or yellow. *D. devosianus* bears dark green leaves, marked white down the center vein, and lilac-and-white flowers. *D. makoyanus* has leaves in olive green, their ribs limned in white or silver gray, their flowers, dark pink or crimson. The pink flowers of *D. portellae* are especially large.

Location: Lightly shaded all year and warm (68°F (20°C)); humid.
Care: Keep evenly moist with soft water, watering less after it has bloomed. Never let the root ball dry out. Spray frequently with warm water or arrange for humid air. Dipteracanthus needs no fertilizer. To make sure the plant stays bushy, prune well.
Propagation: By tip cuttings (3–5 per pot) with bottom heating. Snip tops off new shoots to promote bushy form.
Pests and Diseases: Whiteflies; if the atmosphere is too dry, the leaves will roll up.
Uses: Ground cover for a glass case or window greenhouse, or for a terrarium.

We have to thank Danish gardeners for bringing dipladenia back into vogue after almost one hundred years of neglect; they were the ones to start the cultivation of this plant once again.

Dipteracanthus is not just an interesting ground cover; in a humid conservatory, it can be a beautiful hanging plant.

You may still find *Dipladenia* offered as *Mandevilla*, its former genus name; now only *Mandevilla laxa* actually belongs to that genus.

Dizygotheca – Dracaena

Dizygotheca elegantissima stands out for the delicacy of its leaves. *D. veitchii* has wider leaves; those of its cultivar 'Castor' are darker, and its special appeal is its altogether more compact growth habit.

To enliven a spot in your home where light conditions are less than ideal, use *Dracaena marginata*. It can do wonders in the shade.

Dizygotheca elegantissima

DIZYGOTHECA (SCHEFFLERA)
Dizygotheca (false aralia)

Family: Ginseng, *Araliaceae*
Native Habitat: Australia, Oceania
Flowering Time: Hardly blooms in cultivation

Dizygotheca is an evergreen plant that now belongs in the genus *Schefflera*. *D. elegantissima* has compound leaves; the finely serrated, dark green or reddish green leaflets spread like fingers. *D. veitchii*'s leaves are wider and change from reddish green to dark green as they mature.
Location: Light all year, no sun. Warm (68°F (20°C)) and humid.
Care: Water moderately during growth and reduce in fall and winter. Spray often. Spring to late summer, feed every two weeks.
Propagation: By tip cuttings.
Pests and Diseases: Spider mites and scale insects if the air is too dry; both soggy and dry roots will kill the plant.
Uses: For light, warm rooms and the conservatory; ideal for the greenhouse or enclosed window garden; suitable for hydroponics.

Dracaena marginata

DRACAENA
Dragon tree

Family: Agave, *Agavaceae*
Native Habitat: Tropical and subtropical Africa and Asia; Canary Islands
Flowering Time: Seldom blooms under cultivation

Dracaena is one of the most frequently used potted plants, and it is often mistaken for *Cordyline*. The way to tell is to check the roots: those of *Cordyline* are white, those of the dragon tree are yellowish. Its long green leaves vary in width with the species or variety and may be striped or speckled as well.

Some well-known species and varieties are *D. draco*, native of the Canary Islands, tolerates cold well and has stiff, bluish green leaves that arch as they mature; *D. deremensis* has two colorful, striped cultivars, 'Bausei' and 'Warneckii'. Among the cultivars of the pure green species *D. fragrans*, the most significant are: 'Knerkii,' 'Lindenii,' 'Massangeana,' 'Rothiana,' and 'Victoria'; *D. marginata*, a hothouse plant, has narrower leaves edged in reddish brown, which are especially well marked in the variety 'Tricolor'; *D. reflexa* gained fame through its lovely cultivar 'Song of India'; *D. surculosa*, which loves heat, stands out by its shrubby habit and its broad, spotted leaves.
Location: Year-round light; no sun; variegated plants need more light

than green ones. Keep above 64°F (18°C). *D. draco*, full sun in summer, in winter light at 50°F (10°C).

Care: During growth, water *D. draco* moderately and feed once a week. In winter keep almost dry. Repot when needed, in fertile, humus-rich soil. Keep the other *Dracaenas* evenly but moderately moist. Between spring and late summer feed biweekly and repot as needed in new soil mix.

Propagation: By tip or stem cuttings at 68–75°F (20–24°C), or from seed.

Pests and Diseases: Scale insects, spider mites; both soggy and dry roots will cause leaf damage.

Uses: A decorative plant for living areas and offices. Good for hydroponics. *D. draco* for containers or for the conservatory.

Dracaena draco

The famous dragon tree of the Canary Islands has pure green leaves. Other species, such as *Dracaena reflexa* 'Song of India' or *D. deremensis* and its varieties, bear leaves with assorted markings and colors.

Below is a picture of the almost legendary dragon tree on Tenerife.

Dracaena reflexa 'Song of India'

Dracaena deremensis

Dracaena draco *in its native Tenerife*

Occasionally, *Dracaenas* need to be sprayed well to wash off any accumulated dust. They do not tolerate leaf-polishing products.

Echeveria – Echinopsis

Echeveria develops especially well if it can spend the summer planted out in the rock garden.

Echinocactus grusonii, also known as golden barrel, as well as *E. platyacanthus*, are true echinocacti. Most of the other species of the formerly large genus now have other names.

Echeveria laui

Echinocactus grusonii

ECHEVERIA
Echeveria

Family: Stonecrop, *Crassulaceae*
Native Habitat: Central and South America
Flowering Time: Depending on the species, winter to autumn

Echeveria is a succulent, whose thick, fleshy leaves form rosettes. The leaves have a delicate "bloom." Touching them will leave green "spots." The small flower spikes usually sit on arching stalks. They may be white, yellow, pink, orange, red, or multicolored. Proven species include *E. agavoides, E. derenbergii, E. elegans, E.*

pulvinata, E. setosasowie, E. laui.
Location: Year-round very light; in summer warm, best outside in the sun. Cooler in winter, at 41–50°F (5–10°C).
Care: In summer, water carefully to avoid wetting the rosette. Give some cactus food once a month. In winter keep cool and almost dry. Repot rarely, then into cactus mix or sandy soil.
Propagation: By young rosettes or by leaf cuttings that have dried before being planted, or from seed.
Pests and Diseases: Mealybugs "rot" when water is left standing in the rosette.
Uses: A beautiful flowering and leaf plant for a very light position.

Echeveria derenbergii

ECHINOCACTUS
Echinocactus

Family: Cactus, *Cactaceae*
Native Habitat: Mexico
Flowering Time: Summer

A cactus of globular or squat cylindrical shape that seldom branches. It is densely covered with yellow, white, or brownish thorns. The well-known golden barrel cactus is *E. grusonii*, which, when mature, can reach 3.2 ft. (1 m) in diameter and 4.2 ft. (1.3 m) in height. Only older exemplars produce the silky yellow flowers that can be 2 in. (5 cm) across. *E. platyacanthus* syn. *E. ingens* has a narrowly ribbed, blue-gray body.
Location: Full sun all year; in winter cool, at 50°F (10°C).
Care: Summer into fall, keep evenly moist and furnish with cactus food once a month. Do not water in winter. When needed, repot into cactus soil or into standard potting soil with sand added.
Propagation: Only from seed.
Pests and Diseases: Mealybugs, scale insects, and spider mites.
Uses: For sunny windows and greenhouses.

Echinocereus stramineus

ECHINOCEREUS
Echinocereus

Family: Cactus, *Cactaceae*
Native Habitat: Southwestern United States, Mexico
Flowering Time: Spring

This cactus can form a globe, short column, or rosettes; its thorns also vary, but the flower is always beautiful. Some species are set with white thorns, others are densely matted. *E. acifer* is globular and has red flowers; *E. cinerascens* grows whip-like, with crimson flowers; *E. pectinatus* has a cylindrical body and yellow flowers; *E. cloranthus* has green flowers; those of *E. stramineus* are enormous.

Location: Full sun all year and airy; outdoors in summer. In winter at 41–50°F (5–10°C).
Care: In summer, water moderately and feed only every two months. Keep completely dry in winter.
Propagation: From seed or by offsets.
Pests and Diseases: Spider mites; root rot if too wet.
Uses: For sunny, warm rooms and greenhouses.

Echinopsis oxygona

ECHINOPSIS
Hedgehog cactus

Family: Cactus, *Cactaceae*
Native Habitat: South America
Flowering Time: Spring to summer

These cacti have columnlike, ribbed stems, set with short thorns. The funnel-like flowers open either by day or by night. They are large and predominantly white; they can also be red or white with a pink or red haze. *E. calochlora* and *E. eyriesii* unfold their often fragrant, 6–10 in.- (17–25 cm-) wide flowers in the evening or at night. Day-blooming species are, for example, *E. aurea* (lemon yellow flowers, a rare color with

Echinopsis); *E. mamillosa* var. *kermesina* (6–7 in.- (15–18 cm-) long, red flowers); *E. oxygona* (large, long, white blossoms). *E. frankii* blooms purple, and *E. calorubra*, orange-red.
Location: Night-bloomers, light; day-bloomers, full sun and warm. In winter at 43–50°F (6–10°C).
Care: During growth, always keep moderately moist; in winter dry. Give cactus food once a month. Repot annually in cactus mix with mineral additives.
Propagation: From seed or by offsets.
Pests and Diseases: Mealybugs, spider mites.
Uses: House plant for a light, warm spot; for outdoors in the summer.

Echinocereus is valued for the vivid colors of its flowers—pink, orange, yellow, violet, and red.

It is difficult to believe that the relatively small body of *Echinopsis* can bring forth such enormous flowers.

TIP

Echinocereus plants with densely matted hair are best confined indoors, or—if outdoors—then to a covered terrace to protect them from the rain.

Ensete – Episcia

The Abyssinian banana, *Ensete ventricosum*, full of vitality, needs a large tub, lots of fertilizer, and quantities of water to unfold its full grandeur.

TIP

My two enormous *Ensetes* are planted in bushel baskets. In autumn, when I prepare to take them inside, I cut the ring of roots that have grown over the rim of the containers and place each basket into a large plastic bag. This slows the drying out of the soil. I remove most of the leaves, now 3.2 ft. (1 m) long, leaving just the central core. Out of this "heart," the new, young plant will grow, come spring.

Ensete ventricosum

Ensete ventricosum
Abyssinian banana

Family: Banana, *Musaceae*
Native Habitat: Tropical Africa
Flowering Time: Seldom blooms in cultivation

E. ventricosum comes from forests in mountains 6500 ft. (2000 m) high, so it is not as sensitive as other species of banana. In containers large enough, the leaves of this impressive perennial can reach 8 ft. (2.5 m) in length and 28 in. (70 cm) in breadth, and planted in baskets and with good care, it can grow even bigger. 'Maurelii' is a red-leafed variety.
Location: In summer light to full sun, outdoors if shielded from wind, or planted in a conservatory. In winter light at about 54°F (12°C).
Care: Spring to fall, water very freely and feed every week. While dormant, keep barely moist. Repot in soil rich in humus and nutrients using a very large container, when the old one is completely root-bound.
Propagation: From fresh, imported seeds with bottom heat of 77–86°F (25–30°C).
Pests and Diseases: Spider mites; soil fungi if roots are kept too cold.
Uses: Container plant for large conservatories.

Epiphyllum hybrids
Epiphyllum, orchid cactus

Family: Cactus, *Cactaceae*
Native Habitat: Rain forests of Central and South America
Flowering Time: Spring to summer

Numerous hybrids of this epiphytically growing or shrublike cactus are available. It has long, narrow, leaflike shoots and large flowers. The flowers of cultivars range from 2–14 in. (5–35 cm). Colors vary from white, yellow, orange, pink, red, to violet, and all shades in between.
Location: Year-round light or partial shade. In summer best outside; in winter at 41–59°F (5–15°C).
Care: Keep moderately moist in summer and spray occasionally. Early spring to late summer feed once a week. Planted in a conservatory, it may require little or no water, depending on conditions. Providing ample light prevents the growth of thin "shoots" that have to be removed. Repot annually in flower soil mix with peat added.
Propagation: From seed or by leaf cuttings, 4 in. (10 cm) long; let them dry before planting.
Pests and Diseases: Spider mites and mealybugs if kept too dry in summer; root rot if soil is too wet in winter. Soft, green spots or crooked stems indicate a viral infection.
Uses: Very beautiful flowering cactus for hanging baskets or for high positions, so the long leaflike shoots set with flowers can hang down. In summer for balconies and terraces.

Epiphyllum 'Andromeda'

Epipremnum pinnatum

Episcia cupreata

These three magnificently blooming *Epiphyllum* hybrids are only a small sample of the spectacular array of cultivars offered by American growers. These are now also available in special nurseries in Europe.

Epipremnum spreads fast and can—if need be—tolerate an energetic pruning.

As charming as episcia may be, it will not serve as a houseplant for long: it is too sensitive for our living rooms.

Epiphyllum 'Honeycomb'

EPIPREMNUM PINNATUM
Golden pothos

Family: Arum, *Araceae*
Native Habitat: Pacific Islands
Flowering Time: Seldom blooms in cultivation

Epipremnum is a spreading or climbing plant with leathery leaves, marbled in yellow-white or yellow-green, on shoots 3.2 ft. (1 m) long. The single species in cultivation, *E. pinnatum* (formerly, *Scindapsus aureus* or *Rhaphidophora aurea*), offers the cultivars 'Aureum' and 'Marble Queen.'
Location: Year-round light or shade, no strong sun; warm, at least 68°F (20°C).
Care: Water regularly during growth, less in winter. Feed biweekly. Prune plants that have grown too big when you need to.
Propagation: By tip and stem cuttings.
Pests and Diseases: Scale insects; root rot if soil is too cold in winter. Leaves fade if they receive too much light.
Uses: A hanging plant, it is also very attractive growing on a moss-covered support or on a room-dividing trellis. Good for hydroponics.

EPISCIA
Episcia

Family: Gesneriad, *Gesneriaceae*
Native Habitat: South America
Flowering Time: Summer

These graceful plants have nicely marked, brown-green, velvety leaves. The axial flowers can be red, less commonly bluish, or white. *E. cupreata* presents the largest leaves and flowers; *E. dianthiflora* (now *Alsobia dianthiflora*) displays white, fringed blossoms whose throats tend to be dotted in red.
Location: Light all year, but no sun; warm and airy.
Care: Keep moderately moist; use soft water. Feed lightly every two weeks. Provide high humidity.
Propagation: By tip cuttings or offshoots with bottom heating.
Pests and Diseases: Aphids.
Uses: A plant for pots or a hanging basket inside a glass case, window greenhouse, or warm, humid greenhouse.

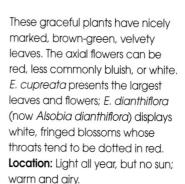

Epiphyllum 'Pegasus'

TIP

Standing in a place too dark for it, the patterned *Epipremnum pinnatum* will revert to green, and the internodal space between its leaves will grow longer and longer.

Erica – Eriobotrya

When the first frost hits your *Erica gracilis* on the balcony or terrace, no need to throw it out yet: for quite a while, it will look very pretty as a "dried" plant. By contrast, the spring heath, *Erica carnea*, is hardy in temperate areas and can be part of a permanent planting.

ERICA
Erica, heath

Family: Heath, *Ericaceae*
Native Habitat: Africa, Europe
Flowering Time: Various, depending on the species

These usually low-growing, evergreen shrubs, with their needlelike leaves are often mistaken for *Calluna*, heather. *Calluna* has scalelike, opposite leaves; *Erica*'s leaves are like needles and they stand in whorls. The white, pink, crimson, or multicolored flowers are shaped like small bells, pitchers, or tubes. *E. gracilis* blooms in late autumn before the frost sets in. Cultivars are offered with bells in white and in assorted shades of red.

Some *Erica* species, i.e., *E. hiemalis* and its hybrids, bloom starting in very early spring, though the hybrids bloom a bit later.

For a permanent planting of balcony boxes, planters, containers, and dishes, *E. carnea*, the spring heath, is best. Called *E. herbacea* for a time, it is hardy in temperate regions and is also offered in many varieties, including 'Kramers White' (white flowers, midwinter to midspring); 'December Red' (light pink, late winter); 'King George' (purplish-pink, winter to early spring); and 'Ruby Glow' (ruby red, late winter to late spring).

Location: Sun to partial shade; always cool.
Care: Keep evenly moist with soft water (except *E. carnea*). Feed with calcium-free fertilizer biweekly. *E. gracilis* needs no food during its short life. Use only (acidic)

Erica gracilis

rhododendron soil for repotting and permanent plantings. Snip off dead blooms.
Propagation: By cuttings (difficult); I had good results from tip layering; I used small, forked sticks to hold shoots down.
Pests and Diseases: Powdery mildew and gray mold.
Uses: A long-lasting flowering plant for cool places, balcony planters, dishes, troughs, and tubs.

Erica carnea

The Most Beautiful Plants from A to Z

Erigeron karvinskianus 'Blutenmeer'

ERIGERON KARVINSKIANUS
Erigeron; fleabane

Family: Aster, *Asteraceae*
Native Habitat: Mexico to Venezuela
Flowering Time: Late spring to fall

This flowering perennial has a low habit (to 8 in. (20 cm)); its creeping shoots are intricately entwined. Lower leaves are serrated, rounded ovals; upper leaves, elongated and smooth-edged. Numerous daisylike star flowers open white and then turn red.
Location: Sunny.
Care: During growth, keep moderately moist and feed every two weeks. Snip off dead blooms to force new ones. Since the plant is not hardy in temperate zones, make sure winter quarters are light and frost free.
Propagation: From seed (they need light to sprout) or by cuttings. The plant will seed itself in a protected location; seedlings bloom the first year.
Pests and Diseases: Rarely.
Uses: A beautiful flowering plant for rock gardens, dishes, troughs, and dry walls. Set out in beds, the plant will tolerate cold down to 25°F (–4°C).

Eriobotrya japonica

ERIOBOTRYA JAPONICA
Loquat

Family: Rose, *Rosaceae*
Native Habitat: China, Japan
Flowering Time: Autumn

Loquat is a small, evergreen tree or shrub with 12 in.- (30 cm-) long, dark green leaves, their undersides densely matted with reddish or silvery hair. In late spring, the tree produces edible, apricot-like fruit, yellow to orange in color. In colder regions the tree only sets flowers and fruit if kept in a greenhouse. In a container it will reach 6.5 ft. (2 m).
Location: Sun to partial shade; in summer outdoors, protected from rain. In winter light, at 43–54°F (6–12°C).

Care: Water regularly, letting the root ball dry each time. Feed weekly till the end of summer. Repot if needed in standard soil enriched with some clay. Pruning is well tolerated. Water little in the winter.
Propagation: From seed or by tip cuttings with bottom heating.
Pests and Diseases: If the leaves cannot dry in a wet summer, a fungus develops (*Eriobotrya* scab).
Uses: Planted in the conservatory or as a container plant.

To the list of the *Erigeron* hybrids we know and love from our perennial borders, now we can add *Erigeron karvinskianus*, a pretty, undemanding, hanging plant.

Planted in a well-protected corner of the garden, the loquat can tolerate cold down to 14°F (–10°C). It looks especially good against a white wall.

Erythrina – Eucomis

To encourage the coral bean to put out more flowers, snip off wilted shoots.

Eucalyptus flowers are very beautiful. The trees bloom only in warm regions, like their native Australia, where the eucalyptus constitutes a characteristic part of the landscape. Trees 330 ft. (100 m) high are common, and they say there are specimens that reach 525 ft. (160 m).

Erythrina crista-galli

ERYTHRINA CRISTA-GALLI
Cockspur coral bean

Family: Bean, *Fabaceae*
Native Habitat: Tropics and subtropics
Flowering Time: Summer to fall

Erythrina is a 6.5 ft.- (2 m-) high, thick-stemmed shrub with long, thorny shoots. These bear racemes of scarlet blossoms at intervals during the summer.
Location: Full sun, warm. In winter dark, at 41–50°F (5–10°C).
Care: Water and feed generously during growth. In the autumn, prune plants back to 8 in. (20 cm), make sure they are not wet, and store them completely dry. The short, thick stem stores enough nutrients to tide the plant over the winter. Repot in spring using standard soil mix. Gradually increase water and light.
Propagation: From seed, if you are willing to wait three to four years for the first flower, or by tip cuttings.
Pests and Diseases: Spider mites and whiteflies.
Uses: Container and garden room plant.

Eucalyptus flower

EUCALYPTUS
Eucalyptus

Family: Myrtle, *Myrtaceae*
Native Habitat: Australia
Flowering Time: Summer

Eucalyptus is an evergreen tree with rough, blue-green or blue-gray leaves alternating along the stems. It is not generally known that the leaves may change shape: those of youthful *E. gunnii*, for example, are small disks; mature trees bear narrow leaves, 5 in. (12 cm) long. In mild areas, the creamy flowers will appear when the tree is young. Fast-growing *E. globulus*, the Tasmanian blue gum, is very attractive, as is *E. ficifolia*, which has rougher, lancetlike leaves and blooms in shades of red.

E. niphophila has 4 in.- (10 cm-) long, silver-blue leaves and grows more slowly.

The bark on older specimens will peel off in patches, creating interesting, contrasting patterns. Eucalyptus contains aromatic oils.

During their first two winters, I treat any young plants of coral bean that I happen to raise from seed as if they were potted houseplants: I place them in a light, warm room and continue to water them.

Eucalyptus tree in native habitat

Location: In summer, sun or partial shade out of doors. In winter, cool and airy at 35–50°F (2–10°C). In its first few years, the tree does better in a greenhouse or conservatory.

Care: Using soft water, make sure that the root ball is moist enough; if it dries out, leaves wilt and wilted foliage does not recover. Feed moderately using calcium-free fertilizer, or the plant will grow too fast. Repot often using humus-rich soil. Though the plant will tolerate pruning, it does not affect its habit.

Propagation: From seed; cuttings are too difficult.

Pests and Diseases: Rarely.

Uses: Container and conservatory plant.

Single flowers of Eucomis bicolor

EUCOMIS
Eucomis, pineapple flower

Family: Lily, *Liliaceae*
Native Habitat: South Africa
Flowering Time: Summer

A magnificent specimen of Eucomis pole-evansi *in a container.*

The large bulb of eucomis produces stemless, long leaves and racemes of small flowers on long stalks. A bunch of bracts crowns the inflorescence. *E. bicolor* grows straplike leaves out of its large bulb. The stalk, 12–20 in. (30–50 cm) long, carries the assembly of light green flowers with violet edges.

E. pole-evansii grows 5 ft. (1.5 m) high and its leaves are 28 in. (70 cm) long. The raceme of attractive, creamy-white flowers is 24 in. (60 cm) long.

Location: Full sun.

Care: During growth, water freely and feed every two weeks. In the autumn, after flowering, the bulb recovers; store it, with or without soil, in a cool, dry place. In early spring, plant it in a pot with much humus in the soil and good drainage. As for *E. pole-evansii*, plant three to four bulbs in one container, using some nutrient-rich soil over sand or pebbles for drainage. Water sparingly at first.

Propagation: From bulbs or seeds. Seedlings take about five years to bloom.

Pests and Diseases: Inadequate drainage will cause rot.

Uses: An interesting plant for pot or container, to be placed on a balcony or terrace, or in a garden room.

Eucomis can be planted in a warm spot of the garden, and its bulbs will overwinter there if they are given a warm cover of dead leaves or chaff. Actually, the plant blooms better under these conditions.

E. pole-evansii has to overwinter in a frost-free environment.

TIP

If you grow some *Eucalyptus gunnii* plants during the summer, you can use their foliage for flower arrangements in the winter. The round, blue-green leaves are really good-looking.

Eugenia – Euphorbia

Eugenia myriophylla is a good candidate for bonsai. *E. uniflora* is raised for its fruit in its native land. Both are close relatives of the clove we use as a spice.

The many varieties of *Euonymus japonica* differ in the patterns and colors of their leaves.

Eugenia myriophylla

EUGENIA MYRIOPHYLLA
Eugenia

Family: Myrtle, *Myrtaceae*
Native Habitat: Brazil
Flowering Time: Seldom blooms in cultivation

Eugenia, an evergreen shrub with narrow leaves, is widely known in bonsai form; its growth rate is appropriately slow. In fact, it can spend appreciable time on the windowsill before it grows large enough for a container. If treated with care, eugenia will make little red berries after it has bloomed.
Location: Full sun; outdoors in the summer. In winter at about 50°F (10°C).
Care: Over the summer, feed biweekly and water sparingly; reduce further in the winter. If needed, repot into standard soil mix. Eugenia likes to be pruned well and can be trained into a standard.
Propagation: By tip cuttings, which will root with bottom heating. Pinch out young plants several times to encourage bushiness.
Pests and Diseases: Scale insects.
Uses: Container and houseplant for light rooms, for a conservatory, and for bonsai.

Eugenia uniflora

Euonymus japonica *and* 'albomarginata'

EUONYMUS
Euonymus

   ☠

Family: Bittersweet, *Celastraceae*
Native Habitat: Japan, Korea, China
Flowering Time: Rarely blooms under cultivation

Euonymus japonica is the only member of its genus to be used as a houseplant. The variegated cultivars of this evergreen are the most beautiful: 'albomarginata' (large, matte, green leaves edged in white); 'aurea' (golden-yellow leaf with a narrow, dark green edge); 'albovariegata' (large, broad leaves with white edges); 'ovata aurea' (leaves dark green along the edge, golden-yellow in the center).

E. fortunei can reach 10 ft. (3 m) and is completely hardy in the temperate zone; the leaves of 'Sheridan Gold' turn yellow-green or show yellow spots in summer; 'Dart's Carpet' has leaves that bronze over or change to brown-violet in winter; 'Dart's Ideal' has spectacular light green leaves; the leaf edges of 'Gold Tip' turn from golden yellow to creamy white. All euonymus species are poisonous.
Location: *E. japonica* light, warm, and humid all year; outside in summer, protected from sun; in winter at 43–54°F (6–12°C). *E. fortunei* outside all year long.
Care: Water moderately from spring to fall; even less in winter. Feed weekly during growth. Repot into standard soil mix or into garden soil rich in humus and clay. Prune as needed or train into shape.
Propagation: By cuttings in spring and summer. Prune young plants several times to ensure bushy growth.
Pests and Diseases: Rarely.
Uses: *E. japonica* is a foliage plant for light, warm rooms, for containers, and for planting in a conservatory. *E. fortunei*, for an outdoor container.

Euphorbia milii *hybrid*

EUPHORBIA
Euphorbia

Family: Spurge, *Euphorbiaceae*
Native Habitat: Worldwide
Flowering Time: Almost all year, more in the winter

E. milii is a succulent shrub about 6.5 ft. (2 m) high, with very thorny, thin shoots and small, egg-shaped leaves. Almost all year, the plant produces little flowers that attract attention by their colorful bracts. Growers have produced colors from red through pink, white, and yellow, to orange. Among the loveliest hybrids of *E. milii* you will find: var. *bevilariensis* (tall, red); var. *tananarivae* (tall, yellow, with red edge).

E. atropurpurea, from Tenerife, has succulent stems that turn woody, topped by a plume of leaves.

E. erythraeae, from Ethiopia,

reaches 30 in. (80 cm), its branches like candelabra.

E. grandicornis, from Kenya and South Africa, has three-sided shoots and very strong thorns.

E. meloformis, from South Africa, is only 4–6 in. (10–15 cm) high, globular in shape, and produces modest, yellow-green flowers.

E. obesa, also a native of South Africa, grows like a spherical cactus with eight ribs.

E. resinifera is from Morocco, has square, thorny shoots and reaches 20 in. (50 cm) in cultivation.

E. submammillaris, about 6–8 in. (15–20 cm) high, grows grasslike. *E. tirucalli* has round shoots that are as thick as a pencil and very poisonous. These last two plants are natives of South Africa.

All euphorbia species are somewhat poisonous.
Location: Light, sunny, warm, all year; in summer outdoors but sheltered.
Care: Water moderately; spring to fall, feed regularly with cactus food. Repot every two years in cactus soil with a clay additive. Prune anytime.
Propagation: By tip cuttings that have dried for one day. Stop the flow of latex by immediately

Euphorbia atropurpurea

Euphorbia obesa

Euphorbia meloformis

holding the cut in warm water.
Pests and Diseases: Leaves fall if too wet or too dry in winter, or if too cold.
Uses: A beautiful houseplant; good for beginners and for hydroponics.

The more than 2000 euphorbia species include annual plants, perennials, shrubs, trees, and succulents; some of these mimic cacti deceptively well.

I have a small collection of succulent euphorbias. Each year I put them outdoors for the summer, and they respond very well. All the pots are sunk into a flattened sand heap, the smaller ones in front and along the sides, larger plants in the back. Visual variety is provided by some rocks and driftwood.

Poinsettias do not have to be red. The breeder's art has created plants with creamy-white, apricot, or pink bracts; even plants with two-colored bracts are available. Similarly, the habit of euphorbias varies from potted cultivars with one or more stems, through bushy hanging plants and charming standards, to tiny "Christmas minis."

Euphorbia pulcherrima *assortment*

EUPHORBIA PULCHERRIMA
Poinsettia

Family: Spurge, *Euphorbiaceae*
Native Habitat: Tropical Mexico
Flowering Time: Late fall to early spring

This herbaceous, intricately branched plant used to be known as *Poinsettia pulcherrima*. With poinsettia, it is not the small, insignificant flowers that matter, but the bracts that surround them. Their colors range from red through pink, apricot, and cream, to white. Beautiful varieties include 'Eckespoint Pink' and 'Eckespoint Red.' Two-colored cultivars are now also available, like 'Jingle Bells.' Usually, the plant is thrown out after it has bloomed. Poinsettia is a short-day plant; it only forms flowers and

colored bracts if, for two months in the fall, it does not receive more than 10 hours of daylight. The best thing is to place an opaque bucket or cardboard box over the plant for 14 hours each day. This is an efficient way to keep all light off the plant; even interior and street lighting will interrupt the rest the plant needs to develop flowers. If you want to try it, read on.

A bushy Poinsettia for a hanging basket.

Location: Year-round light, and not too warm (64°F (18°C)); humid. Avoid drafts.
Care: Prune after it flowers to about 6 in. (15 cm). Keep dry till late spring at 54–59°F (12–15°C). When new shoots appear, repot in standard soil mix and move to a warmer location, later even outdoors. From late spring to late fall, water regularly but sparingly; spray occasionally and feed every two weeks.
Propagation: By tip cuttings in summer.
Pests and Diseases: Scale insects and spider mites if the air is too dry; gray mold and root rot if it is kept too wet and cold.
Uses: Houseplant for light rooms; suitable for hydroponics.

THE MOST BEAUTIFUL PLANTS FROM A TO Z

Eustoma grandiflorum

Exacum affine

Fatshedera lizei

The prairie gentian, *Eustoma randiflorum*, is raised as an annual.

The profusion of flowers *Exacum affine* can produce is surprising.

Fatshedera is an undemanding foliage plant that will thrive in a darker location.

EUSTOMA GRANDIFLORUM
Prairie gentian

Family: Gentian, *Gentianaceae*
Native Habitat: United States, Northern Mexico
Flowering Time: Midsummer to early autumn

Occasionally, two-year-old *Eustoma* plants are still offered under the old name, *Lisianthus russelianus*. This bushy plant has blue-green, oval or elongated leaves and large, showy, bell flowers in crimson, pink, and white. Potted plants are treated with growth retardants to keep them compact.
Location: Very light, no strong sun, warm.
Care: Keep moderately moist. No other care applies.
Propagation: From seed in summer; very challenging. In winter keep the seedlings light and cool; come spring, plant three per pot, leaving room to grow. Flowers open 10–12 months after sowing.
Pests and Diseases: Gray mold at the root crown if too moist and cool.
Uses: House and garden plant.

EXACUM AFFINE
Exacum

Family: Gentian, *Gentianaceae*
Native Habitat: Socotra on the Gulf of Aden
Flowering Time: Summer to autumn

Exacum is a shrubby plant about 12 in. (30 cm) high; its leaves resemble those of tradescantia. Its innumerable small flowers are blue or almost violet, with prominent, bright-yellow stamens. Recently, white cultivars have been introduced. By nature, exacum is biennial, but it is usually treated as an annual.
Location: Light, not sunny, warm. Keep seedlings, sown in the fall, light and cool through the winter.
Care: Water regularly with soft water and feed occasionally. Keep young plants drier over the winter.
Propagation: By cuttings or from seeds, which need light to germinate. Prune young plants often to increase bushiness.
Pests and Diseases: Aphids; gray mold if kept too wet.
Uses: Flowering plant for balcony, terrace, or windowsill.

X FATSHEDERA LIZEI
Fatshedera

Family: Ginseng, *Araliaceae*
Native Habitat: Originated in France
Flowering Time: Hardly blooms in cultivation

This is a cross between *Fatsia japonica* and *Hedera helix* (English ivy). The leaves are three-to-five-lobed, evergreen, and shiny; they are smaller than those of *F. japonica*. 'Variegata' has leaves that are patterned in white.
Location: Light or shady, except for 'Variegata'; room temperature and humid. In summer outdoors, sheltered from the sun. In winter cool at 54–57°F (12–14°C).
Care: Keep evenly and moderately moist; in heated rooms, spray often. Feed once a week during growth. Repot young plants every year, mature ones every two to three years. *x F. lizei* usually does not branch until it has been pruned.
Propagation: By tip cuttings with bottom heating.
Pests and Diseases: Scale insects, spider mites if air is too dry.
Uses: Fast-growing green plant for a room, container, or conservatory. Suited to hydroponics.

In summer, I place my own fatshedera in the shade of a pine tree in the garden. I tie its shoots to the trunk, and after a while, they happily climb up the tree.

Fatsia – Ficus

In England, fatsia is grown as an evergreen garden plant. Since the plant can tolerate short periods of frost, there is no need to hurry moving it back into the house at the end of summer in colder climates, though some people keep it indoors all year.

The flowers of *Felicia amelloides* look good in a vase, and they last a long time.

Fatsia japonica

FATSIA JAPONICA
Fatsia; Japanese aralia

Family: Ginseng, *Araliaceae*
Native Habitat: Ryukyu Islands, South Korea, Japan
Flowering Time: Rarely blooms in cultivation

Fatsia is a foliage plant 3.2–6.5 ft. (1–2 m) in height; its leaves can have seven or nine lobes; they are shiny green and, on mature plants, they can be 16 in. (40 cm) across. The umbels of white flowers appear only on older specimens. Both the green species and its variegated cultivars are available.
Location: Light to shady; cool. In summer outdoors, sheltered from wind; in winter, green plants at 43–50°F (6–10°C), variegated ones at 61°F (16°C). The warmer the air, the more humidity is needed.
Care: In summer, keep evenly moist; in winter, water just enough to keep the root ball from drying out. Feed weekly from spring to fall.
Propagation: From seed, by tip cuttings, or by air layering.
Pests and Diseases: Spider mites if too warm in winter; leaves fall if air is too dry or roots are too wet.
Uses: Ideal for cool, light stairways and lobbies.

Felicia amelloides

FELICIA
Felicia; Cape aster

Family: Aster, *Asteraceae*
Native Habitat: South Africa
Flowering Time: Depending on the species and location, all year

Felicia is a subshrub that grows 8–24 in. (20–60 cm) high. Its rough and hairy leaves can be roundish, elongated, or narrow and lanceolate. The yellow-centered flowers are sky blue or a soft violet, depending on species and variety. *F. amelloides*, the blue felicia, is a perennial that will bloom almost all year if it is kept cool in winter. A particularly pretty variety of *F. amelloides* is 'Santa Anita.' *F.*

bergeriana grows only 6 in. (15 cm) high and blooms in summer, as does the 12 in.- (30 cm-) high *F. tenella.* These two species are annuals and are discarded after they bloom.
Location: Very sunny, warm; in summer outdoors. In winter light, at 50–54°F (10–12°C).
Care: Water sparingly all year; feed every two weeks. Pinch out the plant regularly to achieve bushy habit and profuse flowering. In spring repot in fertile soil.
Propagation: By cuttings in spring.
Pests and Diseases: Powdery mildew if kept too wet and warm.
Uses: House and balcony plant. Thrives under hydroponics.

Ficus elastica

FICUS
Ficus, rubber tree

Family: Mulberry, *Moraceae*
Native Habitat: Tropical Asia, Africa, America
Flowering Time: Seldom blooms in cultivation

Of the more than 800 species of the genus *Ficus*, about 20 are used as houseplants. Of those, the best known is *F. elastica*, the rubber tree and its varieties, e.g., 'Robusta,' with roundish leaves, or 'Abidjan,' whose leaves are reddish underneath. Less frequently seen are the variegated cultivars, for example, 'Doescheri,' 'Schrijveriana,' or 'Variegata.'

F. benjamina, with its more delicate foliage and arching branches, is gaining on *F. elastica* in popularity. Variegated cultivars, like 'Starlight' or 'Variegata,' can now also be found. Another species seen is *F. lyrata*, the fiddle leaf fig, its huge leaves shaped like violin cases. The habit of *F. pumila* is very different: the creeping fig is a low-growing plant with creeping shoots.

Ficus elastica does not remain small for long; in time it will be as large as this magnificent example of the fiddle leaf fig, *Ficus lyrata*, on the left.

TIP

A small assortment of ficus: the weeping fig, an extremely popular foliage plant, is well suited to bonsai; this ancient miniature reveals its exotic tree form. *Ficus pumila*, the creeping fig, is now used both as a hanging plant and for underplanting larger, containerized trees. *Ficus barteri* is one of the narrow-leafed ficus species that have only recently become available and are gaining popularity.

Ficus lyrata

Ficus

Again and again you hear that rubber trees should not be put outside. I cannot agree with this. My two huge *F. elastica* spend summer after summer, right up to the first frost, at the northeast corner of the house. They are in self-watering containers and seem to like it there, as they produce many, many leaves every year. It does not hurt the plants that in their light and cool winter quarters they will drop some of their foliage. As growth sets in once more, the leaves are replaced.

FICUS
Ficus, continued

It is hard to believe that this plant belongs to the fig genus. A few other species worth mentioning: *F. aspera*, has large, rather rough, lanceolate leaves, marbled in green and white; *F. barteri* is a relatively recent species to be offered; *F. deltoidea*, will—with some luck—produce pea-sized mock fruit; *F. religiosa*, the Indian bog tree, has enormous, thin, heart-shaped leaves; *F. rubiginosa*, the rusty fig, branched and low-lying in its habit, has a variegated form called 'Variegata.' *F. sagittata* 'variegata' is an especially attractive hanging plant.

All the species mentioned are evergreen.

Location: Very light all year, but not full sun; humid, warm in summer. In winter at 54–59°F (12–15°C). The plants are able to tolerate heated rooms. Keep *F. benjamina* above 59°F (15°C) in winter.

Care: Spray frequently, especially if the air is heated. Water moderately; in winter when the plants are cooler, reduce watering. Do not let the root ball dry out, especially with *F. pumila*. Feed biweekly during growth.

Propagation: By tip cuttings; air-layering for upright species.

Pests and Diseases: Scale insects, spider mites; leaf loss if too dark or in a draft; yellow leaves if too wet.

Uses: For rooms, offices, and stair-ways, as well as the conservatory. Suited to hydroponics.

Ficus benjamina

Ficus pumila

Ficus benjamina

Ficus barteri

FICUS CARICA
Common fig

Family: Mulberry, *Moraceae*
Native Habitat: Mediterranean region, Asia Minor
Flowering Time: Spring to early summer

The fig is a deciduous shrub with gray-green branches. Its three-or five-lobed, vivid green leaves are very attractive. The modest little flowers are enclosed by the fleshy fruit bottle. The fruit will ripen under favorable conditions in temperate regions.

Location: Sunny and warm; in winter cool, close to freezing. Since the leaves will fall, a dark storage place can be used.

Care: In summer, feed well every two weeks and water amply, letting the soil dry out a bit each time. The fig prefers a well-drained soil with some calcium; standard soil mix with one-third pebbles will do. Young fruit, still on the tree when it is stored for the winter, will continue to grow in the spring and will ripen in the summer.

Propagation: By cuttings in the spring.

Pests and Diseases: Scale insects.

Uses: A container plant good for the conservatory. It is also offered potted for the windowsill. In milder regions of the temperate zone, *F. carica* can be planted out, though in hard winters it will freeze back.

Ficus carica

Ficus carica *at home on one of the islands of the Mediterranean*

If you choose the right species, you can harvest juicy, ripe figs even in the temperate zone—after a long, warm summer, that is.

TIP

In choosing a common fig tree, it is important to pick one of the so-called Adriatic types. Only these will produce fruit without pollination. Tried varieties are: 'Dottato,' 'Fraga,' 'Adriatic,' and 'Mission.'

Fittonia – Fuchsia

Fittonia verschaffeltii

Fortunella margarita

FORTUNELLA
Kumquat

Family: Rue, *Rutaceae*
Native Habitat: China, Japan
Flowering Time: Summer

Fortunella is a very attractive, much-branched shrub with longish, shiny green leaves. The flowers have a less intense scent than those of other citrus trees. *F. japonica's* fruit is round and a pale orange-red, while that of *F. margarita* (variety 'Variegata') is oval and more vividly colored. *F. hindisii*, with its pea-sized fruit, is ideal for bonsai.
Location: In summer, full sun; if possible outdoors. In winter light, at 41–46°F (5–8°C).
Care: Water amply and with soft water. Feed every two weeks. Repot smaller plants annually, larger ones every two to three years in soil rich in humus.
Propagation: By tip cuttings under plastic with bottom heating.
Pests: Scale insects and spider mites.
Uses: For light conservatories and greenhouses. Suited to bonsai.

Fittonias, charming, little leaf plants from the steaming tropical forests of South America, are sensitive to dry, cool, or drafty air.

Fortunella, the kumquat, can tolerate cold down to 14°F (–10°C). You can take the plant out early in the spring and leave it out till late autumn. The fruit can be eaten raw, along with the skin.

FITTONIA
Fittonia

Family: Acanthus, *Acanthaceae*
Native Habitat: South America
Flowering Time: Variable

Fittonia is a low-growing, herbaceous plant with egg-shaped, beautifully marked leaves. *F. gigantea* reaches 24 in. (60 cm), has purple stems, and its leaves are dark green with crimson veins. *F. verschaffeltii* is a creeper and is suited to flat dishes and to hanging baskets. The variety 'Argyroneura' is veined in silvery white, while 'Pearcey' has reddish veins. There also is a variety particularly suited to terrarium planting, called 'Minima,' a dwarf form of 'Argyroneura.'
Location: Light to shade; no sun. Room temperature all year. Air humid and free of drafts.
Care: Always water with lukewarm, soft water and spray occasionally. Give half-diluted flower fertilizer every two weeks. Use a loose, fertile soil for repotting.
Propagation: By cuttings with bottom heating in spring and summer.
Pests and Diseases: Seldom.
Uses: Houseplant for a warm, humid place; for window greenhouses, glass cases, a terrarium, or as ground cover in shady areas of the conservatory.

Fittonia verschaffeltii

FUCHSIA
Fuchsia

Family: Evening primrose, *Onagraceae*

Native Habitat: Mountainous regions of tropical Central and South America

Flowering Time: Depending on the species, spring to autumn

Fuchsia is a subshrub with intricately branched, arching shoots. Its many hybrids are sold as potted, container, and hanging plants for baskets or to cascade from columns. The flowers come in diverse colors, large or small, simple, semi-double, or double. With its 3.5 in.- (9 cm-) long and 4 in.- (11 cm-) wide blossoms, the variety 'Pink Marshmallow' is the current champion in size. At the other extreme is the Mexican *F. minimiflora*; its flower is 0.0015 in. (4 mm) long. Roughly, fuchsias fall into three groups:

1. upright fuchsias
2. hanging fuchsias
3. racemous fuchsias (Triphylla hybrids)

Beautiful upright fuchsias are: 'Beacon,' 'Hanna,' and 'Winston Churchill.' Good hanging fuchsias are 'Berkeley,' 'Cascade,' and 'Red Spider.' Some good fuchsias that grow racemes are 'Erika Koth' and 'Trumpeter.' One species hardy in temperate zones is the scarlet *F. magellanica*, with its varieties 'Gracilis' and 'Ricartonii.'

Location: In summer partial shade or shade, wind-sheltered outdoors. In winter light or dark, at 39–46°F (4–8°C). Keeping it any warmer will stimulate new growth too early. Triphylla hybrids accept full sun.

Care: Water very generously and feed weekly. Keep spraying on very hot days; the plants look best in the fall when the mornings are foggy. Move plants indoors before frost and keep cool and airy till spring, when they are pruned and repotted, ready to set new shoots.

Propagation: By cuttings in summer or by freshly sprouting plants in spring. Prune young plants to encourage bushy growth.

Pests and Diseases: Aphids, whiteflies, spider mites; gray mold, fuchsia rust.

Uses: A very beautiful, profusely flowering plant for a room, the balcony, or a conservatory.

Did you know that, worldwide, there are more than 10,000 fuchsia varieties? This member of the evening primrose family has so many cultivars because it is so beloved all over the world. In Europe, for example, there are fuchsia societies everywhere.

Fuchsia 'Royal Velvet' demonstrates that fuchsia is well suited to standard training. In order for the thin stem to be able to carry the heavy crown of blossoms, however, special supports are required.

TIP

I prune my *Fuchsia magellanica*, in my garden, to 6 in. (15 cm) above ground level and empty two bushel baskets full of dried leaves over it. The plant survives every winter and is getting more and more beautiful; the rigorous pruning rejuvenates it annually.

Fuchsia 'Royal Velvet'

Gardenia – Glechoma

Three different gardenias: an elegant standard, an attractive shrub in a container, and a little potted plant for the windowsill (picture below).

GARDENIA JASMINOIDES
Gardenia

Family: Madder, *Rubiaceae*
Native Habitat: Ryukyu Islands, Japan, China
Flowering Time: Summer and fall

The commonly sold species is *Gardenia jasminoides*, a 5 ft.- (1.5 m-) high shrub with evergreen, leathery, shiny green leaves. The fragrant terminal blossoms are usually double and creamy white. Well-known varieties are 'Fortunei,' 'Plena,' or 'Veitchii,' all of which have large, white flowers. Our

Gardenia jasminoides

grandparents knew the gardenia well because, around the turn of the century, it was a fashionable boutonniere. Now the plant is sought mostly by the owners of conservatories.

Location: Very light all year; no sun; keep at 61–64°F (16–18°C). Outdoors only in the height of summer. If needed, provide bottom heating (64–68°F (18–20°C)).
Care: In winter, during growth, moisten evenly with soft, lukewarm water and feed biweekly with nonalkaline fertilizer. If needed, repot in nonalkaline soil, e.g., rhododendron mix.
Propagation: By tip cuttings in spring or fall, with bottom heating.
Pests and Diseases: Scale insects, spider mites; yellow leaves are due to cold roots or hard water; buds fall if temperatures fluctuate, i.e., if it is too wet, too cold, or too hot.
Uses: For heated conservatories or light, warm rooms.

GASTERIA
Gasteria

Family: Lily, *Liliaceae*
Native Habitat: South Africa
Flowering Time: Spring or summer, depending on location

Gasteria is a succulent with thick leaves that stand in rows or in rosettes. When young, the leaves are often spotted in white or covered with warts. The red flowers are arranged in loose racemes or spikes on a long stalk.

G. armstrongii has short, rounded

Gasteria verrucosa

leaves with small, wrinkled warts on them; it puts forth flowers even as a young plant. *G. humilis*'s 3–4 in.- (8–10 cm-) long leaves show irregular cross-stripes of white speckles. *G. liliputana*'s leaves are about 2 in. (5 cm) long, white-spotted, and grow into a rosette as the plant matures. A larger species, *G. maculata*, has leaves 8 in. (20 cm) long, tongue-shaped, and vividly spotted. The flower stalk is 3.2 ft. (1 m) high. The leaves of *G. verrucosa* are about 8 in. (20 cm) long, tapering, pointed, and covered with little warts.
Location: Light, no direct sun; in summer sheltered outdoors. Keep winter temperatures above 41°F (5°C).
Care: In summer, water normally; reduce water in winter; feed once a week with cactus food. A long, cool rest from fall to spring at 43–54°F (6-12°C), promotes flowering.
Propagation: By offsets or well-dried leaf cuttings.
Pests and Diseases: Mealybugs; if outdoors, slugs; if too wet, root rot, especially in winter.
Uses: An undemanding house-plant for any window or even for a darker position in a room.

Gazania 'Mini Star Mix'

Gerbera jamesonii *hybrid*

Glechoma hederacea 'Variegata'

Compact gazanias will do very well in the cracks between the flagstones of the terrace.

Gerbera is not just a cut flower; planted in large bowls or pots, it can decorate the patio or the balcony.

Glechoma's spreading habit can be taken advantage of in a hanging basket or by using it as a ground cover.

GAZANIA HYBRIDS
Gazania

Family: Aster, *Asteraceae*
Native Habitat: South Africa
Flowering Time: Spring to fall

Gazanias have a moundlike habit. Their leaves are incised, partially or completely, and their undersides are silvery green. The plants generally available are hybrids, grown as annuals, their pretty flowers white, yellow, or orange. Usually, the petals are spotted in black near the center. 'Mini Star Tangerine' comes in several colors; the orange, yellow, bronze, or white flowers of 'Daybreak' remain open even when the weather turns dark.
Location: In summer full sun; in winter light, at 41–50°F (5–10°C).
Care: During growth, water moderately; avoid soggy roots. In winter do not let the root ball dry out completely. Repot and prune the plants in the spring.
Propagation: From seed or by cuttings in late summer.
Uses: A great flowering plant for planters or dishes.

GERBERA
Gerbera

Family: Aster, *Asteraceae*
Native Habitat: South Africa
Flowering Time: Spring to fall; indoors, all year

This herbaceous perennial grows light green, softly hairy leaves that mound near the ground. From them rise long, leafless stalks bearing large, marguerite-like flowers in white, yellow, orange, pink, or red.
 The plants generally available are hybrids of *G. jamesonii* and *G. vindifolia*. Some varieties are double; others are only 12 in. (30 cm) high.
Location: Sunny, light, humid, warm; in winter at 54–59°F (12–15°C).
Care: Keep moderately moist; feed weekly. Inside a room, provide humid air by frequent spraying. Each spring, repot in loose, humus-rich soil or in standard mix with sand.
Propagation: From seed or by division.
Pests and Diseases: Whiteflies; powdery mildew.
Uses: Balcony, garden, or house-

GLECHOMA HEDERACEA
Glechoma

Family: Mint, *Lamiaceae*
Native Habitat: Europe, Asia
Flowering Time: Spring to early summer

Hardy in temperate zones, glechoma is an evergreen and poisonous creeper. The twining shoots bear heart-shaped and tufted leaves, fragrant to the touch, and blue-violet flowers that sit in the leaf axils. As a houseplant, the mottled *G. hederacea* 'Variegata' is offered.
Location: Green varieties, partial shade; variegated ones, light. In summer outdoors; in winter light, at 50°F (10°C).
Care: In summer, water freely and feed every two weeks; in winter, water less. Repot in standard soil mix or garden soil with clay and sand. Prune long shoots at any time.
Propagation: By cuttings or offshoots.
Pests and Diseases: Rarely.
Uses: A hanging plant; for cool conservatories and greenhouses; balconies; ground cover for partially shaded areas.

I have found that gerbera is able to tolerate some frost. My plants overwinter in the garden. I cover them with a thick layer of dried leaves and plastic sheeting, to keep the roots from becoming too wet. I do not remove this protection till the end of spring. In milder regions of the temperate zone, this is worth trying.

Gloriosa – Guzmania

What used to be considered various species of climbing lily are now classified as *Gloriosa superba*. Of these, *G. s. 'rothschildiana'* is the best known.

Cut at the right moment, the flowers of the globe amaranth continue to please as long-lasting, colorful, dried flowers.

Unlike *G. robusta*, the species *Grevillea rosmarinifolia* will bloom under cultivation in a container.

Gloriosa superba *'Rothschildiana'*

Gomphrena globosa

Grevillea rosmarinifolia

GLORIOSA SUPERBA
Glory lily

Family: Lily, *Liliaceae*
Native Habitat: Tropical Asia, Africa
Flowering Time: Summer

The climbing lily is a creeper with a short, tuberous main stem from which emerge shoots 6.5 ft. (2 m) long, set with light green leaves. The tip of the leaf tapers to a tendril. The exotic, 3 in.- (8 cm-) wide flowers are green at first and then turn scarlet. Look for the particularly lovely form 'rothschildiana.'

The tuber is poisonous.

Location: Sunny; if behind glass, light shade; warm.
Care: During growth, water freely and feed once a week; after bloom wilts, give less water. Keep the tubers dry and at 64°F (18°C) over the winter. In early spring plant them upright in 6–8 in. (15–20 cm) pots and let them sprout at 68°F (20°C). Offer climbing support.
Propagation: By offsets.
Pests and Diseases: Aphids.
Uses: Climbing plant for conservatories, greenhouses, and patios.

GOMPHRENA GLOBOSA
Globe amaranth

Family: Amaranth, *Amaranthaceae*
Native Habitat: Tropical and subtropical America
Flowering Time: Summer and autumn

This amaranth is annual. About 12 in. (30 cm) high, its leaves are 4 in.- (10 cm-) long ovals. Its flowers in white, pink, or crimson are terminal globes. There are hybrids for balcony planters, only 6 in. (15 cm) high, such as the Buddy series in white or dark red.

Location: Sunny; outdoors sheltered from rain.
Care: Keep moderately moist and feed every two weeks. Plant in standard soil, clay-sand–enriched garden soil, or in balcony potting soil mix.
Propagation: From seed in early spring with bottom heating to 64°F (18°C).
Pests and Diseases: Powdery mildew.
Uses: A flowering houseplant for a room, balcony, or garden.

GREVILLEA
Grevillea; silk tree

Family: Protea, *Proteaceae*
Native Habitat: Australia
Flowering Time: Hardly blooms in cultivation

Grevillea, a tropical shrub about 10 ft. (3 m) high, is raised for its decorative, fernlike foliage, not for its flower; although interesting, it does not appear in cultivation. *G. robusta* grows fast; its leaves are dark green on top and silvery underneath.

G. rosmarinifolia's foliage is needlelike.

Location: Very light; in winter sunny; in summer shaded if under glass. The plant tolerates heat, but planted in a cold conservatory, it can withstand cold down to 23°F (–5°C).
Care: In spring and summer, keep generously moist with soft water and feed every two weeks; never let the root ball dry out. When needed, repot in sandy standard soil using pots not too large. The plant grows suckers if it is too warm in winter. Prune back in spring if leggy.
Propagation: From seed; cuttings take too long.

TIP

Cut flowers of *Gloriosa superba* will last a long time in a vase.

THE MOST BEAUTIFUL PLANTS FROM A TO Z

Grevillea robusta

Propagation: By removing offsets, or from seed with bottom heating. Do not cover the seeds to sprout!

Pests and Diseases: Scale insects and spider mites.

Uses: Very good for closed window greenhouses and glass cases (as long as they fit in size); also for humid conservatories; with frequent spraying, for living areas. Suited to hydroponics.

With loving care, *Grevillea robusta* can grow to the ceiling in two to three years, even though its roots are in a container.

Although the hybrids created from *Guzmania lingulata* var. *minor* are offered as potted plants, they still can be raised on epiphyte supports.

Pests and Diseases: Aphids, whiteflies; if underfed, the foliage pales.

Uses: A decorative green plant, easy to take care of for a light, airy, and cool position, or a cool conservatory.

GUZMANIA
Guzmania

Family: Bromeliad, *Bromeliaceae*
Native Habitat: Central and South America
Flowering Time: Winter to early spring

A typical bromeliad, guzmania forms a rosette out of its long, narrow, shiny green leaves; from its center arises a stalk of spectacular red or orange-red bracts. The

actual flowers are short-lived and modest.

G. lingulata and its cultivars 'Broadway' and 'Cardinalis' are red-bracted. 'Splendens,' has a creamy-white flower. The lovely red bracts of *G. lingulata* var. *minor* grow no longer than 8 in. (20 cm). Good varieties are: 'Orange,' 'Volkaerts Red,' and 'Citrina.' Crossing *G. lingulata* and *G. lingulata* var. *minor* produces more compact hybrid guzmanias, better suited to living room and greenhouse. Well-known, attractive strains are 'magnifica,' 'intermedia,' 'orangeade,' and 'omer morobe.'

Location: Year round light or partial shade; warm and humid.

Care: Use soft, lukewarm water; after it flowers, fill the funnel as well; spray frequently. Feed lightly every two weeks. Provide moist air by embedding the pot in sphagnum or placing it on wet pebbles. No need to repot, as the mother plant dies off after it flowers.

Guzmania lingulata *hybrid*

Gymnocalycium – Haemanthus

The "strawberry cactus," *Gymnocalycium mihanovichii* var. *friedrichii* f. *rubrum* lacks chlorophyll and is incapable of photosynthesis. A mutation, it cannot survive longer than a few years, nor can mutations that have other strange coloring.

Gymnocalycium baldianum remains short and blooms violet, while *G. gibbosum* reaches 24 in. (60 cm) in height and has white flowers.

Gymnocalycium mihanovichii *var.* friedrichii f. `rubrum'

Gymnocalycium baldianum

Gymnocalycium gibbosum

GYMNOCALYCIUM
Awl cactus

Family: Cactus, *Cactaceae*
Native Habitat: South America
Flowering Time: Spring to fall

Almost all *Gymnocalycia* are flattened spheres with notched or knobbly ribs and brownish black thorns. Their funnel-shaped flowers are 1–2 in. (3–5 cm) wide and glow white, red, or yellow. Reliable varieties are *G. andreae* (yellow flowers); *G. baldianum* (crimson flowers); *G. gibbosum* (white flowers). Best known is the "strawberry cactus," a mutation of *G. mihanovichii* grafted onto *Hylocereus trigonus*.

Location: Light all year, but not full sun; airy; in summer outdoors sheltered from rain. In winter at 46–54°F (8–12°C).
Care: In summer, water moderately; in winter, keep not quite dry. During growth, give cactus food once a month. The plant thrives on soil that is two parts humus and one part sand.
Propagation: By removing side shoots or from seed.
Pests and Diseases: Mealybugs.
Uses: For light rooms and greenhouses.

GYNURA
Velvet plant

Family: Aster, *Asteraceae*
Native Habitat: Tropical Africa, Asia
Flowering Time: Autumn to early winter; *G. scandens*, spring to fall.

The shoots of *Gynura* twine and coil; its serrated leaves are matted with glowing, purple hair.

Best known is *G. aurantiaca* from Java. It will grow about 3.2 ft. (1 m) high; its leaves are 6 in. (15 cm) long. The flowers are small and yellow-orange; they grow in loose spikes.

G. procumbens has 6.5 ft.- (2 m-) long hanging or creeping shoots. The deeply serrated leaves are

Gynura aurantiaca

Haemanthus albiflos

wine red underneath; the orange flowers sit at the ends of the shoots. *G. scandens* has climbing or creeping shoots and roughly toothed leaves.

Location: Year-round very light but not sunny; at room temperature or warmer in summer; needs humid air.

Care: Water regularly and feed lightly once a week. Do not spray the leaves. Force the plant to branch by regular pruning. Since only young plants have the lovely purple coloring, the mother plant is replaced every two years with its own offspring. Repot annually in standard or flower soil mix.

Propagation: By tip or shoot cuttings at 68–77°F (20–25°C).

Pests and Diseases: Spider mites, aphids.

Uses: A houseplant; very decorative in hanging baskets.

HAEMANTHUS
Blood lily

Family: Lily, *Liliaceae*
Native Habitat: Africa
Flowering Time: Summer

Haemanthus is an undemanding bulb plant with white or red flowers, depending on the species.

H. albiflos grows thick, fleshy, broad, straplike leaves; among them rises the creamy-white, umbellate flower on a long stalk; its stamens are yellow. *H. katherinae* forms leaves 12–16 in. (30–40 cm) long. On its 16–20 in. (40–50 cm) stalk is the flower, glowing scarlet,

its stamens protruding. A well-known variety is 'King Albert,' which has lately been reclassified as genus *Scadoxus* by botanists. Both species contain poisonous chemicals, as do all their relatives.

Location: Light, no sun; warm. In winter at a maximum of 59°F (15°C).

Care: In spring, plant single bulbs in smallish pots, using medium-heavy flower soil mix or standard soil with a clay additive. Keep the bulbs at 61–64°F (16–18°C) and water lightly, for slow sprouting. They take some time for root formation. As soon as growth is visible, increase both water and temperature. Feed every two weeks. In fall reduce water just to maintain the leaves.

Propagation: By bulbs for *H. katherinae* and by offsets for *H. albiflos*.

Pests and Diseases: Rarely. If too warm in winter, the development of leaves and flower stalks is arrested.

Uses: A houseplant for light, warm locations.

Scadoxus multiflorus ssp. katherinae
syn. Haemanthus katherinae

Unusual but visually striking is the use of *Gynura* in balcony planters. It looks best against a white wall.

Letting *Haemanthus* dry out during its growth period causes long-lasting damage to the plant.

TIP

It is very easy to propagate a blood lily. Left to itself, any cut leaf will develop bulbils on its cut surface after a while. These little "bulbs" will sprout if they are planted.

Hatiora – Hebe

An enclosed window greenhouse or a glass case provides *Hatiora bambusoides* with accommodation appropriate to its species.

Haworthia guttata is one of those haworthia treasures that can be found only in specialty nurseries.

Hatiora bambusoides

HATIORA
Hatiora; rhipsalis

Family: Cactus, *Cactaceae*
Native Habitat: Brazil
Flowering Time: Winter

Hatoria grows in 0.75–2 in.- (2–5 cm-) long cylindrical or bottle-shaped shoots that harden and frequently divide to form a shrubby cactus. The small, terminal, funnel-shaped flowers are yellow or blue-violet. Well-known species are *H. bambusoides, H. clavata* (Rhipsalis clavata), *H. cylindrica, H. herminiae,* and *H. salicornioides*.
Location: Light or partial shade all year; warm. In winter two months of rest at 50°F (10°C) to promote flowering.
Care: In spring and summer, water freely and feed monthly. Keep it dry during its winter rest.
Propagation: By stem sections.
Pests and Diseases: Root rot if too moist in winter; buds fall if too warm in winter.
Uses: Hanging plant for a light, warm location.

TIP

Given the numerous species, it is a pleasure to collect haworthias. My own collection fits into a 21 in.- (55 cm-) wide, flat dish. A selection of small, colored pebbles provides landscaping.

Haworthia guttata

HAWORTHIA
Haworthia; fairy washboards

Family: Lily, *Liliaceae*
Native Habitat: South Africa
Flowering Time: Early summer to fall, depending on species

Most haworthias are stemless, rosette-forming succulents that grow no higher than 8 in. (20 cm). The small, white bell flowers form a raceme at the tip of a long, bare stalk. The surfaces of the leaves are often knobbly, their edges armed with little teeth. A small selection of species: *H. attenuata* has longish, pointed, green leaves with white tubercles that are grouped into cross-bands. Similarly green-banded *H. baccata* has broader and more rounded leaves than *H. attenuata*. The pale green leaves of *H. bolusii* are tufted at the edges. The small rosettes of *H. cuspidata* look like jewels. *H. fasciata* has fleshy leaves, cross-striped in green on top and set with white tubercles underneath. The leaves of *H. margaritifera* are dark green with upturned tips; they are covered with pearl-white tubercles. The leaves of *H. maughanii* are about 1 in. (3 cm) long; they look like abruptly cut, dark green half-cylinders. *H. reinwardtii* has shoots up to 8 in. (20 cm) long, spiraling, and covered with white tubercles.
Location: Light, no strong sun; in summer outdoors; warm. In winter cool at 50-54°F (10-12°C).

Haworthia baccata

Care: During growth, water moderately (no water into the rosette!) and apply cactus food once a month. In winter keep lightly moist. Haworthias are repotted every spring in cactus soil with a clay additive.
Propagation: By side rosettes or offsets, which have to dry off before being planted; from seed.
Pests and Diseases: Rarely.
Uses: An easy house plant.

Hebe andersonii hybrid

Haworthia cuspidata

Haworthia baccata and Haworthia cuspidata, two more tempting choices for the collection.

If possible, the hybrids of Hebe andersonii should summer out-of-doors. In a closed room, their flowers do not last long.

HEBE ANDERSONII HYBRIDS
Anderson hebe hybrids
Bush Veronica

Family: Figwort, *Scrophulariaceae*
Native Habitat: New Zealand
Flowering Time: Late summer to fall

This is an upright, evergreen shrub with leathery, light green or colored or patterned leaves. Numerous small flowers grow in axial racemes or spikes. A cross between *H. salicifolia* and *H. speciosa* and other species, these hybrids are available in many colors, e.g.: 'Albertine' (purplish pink), 'Imperial Blue' (violet-blue), 'Snowflake' (white). The cultivar 'variegata' has white-edged leaves.

Location: Very light, full sun; in summer outdoors. In winter light at 43–50°F (6–10°C).
Care: Keep evenly moist, avoid waterlogging. During growth, feed every two weeks. Reduce water in winter. In spring, repot into well-draining soil, e.g., potting soil with humus and sand added.
Propagation: By tip cuttings with bottom heating.
Pests and Diseases: Seldom.
Uses: This is a house, balcony, or container plant.

In addition to those listed, there are other less sensitive species of hebe; if sheltered, these can spend the winter in planters and boxes on the balcony: *Hebe albicans* and *H. buxifolia. H. pinguifolia* is especially hardy; the variety 'papagei' has intensely blue leaves.

231

Hedera

It seems to the destiny of English ivy to be the hanging houseplant of choice; its tolerance for shade is an important component of its success.

Hedera algeriensis, recently reassigned to Hedera helix, has to have support for its shoots if you want it to look like this, an upright plant.

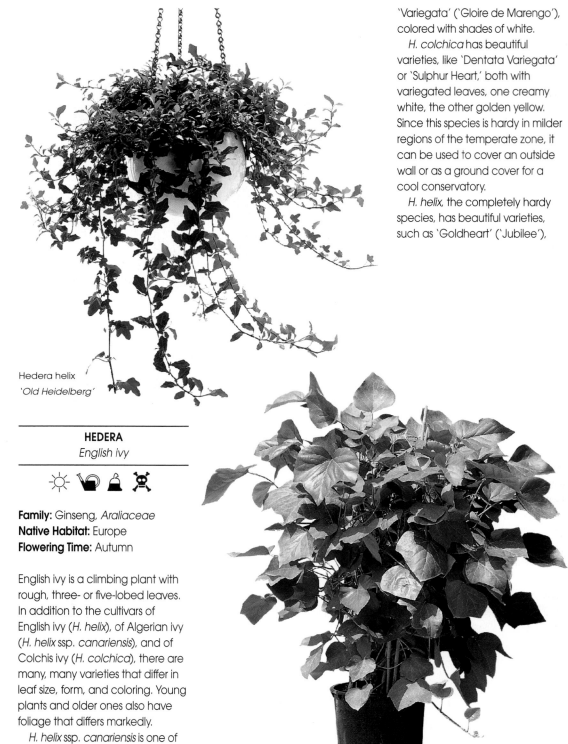

Hedera helix
'Old Heidelberg'

HEDERA
English ivy

☀ 🪣 🔔 ☠

Family: Ginseng, *Araliaceae*
Native Habitat: Europe
Flowering Time: Autumn

English ivy is a climbing plant with rough, three- or five-lobed leaves. In addition to the cultivars of English ivy (*H. helix*), of Algerian ivy (*H. helix* ssp. *canariensis*), and of Colchis ivy (*H. colchica*), there are many, many varieties that differ in leaf size, form, and coloring. Young plants and older ones also have foliage that differs markedly.

H. helix ssp. *canariensis* is one of the larger ivy species; its large (to 8 in. (20 cm)) leaves sit on red petioles. The most beloved variety is

'Variegata' ('Gloire de Marengo'), colored with shades of white.

H. colchica has beautiful varieties, like 'Dentata Variegata' or 'Sulphur Heart,' both with variegated leaves, one creamy white, the other golden yellow. Since this species is hardy in milder regions of the temperate zone, it can be used to cover an outside wall or as a ground cover for a cool conservatory.

H. helix, the completely hardy species, has beautiful varieties, such as 'Goldheart' ('Jubilee'),

Hedera helix

232

'Green Ripple,' 'Hanny,' and 'Heise.' It develops shoots 16 ft. (5 m) long. With protection, it can overwinter outside, in a container. You can also buy English ivy grafted on fatshedera, standard trained.

Warning: the berries that grow on older plants and those that live outdoors are very poisonous.

Location: In summer very light, but not sunny and rather cool; outdoors. Raise atmospheric humidity if it becomes very warm. Variegated plants need more light; green ones tolerate shade. In winter light and cool, at 50°F (10°C). *H. helix* ssp. *canariensis* should be kept warm all year.

Care: During growth, water regularly and feed weekly. In winter cut back watering and feed once a month. Tie the shoots of 'variegata' ('Gloire de Marengo') to its support now and then, as this variety does not grip well. To achieve a bushy habit, prune shoots back in the spring. Repot every two to three years.

Propagation: By tip or stem cuttings with bottom heat.

Pests and Diseases: In a warm room in the winter, spider mites and scale insects; black spot if too wet; pale leaves if too much light. Variegated leaves turn green if too dark.

Uses: A houseplant that will climb or cascade; for cool stairways; suited to hydroponics.

Hedera helix

This English ivy growing on a spiral is a brilliant piece of training. Though a good idea, it has its limits: new growth will have to be cut off, or the spiral will need more and more turns.

TIP

English ivy is very ornamental. In my guest bathroom, where the heating is rarely used, an ivy grows as a decorative frame around the mirror.

Heliotropium – Hippeastrum

The blue-violet of heliotrope may look a bit dark in a balcony planter; companion flowers in white, pink, or yellow bring it to life.

If a hibiscus is well looked after and pruned just like a rose, it will remain compact and bushy and bloom profusely.

Heliotropium arborescens

HELIOTROPIUM ARBORESCENS
Common heliotrope

Family: Borage, *Boraginaceae*
Native Habitat: Peru
Flowering Time: Spring to fall

Heliotrope is a bushy, compact annual (about 24 in. (60 cm) high), with rough, dark green leaves and dark violet, vanilla-scented flowers in terminal umbels. Good cultivars are: 'Marine,' whose color is more toward blue, and 'Marguerite,' with dark blue flowers marked with a white spot. Heliotrope contains poisonous chemicals.
Location: Full sun; sheltered from wind outdoors; the plant can be wintered at 50°F (10°C), but is not worth the trouble.
Care: Water moderately; never let it dry out; feed every two weeks. Remove all dead flowers to encourage further budding.
Propagation: From seed with bottom heat and uncovered; by cuttings from a mother plant that is kept warm till midwinter.
Pests and Diseases: Whiteflies.
Uses: Beautiful flowering plant for balcony planters and dishes.

Hibiscus rosa-sinensis

HIBISCUS ROSA-SINENSIS
Hibiscus, rose mallow

Family: Mallow, *Malvaceae*
Native Habitat: Tropical Asia, probably southern China
Flowering Time: Spring to fall

A very beautiful flowering plant of treelike or shrubby habit, with dark green, shiny leaves that vary in shape. The large flower is funnel-like and its stamens protrude.

With its many varieties, *H. rosa-sinensis* is an example of successful breeding: the plant has become one of the most attractive of house and container plants. Profuse flowering is common even for young plants. Though each flower lives only for one day, new buds are ready to open each day. Colors range from red, through orange and yellow, to white. Double and simple flowers are available; the flower of the pure species is simple and red. Plants are sold treated with a growth-retardant that will wear off after about a year. After that, the rose mallow grows a bit leggy and can reach 10 ft. (3 m).
Location: Inside, very light (but not sunny), and warm; outdoors sunny, sheltered from wind and rain. In winter light, at about 59°F (15°C).
Care: During growth keep evenly moist; never let the root ball dry out. In winter reduce watering. In heated rooms, provide direct and indirect atmospheric humidity. Till the end of summer, feed weekly; in

TIP

When the leaves and flowers of your hibiscus start to become smaller, a good pruning and fresh soil will rejuvenate the plant. By the way, the cooler the plant is kept in the winter (down to 54°F (12°C)), the more richly it will flower.

winter once a month, only if the plant is kept warm.

Propagation: By tip cuttings, with bottom heating. Prune young plants several times to achieve bushy habit and profuse budding.

Pests and Diseases: Spider mites, aphids if roots are dry; buds fall if kept too cold or its position is changed.

Uses: House or container plant; specimen for the conservatory; suited to hydroponics.

An assortment of Hippeastrum varieties

If you start many *Hippeastrum* bulbs at one time, you will be able to enjoy a bountiful show of spring blossoms.

HIPPEASTRUM
Hippeastrum, "amaryllis"

Family: Lily, *Liliaceae*
Native Habitat: South America
Flowering Time: Winter to spring

Hippeastrum is a bulb plant; only its cultivars are generally available. After it sprouts in winter or spring, a tall, hollow stalk rises up to 31 in. (80 cm), carrying three to four large, funnel-shaped blossoms. Two or three flower stalks are quite common. Colors include white, pink, and red; there are also many-colored corollas with stripes or contrasting throats. Newer hybrids are the result of re-crossing large hybrids with the wild species; these

cultivars are smaller, have several stalks, and each stalk carries up to six blossoms.

"Amaryllis" contains poisonous substances.

Location: While blooming, light, at about 64°F (18°C). In summer outside.

Care: Sprout the bulbs in late fall or winter at about 68°F (20°C), at a window, after you have planted them in a relatively large pot in standard or flower soil mix. Half the bulb must be above ground. Water very lightly at first; once sprouted, increase water gradually, till the stalk is hand-high; then water freely. Keep bulb dry when watering. Spray till the flower appears. After the flower wilts, cut the stalk at soil level; continue to water regularly and feed biweekly

till the late summer. Allow leaves to dry slowly by placing the pot in a rain-free spot; then rest the bulb in a cool, dark spot for two months before sprouting it again.

Propagation: By bulb offsets; they flower in two to three years.

Pests and Diseases: Soft-bodied mites, thrips, amaryllis rust.

Uses: An attractive flowering plant. Suited to hydroponics.

When buying bulbs, look for size and firmness because the rule is the larger the bulb, the more flowers can be expected. My five *Hippeastrum* bulbs are sprouted at three-week intervals; this way I have one blooming throughout the winter.

Howeia – Humulus

This magnificent specimen of *Howeia forsteriana* shows just how elegant this palm becomes with increasing maturity.

The flower umbels of *Hoya multiflora* resemble little bundles of gleaming pearls.

Howeia forsteriana

Hoya multiflora

HOWEIA (KENTIA)
Howeia, sentry palm

Family: Palm, *Arecaceae*
Native Habitat: Lord Howe Island in the South Pacific
Flowering Time: Rarely blooms under cultivation

The compound leaf of the sentry palm is 6.5–10 ft. (2–3 m) long. The two best-known species, *Howeia belmoreana* and *H. forsteriana*, differ in size and habit: *H. belmoreana* is shorter and grows upright; the habit of *H. forsteriana* is bushier, and it grows slowly. Both species are raised in pots with multiple stems.
Location: Light or partial shade all year, no direct sun; warm (61–70°F (16–21°C)). Older plants outdoors in summer.
Care: Water regularly with soft water, letting the soil dry in between; administer light, nonalkaline plant food every week. Repot only when roots completely fill the container; use deep tubs and peat-rich soil.
Propagation: From seed; sprouting time is two to twelve months.
Pests and Diseases: Scale insects; spider mites and thrips if the air is too dry.
Uses: A decorative house and container plant; for conservatories; good for hydroponics.

HOYA
Hoya; wax plant

Family: Milkweed, *Asclepiadaceae*
Native Habitat: China, Malaysia, Australia
Flowering Time: Late spring to autumn

Hoya is an evergreen vine with shoots 3.2 ft. (1 m) long and slightly succulent, dark green leaves. The plant bears groups of 12–20 waxy-looking, star-shaped, umbellate flowers. They are white, sometimes tinted with pink, with a central eye. When it is hot they exude honey-sweet nectar and have a strong fragrance. Each blossom lasts for weeks. The most important species is *H. carnosa*, which also has a Variegata form.

H. bella is more dainty and pendulant. It cascades well and thrives in orchid baskets.

Other species are *H. lacunosa*, a spring bloomer, and *H. multiflora*, with greenish yellow flowers.
Location: In summer light and warm; in winter at only 54–59°F (12–15°C). to promote flowering.
Care: Keep evenly and lightly moist; spray often. After

Hoya carnosa

Humulus japonicus

Hoya carnosa can become very large over the years; eventually, you may be forced to prune it. For the windowsill, the more compact *Hoya bella* is better suited.

midautumn, cut back on water, but the root ball should not be dry in its cool winter position. Feed biweekly during growth. Repot older plants if needed in standard soil mix with drainage, using pots just a little larger. Once buds appear, do not move hoya, to prevent the buds from falling. Provide support for climbing.
Propagation: In spring by tip or stem cuttings with bottom heating.

Hoya bella

Rooting takes six to eight weeks.
Pests and Diseases: Scale insects, aphids, or spider mites if too warm in winter; leaves fall if roots are soggy.
Uses: Climbing or hanging plant for light rooms. Good for hydroponics.

HUMULUS JAPONICUS
Japanese hop

Family: Mulberry, *Moraceae*
Native Habitat: Japan, Taiwan, China
Flowering Time: Late summer

Japanese hop is an annual that climbs up to 13 ft. (4 m) high; its leaves are five- or seven-lobed. The small, yellow-green flowers go unnoticed. A fast-growing variety is the white-patterned 'Variegatus.'
Location: Sun to partial shade.
Care: During growth, water freely and feed monthly, but avoid waterlogging. *Humulus* grows fast and vigorously: it needs good climbing support.
Propagation: From seed in early spring.
Pests and Diseases: Rarely.
Uses: Fast-growing screen for balconies and terraces.

TIP

When snipping dead flowers off hoya, remove only a single blossom and its little stalk. Do not take off the whole umbel, as the shoots of older wood will produce ever new flowers.

Hyacinthus – Hymenocallis

Hyacinthus arrived in Europe from the Orient in the middle of the sixteenth century. Forcing hyacinths to bloom on glasses is a far more recent development.

The inflorescence of hydrangea consists of small, insignificant flowers and spectacular, colored sepals.

Hyacinthus orientalis

Hydrangea macrophylla

Hyacinths on their glasses

In specialty nurseries, you can obtain bulbs of *Hyacinthus orientalis* that have received temperature treatment after they were harvested; thus they are more advanced and will bloom earlier.

HYACINTHUS ORIENTALIS
Hyacinth

Family: Lily, *Liliaceae*
Native Habitat: Mediterranean region, Asia Minor
Flowering Time: Midwinter and late spring

An 8–12 in.- (20–30 cm-) high bulb plant, hyacinth has upright, light green leaves and large flower spikes of numerous, fragrant blossoms in different colors. For forcing indoors, choose among: 'City of Harlem' (light yellow); 'Delft Blue' (porcelain blue); 'Jan Bos' (light red); 'L'Innocence' (ivory white); 'Ostara' (dark blue); 'Pink Pearl' (deep, dark pink); and 'Gipsy Queen' (apricot). To force hyacinths to bloom early indoors, there are two methods.

Forcing in Soil
Plant the bulbs, starting in the fall, in pots or bowls with sandy garden soil. The tip of the bulb should be about 0.4 in. (1 cm) above soil level. Bury the pots about 8 in. (20 cm) deep in your garden and cover with a thick layer of leaves. Alternatively, if temperatures are under 54°F (12°C), place them in a dark box on the balcony. After

about 10 weeks, when the buds begin to form, move them to a cool, darkish place and gradually accustom them to more and more light.

Forcing on Glasses
Fill the glasses in midautumn with boiled water, preferably adding a few pieces of charcoal. There has to be a gap of 0.75–1.5 in. (2–4 cm) between the bottom of the bulb and the water. Cap the bulbs and move the glasses to a dark, cool place (under 50°F (10°C)). Occasionally add boiled or rainwater to maintain the level. When shoots reach about 4 in. (10 cm), move them gradually to a warmer place. Remove the cap when the shoot lifts it off.
Location: The cooler the location, the longer the flowers will last.
Care: Water normally. Plant bulbs in your garden after they have flowered; they cannot be forced again.
Propagation: From bulbs.
Pests and Diseases: If the period of darkness is too short, no flower develops.
Uses: As a flowering plant indoors; otherwise, as a garden plant.

HYDRANGEA MACROPHYLLA
Hydrangea

Family: Saxifrage, *Saxifragaceae*
Native Habitat: China, Southeast Asia
Flowering Time: Spring and summer

Hydrangea is a shrubby plant with large, dark green, roughly serrated leaves. The huge umbels of its flowers come in shades of white, pink, and light blue. The blue color is the result of acidifying the soil with aluminum sulfate or potash. It is really the sepals that color, while the flowers themselves are small, yellow-green, and go unnoticed. Over the years, hydrangeas can become magnificent container plants and huge shrubs outdoors. Good varieties are: 'Blue Wave,' 'Lilacina,' 'Veitchii,' 'Mme E. Mouillere,' and 'Blue Bonnet.' Hydrangeas are long-lived. The ones planted in 1923 for my father's confirmation in front of his parents' house on the Moselle River grew into enormous shrubs that bloomed profusely each year. They were there in 1968 and may still be blooming today.
Location: Light but no direct sun; cool all year; in summer outdoors, shaded.

Care: Water well, from below, with soft water; administer rhododendron or other nonalkaline food once a week till late summer. Avoid dry root ball. After leaves fall in the autumn, reduce watering and store cool and free of frost. Gradually move to warmer locations starting in late winter. Pruning should take place in spring, as hydrangeas bloom on two-year-old wood.

Propagation: By tip cuttings.

Pests and Diseases: Aphids, spider mites; yellow leaves mean calcium in the water.

Uses: An attractive house and container plant.

HYMENOCALLIS
Hymenocallis

Family: Lily, *Liliaceae*

Native Habitat: Southern United States, Central and South America

Flowering Time: Summer; depending on the species, at other times of the year

Between the tall, straplike leaves of this bulb plant appears a long, bare stalk, tipped with four to twelve enormous, fragrant flowers. The plant is poisonous. *H. x festalis* is a somewhat smaller, white-blooming hybrid.

The most commonly grown species is *H. narcissiflora*. Its stalk is 3.2 ft. (1 m) high and bears 5–6 flowers.

H. speciosa is a species that does not go into dormancy in winter.

Location: Light and warm.

Care: Plant the bulb in late winter or spring; set aside at 61–64°F (16–18°C). Gradually increase both temperature and water; feed once a month, increasing to once a week. In autumn, allow bulbs that will lose their leaves to slow down gradually. Store them in wood shavings at 50–59°F (10–15°C) over the winter. Maintain plants that keep their leaves just barely moist at 59–68°F (15–20°C).

Propagation: From bulbs.

Pests and Diseases: Rarely.

Uses: A decorative and unusual potted plant.

Hydrangea can reach respectable proportions in a container and will last for many years.

Hymenocallis x festalis stays more compact than the better-known species, *H. narcissiflora*. Here it is underplanted with *Exacum affine*.

Hydrangea macrophylla *in a container*

Hymenocallis x festalis

TIP

The old name of hymenocallis, *Ismene*, is still in use among some nursery persons.

Hypocyrta – Impatiens

You can grow *Hypocyrta glabra* in a pot and later move it to a hanging basket.

The American name of *Hypoestes phyllostachya*, "pink polka-dot" is appropriate to this charming, colorful leaf plant.

Hypocyrta glabra

Hypoestes phyllostachya

I use *Hypoestes* outdoors, perhaps in a balcony planter. The flower looks especially good when varieties of different colors are planted together.

HYPOCYRTA GLABRA
Hypocyrta; pouch plant; guppy fish plant

Family: Gesneriad, *Gesneriaceae*
Native Habitat: Brazil
Flowering Time: Spring to summer

This is a low-growing, bushy plant with leathery, dark green, shiny leaves that remind one faintly of boxwood. The branches of this small shrub begin to arch when it is mature, and they open small, orange-yellow flowers. Their petals balloon, as if blown up.
Location: As light as possible all year, but not full sun; in summer outdoors. A cool winter position, at about 59°F (15°C), helps bud setting.
Care: Keep moderately moist in summer with soft water; feed every two weeks. In winter, water rarely. Prune after it has flowered; this promotes both flowering and bushiness.
Propagation: By tip cuttings.
Pests and Diseases: If too warm in winter, aphids.
Uses: An undemanding plant for light rooms; a good hanging plant.

HYPOESTES PHYLLOSTACHYA
Pink polka-dot plant

Family: Acanthus, *Acanthaceae*
Native Habitat: Madagascar
Flowering Time: Autumn

It is the leaves of this small, 16–20 in.- (40–50 cm-) high shrub that attract attention: they are olive green and covered with pink, red, or white dots or spots. The pale crimson, tubular flowers are small and insignificant.

Several varieties are good, among them, 'Pink Splash,' with leaves marked in an almost mauve color, and 'Pink Dot,' with particularly pretty pink spots.

Generally, this good-looking little tropical plant is grown as an annual and consequently is herbaceous rather than woody. This is due to the fact that it does not get enough light in the winter. Under optimal light conditions (e.g., under a plant light), the plant will become shrubby in colder latitudes, as you will find with *Hypoestes* kept in botanical gardens.
Location: Very light all year, so the leaves keep their colors, but no strong sun. Warm (68°F (20°C)) and humid.
Care: Keep well moistened with soft water; spray a lot. Feed every two weeks during growth and once a month in winter. Prune leggy plants radically before they start putting out shoots.
Propagation: From seed in spring or by tip cuttings with bottom heating. Rooting takes eight weeks. Prune young plants several times to create bushy form.
Pests and Diseases: Root rot and leaf loss through soggy roots. Pale leaf colors if too dark.
Uses: A wonderful foliage plant for light, warm rooms, greenhouses, glass cases, and window gardens. Well suited to use as a ground cover in warm conservatories. Young plants can be used for underplanting.

The Most Beautiful Plants from A to Z

Impatiens-Neuguinea *hybrids*

Impatiens walleriana

IMPATIENS WALLERIANA
Impatience; busy Lizzy

Family: Touch-me-not, *Balsaminaceae*
Native Habitat: Tropical East Africa, subtropical Asia
Flowering Time: All year

The *Impatiens* is a bushy flowering plant with fleshy stems and leaves. This plant is usually raised as an annual. It has become one of our most frequently used balcony and houseplants because it has a very long flowering time.

I. walleriana is the parent of many varieties. Many contemporary cultivars, such as 'Miss Smiss' or 'Futura,' are able to tolerate sun. As houseplants, the New Guinea hybrids, with beautifully marked leaves, have become popular. The vivid flowers come in white, orange, pink, purple, and red, as well as all colors in between. Lovely varieties are, for example, 'Spectra' and 'Tango,' for which seeds are also available. In addition there are double varieties that resemble tiny roses.

Location: Light but not sunny; at normal room temperatures, outdoors in summer. In winter at 50–61°F (10–16°C).

Care: Keep moist in summer, avoid waterlogging. During its winter rest, water sparingly with soft water. Spring to fall feed every two weeks with half-diluted plant food. Provide extra humidity if temperatures rise above 70°F (21°C). Prune leggy plants back in the fall.

Propagation: From seed in midwinter; seeds require light to germinate: place them uncovered on the windowsill and provide extra plant lighting for flowers in late spring. Tip cuttings root very easily.

Pests and Diseases: Spider mites, whiteflies, aphids; stem rot if kept too wet and cold .

Uses: Popular flowering plant for balconies, patios, and indoors; good for underplanting containers and for hydroponics.

There is one disadvantage in using New Guinea *Impatiens* hybrids: they do not bloom right through; their flowers appear at intervals. There are always times when there are no flowers.

Contemporary varieties and cultivars of *Impatiens walleriana* are able to tolerate sun, as long as their roots are well watered before the hottest part of the day.

Mixed 'Belizzy' Impatiens

241

Iochroma – Jacaranda

A rare shade of blue-violet is the hallmark of *Iochroma cyaneum* 'grandiflorum.'

The flowers of *Ipomoea* are open only in the morning if the sun shines; on cloudy days, however, they may stay open into the afternoon.

Emphasized by back-lighting, the red coloring of the iresine is very obvious .

I plant iresines in my balcony boxes, where they thrive during the summer and provide a spectacular show.

Iochroma cyaneum '*Grandiflorum*'

IOCHROMA CYANEUM
Violet bush

Family: Nightshade, *Solanaceae*
Native Habitat: Colombia
Flowering Time: Late summer; depending on care and location, all year

The *Iochroma* is a 6.5–8 ft.- (2–2.5 m-) high shrub with brittle branches. Its elliptical leaves are covered with fine gray hair. The long, tubular flowers hang in clusters on the tips of the shoots. The violet bush blooms blue to violet and also pink. A new variety, 'Samba,' blooms red.
   Iochroma is poisonous in all its parts.
Location: In summer, light to partial shade; outdoors if sheltered. In winter, light or dark at 43–54°F (6–12°C).
Care: Water generously and feed well every week. Tie up the shoots as they grow.
Propagation: By soft cuttings in summer.
Pests and Diseases: Spider mites, whiteflies; young plants are susceptible to fungi during prolonged wet weather.
Uses: Container plant.

Ipomoea purpurea

IPOMOEA
Morning glory

Family: Morning glory, *Convolvulaceae*
Native Habitat: Tropical America
Flowering Time: Late summer to late autumn

A very fast-growing climber with entwined shoots and heart-shaped leaves. It is raised as an annual. The blossoms of the morning glory can be 4 in. (10 cm) across; they can be blue, purple, pink, or white, or they may be patterned in several colors. Best known is *Ipomoea purpurea*, which now goes under the name *Pharbitis purpurea*.
   The plant is poisonous.
Location: Sunny and sheltered against wind, outdoors. Does not last over winter.
Care: Never allow the roots to dry out while the plant is growing. Feed weekly. Provide trellis for climbing.
Propagation: From seed in spring.
Pests and Diseases: Spider mites; in cold, wet summers it does not grow well.
Uses: A pretty screen for balconies and terraces.

Iresine herbstii

IRESINE HERBSTII
Iresine, blood leaf

Family: Amaranth, *Amaranthaceae*
Native Habitat: Brazil
Flowering Time: Does not bloom in cultivation

This bushy, 12 in.- (30 cm-) high foliage plant is raised as an annual. Its leaves are rounded or pointed ovals, fleshy, and very colorful; they have red petioles. The most gorgeous variety is 'aureo-reticulata': its petiole and leaf veins are wine red, while the leaf blade is variegated in green and gold.
Location: Year-round strong light, even full sun; warm and airy.
Care: Keep evenly moist; in spring and summer, feed every two weeks. Prune young or leggy plants frequently. It is best to raise new plants every year.
Propagation: By tip cuttings in water or soil. Very easy.
Pests and Diseases: Rarely; leaves revert to dark red if they do not have enough light.
Uses: A magnificent pot or container plant for the balcony or patio; good for planting in a conservatory that is not too cold.

Ixora coccinea

Jacaranda mimosifolia

IXORA COCCINEA
Ixora coccinea

Family: Madder, *Rubiaceae*
Native Habitat: India
Flowering Time: Early spring to autumn

Ixora is an evergreen shrub, about 3.2–5 ft. (1–1.5 m) high. Its leaves are like leather; its flowers stand in terminal clusters and they are luminously scarlet. Numerous hybrids exist.

Location: Light all year, no direct sun; humid and warm. The soil should be at 64–68°F (18–20°C).
Care: During growth, water regularly, in winter more sparingly, with soft water; spray very frequently and feed biweekly. Once buds have set, do not move the plant or they will fall.
Propagation: By tip cuttings in spring with bottom heating.
Pests and Diseases: Scale insects if too dry; chlorosis if hard, cold water is used.
Uses: For enclosed window gardens, glass cases, or planted in warm conservatories.

JACARANDA MIMOSIFOLIA
Jacaranda, fern tree

Family: Trumpet creeper, *Bignoniaceae*
Native Habitat: Central and South America
Flowering Time: Spring

Because of its 18 in.- (45 cm-) long, delicately compound leaves, *J. mimosifolia* goes under the common name fern tree. Actually,

Blooming jacaranda tree on Tenerife

the name is very descriptive. In cultivation only older specimens will bloom, but in its native habitat, the jacaranda tree does put out flowers. They appear just before the new shoots, in terminal, spherical racemes. The individual blossoms are about 2 in. (5 cm) long and bell-shaped.

Location: Very light but not sunny; warm and humid. In winter, light and cooler at 59°F (15°C).
Care: Year-round, keep evenly moist; spray frequently; feed very moderately. Prune any time.
Propagation: From seed with bottom heating, after soaking seeds for 24 hours. Sprouting takes two to three weeks. Keep young plants cool in winter.
Pests and Diseases: Aphids and whiteflies if too warm in winter.
Uses: When young, as houseplant; otherwise, a container plant; very beautiful for the conservatory.

Ixora coccinea tends to grow leggy, which makes us want to prune it. Always remember that the flowers appear at the tips of the shoots.

As an indoor plant in colder regions, *Jacaranda mimosifolia* is valued mostly for its fernlike compound leaves. In its own habitat, it becomes an impressive tree.

TIP

Because in winter the intensity of the light decreases in northern latitudes, jacaranda drops many of its leaves; remove fallen leaves immediately, as they have a disagreeable smell.

Jacobinia – Jatropha

Jacobinia carnea is a tropical beauty, sensitive to dry air and dry roots.

The evergreen *Jacobinia pauciflora* is an ideal conservatory plant.

Jacobinia carnea

Jacobinia pauciflora

JACOBINIA
Jacobinia

Family: Acanthus, *Acanthaceae*
Native Habitat: South America
Flowering Time: *J. carnea*, summer through fall; *J. pauciflora*, winter through spring

The genus *Jacobinia* was formerly known as *Justicia*; it provides us with two very different houseplants. *J. carnea* is about 5–6 in. (12–15 cm) high, has broad, elliptical, dark green leaves, and grows spikelike clusters of pink to orange flowers.

J. pauciflora is an evergreen, about 20 in. (50 cm) high, and bears pendant, red-and-yellow flowers in great profusion.
Location: *J. carnea*: light, no direct sun all year; warm and humid. *J. pauciflora*: full sun all year, in summer outdoors. In winter at 50–54°F (10–12°C).
Care: Keep both species moist during the summer, but

J. pauciflora needs a cooler spot and less water. Feed both species during active growth once a week. *J. carnea* can be pruned back in early fall, after it has bloomed, though in the first year or so this will hardly be necessary, as plants are treated with growth retardants.
Propagation: By tip cuttings in the spring, with bottom heating. Rooting takes about three weeks. Prune young *J. carnea* plants quite vigorously to achieve a bushy habit.
Pests and Diseases: Spider mites and aphids; *J. pauciflora* loses its leaves as soon as its roots dry out.
Uses: Very nice, flowering house-plants; *J. carnea* for warm, *J. pauciflora* for cold conservatories.

JASMINUM
Jasminum

Family: Olive, *Oleaceae*
Native Habitat: Tropical and subtropical Africa, Asia, and the Americas
Flowering Time: Depending on the species, any time of year

Jasmine is a climbing or twining evergreen or deciduous shrub. Its leaves are alternate and pinnately compound. The flowers can be white, pink, or yellow in umbellate, terminal clusters. *J. mesnyi* blooms through winter into spring, bearing numerous yellow blossoms; it is suitable to a cold conservatory. In a container, this species of jasmine can tolerate 14°F (–10°C) frost; it can be stored for a short, hard winter in a garage, to be put outside again as soon as the worst frosts are over, ready for early flowering.

J. officinale has white blooms summer through fall. This species can be in a container and inside a room all summer.

J. polyanthum has white flowers tinged pink on the outside; 30–40 of them clustering together. This jasmine grows fast and, planted in the conservatory, can reach 16 ft. (5 m) in height. It flowers summer and fall.

J. sambac has leathery, ever-green leaves up to 5 in. (12 cm) long. The pure white flowers open three to twelve to a cluster, from early spring to late fall. This species needs to be tied up and grows very slowly to 10 ft. (3 m); it is best off in a con-servatory all year. `plenum` is a double variety.

Warning: the strong fragrance of some jasmines can cause

Jasminum polyanthum

Jatropha podagrica

Jasminum polyanthum glows pink in bud and white in bloom. Once in a while, the plant retains its foliage in winter.

Jasminum officinale, which grows very well on an arch, gives the perfume industry one of its most exquisite and precious fragrances.

Jatropha podagrica, the nettle spurge, is often seen in nurseries because of its bizarre form; it is very easy to take care of.

headaches and migraines.

Location: Full sun, airy; in summer outdoors (except *J. sambac*). In winter 46-50°F (8-10°C).

Care: In summer, keep the root ball evenly moist with soft water. Feed every 14 days. In winter, water just enough to keep the plant from drying out. If needed, repot in the spring into large containers.

Propagation: By semihardwood cuttings in spring and summer with bottom heating.

Pests and Diseases: Aphids if too warm in winter; leaf loss in winter is natural with *J. officinale*.

Uses: An exquisite, flowering climber for a room, container, or conservatory.

JATROPHA PODAGRICA
Nettle spurge

Family: Spurge, *Euphorbiaceae*
Native Habitat: Central America
Flowering Time: Late spring

The nettle spurge is a 12–24 in.- (30–60 cm-) high succulent shrub with a thickened, bottle-shaped stem and leaves 8 in. (20 cm) wide, with three or five lobes. During the rest period in winter, small, coral flowers develop on long, red stalks.

The plant is poisonous in all its parts.

Location: Year-round light and sunny at room temperature.

Care: Water little, somewhat more while in bloom. Keep almost dry after the leaves fall, which is quite natural. In winter give cactus food once a month.

Propagation: From seed with bottom heating or by cuttings from mature plants.

Pests and Diseases: Root rot if too wet during winter rest.

Uses: A somewhat bizarre but problem-free houseplant for aficionados.

Jasminum officinale

Kalanchoe – Laelia

Both *Kalanchoe porphyrocalyx* and the similar *K. manginii* are marvelous cascading plants. They both come from Madagascar.

K. pinnata and *K. daigremontiana* both carry tiny, adventitious plants on the edges of their leaves.

The leaves of *Kalanchoe beharensis* are very impressive: this plant grows to 13 ft. (4 m) high in its native land.

Kalanchoe porphyrocalyx

KALANCHOE
Kalanchoe

Family: Stonecrop, *Crassulaceae*
Native Habitat: Madagascar
Flowering Time: Spring

We are offered an amazing variety of species and forms by the genus *Kalanchoe*: there are herbaceous perennials, shrubs, and subshrubs, all with succulent leaves. You probably would recognize *K. blossfeldiana*. The pure form is not sold any more, but some of its many cultivars are: 'Bali' (red flowers); 'Mini' (dwarf, red); 'Calypso' (dark pink); 'Nugget' (orange); and 'Fortyniner' (yellow). A yellow-blooming novelty is 'Gold Jewel.' In its native Madagascar, the plant blooms in the spring, but by controlling the length of its day (it is a short-day plant), modern growers can make it bloom at just about any time.

New on the market is *K. porphyrocalyx*. With its pendulant flowers it is as good a hanging plant as *K. manginii*. A pretty green plant is *K. tomentosa*; its thick leaves are covered with a white mat of hair, their edges turning color to dark brown or fox-red. *K. pinnata*, the air plant, literally bears living young: they grow between the lobes along the edges of its leaves, complete with tiny aerial roots, which fall off and take root. Other species encountered in succulent collections are *K. daigremontiana*, with its leaves like long triangles that curl at the edges. As the name implies, the leaves of *K. tubiflora* are rolled up, the tiny adventitious plantlets sitting at the tip. The flowers are small, bell-like, and usually reddish.

Location: Light or sunny all year; in summer warm. *K. blossfeldiana* best out-of-doors. In winter cool, not under 54°F (12°C). *K. blossfeldiana* not under 59°F (15°C).

Care: In summer, water moderately, letting the surface of the soil dry each time. Keep almost dry in winter. *K. blossfeldiana* requires more moisture in winter, too. Feed every two weeks from spring to late summer. If need be, repot in spring in ordinary soil mix.

Propagation: By tip or leaf cuttings,

Kalanchoe pinnata

Kalanchoe beharensis

Kalanchoe daigremontiana

TIP

Kalanchoe is a short-day plant. Flowers will form only if the plant is kept completely dark (covered with a cardboard box) for 16 hours every day for two full months.

Blossfeldiana *hybrid kalanchoe*

letting the cut surface dry out before planting, or from seed (seeds need light to germinate). Where present, adventitious plants can be removed from their mother plants and set in a sandy growing medium.

Pests and Diseases: Aphids; gray mold if kept too wet and cool.

Uses: A good-looking flowering plant for a light spot in a room; good for hydroponics.

LAELIA
Laelia

Family: Orchid, *Orchidaceae*
Native Habitat: Tropical America
Flowering Time: Depending on species and variety, any time of year

With respect to looks and care requirements, laelia has much in common with cattleya, a genus it is closely related to and with which it is often cross-bred (*x Laeliocattleya*). The most lovely species are: *L. pumila* (flower light rose, lip lighter with black-red edge); *L. purpurata* (petals reddish, lip crimson); *L. rubescens* (flower white or pink, lip speckled

red and black); and *L. tenebrosa* (a relatively narrow flower, yellow-brown to bronze, lip with a dark crimson throat opening).

Attractive hybrids are *Laeliocattleya* Chitchat 'Tangerine' (yellow-orange, 2 in.- (5 cm-) wide, flowers in umbels); *x Laeliocattleya* Culminant 'La Tuilerie' (with pink flowers, a darker lip with a lighter edge); *x Laeliocattleya* Rogo, 'Mont Millais' (with reddish-orange flowers).

Location: Very light, but no noon sun; humid and warm at 64–75°F (18–24°C). In winter if possible 7°F (4°C) cooler.

Care: During growth, water freely with soft water; in the winter, just enough to keep the pseudobulbs from shrinking. Spray often. Add orchid food to every third can of water. Every two to three years repot after flowering in orchid soil. Tie up epiphytic laelias.

Propagation: By division into groups of three or four pseudobulbs, at the beginning of the main growth period, or from seed.

Pests and Diseases: Rarely.

Uses: Magnificent, large-blooming orchids for the home or the greenhouse.

Laelia tenebrosa

Kalanchoe hybrids can be pruned after they bloom to promote bushy form.

The Brazilian *Laelia tenebrosa* has flowers 5.5 in. (14 cm) across with bronze petals.

TIP

While laelias love fresh air, they react badly to drafts.

Lagerstroemia – Lantana

Long, hot summers are required for the crepe myrtle to bloom well.

Lampranthus spectabilis, as its name implies, offers spectacular colors.

Lagerstroemia indica

Lampranthus spectabilis

Once I forgot one of my crepe myrtles when it came to moving it indoors. It was a fairly hard winter, and the plant lost its above-ground parts; in spring, however, it sprouted new ones. Since then, I prune it back in the fall and cover it with lots of dry leaves. It always blooms the next summer on shoots 30 in. (80 cm) long. In regions where the climate is not too severe, this treatment is worth a try.

LAGERSTROEMIA INDICA
Crepe myrtle

Family: Loosestrife, *Lythraceae*
Native Habitat: China
Flowering Time: Late summer to midautumn, or even later

The crepe myrtle is a small, deciduous tree or shrub with elliptical leaves. The flowers, usually pink but occasionally white or crimson, appear in terminal panicles on year-old shoots. Only *Lagerstroemia indica* is in cultivation.
Location: During summer and fall, outdoors in a sheltered but very sunny place, preferably in front of a white wall to reflect the heat. In winter at 35–46°F (2–8°C) in a cold conservatory or in a dark cellar.
Care: Water very well in summer, especially while it sets buds and blooms. Feed biweekly till the end of summer. Move indoors as late as possible; the plant tolerates cold to 5°F (–15°C). In late winter, prune well and repot in rich soil.
Propagation: By tip cuttings in late summer.
Pests and Diseases: Aphids on young shoots; powdery mildew in rainy summers; buds and blossoms

fall if kept too dry at that time.
Uses: A beautiful, flowering container plant.

LAMPRANTHUS
Ice plant

Family: Mesembryanthemum, *Aizoaceae*
Native Habitat: South Africa
Flowering Time: Summer

This is a low-growing, succulent perennial with creeping shoots. Its leaves are fleshy and narrow, almost cylindrical in shape. The relatively large flowers open only when the sun shines. Colors range from white through yellow and orange to crimson red. Some beautiful species are *L. aurantiacus* (orange flowers); *L. blandus* (pale pink); *L. conspicuus* (crimson); *L. rupestris*, and *L. spectabilis* (crimson).
Location: Sunny; in summer outdoors. In winter at 41°F (5°C) or warmer.
Care: In summer, water moderately, in winter not at all. Feed every two weeks during growth. A light pruning after flowering promotes next year's bloom.
Propagation: From seed, cuttings, or by division.
Pests and Diseases: Aphids, if too shady.
Uses: An outstanding flowering plant for balconies and dishes in very sunny places.

The ice plant displays its colors in South Africa's Namaqualand.

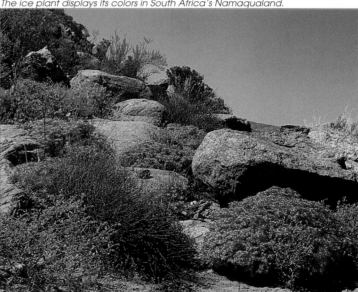

LANTANA CAMARA HYBRIDS
Hybrid lantana

Family: Verbena, *Verbenaceae*
Native Habitat: Parent species stem from the tropical Americas
Flowering Time: Late spring to autumn

These hybrids of lantana grow 12–40 in. (30-100 cm) high. Their leaves are egg-shaped or elongated, and wrinkled. Numerous small flowers crowd into rounded umbels. The plant covers itself in colors from white, through yellow and orange, to pink; even two-colored flower clusters happen. Moreover, these colors will change continuously over the flowering period because few of these hybrids are stable. Some good varieties are 'Arlequin' (flower dark pink with yellow); 'Goldsonne' (pure yellow); 'Naide' (white with a yellow eye); 'Raoux' (scarlet with orange); and 'Schloss Ortenburg' (brick-red with yellow-orange). The variety 'Aloha' is new: its leaves are variegated yellow and green, its flowers are yellow. Lantana is poisonous in all its parts.
Location: Full sun; winter at 43–50°F (6–10°C), dark or light.
Care: Keep moderately moist and feed biweekly. Remove all fruit immediately to encourage further flowering. Before winter storage, prune vigorously.
Propagation: By tip cuttings.
Pests and Diseases: Whiteflies and spider mites.
Uses: Profusely blooming plants for balconies and terraces. Pretty when trained as standards.

Lantana camara hybrid

Standard trained, lantana looks especially good, but the little tree needs extra supports to carry the heavy crown of flowers.

TIP

With maturity, lantana will produce fewer and fewer flowers. Make sure to make tip cuttings in time or to prune the plant well to stimulate new growth.

Lathyrus – Leptospermum

With *Lathyrus odoratus,* the sweet pea, it is possible to create a delicately blooming and fragrant screen in a very short time.

This is a globe-shaped laurel, but the cut is not required: a natural specimen is just as attractive.

Lathyrus odoratus

LATHYRUS ODORATUS
Sweet pea

Family: Bean, *Fabaceae*
Native Habitat: Sicily, Italy
Flowering Time: Summer through autumn

The sweet pea is an annual climber that can reach about 6.5 ft. (2 m). Its large flowers are fragrant, and their colors range over shades of white, yellow, pink, red, and mauve. Good varieties include: 'Cutherson,' 'floribundus,' 'Royal' (high-growing), 'Knee-high' (bushy), 'Little Sweetheart,' 'Bijou,' and 'Cupido' (low-growing).
    Warning: the seeds of the sweet pea are poisonous.
Location: Full sun and airy, but sheltered from wind, outdoors.
Care: Plant in loose, fertile garden soil or standard soil mix. Keep evenly moist and feed weekly. Snip off dead flowers.
Propagation: From seed, sown outdoors in spring.
Pests and Diseases: Aphids.
Uses: Very pretty flowering climber for a trellis, as a screen for balcony or terrace, or (bushy varieties) for planters.

Fruit of the laurel

When your laurel has been pruned, remove cut leaves, as their cut edges will darken and mar its appearance.

Laurus nobilis

LAURUS NOBILIS
True bay, laurel

Family: Laurel, *Lauraceae*
Native Habitat: Mediterranean region, Asia Minor
Flowering Time: Spring

The laurel is an evergreen shrub with leathery, aromatic leaves that are used as a spice and in making pharmaceuticals. Flowers and fruit appear only on unpruned specimens, never on pruned ones. Laurel is often trained as a spherical standard.
Location: Sunny or shady, in summer outdoors; in winter at 32–43°F (0–6°C).
Care: Keep lightly moist, especially during growth; feed weekly, using dry fertilizer dissolved in water. Pruning and shaping are tolerated. Laurel also can bear short spells of frost, so you can bring it inside for the winter relatively late.
Propagation: By tip cuttings in fall or spring; they are very slow.
Pests and Diseases: Scale insects if too warm in winter; mealybugs, spider mites.
Uses: A classical, evergreen container plant; good for cool stairways.

THE MOST BEAUTIFUL PLANTS FROM A TO Z

Leea amabilis

Leonotis leonurus

Leptospermum scoparium

LEEA
Leea

Family: Leea, *Leeaceae*
Native Habitat: Tropical Asia
Flowering Time: Autumn

Leea is a small shrub, up to 3.2 ft. (1 m) high. Its leaves can be up to triply pinnately compound. The small flowers appear in terminal, umbrella-shaped clusters.

L. amabilis has bronze-colored leaves. *L. rubra*, still often referred to under its old name, *L. coccinea*, has wine-red foliage.
Location: Light or partial shade; humid and warm. Even in winter at least 61°F (16°C).
Care: Keep evenly and lightly moist; feed every three weeks. Mix Styrofoam bits into the soil to avoid waterlogging.
Propagation: By tip or stem cuttings with bottom heat and high atmospheric humidity.
Pests and Diseases: Aphids, spider mites; soggy or dry roots will cause leaves to fall.
Uses: For window greenhouses, large glass cases, humid and warm greenhouses, and conservatories.

LEONOTIS LEONURUS
Lion's ear

Family: Mint, *Lamiaceae*
Native Habitat: South Africa
Flowering Time: All autumn

The lion's ear is a subshrub that grows 3.2–6.5 ft. (1–2 m) high. In a conservatory it is an evergreen. It has incredible, hairy, 2 in.- (5 cm-) long, tubular, dark-orange flowers; they stand in whorls around upright stems. For outdoor flowering in a container, *Leonotis* blooms too late in the year, but it is a valuable and beautiful plant for the conservatory.
Location: In summer, full sun, wind-sheltered, out-of-doors. In winter, light or dark, at 41–50°F (5–10°C), somewhat warmer inside.
Care: During growth, water generously; otherwise, moderately. Feed once a month till the end of summer. Prune back to 4–8 in. (10–20 cm) before putting in cool winter storage. In late winter, repot if needed in good potting soil.
Propagation: From seed or by cuttings; pinch out young plants several times to aid bushy habit.
Pests and Diseases: Rarely.
Uses: Winter-blooming conservatory plant.

LEPTOSPERMUM SCOPARIUM
Tea tree

Family: Myrtle, *Myrtaceae*
Native Habitat: New Zealand
Flowering Time: Late spring, early summer

The tea tree is an evergreen, flowering shrub with myrtlelike foliage. The flowers are small but numerous. They are white, pink, or red, double or simple. Well-known varieties: 'Album Plenum' (white, double); 'Boscawenii' (pink flowers, compact habit); 'Chapmanii' (leaves reddish, flowers pink); 'Keatleyi' (1 in. (2.5 cm) flowers in pink); and 'Red Damask' (leaves red, flowers crimson, double).
Location: In summer, sunny and warm, outside. In winter light, at 39–50°F (4–10°C).
Care: Water well during growth with soft water. Administer rhodo-dendron food every two weeks. Prune after it flowers.
Propagation: From seed or by cuttings. Pinch out young plant several times.
Pests and Diseases: Rarely; dry root ball leads to leaves dropping off.
Uses: Potted or container plant for the house or the conservatory.

Leea, a well-articulated foliage plant, will occasionally produce umbellate inflorescences.

The soft, hairy, opposed leaves of the lion's ear are responsible for its name.

By moving the tea tree in late winter to a warm location (not over 58°F (14°C)), you can encourage it to bloom several weeks earlier.

TIP

The branches of *Leonotis* are brittle; to avoid major damage to the plant, keep it away from traffic areas so it will not be touched and broken.

Lilium – Lobelia

If you keep lilies on your balcony or patio, make sure that their stamens cannot touch anything; the pollen leaves behind yellow spots that cannot be removed from clothing or skin.

Lithops resemble the stones among which they live; indeed they look like a living stone.

The color of the flower to come can be predicted in very small lithops plants. The groove between the two halves extends all the way with the white-blooming species, but is short of the edges with those that bloom yellow.

Lilium *Midcentury hybrid*

LILIUM
Lily

Family: Lily, *Liliaceae*
Native Habitat: Originally from Asia, America, Europe
Flowering Time: Summer

Do lilies make good houseplants? I will leave it open. For short periods of time, they certainly bring life into a room. For this purpose we will consider the hybrids of *Lilium tigrinum* and the related Midcentury hybrids, with their range of varieties. For containers, some of the many hybrids of *L. auratum, L. longiflorum,* and *L. speciosum* are also being used. The genus *Lilium* contains about 100 species and uncounted varieties and hybrids, which continue to be refined, especially in the United States. Here we give only a small sample: *L. lancifolium* hybrids (syn. *Lilium tigrinum*): 'Golden Tiger' (yellow flowers); 'splendens' (red-orange); 'flaviflorum' (light orange with red dots).

Midcentury hybrids: 'Cinnabar' (bright red); 'Croesus' (golden yellow); 'Enchantment' (orange-red).

Warning: the bulbs of the lily are poisonous.

Location: Very light; till the bulbs root at 41–54°F (5–12°C). As soon as the plants start growing, 54–68°F (12–20°C).

Care: If you desire early-blooming lilies, plant the bulbs in autumn over a layer of drainage (sand or pebbles) into pots a bit too large. Use either standard soil mix or garden soil with clay and humus, improved with bone meal. Give the bulbs a soil cover of about 4 in. (10 cm). Store the pots cool but free of frost. Starting in late winter, gradually increase the temperature and adjust the watering to it. Occasional feeding is then in order. As soon as the shoots reach 4 in. (10 cm), move them to a very light and airy place at 54–68°F (12–20°C). Continue care until after blooming. Then, plant them in the garden and continue watering and feeding so that the bulbs can gain strength for next year. For normal summer flowering, plant the bulbs only after winter is completely over.

Propagation: From seed, by division, or from bulbs.

Pests and Diseases: Lily bulb borers—red beetles that gnaw into the bulbs; gray mold.

Uses: Houseplant for light, cool rooms; container plant.

Lithops karasmontana

LITHOPS
Lithops

Family: Mesembryanthemum, *Aizoaceae*
Native Habitat: South and southwest Africa
Flowering Time: Midsummer to late fall

Lithops look like stones. They are succulent plants that consists of two, fleshy, flattened leaves on a short, subterranean stem. Between the two leaves, the relatively large flower arises, like a white or yellow sunburst.

Location: Full sun all year. With good protection from rain, outdoors in summer. In winter at 54–59°F (12–15°C).

Care: Spring to fall, water very carefully. Too much moisture will cause the leaf bodies to burst. No fertilizing needed. Keep quite dry after the beginning of fall until the old leaves have completely shriveled.

Propagation: From seed. Young plants start blooming after two to three years.

Pests and Diseases: Mealybugs; root rot sets in if too wet.

Uses: An interesting succulent for a sunny location.

The Most Beautiful Plants from A to Z

Livistona chinensis

Lobelia erinus *'Kaiser Wilhelm'*

LIVISTONA
Fan palm

Family: Palm, *Arecaceae*
Native Habitat: Australia, China, Ryukyu Islands
Flowering Time: Rarely blooms under cultivation

At one time, the fan palm was extremely fashionable. Its leaves can reach 24–35 in. (60–90 cm) in diameter even in young plants. They stand stiffly upright; their stems are serrated. Important species are: *L. australis*, whose shiny, fan-shaped leaves reach 6.5 ft. (2 m) in breadth, and *L. chinensis*, with a thicker stem and leaves just as large; this plant has less need of light. These two palm trees used to be seen in hotel lobbies the world over.

Location: Full sun; in summer outdoors. In winter light at 54–57°F (12–14°C).
Care: During growth, water freely, spray often, and feed every two weeks. Keep the plant rather dry in winter. If needed—that is, when the container is filled with roots—repot in standard soil with one-third sand added. Use deep containers.
Propagation: From seeds that were soaked for one day. Bottom heating and light are needed for sprouting.
Pests and Diseases: Aphids, scale insects, if the air is too dry or it is too dark in winter.
Uses: When small, a beautiful foliage plant for a room; when larger, planted in the conservatory.

LOBELIA ERINUS
Lobelia

Family: Bellflower, *Campanulaceae*
Native Habitat: South Africa
Flowering Time: Summer through fall

Lobelia is a 10 in.- (25 cm-) high, upright annual with narrow, light-green leaves and blue-and-white flowers. To the bushy Compacta series belong, among others, 'Kaiser Wilhelm' (cornflower blue); 'Mrs. Clibran Improved' (white and blue); and 'Rosamunde' (crimson and white). The hanging Pendula series includes 'Blue Cascade' (light blue) and 'Saphir' (dark blue and white).
Location: Sun to partial shade.
Care: Water freely, never letting the root ball dry out; give half-diluted plant food once a week. Prune the plants after their first flowering; they will bloom again, right up to the first frost.
Propagation: From seed in winter or spring; seeds need light to sprout.
Pests and Diseases: Rarely.
Uses: Balcony planters and dishes; for underplanting standard-trained plants.

Livistona chinensis grows very slowly at first, but it can reach 30 ft. (9 m) in time.

Hanging lobelias make a good underplanting for fuchsia or woody chrysanthemums trained as standards.

Livistona chinensis

TIP

Livistona can tolerate short frosts down to 21°F (–6°C). If planted in an unheated conservatory, it should do fine, unless it gets even colder there.

Lobivia – Mandevilla

Lobivia is an anagram on Bolivia, the native habitat of many lobivia species.

Lotus maculatus and *Lotus berthelotii* are both lovely, richly blooming hanging plants. They look equally good when not in flower. Both plants require a sunny and airy location.

Lobivia winteriana

LOBIVIA
Lobivia

Family: Cactus, *Cactaceae*
Native Habitat: Northern Argentina, southeastern Peru
Flowering Time: Spring to summer

Lobivia is a globular cactus with strong brown or yellow thorns. The plants tend to grow in mounds. The flower resembles a flat bell or funnel; it is red, yellow, or white, with many yellow stamens. Most lobivias are now reclassified as *Echinopsis*; here are some good species and their varieties: *L. backebergii* (crimson with a blue gloss); *L. cinnabarina* (scarlet); *L. hertrichiana* (bright red); *L. pugionacantha* var. *rossii* (yellow and orange-red); and *L. winteriana* (ruby red).
Location: Sunny and warm; in winter cool, at 43–46°F (6–8°C).
Care: In spring and summer water freely and feed every two weeks. In winter keep cool and dry to stimulate the formation of buds.
Propagation: By removing the offsets.
Pests and Diseases: Mealybugs.
Uses: For bright rooms, green-houses, and cactus collections.

Lotus maculatus

LOTUS
Deer vetch

Family: Bean, *Fabaceae*
Native Habitat: Canary and Cape Verde Islands
Flowering Time: In the spring; *Lotus maculatus*, the whole summer

Deer vetch is a handsome hanging plant that deserves more attention. *L. berthelotii* has gray-green, needlelike leaves; its flowers—strangely arched, scarlet forms—cluster at the tips of the branches. *L. maculatus* 'Golden Flash' has coppery-yellow flowers and has the advantage that it blooms all summer. Both species are low-lying, or hanging, and both look good even when not in bloom.
Location: Sunny and light all year; in summer outdoors if sheltered. In winter at 46–50°F (8–10°C).
Care: Keep evenly moist during the time of growth; water less in winter.

Up to the end of fall, feed weekly.
Propagation: By tip cuttings taken either in spring or in the fall, with bottom heating.
Pests and Diseases: Aphids; leaves will drop if the root ball dries out.
Uses: Magnificent flowering and foliage plant for hanging baskets, balcony planters, columns, and pedestals, or for underplanting in the conservatory.

Lotus berthelotii

TIP

My deer vetch is planted in a flat dish that is perched on top of a piece of tubing. The tube itself is anchored in the ground beneath my garden pond. The plant enjoys the humidity it needs without getting its roots wet. It thrives very nicely.

THE MOST BEAUTIFUL PLANTS FROM A TO Z

Mammillaria assortment

Mandevilla laxa

It is no wonder that mammillarias are the most frequently sold cactus genus; their small circle of flowers is quite enchanting.

Mandevilla laxa thrives in cool conservatories as well as in warm ones.

MAMMILLARIA
Mammillaria

Family: Cactus, *Cactaceae*
Native Habitat: Mexico, United States, South America
Flowering Time: Predominantly in spring and summer

Mammillaria is a small globe cactus that is extraordinarily variable in its shape, color, and thorns. The flowers tend to form a wreath around the plant; they are followed by little red fruits, no less charming. Only specialists know the over 300 diverse species in this genus. Many of them are under cultivation, but we can mention only a few:

M. bocasana: globular; flowers yellow-white with reddish brown central line; grow in groups.

M. gracilis: short, cylindrical; flowers yellow-white; orange fruit.

M. hahniana: flattened globe; flowers and fruit both crimson.

M. sempervivi: Globular or compactly cylindrical; flowers white to light pink

M. surculosa: diameter of each head less than 0.8 in. (2 cm); flowers yellow.

M. zeilmanniana: diameter of globe 3 in. (8 cm); flower bright crimson, pink or white; will bloom as a young plant.
Location: Sunny for almost all species; in the summer outdoors, if protected; in winter 43–46°F (6–8°C). Mammillaria's ability to form flowers and thorns depends on the amount of sunshine it receives.
Care: In summer, water freely with soft water; administer cactus food monthly. Keep almost dry in winter. My own mammillarias are watered from below: once a week, I place their pots into a bowl of rainwater. They absorb what they need.
Propagation: From seed or by offsets.
Pests and Diseases: Mealybugs and spider mites.
Uses: For sunny rooms, greenhouses, and cactus collections.

MANDEVILLA LAXA
Chile jasmine

Family: Dogbane, *Apocynaceae*
Native Habitat: South America
Flowering Time: Early summer to fall

Chile jasmine is a deciduous, fast-growing, twining plant; its leaves are 2–6 in. (5–15 cm) long, its snow-white, funnel-shaped flowers form small clusters at the ends of new shoots. They are intensely fragrant. All *Mandevilla* species and varieties are poisonous. Some people get a headache from the scent.
Location: Full sun and warm in summer; in winter light or dark, at 39–46°F (4–8°C).
Care: During growth, water and feed freely. Provide strong climbing support. If you overwinter the plant in the dark, cut it back to soil level and keep it almost dry.
Pests and Diseases: The plant attracts aphids; spider mites; danger of root rot if too wet in winter.
Uses: Splendid climbing plant for balconies, terraces, and cool or warm conservatories.

TIP

Mandevilla can tolerate down to 5°F (−15°C) of frost. In milder regions of the temperate zone, the plant can overwinter outside, provided that it is kept warm with a thick layer of leaves. In that case, all its shoots have to be cut at ground level before it is covered. My own *Mandevilla* is so lovely, I shine lights on it at night.

Maranta – Miltonia

Maranta 'Fascinator'

Maranta 'Fascinator' is a new cultivar. In the picture below one sees how exquisite the markings of *Maranta leuconeura* really are.

Occasionally, you come across a medinilla of compact habit; usually it turns out that it was bred in Holland.

Maranta leuconeura

MARANTA
Maranta; prayer plant

Family: Prayer plant, *Marantaceae*
Native Habitat: Brazil, tropical Americas
Flowering Time: Seldom blooms in cultivation

Maranta is a bushy rain forest plant with tuberous roots and large, oval, vividly colored leaves on upright petioles. *M. bicolor* and *M. leuconeura* are two beautiful species; some of their better-known varieties are 'erythroneura,' 'kerchoviana,' 'massangeana,' and 'Fascinator.'
Location: Light or partial shade all year; no strong sun; warm and humid. Shelter from all drafts.
Care: Avoid chilling the root ball; use soft water at room temperature and never allow the roots to dry out. To achieve the necessary humidity, set the pot over a dish of water, since spraying can spot the leaves. Give half-diluted plant food every two weeks; less in often in winter.
Propagation: By division when repotting.
Pests and Diseases: Spider mites; if too wet, danger of root damage; pale leaves indicate too much light.
Uses: Attractive foliage plant for enclosed window greenhouses, glass cases, or warm conservatories. Because of the plant's slightly creeping habit, it does well in larger bowls. Suited to hydroponics.

MEDINILLA MAGNIFICA
Medinilla

Family: Melastome, *Melastomataceae*
Native Habitat: Philippines
Flowering Time: Spring to summer

Medinilla bears pink flowers with violet stamens; they grow in hanging clusters up to 20 in. (50 cm) long, hooded by pale pink bracts. The leaves are also large; thick and leathery, they are 12 in. (30 cm) long. In its own habitat, the plant reaches 3.2–5 ft. (1–1.5 m), a stature it can achieve elsewhere only if planted in a warm conservatory.

Location: Light, some sun, but not strong noon sun; warm and humid. Over the winter, cooler, but not under 59°F (15°C).
Care: Once buds have set, water with soft water and give nonalkaline fertilizer once a week. Spray with soft water. To set buds, medinilla needs two months of complete rest with a drop in temperature of about 9°F (5°C) and very minimal watering. When buds are visible, move to a warmer location and—very important—do not turn any more.
Propagation: By cuttings with bottom heating of 86–95°F (30–35°C) or by air layering.
Pests and Diseases: Spider mites if air is too dry.
Uses: Splendid plant for an enclosed window, greenhouse, or a warm, humid conservatory, where it can also be in a container.

Medinilla magnifica

Microcoelum weddelianum

Miltonia *hybrid*

MICROCOELUM WEDDELIANUM
Microcoelum

Family: Palm, *Arecaceae*
Native Habitat: Tropical Brazil
Flowering Time: Seldom blooms in cultivation

This filigreed palm tree comes from the tropical rain forest; accordingly, its requirements for humidity are very high. Fully grown, the palm is 5 ft. (1.5 m) high, its compound leaf up to 3.2 ft. (1 m) long. In the temperate zone, these noble proportions are achieved only if it is planted in a warm and humid conservatory.
Location: Never under 64°F (18°C); no direct sun and high humidity.
Care: Keep evenly moist and mist often. Water somewhat less in winter, but keep spraying. During cooler periods, allow the soil surface to dry somewhat before watering again. Avoid water-logging. During growth, feed once a month. If it is in a container, repot every two to three years.
Propagation: From seed with bottom heating at 86°F (30°C). Sprouting time is two to three months.
Pests and Diseases: Spider mites; brown leaf tips are usually a sign of dry roots or dry air. Keeping the plant's roots too cold will stunt its growth.
Uses: It is best to keep this plant in an enclosed window greenhouse or glass case, or a warm and humid conservatory.

MILTONIA
Miltonia, pansy orchid

Family: Orchid, *Orchidaceae*
Native Habitat: South America
Flowering Time: Depending on the species, at different times

The pseudobulb of miltonia is egg-shaped and compressed; it has three leaves. At its base appear, on 6–20 in.- (15–50 cm-) high stalks, the pansylike flowers, singly or in groups. In addition to the 40 species, there are many hybrids.
Location: Year-round light, but not too sunny; in summer to 77°F (25°C), in winter about 68°F (20°C), a bit cooler at night. Humid.
Care: Once it has sprouted, water the plant freely and feed every two weeks, hybrids more often. During flowering and resting, give less water. Do not spray directly onto the plant.
Propagation: By division of the bulbs at repotting time.
Pests and Diseases: Spider mites, scale insects; the leaves turn red if the plant gets too much sun.
Uses: An orchid for a greenhouse or for a suitable spot in a living room.

This mature specimen of *Microcoelum weddelianum* is in the botanical garden at Freiburg.
To prolong the life of this sensitive, tropical palm, it is a good idea to sink its container into another, larger one and to fill the space with clay granular. It is easier to keep miltonia hybrids than plants of the pure species.

TIP

It takes some sensitivity and special attention to water, feed, and spray miltonias without damaging them: the pseudobulbs rot easily when wet, and the roots can also be hurt by the salts contained in orchid food.

Mimosa – Musa

Small but lovely is the flower of *Mimosa pudica*. When the leaves (below) are touched, they close, but if this mechanism is activated too often it becomes paralyzed. It does recover in time, however.

Monstera deliciosa must surely be one of the most beloved tropical houseplants in the world.

Mimosa pudica

MIMOSA PUDICA
Mimosa, sensitive plant

Family: Bean, *Fabaceae*
Native Habitat: Brazil
Flowering Time: Late summer

The sensitive mimosa is a subshrub that is raised as an annual in the temperate zone. The leaf, on its long petiole, divides into fingers, which are in turn set with narrow leaflets. The slightest touch causes the leaflets to snap together; a harder touch causes the whole leaf to sink down, as if wilted. The small, mauve, globe flowers sit in the leaf axils.
Location: Light to sunny all year; room temperature; humid.
Care: Keep evenly moist and feed every two weeks; avoid dry root ball. Spray to keep the air moist. Prune long shoots in the fall.
Propagation: From seed in spring with bottom heating. Do not prune young plants.
Pests and Diseases: Aphids and spider mites if exposed to draft.
Uses: An interesting green plant for warm, light rooms.

Mimosa pudica

Monstera deliciosa

MONSTERA
Breadfruit; Swiss cheese plant

Family: Arum, *Araceae*
Native Habitat: Tropical Central and South America
Flowering Time: Seldom blooms in cultivation

Monstera is a most imposing and undemanding foliage plant. The huge, shiny, dark green leaves of young plants are elegantly perforated; those of older plants are deeply cleft. The plant grows shoots up to 16 ft. (5 m) long and numerous aerial roots; it needs twining or epiphyte support.

M. deliciosa is the best-known species; 'Bonsigiana' is a somewhat more compact variety. You seldom see 'Variegata,' which is more sensitive, grows more slowly, and has white-variegated leaves.

A good-looking, fast-climbing species is *M. adansonii*: its leaves are more oval; it needs more warmth.

Occasionally, *Monstera* will bloom; subsequently, its large spadix, typical of plants of the arum family, is covered with violet berries.

Although the fruit is said to taste of pineapple and can be used to flavor mulled wine, it can irritate mucous membranes. Better abstain.

Location: Light, no sun; warm and humid all year. In summer, in partial shade, outside.
Care: Keep evenly moist and feed

every two weeks. Wipe the leaves now and then, so that respiration is not restricted. Do not cut the pencil-thick aerial roots that older plants will form. If possible, put them into the soil, where they will take hold.

Propagation: By tip or stem cuttings with bottom heating; or by air layering. Seeding is possible.

Pests and Diseases: Scale insects, spider mites; if too dark, the leaves are not perforated; brown leaves and tears indicate too much water; small leaves with long petioles point to a light deficiency.

Uses: A very popular houseplant; can be used to climb a trellis; ideal for a heated conservatory. Suited to hydroponics.

Ornamental banana with red leaves

in wine-growing regions of the temperate zone. Even with perfect winter protection, the plant dies back (the old leaves are cut back anyway); with warmer weather, it sprouts new shoots and in a few months is its usual enormous self. It does best, however, planted in a high-ceilinged conservatory. There, the stature of the plant may still necessitate pruning, and its tendency to spread has to be controlled.

Even *M. acuminata*, the dwarf banana, reaches 6.5 ft. (2 m) in height. *M. x paradisiaca* refers to various hybrids and ornamental forms.

Location: Very light, full sun; in winter not under 66°F (19°C). *M. acuminata* at 64–69°F (18–21°C) all year.

Care: During growth, water and feed freely. Replant often in rich soil and large containers. Using plastic is convenient, given the sizes needed: the soil dries out more slowly and they are easier to bury in the garden for the summer. As the plant ages, lower leaves will wilt; remove yellow leaves.

Propagation: From seed with bottom heating or by offshoots.

Pests and Diseases: Spider mites, scale insects; fungi with prolonged wetness.

Uses: Majestic plant for a conservatory, large greenhouse, or pool area. Young plants for the home.

Even the dwarf form of *Musa* needs lots of room. The banana is best off planted in a roomy conservatory. For container cultivation, use *Ensete ventricosum*, the Abyssinian or ornamental banana, which is here shown with red foliage.

MUSA
Banana

Family: Banana, *Musaceae*

Native Habitat: Tropical regions of the Old World.

Flowering Time: Seldom blooms in cultivation

The banana is a perennial; it develops pseudostems from the sheaths of older leaves. Leaves grow to a stately 3.2 ft. (1 m) long. The plant also makes offsets. The hardiest species is *M. basjoo*, the fibrous Japanese banana, which has been known to survive winters

Musa x paradisiaca

Myrtus – Neoregelia

A young specimen of *Myrtus communis.* Older and standard-trained plants can be moved indoors late in the fall, as they are able to withstand temperatures down to 23°F (–5°C).

Forced narcissus plants are offered for sale in very early spring. If you accustom them to the cold gradually and if the spring is mild, they can then be planted in the flower boxes on your balcony.

Myrtus communis

MYRTUS COMMUNIS
True myrtle

Family: Myrtle, *Myrtaceae*
Native Habitat: Mediterranean region
Flowering Time: Summer through fall

The true myrtle is a traditional container plant. It is an evergreen shrub, 16.5 ft. (5 m) high in its native setting, about 3.2 ft. (1 m) in a container. It has small, dark green, leathery leaves and little white fragrant flowers. Some lovely varieties are 'Hamburger Brautmyrte' and 'Konigsberger Brautmyrte,' as well as the colorful 'variegata.'
Location: In summer, sunny and warm, outdoors; in winter light at 41–50°F (5–10°C).
Care: Keep evenly moist with soft water. Till the end of summer feed weekly. Water sparingly in winter. The plant withstands pruning, so that standard or pyramid shapes can be produced. Repot every two to three years. Choose slightly larger containers and do not plant too deep; leave the trunk free.
Propagation: By tip cutting in winter or summer, at 61–68°F (16–20°C). Pinch out young plants regularly to stimulate bushiness.
Pests and Diseases: Scale insects and aphids if too warm in winter; root rot if too wet. Leaves will drop if kept too dark and too warm.
Uses: An evergreen container and conservatory plant. Suited to bonsai.

Standard-trained myrtles

Narcissus hybrids

NARCISSUS
Narcissus

Family: Lily, *Liliaceae*
Native Habitat: Central Europe, Mediterranean region
Flowering Time: Spring

Narcissus is one of those spring flowers that bring color into our homes during the darker months. Many species and hybrids can be used in this way. Very good are *N. pseudonarcissus* varieties (daffodils) or the many-blossomed varieties of *N. tazetta* (paper whites). Especially suitable is a variety of *N. cyclamineus,* called 'Tête-à-tête'; it is only 6–8 in. (15–20 cm) high and puts out 2–3 blooms per stalk in late winter.

Neoregelia carolinae *'Flandria'*

Narcissus is poisonous in all its parts.

Location: Keep blooming narcissus in the warm living room only for short periods of time, as the flowers last longer in a cool place.

Care: In fall, place the bulbs in a flat dish filled with soil and let them sprout in a dark, cool location. After ten to twelve weeks, move them to a warmer place (59–64°F (15–18°C)) to set buds and keep them moist. After they have bloomed, plant them in the garden.

Propagation: By offset bulbs or from seed.

Pests and Diseases: Rarely.

Uses: Spring decoration for cool rooms, lobbies, terraces, and cool conservatories.

NEOREGELIA
Neoregelia

Family: Bromeliad, *Bromeliaceae*
Native Habitat: Brazilian rain forests
Flowering Time: Varies with the species

Neoregelias grow more often as epiphytes than as terrestrial plants. They form a leafy rosette in which the flowers develop. After blooming, the rosette dies back. During flowering, the leafy bracts of the rosette take on intensive colors that often last for months.

N. binotii has leaves 12 in. (30 cm) long, leathery, thorny, and spotted in red near the tips. They are green below and banded in white above.

N. carolinae forms flat rosettes out of 12–16 in.- (30–40 cm-) long, green, prickled leaves. Their inner leaves are bright red during flowering. Usually, only cultivars are available, such as 'tricolor,' 'Marechalii,' and 'Meyendorffii.'

N. concentrica has leaves 5 in. (12 cm) wide, 12 in. (30 cm) long, and irregularly speckled on top. The inner leaves are shorter and violet in color. This species also offers cultivars, such as 'Plutonis,' with bracts tinged in red.

Location: Very light, no direct sun; year-round warm and humid.

Care: Water and spray only with soft water; the rosette can have lukewarm water in it. Feed every two weeks, in part in the rosette funnel. The rosette can be rinsed now and then to remove any salt deposits. Provide high humidity. If a neoregelia with fully developed bract coloring is kept cooler (54–57°F (12–14°C)), the rosette and its color will last for three to six months before it dies.

Propagation: By offsets; remove only when they have formed roots.

Pests and Diseases: Scale insects, thrips; the plant rots if it is too wet.

Uses: A splendid flowering plant for enclosed window greenhouses and glass cases; if humidity is sufficient, for the living room. Suited for hydroponics.

Neoregelia means "new Regelia"; it refers to the name of the director of the St. Petersburg botanical gardens, E.A. von Regel.

Some *Narcissus tazetta* are specially grown to flower in water. Their bulbs can be set in a flat dish with rough sand or pebbles, where the roots can take hold. The dish is then filled with water to just below the bottom of the bulbs. With this method, the plants do not have to be kept in the dark cellar to sprout, but the bulbs of these paper whites do have to be thrown out after they have bloomed.

Nepenthes – Nerine

Provided that you are willing to spend a lot of time and invest in a humidifier, you can try growing nepenthes in your home.

To give it the needed humidity during warm summers, *Nephrolepis* can be placed in the shallow end of the garden pond; or, should you happen to have a rivulet flowing through the bottom of your garden, you can let it wash over the foliage of the plant in the summer.

TIP

My own sword fern is embedded in a tub with a layer of wet peat and does very well.

Nepenthes *hybrid*

NEPENTHES
Nepenthes

Family: Pitcher plant, *Nepenthaceae*
Native Habitat: Ceylon, Sumatra, Borneo, Malaysian archipelago
Flowering Time: Seldom blooms in cultivation

This insectivore is a climbing or bushy plant, usually epiphytic. The plant's pitcherlike insect traps have lids and are really adapted leaf blades.

As a rule, only hybrids of nepenthes are sold commercially, since these are faster-growing and much more robust than the pure species.

Location: Very light, but not sunny; Never under 68°F (20°C); humid.
Care: Always water and spray with soft water. Feed biweekly during growth with organic-based fertilizer such as fish emulsion. Repot annually in a mixture of rough peat, pieces of bark, and charcoal.
Propagation: By cuttings, in very rough peat at 95°F (35°C). Rooting takes about two months.
Pests and Diseases: Rarely; dry room air is not tolerated.
Uses: For use in baskets or dishes, so that the pitchers can hang over the edge. For enclosed window greenhouses, hot, humid greenhouses, and glass cases.

Nephrolepis exaltata *'Teddy Junior'*

NEPHROLEPIS
Boston fern

Family: Polypody, *Polypodiaceae*
Native Habitat: Tropics
Flowering Time: Not a flowering plant

This is a fern with light green, compound fronds; those of *N. biserrata* can grow to 3.2 ft. (1 m) long. They form a rosette right on the ground and grow upright or arched.

N. cordifolia produces offshoots; its fronds are narrow and light green. The fronds of the variety 'Plumosa' are dark green, and its leaflets are also compound.

N. exaltata is the most important species for our purposes; it has numerous cultivars, some very old. There are varieties with wavy, curly, and twisted fronds, e.g., 'Boston Dwarf' (small, upright); 'Teddy Junior' (adaptable, wavy); 'Rooseveltii' (large and expansive); 'Rooseveltii Plumosa' (large with curly fronds); 'Bornstedt' (triply compound, leaf tip rounded off).
Location: Light, almost sunny; warm and humid all year. *Nephrolepis* can tolerate more light than other ferns.

Care: Never allow the root ball to dry out. Use only soft water in watering and spraying. Provide also for indirect humidity. Feed lightly from early spring to late summer.

Propagation: By offshoots or by division; From spores for pure species.

Pests and Diseases: Spider mites if too dry; brown leaf tips if air or roots are too dry or waterlogged.

Uses: A dignified hanging plant, especially good for pedestals. Suited to hydroponics.

NERINE
Nerine

Family: Lily, *Liliaceae*
Native Habitat: South Africa, the Cape
Flowering Time: Autumn; a few species bloom earlier

Nerine is a bulb plant whose handsome, usually pink, flowers appear in umbels before the leaves.

N. sarniensis is the parent form of many nice hybrids, such as `corusa major' (large, red-tinted flowers); `Harlem' (salmon-colored); `Miss E. Cator' (pink blossoms); `Bettina' (big, pink umbels). *N. bowdenii* forms umbels of eight or more tubular flowers on stalks 18 in. (45 cm) long. Certain storage procedures now yield bulbs that bloom later. In England, where this flower is very popular, there is a Nerine Society. The plant is poisonous.

Location: Light to partial shade; rather cool in winter.

Care: In early fall, plant the bulbs in calcium-free soil with humus and sand added. Place the bulbs close together, with the tips protruding. After sprouting occurs, begin watering gradually. While plants are in flower, water evenly and feed lightly every week. So that the leaves can nourish the bulb, continue watering and feeding to late spring. Then allow the leaves to dry, watering just to moisten the soil. To encourage sprouting again, in late summer carefully scrape the soil off the tops of the bulbs and replace it with fresh soil, enriched with bone meal.

Propagation: From young bulbs or from seeds that have freshly ripened. The seedlings are cultivated without a winter rest for three years.

Pests and Diseases: Freshly planted bulbs should be watered carefully as they rot very easily.

Uses: Nerine is a houseplant. It looks good in early winter with pine boughs and candles.

Ever since a ship bearing nerine bulbs capsized off the coast of Guernsey in the Channel Islands, nerine has grown wild there. *Nerine bowdenii* is the strongest species; it blooms in the autumn.

Nerine bowdenii

Nerium – Nidularium

Oleander is one of those container plants that can withstand frost down to 23°F (–5°C). It can be left outside till late in the fall and can be returned outdoors again early in the spring. The shorter the time in winter quarters, the better for the plant.

Nerium oleander

NERIUM OLEANDER
Oleander

Family: Dogbane, *Apocynaceae*
Native Habitat: Mediterranean region, Portugal, Iran
Flowering Time: Summer through autumn

Oleander is a tall, upright shrub with leathery, lanceolate leaves. Its attractive, umbellate flowers can be simple or double, white, pink, red, or yellow. Many varieties are available, for example: Pink varieties: 'album,' 'grandiflorum,' 'Louis Pouget,' 'Cherry Ripe,' 'Nano Rosso,' 'Provence.'

Red varieties: 'Agnes Durac,'

Nerium oleander

'Alassio,' 'Algier,' 'Etna.'
Yellow varieties: 'flavescens,' 'Maria Gambetta,' 'Soleil d'or.'
White varieties: 'album grandiflorum,' 'Casablanca,' 'Mont Blanc.'
Oleander is poisonous in all its parts.

Location: In summer sunny and as hot as possible, e.g., in front of a light southern wall. In winter at 39–41°F (4–5°C), light and airy in a pinch, a cellar that gets some light will do.

Care: It is easy to grow oleander if you know that its native habitat is a sunny river bank. Water freely in summer and feed weekly. Water can stand in the saucer. Before overwintering, do not remove either fresh flower shoots (they will open next spring) or dead blooms (the first flowers will grow from them). If the plant is leggy, prune a few older shoots right down to the ground each year.

Propagation: By cuttings in water.
Pests and Diseases: Scale insects; *Ascachyta*, a fungal disease, and oleander cancer, a virus disease.
Uses: A very lovely and profusely blooming container plant for sunny locations.

THE MOST BEAUTIFUL PLANTS FROM A TO Z

Nertera granadensis

Nicotiana *varieties*

Nidularium *hybrid 'tricolor perfecta'*

NERTERA GRANADENSIS
Nertera; bead plant

Family: Madder, *Rubiaceae*
Native Habitat: Central and South America, New Zealand, Australia
Flowering Time: In the spring

Nertera is a small houseplant, grown as an annual, that forms a dense mat. Its flower is modest, but is followed by numerous pea-sized, orange-red berries.
Location: Light, shielded from strong sun; in summer best outdoors. If it is kept over winter, light and cool: before and during flowering, below 55°F (13°C).
Care: Because of the danger of rot, water from below with tepid water to which you add liquid fertilizer every two weeks. Spray often, except when in bloom. Keep drier in winter.
Propagation: By division or seeds.
Pests and Diseases: Aphids if too warm in winter; wilt if it is watered from above.
Uses: A low, mounding potted plant with pretty fruit.

NICOTIANA
Tobacco

Family: Nightshade, *Solanaceae*
Native Habitat: Parent forms: South America
Flowering Time: Summer to autumn

Tobacco is a 12–31 in.- (30–80 cm-) high flowering plant with many, fragrant flowers in various colors.
 N. alata comes in several good varieties: 'Daylight' (white, 31 in. (80 cm) high); 'Nico White' (large flower, 12 in. (30 cm) high); 'Nico Red' (scarlet, 12 in. (30 cm)); 'Nicki Rose' (carmine, 16 in. (40 cm)); 'Nicki White' (pure white, 16 in. (40 cm)); Nicki Red' (dark pink, 16 in. (40 cm)).
 Outstanding varieties of *Nicotiana x sanderae* are 'Idol' (bright red, 80 cm) and 'Scharlachkonigin' (red with dots, 31 in. (80 cm)).
 Tobacco is poisonous in all its parts.
Location: Full sun outdoors.
Care: Water freely and feed weekly: it needs a lot of nutrients. Remove dead flowers regularly.
Propagation: From seed.
Pests and Diseases: Aphids.
Uses: For balconies and patios, in dishes.

NIDULARIUM
Nidularium

Family: Bromeliad, *Bromeliaceae*
Native Habitat: Brazil
Flowering Time: Summer

The best-known species is *N. fulgens*, an epiphytic, green, funnel-shaped bromeliad; its dark-spotted leaves turn bright red in the center of the rosette before the flower appears. The colored bracts of *N. billbergoides* are yellow, and its flower is slightly forward-bent. It is easily mistaken for *Neoregelia*.
Location: Light, humid, and warm, not under 64°F (18°C), all year.
Care: Water only with tepid, soft water. Keep the funnel filled with water, particularly in summer. In summer, feeding the plant lightly is in order, as well as spraying the leaves with orchid food solution. Reduce watering in winter.
Propagation: By well-developed offsets. First flower in two to three years.
Pests and Diseases: Root rot if soil is too wet or too cold; brown leaf tips if the air is too dry from heating.
Uses: Mostly for enclosed glass cases and window greenhouses.

When *Nertera granadensis* spends the summer in the garden, its pot is best placed on a perch: slugs love this plant and come from far and wide to eat it up.

While the wild species of tobacco bloom at night and are pollinated by night-flying insects in their native habitats, the ornamental varieties bloom by day.

In order to enjoy nidularium in your home, you will have to embed its pot in another, larger one and fill the gap with wet pebbles, or you will have to buy a room humidifier.

Tobacco is relatively sensitive to cold and should not be set out too early in the spring.

Notocactus-Odontoglossum

Notocactus blooms freely as a young plant and has low care requirements. For these reasons, it is a good cactus for the beginner.

Although strictly speaking *Odontioda* hybrids require no rest period, they should still get a chance to recover after blooming. Reducing water and fertilizer for a few weeks helps them rest.

Notocactus magnificus

x Odontioda *'Brutus'*

ODONTIODA
Odontioda

Family: Orchid, *Orchidaceae*
Native Habitat: Parents: South America
Flowering Time: No set time

This orchid is a cross between *Cochlioda* and *Odontoglossum*. Notable are the red-blooming *Odontioda* hybrids, but recrossing these hybrids has also produced plants with deep orange flowers. Another gorgeous cultivar is *Odontioda* Dalmar 'Lyath Bachus'; its 4 in. (10 cm)-wide, deep red flower is edged in mauve and the lip is mauve with deep red markings.
Location: Light, cool, airy, and humid; in winter not under 54°F (12°C).
Care: Water frequently in summer and spray. Add orchid food to every third watering. Reduce water after it has bloomed.
Propagation: By division.
Pests and Diseases: Aphids, scale insects.
Uses: An easy orchid for living areas and window greenhouses.

NOTOCACTUS
Notocactus

Family: Cactus, *Cactaceae*
Native Habitat: Chile, Uruguay, southern Brazil
Flowering Time: Late summer

Notocactus is a globular-to-columnar cactus that has recently been assigned to *Parodia*. *N. haselbergii* looks like a silver sphere because its many ribs are densely set with soft, white thorns. It has small, red flowers, about 0.4 in. (1 cm). *N. herteri,* also globular, carries reddish brown thorns on its ribs; it blooms deep violet. *N. leninghausii* grows columnar and can reach 3.2 ft. (1 m) in height.

The close-fitting ribs are covered with soft, yellow thorns; the flowers are bright yellow. Those of *N. magnificus* are also yellow and very large. *N. mammulosus* bears light brown thorns; the flower is yellow with a violet stigma. *N. ottonis* is the smallest species.
Location: Sunny and warm; in winter at about 50°F (10°C).
Care: During growth, water freely and, as soon as flower buds appear, feed every two weeks. Avoid waterlogging. Keep cool and dry in winter.
Propagation: From seed.
Pests and Diseases: Mealybugs; rot sets in if too wet and cold.
Uses: A very beautiful cactus for a room, even when not in flower.

If you have a garden, you can hang odontioda in its basket from a tree with light foliage and leave it there till fall. In dry weather, make sure to water it. In very rainy summers it is best not to move it outside.

x Odontocidium tigersun `Nutmeg`

Odontoglossum `Paradise`

The x Odontocidium blossom's tigerskin markings are amazing and exotic. This orchid is also easy to care for.

The Odontoglossum hybrid `Paradise` is able to charm with no less than three colors.

Odontoglossum grande, called the "tiger orchid," has the most spectacular flowers of the genus. They become 2–3 in. (5–8 cm) long and 7 in. (18 cm) wide. They last for a long time.

X ODONTOCIDIUM
Odontocidium

Family: Orchid, Orchidaceae
Native Habitat: Parents from South America
Flowering Time: No set time

This hybrid orchid is a cross between Oncidium and Odontoglossum. x Odontocidium Jacobert has a deep red blossom, its rippled lip marked with a large red dot in the center. It lasts six to eight weeks. The strong, yellow, 3.5 in.- (9 cm-) wide, blooms of x Odontocidium tigersun `Nutmeg` are spotted in white and brown.

Location: Partial shade; in summer 64–77°F (18–25°C) by day and about 64°F (18°C) by night. In winter at 55–61°F (13–16°C).

Care: In summer provide fresh air and high humidity; possibly you can hang the plant in a tree. Use only soft water, letting the soil dry off before watering again. Make sure it drains well. Add orchid food with every third watering. Repot after flowering.

Propagation: By division, with at least two pseudobulbs per piece.

Pests and Diseases: Aphids, spider mites.

Uses: An easy orchid for the living room or the cool greenhouse.

ODONTOGLOSSUM
Odontoglossum

Family: Orchid, Orchidaceae
Native Habitat: Central America
Flowering Time: Depends on the species

These epiphytic orchids are often used for breeding because of their large flowers. Their pseudobulbs are egg-shaped and grow up to three leaves. The racemous, upright inflorescences grow at their base.

O. cariniferum blooms in spring; its red-brown to olive-green flower clusters can be up to 3.2 ft. (1 m) long. Lips are kidney-shaped. O. crispum has flower stands much shorter; its large, rippled flowers are white to pink, the colors varying in tone. The tongue-shaped lip has a central yellow spot. It blooms from late winter through spring. O. pulchellum also blooms at that time of year in white panicles; flowers have yellow-red dotted lips.

Location: By an east or west window; in summer, as airy as possible. In winter at least 54°F (12°C).

Care: During growth keep plant evenly moist with soft water, allowing the soil to dry somewhat in between. Give orchid food once a month. After blooming, water just enough to keep the pseudobulb from shrinking and the soil from drying out.

Propagation: By division, three pseudobulbs per piece.

Pests and Diseases: Aphids, scale insects; rotten spots indicate soggy roots.

Uses: For conservatories and warm greenhouses. A few species also for living areas if not very warm.

Odontoglossum grande

TIP

Odontoglossum grande now belongs to Rossioglossum, but is kept and cared for like the other Odontoglossum species.

Olea – Ophiopogon

The olive makes one think of the olive groves all over the Mediterranean region, of deep blue skies and vacations. Such simple garden plants as forsythias, privet, and lilac also belong to the olive family.

Unless you know exactly what you are about, it is better not to cut off the wilted blooms of oncidias, as some species bloom again and again on the same stalk.

Olea europaea

OLEA EUROPEA
Common olive tree

Family: Olive, *Oleaceae*
Native Habitat: Mediterranean regions, North and South Africa, Asia
Flowering Time: Late summer

The evergreen olive has willowlike leaves that are rough, blue-green on top, and silvery-white underneath. Its modest flowers are small and creamy white; they sit in axial racemes. The olive seldom sets fruit in northern regions. Larger olive trees are not cheap, since they grow slowly, but they can reach a venerable age of several hundred years.

Location: Sunny and warm, in summer outdoors. In winter light, at 35–50°F (2–10°C), though for short periods it can be in a dark cellar.
Care: During growth, water regularly and feed every two weeks. Repot in spring if needed. Since the olive can bear some frost, it can be moved indoors late and out again early. On warm winter days, air out the place where it is stored. Pruning and training to shape are always possible.
Propagation: By herbaceous cuttings and or from scarified seeds.
Pests and Diseases: Rarely.
Uses: Evergreen container plant or for the conservatory.

TIP

The butterfly orchid, *Oncidium papilio*, loves warmth; it does not want a cold winter rest, but prefers the same temperatures all year.

ONCIDIUM
Oncidium

Family: Orchid, *Orchidaceae*
Native Habitat: Central and South America
Flowering Time: Varies with the species

Most of the 530 species of the genus are epiphytic; their habitats range from tropical river valleys to high mountains. The pseudobulbs vary in their form and leaves; some species have large, single, fleshy leaves. Equally variable are the form and arrangement of the flowers, which are often found in very long racemes. This genus of orchid has knoblike growths at the base of the lip. When buying one, it is vital to determine the temperature needs of the species in question.

For a warm greenhouse or room, choose: *O. bicallosum,* for example, with small, paired knobs on the lip. It blooms in winter.

Oncidium kramerianum

Oncidium 'Rotkappchen

O. forbesii, with long clusters of large butterfly flowers, blooms in early winter.

O. ornithorhynchum has a flower resembling a bird's beak, smells of vanilla, and blooms in autumn,

Hybrids for heated greenhouses are: 'Goldrush,' 'Little Red Ridinghood,' and 'Thilo.'

Location: Light to partial shade and humid; in summer outdoors. In winter, after flowering, cool, at 54°F (12°C).

Care: Water well in summer with soft water, letting the soil dry before each watering. Add some orchid food every two weeks. Arrange for high humidity. After flowering, keep only slightly moist, to prevent bulbs from shrinking.

Propagation: By division, in groups of at least three pseudobulbs.

Pests and Diseases: Aphids.

Uses: A few species are worth trying in living areas; others are for a heated greenhouse or window greenhouse.

Ophiopogon jaburan 'Variegatus'

OPHIOPOGON
Mondo grass

Family: Lily, *Liliaceae*
Native Habitat: Japan, China, Ryukyu Islands
Flowering Time: In summer

Mondo grass is a marvelous evergreen perennial with long leaves colored dark green, striped either white or yellow-green. Its white or violet flowers stand in spikes. *O. jaburan* has narrow leaves, 16–31 in. (40–80 cm) long; its flowers open in summer. They are white to violet and sit within bracts on a long spike. There also are varieties with yellow or white striped or speckled leaves; they

are subsumed under the general name 'Variegatus.'

The species *O. japonicus* has shorter, dark green leaves; they are only 2 in. (5 cm) long in the variety 'Minor.'

Location: *O. japonicus*, shade or partial shade; *O. jaburan*, light. In winter at least 50°F (10°C). *O. japonicus* down to 32°F (0°C).

Care: Keep moderately moist and water every two weeks.

Propagation: By division or from seed.

Pests and Diseases: Spider mites, thrips.

Uses: A handsome flowering plant for any room; *O. japonicus* as underplanting in the conservatory, greenhouse, or terrarium.

The *Oncidium* hybrid 'Little Red Ridinghood' displays its elegantly arching spike, densely set with blossoms.

While *Ophiopogon jaburan* cannot be called hardy, with some protection, *Ophiopogon japonicus* can overwinter outside in milder regions of the temperate zone. My own plants of *O. japonicus* serve as underplanting for tall bamboo.

Opuntia – Pachira

Among the most beautiful of prickly pears is *Opuntia robusta*, with its blazing yellow flower and deep red fruit. By the way, some prickly pears, such as *O. fragilis*, *O. polyacantha*, and *O. vulgaris*, are hardy in the temperate zone, but they have to be protected from becoming waterlogged.

Osmanthus x burkwoodii is the best species for container gardening. In the wine-growing regions of the north, *O. delavayi* has been known to thrive planted outside; *O. fragrans* is also able to withstand cold down to 14°F (–10°C).

Opuntia robusta

Osmanthus x burkwoodii

OPUNTIA
Prickly pear, cholla

Family: Cactus, *Cactaceae*
Native Habitat: North and South America
Flowering Time: Summer

Opuntia is a cactus that has a segmented main stem. Formerly, what are now *Opuntias* were assigned to other genera, depending on their habit. As houseplants, three subgenera are important: *Cylindropuntia*, with cylindrical segments, *Platyopuntia*, with disc-like segments, and *Tephrocactus*, with spherical segments. As a rule, *Opuntias* have sharp thorns and tufts of small, barbed bristles that catch and stay in the skin. Many *Opuntias* bloom profusely; some produce edible fruit. Well-loved are *O. microdasys*, with yellowish glochids, its variety 'albaspina' with snow-white ones, and *O. rufida* with red-brown glochids. Also interesting are the 'cristata' forms that produce strange, banded shapes.

Beautiful *Cylindropuntias* are *O. bigelovii* (carmine-yellow, 3.2 ft. (1 m) high, thorns yellowish white);

O. imbricata (scarlet, 10 ft. (3 m) high, thorns brown); *O. subulata* (reddish to red, 13 ft. (4 m) high, thorns yellowish); *O. tunicata* (yellow, low-growing, thorns reddish, 2 in. (5 cm) long).

Well-known *Platyopuntias*: *O. azurea* (yellow with red center, shoots blue-green); *O. elata* (orange, 10 in. (25 cm) long, green); *O. compressa* (sulfur yellow, creeping); *O. robusta* (yellow, shoots large, circular).

Tephrocactus forms: *O. alexandri* (pink-white, thorns white, dark tips); *O. dactylifera* (orange-yellow, red to yellow-brown thorns); *O. floccosa* (yellow or orange, shoots wrapped in white wool).

Location: Full sun, warm; in summer outdoors. In winter at 35–41°F (2–5°C); smaller species warmer.
Care: *Opuntia* needs a lot of water in the summer, particularly *Cylindropuntia*, which has to have some water even in winter, while other species go almost dry. Feed weekly with cactus food. Repot with good drainage in spring.
Propagation: By separated segments that have to dry well before being planted.
Pests and Diseases: Mealybugs, scale insects, spider mites.
Uses: For sunny, warm rooms, larger species for containers.

OSMANTHUS
Osmanthus

Family: Olive, *Oleaceae*
Native Habitat: China, Japan
Flowering Time: Spring, summer

Osmanthus is an evergreen shrub with leathery leaves that can take various shapes; its flowers tend to be small, white, clustered, and intensely fragrant. *O. x burkwoodii* is best known; it blooms in midsummer. *O. delavayi* has a broad habit and starts blooming in spring. The leaves of *O. fragrans* are 4 in. (10 cm) long ovals; its flowers are white. Those of the variety 'Rubra' are orange; they smell like apricots.
Location: Sun to partial shade; in summer partial shade outdoors. In winter cool.
Care: Young plants need more water; later, water moderately. Feed once a month.
Propagation: From seed or by cuttings.
Pests and Diseases: Rarely.
Uses: Container plant for unheated or warm conservatories; for espalier.

Oxalis deppei

Pachira aquatica

The Cape shamrock, "lucky clover" *O. deppei*, is not an ideal houseplant: it gets too warm in closed rooms. Pretty varieties of *O. deppei* are 'Braunherz' and 'Iron Cross.'

The botanical family of the kapok trees, to which pachira belongs, also includes *Durio zibethinus*, the civet durio. It is said that of all delicious fruits, the fruit of the civet durio smells worst.

OXALIS
Oxalis, Cape shamrock

Family: Wood sorrel, *Oxalidaceae*
Native Habitat: South Africa, Central and South America
Flowering Time: Varies with species and handling

Oxalis is a perennial, about 10 in. (25 cm) high. Its leaves, on long petioles, are four-lobed; its small, pink flowers stand five to twelve to a cluster. Leaves and flowers grow out of a bulblike tuber. *O. deppei*, the Cape shamrock, blooms between summer and midwinter. Bulbs from the previous year can be purchased in early fall. Place several in a small pot and store them at about 46°F (8°C). *O. bowiei* blooms in summer, so it is started in spring. Its light green leaves are three-lobed and its flower is dark pink.
Location: *O. deppei*, full sun and cool; planted in the garden in late spring. *O. bowiei*, sun to partial shade. Store the tubers in the fall free of frost, like gladiolus or dahlia bulbs.
Care: Keep relatively dry, but do not dry out. Feed *O. bowiei* occasionally; in late summer allow the leaves to die off.
Propagation: By bulbs.
Pests and Diseases: None.
Uses: *O. deppei* for a cool conservatory; *O. bowiei* for planters, bowls, hanging baskets.

PACHIRA AQUATICA
Pachira

Family: Kapok tree, *Bombacaceae*
Native Habitat: Mexico, Ecuador, Brazil
Flowering Time: Seldom blooms in cultivation

This dainty little tree is a close relative of the bizarre baobab tree (*Adansonia digitata*); both trees store water in their trunks. This is the reason for pachira's name *aquatica*, an old name restored after it had been *P. macrocarpa* for a while. The leaves are leathery and lobed like a hand. In colder regions the 14 in.- (35 cm-) wide flowers, reminiscent of heron feathers, never appear.
Location: Full sun or partial shade all year; humid. In summer at room temperature; in winter somewhat cooler.
Care: Keep moderately moist all year. During growth feed lightly once a week. Provide indirect atmospheric humidity.
Propagation: By tip cuttings at about 77°F (25°C) or from seed.
Pests and Diseases: Leaves drop if air is too dry.
Uses: A distinguished foliage plant for the house.

Pachyphytum – Pachypodium

Because of its lovely, white-dusted leaves, *Pachyphytum oviferum* is a succulent for a collector's heart.

For a while, pachypodium was a rather fashionable plant and people would show it to visitors as a "rare cactus with leaves."

Never feed *Pachyphytum* with nitrogen-rich fertilizers or the leaves will explode.

PACHYPHYTUM
Pachyphytum

Family: Stonecrop, *Crassulaceae*
Native Habitat: Mexico
Flowering Time: Spring

This succulent has a short-stemmed habit and thick, ovoid or elongated leaves that are delicately coated, as if covered with hoar frost. The large, reddish or white flowers stand in clusters on 2–6 in.- (5–15 cm-) long stalks. The best-known and probably the loveliest species is *P. oviferum* (the "egg-bearing" pachyphytum); its leaves are powdered in gray-white, often shaded in red. The flowers are greenish white. *P. bracteosum*, not quite so handsome, has red flowers. *x Pachyveria* is a cross between *Pachyphytum* and *Echeveria*. The succulent leaves are narrower, pointed, and more clearly arranged in rosette formation. In spring the flowers appear in one or

Various Pachypodium species

two colors of white, yellow, reddish, or orange.

Location: Light to full sun and warm; in summer outdoors. In winter at room temperature, but even better at 46–50°F (8–10°C).
Care: Water rarely in summer and never on the plant. Give cactus food once a month. In winter keep cool and almost dry. Avoid soggy roots at all costs. Remove shrunken leaves regularly.
Propagation: By leaf cuttings or from seed.
Pests and Diseases: Root rot from waterlogging in winter.
Uses: Trouble-free plant for hot south windows. Several specimens are very attractive grouped in a flat dish with small stones.

PACHYPODIUM
Pachypodium

Family: Dogbane, *Apocynaceae*
Native Habitat: Madagascar
Flowering Time: Spring

Pachypodium resembles a columnar cactus with a bunch of leaves on top. Above a height of 4 ft. (1.2 m), this succulent plant produces numerous, white, star flowers.

The leaves of *P. geayi* are narrow and silver-gray, those of *P. lamieri*, broader and fresh green. The plant's natural rest period is in summer, when the leaves will drop, but in cultivation it is possible to forgo this rest, and thus to preserve the leaves.

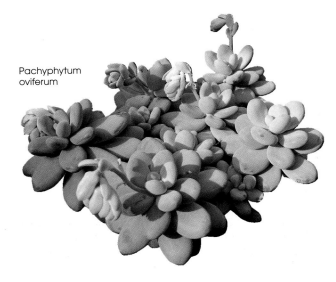

Pachyphytum oviferum

272

THE MOST BEAUTIFUL PLANTS FROM A TO Z

The latex of pachypodium is very poisonous.

Since 1948, botanical collections have included *Pachypodium brevicaule*, a strange Madagascan succulent with petioled leaves in rosettes, two thorns (modified stipules) to either side of each leaf, and yellow flowers. The plant forms low stems that clump up and can grow up to 24 in. (60 cm) in diameter.

Location: Light, sunny, with bottom heat all year. Ideal location: a window bench over the heater.

Care: During growth water freely, less in winter. Avoid soggy roots. Once a month, from spring to fall, give cactus food.

Propagation: From seed.

Pests and Diseases: Root rot and black, slimy spots if roots are waterlogged in winter. If lower leaves drop, stop watering for several weeks till new leaves appear.

Uses: Pachypodium is a problem-free houseplant. Suitable for hydroponics.

Pachypodium namaquanum
(Picture on right)

Pachypodium brevicaule

Pachypodium brevicaule means short-stemmed *Pachypodium*. The plant is native to Madagascar. Its knotted stem resembles a stone on which appear the yellow flowers, 0.8–2 in. (2–5 cm) long.

Almost 6.5 ft. (2 m) high, *Pachypodium namaquanum* is pictured here in its native Namibia. This impressive plant form puts forth numerous red-brown speckled flowers; its stems always turn toward the sun. This strange succulent is called "club-foot" by the native Nama.

It is best to deal gently with pachypodium: its thorns can hurt.

Pachystachys – Paphiopedilum

The candlelike flower spikes of *Pachystachys lutea* resemble those of *Aphelandrai*, a related plant.

If you are thinking of buying a screw pine, consider that the plant grows very large; if it is healthy—and it does not take too much care to keep it so—it soon becomes too big for most living rooms.

Pachystachys lutea

PACHYSTACHYS LUTEA
Cardinal's guard

Family: Acanthus, *Acanthaceae*
Native Habitat: Peru
Flowering Time: Spring to fall

Pachystachys is a 16 in.- (40 cm-) high flowering plant with dark green, oval, slightly wrinkled leaves and large white blossoms in spikelike clusters. Brilliant yellow bracts intermingle with the flowers. Nurseries treat the plant with growth-retardants to keep it compact.
Location: Light, humid, and warm all year; never have the air, and particularly the soil, under 64–68°F (18–20°C).
Care: Keep moderately moist and spray often, summer and winter. Spring to fall, feed every two weeks, in winter only rarely.
Propagation: By tip cuttings at 77°F (25°C). Prune young plants often to stimulate bushy habit: only densely branched plants bloom well.
Pests and Diseases: Aphids, whiteflies, spider mites; cold soil (under 64°F (18°C)) damages the plant.
Uses: Houseplant for light, warm rooms.

TIP

It is a good idea to grow some new young cardinal's guard plants from cuttings before the more mature one becomes too leggy, as it will in time.

Pandanus veitchii

PANDANUS
Screw pine

Family: Screw pine, *Pandanaceae*
Native Habitat: Malaysian archipelago, Madagascar, Africa
Flowering Time: Seldom blooms in cultivation

Pandanus grows into a tall evergreen tree or shrub. Its common name suggests the spiral arrangement of the leaves around its trunk, which is quite obvious in older plants. The aerial roots, which give added support to the trunk that carries many leaves 3.23 ft. (1 m) long, are also typical. *P. sanderi* has toothed leaves with white or yellowish longitudinal stripes. The gray-green leaves of *P. utilis* are edged with red prickles. The best-known variety is *P. veitchii*, with creamy-white stripes along its leaves.
Location: Light and sunny all year; never under 64°F (18°C). In summer, in a protected spot outdoors.
Care: Keep evenly moist, spring to the end of summer, and feed weekly; in winter, monthly. Repot if needed in garden soil with one-third sand.
Propagation: By offsets with roots; *P. utilis* only from fresh seeds.
Pests and Diseases: Wetness and bottom cold can kill the plant.
Uses: Foliage plant for warm rooms; for a heated conservatory.

Pandorea jasminoides

Paphiopedilum *hybrid*

Pandorea jasminoides, one of the most beautiful climbing plants for a container, is at this time sold only in nurseries that specialize in rare container plants.

Though lady slipper species, such as *Paphiopedilum concolor*, offer a great range of choices, the hybrids are easier to care for. If you have a garden, you can hang your lady slippers in the partial shade of a tree and leave them there till the nights start being cool.

PANDOREA JASMINOIDES
Pandorea

Family: Trumpet creeper, *Bignoniaceae*
Native Habitat: Australia
Flowering Time: Summer and autumn, earlier in a conservatory

Pandorea is a slow-growing, evergreen shrub with shiny, green, compound leaves and funnel-shaped flowers up to 2 in. (5 cm) wide. Two good varieties are 'Alba,' white, and 'Rosea,' pink.
Location: Light to sunny all year; in winter at 59°F (15°C).
Care: Plenty of water, fertilizer, and sun during growth are the necessary prerequisites for lavish flowering. The plant twines around itself, but needs a trellis to climb upward. Keep cool and light in winter.
Propagation: By cuttings in spring and summer.
Pests and Diseases: Aphids; young plants endangered by excessive wetness.
Uses: Ideal climbing plant for a heated conservatory, best planted in the ground.

PAPHIOPEDILUM
Lady slipper

Family: Orchid, *Orchidaceae*
Native Habitat: India, Philippines, Thailand
Flowering Time: Varies according to species

The lady slipper is the best-loved orchid after *Phalaenopsis*. The lip of the flower really does look like a shoe. Most species are terrestrial and have no pseudobulbs. *Paphiopedilum* blooms mostly in winter and spring; individual flowers can last for weeks, even months. The plant has two to four pairs of leaves. Each pair grows one flowering stem of one or more blooms. After blooming, the plant develops a dense group of offsets that will bloom in turn. The flower can be white, yellow, green, brown, or reddish; often it is striped, speckled, or spotted. Beautiful species are *P. barbatum, P. bellatulum, P. concolor, P. glaucophyllum, P. malipoense,* and *P. spicerianum*.
    Very well-known *Paphiopedilum* hybrids are 'China Girl,' 'Goliath,' 'King Arthur,' and 'Maudiae.'
Location: In summer partial shade; can be outdoors. In winter light, not under 64°F (18°C).
Care: Keep evenly moist with tepid, soft water. Allow soil to dry somewhat before watering again. Spray the leaves often and provide high atmospheric humidity. Spring and summer, give orchid food every 14 days. Repot every two to three years.
Propagation: By division.
Pests and Diseases: Aphids, scale insects, spider mites; make sure the pot does not cool off too much: cold soil will hurt the plant.
Uses: An orchid that requires much care.

Paphiopedilum concolor

TIP

The care a lady slipper requires can be deduced from the color of its leaves; if the leaves are pure green the plant requires moist, cool conditions. Plants with marbled leaves, however, prefer it moist and warm.

Parodia – Pavonia

The majority of parodias grow slowly and take up little room. They bloom freely (see *P. microsperma* on the right) and they require relatively little care. Altogether, a good cactus for a collection.

Passiflora caerulea is readily available, usually for planting right in the soil.

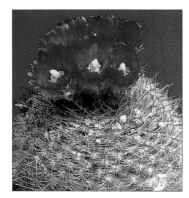

Parodia microsperma

PARODIA
Parodia

Family: Cactus, *Cactaceae*
Native Habitat: South America
Flowering Time: Spring to fall, depending on the species

Parodia can be globular or columnar in growth; its ribs spiral around its body and are often set with barbed thorns. Near the apex appear the flowers in red and yellow shades. Most species are not higher than 8–10 in. (20–25 cm) with a diameter of 6 in. (15 cm).
Location: Sun and fresh air; species with rough thorns under glass; those with soft thorns by a window. In winter at 39–46°F (4–8°C).
Care: During growth keep moist, but let soil dry somewhat before each watering. Administer cactus food every three weeks. Keep dry from midautumn to spring.
Propagation: From seed, but it is slow and difficult.
Pests and Diseases: Avoid overfertilizing, overwatering, stale air, and inappropriate winter treatment.
Uses: A cactus with complex care requirements.

Passiflora caerulea

PASSIFLORA
Passion flower

Family: Passion flower, *Passiflora-ceae*
Native Habitat: Tropical and subtropical America, Asia, Australia
Flowering Time: Spring to fall

This is an evergreen plant with twining, spiraling shoots that bear leaves with three to seven lobes. It is called passion flower because parts of the flower are said to symbolize Christ's passion: the corolla shows the crown of thorns, the five stamens stand for the five wounds, the flower's three stigmata for the nails.

The most widespread species is *P. caerulea*, the blue passion flower

with its excellent hybrids, 'Kaiserin Eugenie,' with purple flowers, and 'Constanze Eliott,' with creamy-white ones. The flowers of *P. incarnata* and *P. edulis* are similar, though more modest; the latter species produces edible fruit. *P. quadrangularis*, the giant grana-dilla, is a powerful climbing shrub. Its flowers are 4–5 in. (10–12 cm) in diameter, reddish in the center, ringed by scarlet petals. *P. racemosa* and *P. manicata* both bloom scarlet. The first is a slow climber and loves heat, while the second grows fast and likes it cool and airy.
Location: Very light, in summer outdoors. In winter light and airy at 43–46°F (6–8°C).
Care: Once growth has begun, keep as light and warm as you can. Plenty of water and fertilizer are prerequisites for rich flowering.

TIP

My own *Passiflora caerulea* is planted in a flower bed on the patio. We live in the wine-growing region of the north, so the plant survives the winter if I tie pine boughs to the trellis to protect the foliage. Even in hard winters, when the above-ground parts of the plant freeze right down to the soil, they grow back in the spring and again cover 21–32 square feet (2–3 m²) by the end of the season.

The Most Beautiful Plants from A to Z

Pruning, even during growth, assists the formation of new shoots and of flowers. Provide a strong trellis. Prune back long shoots to 20 in. (50 cm) above the soil before moving the plant for the winter. Repot young plants every year; older plants only as needed.

Propagation: By tip cuttings with bottom heating or by offshoots of older plants. Flowering of plants raised from seed is often late and meager.

Pests and Diseases: Spider mites, thrips; root and stem rot if soil is kept too cold and wet, particularly for the heat-loving species *P. quadrangularis* and *P. racemosa*, while *P. caerulea* is less sensitive that way.

Uses: Splendid climber for the patio, balcony, conservatory, or the windowsill. *P. quadrangularis* only for a heated greenhouse.

Passiflora manicata

Passiflora incarnata

Passiflora quadrangularis

Pavonia multiflora

PAVONIA MULTIFLORA
Pavonia multiflora

Family: Mallow, *Malvaceae*
Native Habitat: Brazil
Flowering Time: Autumn to late spring

The many-flowered pavonia, now called *Triplochlamys multiflora*, is a winter-blooming shrub with large, evergreen leaves. The scarlet calyx of the flower is surrounded by large red upright bracts. Flowers appear in higher leaf axils, a good reason for pinching out young plants.

Location: Very light but screened from direct sun all year; humid. In winter light and cool but not below 54°F (12°C).

Care: Keep moderately moist with soft water, spring and summer. In winter, reduce water according to position; spray often. Spring and summer, give calcium-free fertilizer biweekly. Prune after flowering.

Propagation: By tip cuttings at 86–95°F (30–35°C). Difficult.

Pests and Diseases: Rarely.

Uses: For the conservatory.

Three *Passiflora* species, one more spectacular than the other: *Passiflora manicata* from South America; *Passiflora incarnata*, which is cultivated for pharmaceutical reasons in the United States—namely, for the sleep-inducing properties of its juices; and *Passiflora quadrangularis*, the giant granadilla.

The chances of succeeding with cuttings of *Pavonia* are somewhat improved if they are treated with a growth hormone.

TIP

I have tried planting *Passiflora quadrangularis* in the garden for the summer and even had a few flowers to show for it, but in most areas such an experiment may not end so well.

277

Pelargonium

The different scents of the scented geranium are the result of various aromatic oils and other substances within the plant, such as citronellol, geraniol, menthol, terpentes, and alcohol.

Pelargonium tomentosum

Pelargonium 'Little Gem'

Pelargonium graveolens

Pelargonium 'Mable Grey'

PELARGONIUM
Geranium

Family: Geranium, *Geraniaceae*
Native Habitat: South Africa, Mediterranean region
Flowering Time: Spring to fall, some species all year

The genus *Pelargonium*, commonly called geranium, encompasses about 250 species, which are now grouped into five major divisions:
• Leafy geranium
• Scented geranium
• Regal geranium or English geranium
• Ivy geranium or "hanging geranium"
• Zonal geranium
Less well-known is a sixth group, the succulent pelargonium. Its fleshy stems and rather bizarre appearance make it a good candidate for bonsai training. It is treated like other succulents.

PELARGONIUM
Leafy geranium

These geraniums have multicolored leaves; the mutations are due to chlorophyll defects in their foliage. There are at least fifty varieties. Some of the best come from England, such as 'Masterpiece,' 'Dolly Vardon,' 'Freak of Nature,' and 'Chelsea Gem.'
Care: Treat these varieties like zonal pelargonia, but pinch out flower buds to allow the plant to use all its strength for leaf building.

PELARGONIUM
Scented geranium

Some of these species are not found in nurseries, though some specialty nurseries may have them. Ask for cuttings from your friends. The flower of this geranium is less interesting than the scented leaves that remind you of lemons, roses, mint, almonds, lilac, or apples.

The most important species are P. capitatum (rose-scented); P. crispum (lemon-scented); P. x citrosum (also lemon-scented); P. extipulatum (mint-scented); P. graveolens (rose-scented); P. 'Marble Grey' (strongly lemon-scented); P. papilionaceum (fir-scented); P. 'Royal Oak' (pepper-scented); P. tomentosum (mint-scented). Nurseries that carry scented pelargonia are listed starting on page 376.
Location: Light and sunny; can be outside. If you are willing to forgo flowers, the plant can be warm all year; otherwise keep at 46–54°F (8–12°C) in winter.
Care: In summer, water regularly. Keep rather dry in winter. Prune and repot in spring.
Propagation: By tip cuttings.
Pests and Diseases: Whiteflies, aphids.
Uses: For living areas, balconies, troughs; *P. crispum* is suitable for bonsai.

PELARGONIUM GRANDIFLORUM HYBRIDS
Regal or English geranium

These hybrids usually grow on somewhat woody stems. The leaves are large and serrated. Flowers come white, pink, red, and speckled, streaked, or with darker markings.

Very attractive varieties are 'Jasmin' (white); 'Jupiter' (lilac with red markings); 'Muttertag' (orange-red with dark red markings); 'Mikado' (dark salmon with one dark red spot on each petal).
Location: At an eastern or western window all year; summer outside is tolerated. In winter at 50–54°F (10–12°C), never over 59°F (15°C).
Care: Water freely, but do not leave water in the saucer. After flowering (early spring to early summer), prune lightly and repot. Buds are set when days are 12 hours long and it is 46–54°F (8–12°C), as a rule in winter. When the days get longer and it is warmer, the flowers are formed. English geraniums should be replaced after the third year, when flowering markedly diminishes.
Propagation: By tip cuttings, e.g., from pruning, with soil at 50°C (10°C). After sprouting at 54°F (12°C); any warmer and it will not bloom.
Pests and Diseases: Aphids, whiteflies; frequently fungus diseases.
Uses: Exquisite houseplant; may flower too early for the balcony in the temperate zone.

Pelargonium 'Chelsea Gem'

PELARGONIUM PELTATUM HYBRIDS
Ivy or "hanging" geranium

Ivy geranium has low-lying, or hanging shoots with ivylike, fleshy, smooth leaves. There are half-hanging, hanging, simple, semi-double, and double varieties to choose from. Colors range from white through red-and-white, salmon, pink, and bright red, to lilac. The length of shoots varies between 16 in. (40 cm) and 5 ft. (1.5 m), with 'Ville de Paris.' The so-called Cascade varieties are self-cleaning. They bloom for a long time and very profusely.

'Chelsea Gem' is a fast-growing leafy geranium. It thrives in a room as well as on a balcony or terrace.

Many scented geraniums, such as *Pelargonium tomentosum* or the rose geranium, *P. graveolens,* grow into substantial shrubs in a container.

Because the time of flowering can be controlled, regal pelargonium is available for sale all year round.

A selection of scented geraniums in containers and pots

Hybrid Pelargonium grandiflorum

279

Pelargonium

Zonal geraniums, as they are commonly called (right), are all-time favorites for balcony planting. They bloom plentifully, and they do not take damage from a heavy rain—unlike petunias, which can be completely crushed by a sudden downpour. Elegant alternatives to the rustic bright red geranium are newer burgundy and lilac-toned plants.

Here are some good varieties: 'Amethyst' (blooms lilac, double shoots 31 in. (80 cm) long); 'Cocorico' (red, simple, 4 ft. (1.2 m) long); 'Mexican' (red-and-white, double, 3.2 ft. (1 m)); 'Ville de Paris' (pink, simple, 5 ft. (1.5 m)).

Location: Light, even full sun; in winter not quite as cool as zonal geranium.

Care: Treat like zonal geranium hybrids. Double varieties need rain protection.

Propagation: By cuttings in the fall or from seed in winter. (Some seeds have recently become available.)

Pests and Diseases: Double varieties tend to rot in very wet summers.

Uses: One of the loveliest and least demanding balcony and hanging plants.

Pelargonium zonale *hybrid*

PELARGONIUM ZONALE HYBRIDS
Zonal geranium hybrids

This geranium grows upright to 12–16 in. (30–40 cm), is densely branched and bushy, and has velvety leaves with often spectacular brown markings. The spherical umbels of simple or double blossoms show fine colors from white through all shades of pink and salmon to fire-engine red. With some work, you can train a zonal geranium into a standard or pyramidal form.

Some good varieties are 'Alba' (white, double); 'Casino' (dark salmon, double); 'Gloria' (orange-salmon, simple); 'Irene' (light red, double); 'Kardinal' (crimson, simple); 'Rio' (pink with an eye, simple); 'Vulkan' (red, simple); 'Wienerblut' (orange-salmon, simple).

The leaves of the following varieties are very decorative: 'Goldpapa' (golden leaves marked in red-brown); 'Cloth of Gold' (yellow, unmarked); 'Friesdorf' (black-mottled leaves, simple, scarlet flowers). The name zonal geranium conjures up leaves with concentric markings, but this group also includes the Miniature pelargonia, whose smallest representative is no taller than 5 in. (12 cm).

Location: Light or full sun; in winter at 41–46°F (5–8°C). Without a cool rest, the plants will bloom in winter, too.

Care: During growth water freely, but avoid waterlogging; feed well to the end of summer or longer, if the plant will overwinter. Remove dead flowers regularly.

Propagation: By cuttings in late summer; they are possible all year; winter cuttings will produce flowers in late spring.

Pests and Diseases: Aphids, spider mites; gray mold and geranium rust; viral mosaic diseases.

Uses: Valuable balcony plant.

Rustic charm using Pelargonium

The Most Beautiful Plants from A to Z

Pelargonium stands for idyllic country life, for a healthy world, for romantic summers. It has enjoyed the affection of people all over the world for a very long time. The history of pelargonium, which brightens our homes under the name "geranium," goes back a long way. In 1631, John Tradescant, gardener to the King of England, brought the first pelargonium from the Cape of Good Hope to Great Britain. Another genus of plants, *Tradescantia*, is named after him. In the eighteenth century, the *P. peltatum* and *P. zonale* hybrids were created, also by English gardeners.

Pellaea rotundifolia

Family: Madder, *Rubiaceae*
Native Habitat: Tropical Africa, Arabia
Flowering Time: Fall through winter

Pellaea rotundifolia is called button fern because of its little round leaves.

When a *Pentas lanceolata* plant that is kept inside a room has set buds, it should be sprayed very frequently.

Because the button fern has a shallow root system, it is best planted in flat dishes.

PELLAEA
Button fern

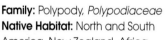

Family: Polypody, *Polypodiaceae*
Native Habitat: North and South America, New Zealand, Africa, Australia
Flowering Time: Not a flowering plant.

Button ferns, unlike other ferns, like it dry. *Pellaea rotundifolia* has 8–12 in.- (20–30 cm-) long fronds, set with small, round, leathery leaflets. A more common form is *P. altropurpurea*, a species with reddish leaves; it is able to tolerate more cold and harder water. Its 10 in.- (25 cm-) long fronds are covered with fluffy hair. *P. falcata*, the sickle-shaped *Pellaea*, looks like a larger edition of *P. rotundifolia*. *P. viridis* has up to 24 in.- (60 cm-) long, twice or thrice

pinnately compound green fronds with reddish black petioles. This is considered the most hardy species.
Location: Light, sunny, but no strong noon sun; in summer, outdoors. In winter light and airy at 54–59°F (12–15°C).
Care: In summer keep moderately moist; in winter drier, but not dried out. During growth, feed lightly every three to four weeks.
Propagation: By division of older plants or from the spores that form underneath the leaves on older specimens. They are sown and sprouted under glass at 64°F (18°C).
Pests and Diseases: Rarely; waterlogging is not tolerated.
Uses: Evergreen, undemanding fern for the house; some species are appropriate as hanging plants.

Pentas is a subshrub that grows about 24 in. (60 cm) high. Its lanceliolate leaves are light green, about 2 in. (5 cm) long. The flowers appear in dense, terminal umbels; they can be white, pink, red or violet.
Location: Sunny, warm and airy; in summer outdoors. Starting in mid-autumn, keep at 54–59°F (12–15°C).
Care: During growth, water amply and feed every week. Keep slightly drier in the winter. Pentas need pruning after the growth retardants (which are routinely applied in the nursery) wear off and the plant begins to look leggy.
Propagation: By tip cuttings with bottom heating or from seed, in which case the color of the flowers cannot be controlled. Young plants have to be pruned several times to ensure fullness of form.
Diseases: Yellow leaves are due to waterlogging or cold root ball.
Uses: House or greenhouse plant that blooms in winter.

Peperomia caperata

PEPEROMIA
Peperomia

Family: Pepper, *Piperaceae*
Native Habitat: Tropical and subtropical America
Flowering Time: Varies

Peperomia is a low-growing, bushy plant with whitish green flowers reminiscent of mousetails. The leaves are slightly succulent, and they vary from species to species in color, form, and structure. This wealth of species and varieties stimulates the plant collector. The leaves of *P. argyreia* are shieldlike, marked in a silvery half-moon pattern. *P. caperata* has a wrinkled, broken-up leaf surface. The white flowers reach far above the foliage. This species also has spotted forms, like 'variegata' and 'tricolor.' A red leaf edge characterizes *P. clusifolia*, which also is available in its white-green 'Variegata' form. *P. griseoargentea* has dark veins; between them, the green leaf blade is rippled. The veins of the leaves of *P. metallica* show red underneath the gray-green surface. The leaf axis is marked in white. *P. puteolata* has lanceolate, leathery, dark green

leaves 4 in. (10 cm) long, to which the light grooves on top are in brilliant contrast *P. rotundifolia* is round leafed.

Location: Light to partial shade; all year at 55–64°F (13–18°C). Keep species with delicate foliage humid in summer.

Care: Water moderately with soft water. Feed every two weeks from spring to midsummer.

Propagation: By tip, stem, or leaf cuttings.

Pests and Diseases: Wetness and cold can cause serious damage, particularly in winter.

Uses: A very lovely and versatile foliage plant for hanging baskets or epiphytic supports; delicate species for use as a ground cover in glass cases and window greenhouses. Suited to hydroponics.

Peperomia rotundifolia

The leaves of various peperomia species

Peperomia caperata is the most commonly offered species.

The leaves of *Peperomia rotundifolia* develop out of disks the size of a pinhead.

With the multiplicity of forms and colors it offers and its relatively compact habit, peperomia is an ideal species both for collecting and for grouping.

Pereskia – Petunia

Pereskia is the cactus that stopped halfway in the course of evolution. On the one hand, it still has leaves, like any cotyledonous flowering plant with two cotyledons. On the other hand, it also has areolae and thorns, like the cacti farther along the evolutionary path. It used to be customary, by the way, to use pereskias as graft stock for Christmas and Easter cacti trained as standards.

About 25 species of *Pernettya* grow in Central and South America, from Mexico to the Antarctic. Only one species, *P. tasmanica*, occurs in Tasmania and New Zealand.

The full beauty of *Persea americana*, the avocado tree, becomes evident only when the plant grows mature enough to be moved from a pot to a container.

Because of their sensitivity to salts, avocado trees prefer natural fertilizers.

Pereskia aculeata

Pernettya mucronata

Persea americana

PERESKIA
Pereskia

Family: Cactus, *Cactaceae*
Native Habitat: Tropical and subtropical South America
Flowering Time: Autumn

Pereskia can take the form of a tree, a shrub or a creeper. *P. aculeata* grows shoots up to 33 ft. (10 m) long with strong, curved thorns and oval, slightly waxy leaves 2–3 in. (6–8 cm) long. The flowers, creamy white to pink, appear in clusters and smell of lemons. The variety 'Goldseffiana' has olive-green leaves, scarlet underneath. Those of *P. grandifolia* are larger, and its flower is pink, 3 in. (8 cm) across.
Location: Sunny, airy; best off in a greenhouse. In winter cooler by 18°F (10°C).
Care: Water regularly in summer, less in winter. The shoots will need pruning.
Propagation: By herbaceous tip cuttings or from seed.
Pests and Diseases: The plant reacts negatively to waterlogging; leaves fall if it is kept too cold.
Uses: For a heated conservatory.

PERNETTYA MUCRONATA
Pernettya

Family: Heath, *Ericaceae*
Native Habitat: Chile to Tierra del Fuego
Flowering Time: Late spring, early summer

An evergreen shrub 20–40 in. (50–100 cm) high, pernettya has small lanceolate leaves and little, nodding flowers in white. After pollination, these turn into 3/8 in.–5/8 in.- (8–12 mm-) wide berries, which are white, pink, red, or mauve, according to the variety: 'alba' (white fruit); 'Bell's Seedling' (deep red fruit, long-lasting); 'lilacina' (lilac fruit); 'Stag River' (pink fruit). To make berries possible, you will need at least one male and one female plant.
Location: Light all year; in summer best outdoors. In winter in a cool greenhouse or room.
Care: Keep evenly moist with soft water and feed every 14 days.
Propagation: By tip cuttings in a peat-sand soil mix.
Pests and Diseases: Rarely.
Uses: A container plant for cold or heated conservatories.

PERSEA AMERICANA
Avocado

Family: Laurel, *Lauraceae*
Native Habitat: Mexico, Brazil, Peru
Flowering Time: Seldom blooms in cultivation

The avocado is an evergreen tree or shrub with dark green, leathery, oval, pointed leaves. Its flowers are small and appear in clusters.
Location: Humid, light, and sunny all year; in summer outside. In winter cool but not under 50°F (10°C).
Care: In summer, water very freely and spray occasionally. In winter, water just to prevent too many leaves from falling. Prune to prevent legginess.
Propagation: From seed: place the lower third of the avocado stone in damp soil and cover with a plastic hood. Keep light and warm; remove the hood occasionally.
Pests and Diseases: Scale insects, spider mites.
Uses: Evergreen container plant; for a conservatory, for example.

PETUNIA
Petunia

Family: Nightshade, *Solanaceae*
Native Habitat: Parent forms from South America
Flowering Time: Late spring into fall

For the past 150 years, the annual petunia has been one of the most successful flowers on the market. No one knows how many varieties and hybrids have been developed during this time. Petunia tends to have a compact, upright habit, but there are cascading hybrids with shoots as long as 5 ft. (1.5 m). Stems and leaves are roughly hairy and sticky. There are large- and small-blooming, double and simple varieties. Colors include white, yellow, pink, red, and violet; some cultivars are veined, striped, or rippled at the edges. For a long time there was no yellow petunia, but now we have 'Summersun,' 'Ruban,' 'Yellows,' 'Magic Yellow,' and 'California Girl.'

Some years ago, a new petunia, the so-called 'Surfinia,' became popular. The two-colored 'Surfinias' come from Japan, and at first only white with light or dark violet was available, e.g., 'Surfinia White' and 'Shihi Purple.' Now other cultivars are to be had: 'Pink Mini' (magenta-pink); 'Pink Vein' (mauve-pink with violet markings in the throat); and 'Blue Vein' (white with dark violet markings).

Recently, yet another petunia, (*P. violacea*), has come on the market. It is small-flowered and ranges in tone from pink to crimson. It grows shoots 3.2 ft. (1 m) long over the course of the summer.

Petunia riches spill over a balcony railing

Petunias are poisonous.
Location: Sunny; outdoors; protected from rain and wind.
Care: Water freely and feed weekly. Pinch off all dead flowers quickly, since seeds are formed fast and that takes energy from flowering. Prune leggy plants back by one-half.
Propagation: From seed in winter with bottom heating.

Surfinias only by cuttings; newer hybrids set seeds.
Pests and Diseases: Aphids.
Uses: A gorgeous flowering plant for balconies and hanging baskets; good also for borders.

Petunias are damaged by rain and wind. Under the eaves is the best place for them. It is possible to buy protective awnings that fit over the planters, but you may find these unattractive.

Breeders worked for years to produce a yellow petunia. The results are astonishing.

A yellow petunia hybrid

Phalaenopsis – Philodendron

Like most other orchids, *Phalaenopsis* was considered impossible to keep in the normal living areas of a home. Its modern hybrids, however, are able to thrive and bloom freely and regularly on a windowsill.

Philodendron scandens is a tireless climbing or hanging plant. Even in darker locations it continues growing, but its leaves will revert to green under such conditions and the spaces between leaves will get longer and longer.

Phalaenopsis *hybrid*

Philodendron scandens

PHILODENDRON
Philodendron

Family: Arum, *Araceae*
Native Habitat: Tropical rain forests of the Americas
Flowering Time: Seldom blooms in cultivation

There are climbing and upright philodendrons; they all have aerial roots and shiny, dark green or purple leaves. Leaf shapes vary by species: small or large, narrowly pointed, arrowlike, heart-shaped, deeply incised, or red underneath. Even botanists can be hard pressed to identify philodendrons, since leaves can vary markedly between young plants and older ones of the same species. Plants grow well with a mossy support or from a hanging basket. The white flower spadix with its white, yellow, or red spathes never appears except in very mature plants. Only the Colombian *P. erubescens* blooms willingly. It has a greenish red stem, and arrow-shaped, shiny, dark green leaves with red undersides (young leaves are dark red-brown). The foliage of 'Red Emerald' and 'Burgundy' is reddish, that of 'Green Emerald' is dark green.

PHALAENOPSIS
Moth orchid

Family: Orchid, *Orchidaceae*
Native Habitat: Tropical Asia, Australia, and Oceania
Flowering Time: Varies with the species

Phalaenopsis, which tends to grow epiphytic in the wild, has broad, dark green or spotted leaves. The flowers, in racemes or spikes, are often spectacularly colored and last a long time. *Phalaenopsis* is without pseudobulbs because temperatures in its native habitat fluctuate hardly at all; it has fleshy roots, instead. The many hybrids outdo the species in size and color and are much better adapted to our heated living areas.
Location: Year-round, light to partial shade. By day at 68–77°F (20–25°C). By night not under 61°F (16°C).

Care: Keep moderately moist with soft water all year. Allow the soil to dry up a little but never to dry out completely between waterings and provide orchid food every 14 days. High humidity is an advantage, and for the pure species, a necessity. The roots need a lot of air, so use orchid mix to repot and avoid injuring the roots. Lowering night temperatures to 55–61°F (13–16°C) for three to four weeks in late fall or winter will improve flowering.
Propagation: By adventitious plantlets that can be potted when they have grown strong little roots.
Pests and Diseases: Scale insects if kept too dry; root rot if roots are damaged.
Uses: A beautiful orchid; good for beginners; excellent for hydroponics.

Never cut off the stalk of wilted moth orchids completely. If you leave a few "eyes" you give the plant a chance to sprout anew.

P. angustisectum syn. *P. elegans* is a climbing species, its leaves deeply incised, green, and long-stemmed.

P. domesticum, with its dark green, narrow-pointed leaves, does not climb. Well-known varieties are: 'Imperial Green' and 'Tuxla,' with green leaves and 'Valerie,' with red ones.

The leaves of *P. ilsemannii* can be oval or arrow-like; they are irregularly mottled, white, gray-white, and green. A lovely variety is 'Royal Queen.'

P. pedatum has leaves 12 in. (30 cm) long, dark green, divided, and deeply incised. Their outline is almost triangular. Similar leaves are borne by the hybrids 'florida' and the white-streaked 'variegata.' This species climbs slowly.

Another slow climber is *P. rugosum*; its leaves are heart-shaped and slightly wrinkled. A band of transparent, whitish tissue edges the leaf.

The best-loved species is *P. scandens*. In youth its heart-shaped leaves are small; with maturity they reach 8 x 12 in. (20 x 30 cm). This species is easy to take care of and will twine up a support.

Location: Light or partial shade all year; at room temperatures.

Care: Using soft water, keep moist without drowning or drying out. Spray or wipe the leaves often with a damp cloth. Varieties with velvety leaves need more humid air. Feed fast-growing plants weekly, spring to fall, others every two weeks; in winter, monthly or even less often. The plant tolerates pruning, but never cut the aerial roots.

Propagation: By tip or stem cuttings (after pruning); by air layering; by the occasional young plants that appear in the root area; or from seed.

Pests and Diseases: Scale insects; root rot if the roots are kept too cold; brown spots and dry leaves with direct sun. Some species react to the chemicals in leaf cleaners.

Uses: A foliage plant for living areas, hothouses, warm conservatories, and offices, and for hanging baskets. Suited to hydroponics.

Philodendron erubescens *'Red Emerald'*

Philodendron elegans

Philodendron rugosum

Philodendron *'Lynette'*

Philodendron pedatum *'florida'*

Hardly any other species offers so many foliage plants for the house as philodendron does. The most beautiful species can be seen in the greenhouses of botanical gardens. One of the most incredible is *P. melanochrysum*. It has vertically hanging leaves 31 in. (80 cm) long. They are green and bronzed over, as if they were powdered with gold dust.

Phoenix – Phyllostachys

Phoenix canariensis is a date palm from the Canary Islands. It is well liked for its tendency to form a container plant of stature as it matures.

The fibers of *Phormium tenax* are the strongest in the plant kingdom. The leaves of this New Zealand plant are so tough that you will find it impossible to tear them in half crosswise.

Phoenix canariensis

Phormium tenax

PHORMIUM TENAX
Phormium

Family: Lily, *Liliaceae*
Native Habitat: New Zealand
Flowering Time: Late summer

This evergreen member of the lily family has narrow, swordlike leaves up to 6.5 ft. (2 m) long. The plant forms a dense cluster and, in very warm summers, a flower stalk emerges, lifting the matte red flowers above the leaves. Well-known varieties include 'atro-purpureum' (dark purple to red foliage); 'Bronze Baby' (wine-red foliage); 'Dazzler' (yellow or with salmon or orange-red stripes); 'Aurora' (striped red, bronze, salmon pink, and yellow); and 'Veitchii' (striped creamy white).
Location: Sun to partial shade; in summer warm to hot, outdoors. In winter light at 43–46°F (6–8°C). Cooler and darker will serve as well.
Care: Water freely and feed weekly in summer. Fast-growing varieties need frequent repotting and division.
Propagation: By division.
Pests and Diseases: Rarely.
Uses: An imposing and very decorative container plant.

Since phormium in its native New Zealand grows along river banks, my own plant is immersed in the shallow end of the garden pond every spring. I put an occasional fertilizer stick into its container, and the summer care of my phormium is complete, to the plant's full satisfaction.

PHOENIX
Date palm

Family: Palm, *Arecaceae*
Native Habitat: Arabia, North Africa, Canary Islands
Flowering Time: Seldom blooms in cultivation

The best-known species of *Phoenix* is the true date palm, *P. dactylifera*. Many a home gardener has grown it from the seeds of dried dates. The most commonly cultivated species is *P. canariensis*. In youth its dark green, compound, leathery leaves are upright, but with age they arch and spread out mightily.

The compound leaves of the dwarf species *P. roebelenii* are less stiff and leathery than those of the other Phoenix species.
Location: Light, airy, and sunny all year. In summer best outdoors; in winter cool, at 41°F (5°C); *P. roebelenii* at 59°F (15°C).
Care: Keep evenly and lightly moist. Provide adequate humidity for *P. roebelenii*. Feed once a week, spring to summer.
Propagation: From seed.
Pests and Diseases: Scale insects if too warm in winter; brown leaf tips are a sign of cold, alkaline, or insufficient water.
Uses: House, container, or conservatory plant. Suited to hydroponics.

Phyllitis scolopendrium

PHYLLITIS SCOLOPENDRIUM
Hart's tongue fern

Family: Polypody, *Polypodiaceae*
Native Habitat: Europe, Asia Minor, North Africa, Japan
Flowering Time: Not a flowering plant

This fern is hardy in most of the temperate zone. It was once a very popular houseplant because of its tongue-shaped, slightly wavy, shiny, light green leaves. Today it is sought again for cool conservatories and other light, cool, glassed-in spaces. English growers produce astounding varieties, with curly, fringed, and perforated leaves, such as *P. scolopendrium* 'undulata' and 'digitata.' The variety 'capitata' is particularly splendid: it grows remarkably distorted leaves. There even are varieties with parsleylike leaves, such as 'ramosa margin-ata' and 'ramosa cristata.'
Location: Partial to complete shade and humid air, all year. Late spring to midautumn outside. In winter at 50°F (10°C).
Care: Keep evenly moist, but not wet. If in a room, spray often with soft water. Feed lightly from late spring to midfall. In heated rooms increase humidity by placing the plant in wet peat or over, not in, a bowl of water.
Propagation: From spores; cultivars by division; petiole cuttings with a piece of rhizome can be rooted.
Pests and Diseases: Scale insects, thrips if air is too warm and dry.
Uses: Houseplant for light cool rooms; for underplanting shady parts of a conservatory; for outdoor planting.

PHYLLOSTACHYS
Golden bamboo

Family: Grass, *Poaceae*
Native Habitat: China, Japan
Flowering Time: Not a flowering plant

This species of bamboo grows tall and produces offshoots. Its leaves are light green and delicate, its stems can be variously colored.

P. aurea grows to 10 ft. (3 m) in a container. The color of its foliage is like that of corn; the stems are light green at first and brilliant yellow in later years. The variety 'holochrysa' has yellow-orange stems.

P. aureosulcata 'spectabilis' is one of the loveliest bamboos: light yellow stems with green grooves.

P. nigra is less spreading. Its stems are green in the first year; then they become spotted green and brown, and in a sunny location, they turn completely black. It grows to 6.5–13 ft. (2–4 m) in a container. Two of its beautiful

Phyllostachys aurea

varieties are 'Baryana' and 'Henonis.'
Location: Sunny; in mild winters outdoors or cool and light inside the house.
Care: During growth, water generously and feed every two to three weeks with nitrogen-rich fertilizer. Mulch between the stems with dry leaves. If the plants are to remain outdoors for the winter, their containers can be put into the ground in a wind-sheltered corner. On frost-free days, they can be watered with lukewarm water. The plant can survive down to –4°F (–20°C); *P. nigra*, to –9°F (–23°C). Usually the plants do not freeze in winter; they dry out because they receive no water during long periods of frost.
Propagation: By division.
Pests and Diseases: Rarely.
Uses: Large specimen plant for cool, high, glass structures or stairwells. Because of its height and tendency to spread, it is not a good plant for conservatory planting; a good container plant.

If you cannot find the varieties of *Phyllitis scolopendrium* mentioned here in your garden center, inquire in a nursery that specializes in perennials.

Bamboo is very decorative and is becoming more and more accepted as a container plant.

I have transplanted specimens of *Phyllostachys nigra* and *Phyllostachys aurea* into the ground, near the edge of the pond. They have been there now for 13 years. They survived even the cold winters of 1981–82 and 1982–83, when temperatures went down to –9°F (–23°C).

Pilea cadierei

Clear weed is a charming foliage plant that remains small.

Pepper, particularly in its variegated forms, is one of the loveliest foliage plants for window greenhouses and glass cases.

More mature Pileas will drop their lower leaves, leaving bare stems. Since this cannot be avoided, prepare in advance by growing replacements.

PILEA
Clear weed

Family: Nettle, *Urticaceae*
Native Habitat: Australia, tropical regions of the world
Flowering Time: Varies with the species.

Pilea is an annual or perennial herbaceous plant up to 16 in. (40 cm) in height. Leaf color and shape vary with the species. The clear weed's reproductive process is extraordinary: if you spray a plant that is about to flower on a hot day, all buds that are ready open at once and throw off their pollen in little clouds. *P. cadeierei* is the most common species. It comes from Vietnam and grows to 16 in. (40 cm). Its leaf is covered with raised, silvery spots. The variety 'Minima' is an appealing dwarf form, hardly half that height.

The round leaves of *P. involucrata* are wrinkled and veined in dark green, but their undersides are a dark scarlet. Pink flowers appear in summer.

P. microphylla has fine, compound leaves, like a fern. *P. nummularifolia* makes a pretty hanging plant with its threadlike, red shoots and its 0.4 in.- (1 cm-) wide leaves, violet underneath.

The Peruvian *P. spruceana* is only 4 in. (10 cm) high. It produces spectacular light green nettle flowers.

Location: Moderately light or partially shaded all year; warm and humid.
Care: Water well in spring and summer, less in winter. Spring to fall, feed every week.
Propagation: By tip cuttings. Prune young plants to achieve bushy form.
Pests and Diseases: Spider mites if too dry.
Uses: *P. nummularifolia* as a hanging plant; the others as ground cover for not-too-warm window greenhouses and conservatories; nice in dishes and for hydroponics.

Pilea spruceana

Piper crocatum

PIPER
Pepper

Family: Pepper, *Piperaceae*
Native Habitat: Tropical regions
Flowering Time: Seldom blooms in cultivation

The genus pepper includes plants that have green or colored leaves, that grow upright, climb, or have a shrubby habit. Most attractive are the multicolored climbers *P. crocatum*, a Peruvian species, and *P. ornatum*, with broadly heart-shaped, waxy leaves.

Location: Species with colored leaves: very light, no sun, humid, and warm all year. In winter not under 64°F (18°C). Bottom heat is important.
Care: Keep moderately moist with soft water. Early spring to early fall, feed every 14 days; if growth is fast, every week. Provide a humid atmosphere and climbing support.
Propagation: By stem cuttings at 77°F (25°C) with plastic cover.
Pests and Diseases: Rarely.
Uses: Variegated plants for an enclosed glass case, a window greenhouse, a warm conservatory. For hanging baskets, for climbing, or for ground cover.

The Most Beautiful Plants from A to Z

Pistacia lentiscus

Pittosporum crassifolium

PISTACIA
Pistachio

Family: Sumac, *Anacardiaceae*
Native Habitat: Mediterranean region, tropics and subtropics
Flowering Time: Early spring to summer

Pistachio is a dioecious shrub; it can be evergreen or deciduous. *P. lentiscus*, the mastic tree, has leathery, pinnately compound leaves. The flowers appear in dense racemes at the leaf axils. Red stamina characterize the blossoms, especially those of the male plant. The true pistachio, *P. vera*, a native of Asia Minor, is semievergreen.
Location: Sun to partial shade all year. In winter light, 41–50°F (5–10°C) or warmer. The plant tolerates dry air.
Care: Water moderately and feed weekly.
Propagation: By herbaceous cuttings in summer.
Pests and Diseases: Rarely.
Uses: An easy container plant for terraces, balconies, and unheated garden rooms. Suited to bonsai.

PITTOSPORUM
Pittosporum

Family: Pittosporum, *Pitto-sporaceae*
Native Habitat: Australia, New Zealand, tropics and subtropics of the Old World
Flowering Time: Spring to summer

Pittosporum is an evergreen tree or shrub with dense foliage. The leaves are smooth-edged, leathery, shiny, and green. The flowers are creamy-white, perhaps pink or reddish; they are borne in clusters. They are fragrant. A sticky substance surrounds the seed capsules. *P. crassifolium*, from New Zealand, blooms in late summer. The foliage of *P. tenuifolium* is dense, the leaves light green and rippled, the flowers dark red. It blooms in the spring. The variety 'variegatum' has smooth leaves, unevenly edged in white. The green-speckled leaves of 'Irene Petersen' are almost white when the plant is young. *P. tobira*, an important hedge plant in China and Japan, has leathery leaves 4 x 1.5 in. (10 x 4 cm). Creamy-white, fragrant flower umbels open at the tips of the shoots in the spring. This species also has a 'variegatum' with leaves marked in white. Its variety 'Nanum' grows slowly to only 20 in. (50 cm) high. It rarely blooms, but it has a spreading habit.

The wavy leaves of *P. undulatum* are up to 6 in. (15 cm) long. The plant grows slowly, cannot tolerate much frost, and blooms in late spring.
Location: Year-round, sun to partial shade; in summer outdoors. In winter at 41–50°F (5–10°C).
Care: In summer, water freely and feed every two weeks. In winter just keep the root ball moist. Like the laurel, pittosporum can be pruned into shape.
Propagation: From seed or by herbaceous cuttings.
Pests and Diseases: Scale insects; brown leaf edges indicate lack of water or too intense sun.
Uses: A decorative container plant. *P. tobira* 'Nanum' as a ground cover for a cool conservatory.

Pistachio makes a good bonsai, as can be seen here. The resin of the mastic tree is used in industry, e.g., for plasters, dressings, adhesives, and lacquers. In the past, mastic was chewed as a dental and mouth cleanser. In Greece it is used to preserve wine.

Pittosporum, like the laurel, is well suited to pruning into shapes.

The dwarf variety, 'Nanum,' of *P. tobira* looks very good in a bed of pebbles since its habit is very regular, low and spreading. It is used in this fashion in Japanese gardens.

Pittosporum tobira

Platycerium – Podranea

Plectranthus fruticosus

The staghorn fern is one hanging plant that everyone will notice.

Although it is quite possible to overwinter your *Plectranthus*, it is not worth it. For one thing, raising young plants from cuttings is no trouble at all.

TIP

Since it is often difficult to water a staghorn fern, I tend to immerse mine in water or—when it is time to feed it—in water with plant food dissolved in it. I use what is left for my other plants.

PLATYCERIUM
Common staghorn fern

Family: Polypody, *Polypodiaceae*
Native Habitat: Tropical South East Asia, Australia, Africa
Flowering Time: Not a flowering plant

This epiphytic fern has two distinct leaf forms, each with its own function. The smaller leaves that cover the root crown serve to take up water and nutrients; they are sterile, i.e., bear no spores. After some time they rot away, giving the plant humus. The spore-bearing fronds can grow to 3.2 ft. (1 m) in length. They are incised, like a stag's horns, although their shapes vary according to the species. The two-forked stag horn fern, *P. bifurcatum*, is easy to grow in a room. The leathery leaves can be 35 in. (90 cm) long. The fronds grow upward on an angle; the lobes arch downward. Each new basal leaf rolls up over the last one

and turns upward. This rather variable species is sold in many forms, e.g.: 'Majus,' 'Roberts,' 'Ziesenhenne,' and 'San Diego.'

The name of *P. grande* is justified by its fronds' reaching 4 ft. (1.2 m) in length. Two species that grow too large for all but vast greenhouses are *P. wilhelminae-reginae* and *P. willinckii*, with their varieties 'Kingii' and 'Payton.'
Location: Year round, light to partial shade; humid and warm. In winter not under 57°F (14°C).
Care: Water moderately with soft, lukewarm water; prevent dry roots, especially in winter. Spring through summer feed with half-diluted plant food. Do not spray; provide indirect humidity. Never remove dead basal leaves. Tie young plants to epiphytic supports; older plants are planted in orchid soil in shallow baskets or bowls.
Propagation: Occasionally, it is possible to remove an offset. Spores are formed, but they seldom sprout.
Pests and Diseases: Scale insects from dry conditions.
Uses: Exotic hanging plant for window greenhouses and for living areas, if indirect humidity is provided.

PLECTRANTHUS
Swedish ivy

Family: Mint, *Lamiaceae*
Native Habitat: Tropics and subtropics worldwide, except in the Americas
Flowering Time: Late fall to winter; *P. fruticosus*, late winter to spring

Plectranthus is an upright or low-growing and spreading perennial or subshrub, not hardy in temperate regions. The leaves may give off a strong scent if rubbed. *P. fruticosus*, well known to our grandparents, has been super-seded by *P. coleoides* 'Marginatus,' grown as an annual. Its leaves are edged in white; its shoots are 3.2 ft. (1 m) long.
Location: Light or sun all year and airy; in summer outdoors. In winter not under 59°F (15°C).
Care: During growth, water moderately; in winter keep rather dry. Feed every two weeks.
Propagation: By tip cuttings; prune young plants often for bushiness.
Pests and Diseases: Scale insects if kept too dry and warm.
Uses: An exotic hanging plant for window greenhouses; a house-plant only if an air humidifier is used.

Plumbago auriculata

PLUMBAGO AURICULATA
Plumbago

Family: Leadwort, *Plumbagin-aceae*
Native Habitat: South Africa
Flowering Time: Late spring through fall; in the conservatory to early winter

Plumbago is a deciduous, low-lying or creeping shrub with long, stiff shoots. Its flowers are terminal and resemble phlox, but are blue or occasionally white. The shrub's leaves are oval and small. It blooms almost continuously. Usually you will find the sky-blue variety 'caerulea'; less often, the pure white form 'Alba.'

Location: In summer sunny and warm, but sheltered from wind, as the branches break easily. In winter at 39–46°F (4–8°C) or in a cool conservatory,
Care: Water generously in summer; keep moist in winter. Feed weekly to the end of summer. Snip off dead flowers. Prune anytime. In winter, all or part of the leaves will wilt but not fall, so they have to be removed.
Propagation: By herbaceous cuttings in summer.
Pests and Diseases: Both a dry root ball in summer or wetness in winter will diminish flowering.
Uses: Long-blooming container plant that is easy to look after.

Podranea ricasoliana

PODRANEA RICASOLIANA
Podranea

Family: Trumpet creeper, *Bignoniaceae*
Native Habitat: South Africa
Flowering Time: Late summer through fall, longer in a conservatory

Podranea is a most beautiful and fast-growing climbing plant. It is an evergreen with pinnately compound leaves. Planted in the ground, *P. ricasoliana* is said to grow 10 ft. (3 m) a year. The 2 in.-(5 cm-)wide, pink-and-red-striped trumpet flowers open in terminal spikes 12 in. (30 cm) long. In a sunny location they will last till the late fall.
Location: Light to full sun; in winter at 43–50°F (6–10°C) or cooler, and dark, if need be.
Care: Water freely and feed weekly through the summer. Tie to a trellis. In the fall (and in the conservatory) prune firmly or the plant will lose all its bottom leaves. In winter keep cool and dark.
Propagation: By herbaceous cuttings in summer or from seed.
Pests and Diseases: Aphids.
Uses: A splendid container plant.

Plumbago can be trained to a trellis, where it will grow to 13 ft. (4 m) in height. It can also be standard trained or planted in balcony boxes, where it looks very attractive.

Podranea ricasoliana, a near relation of the trumpet creeper, can be found only in nurseries that specialize in container plants. They may have it trained as a standard.

TIP

My own plumbago grows with a datura in a large plastic bushel basket. For the summer I bury it in the garden till the late fall, when it is dug up. The roots are cut off all around, and the container is taken indoors, still in full bloom.

Pogonatherum – Polystichum

With its elegant, thin blades, pogonatherum is as suited to set off flower arrangements and bouquets as the better-known asparagus fern.

Pogonatherum paniceum

POGONATHERUM PANICEUM
Pogonatherum

Family: Grass, *Poaceae*
Native Habitat: East Asia, China, Australia
Flowering Time: Summer

This plant, which looks like bamboo, is related to it only in that both species are sweet grasses. It is much closer to *Saccharum officinarum*, sugar cane; it used to be in the same genus (*Saccharum paniceum*). The plant does not grow tall, but it is bushy. Its blades, with their 2.7 in.- (7 cm-) long leaves arch slightly.

Pogonatherum paniceum has been for sale only since 1980.
Location: Light to sun all year; in summer outdoors; warm.
Care: Never let it dry out, not even in winter: a dry root ball can kill it. In summer, water very freely; water in the saucer is allowed. Feed every two to three weeks.
Propagation: By division or off-shoots.
Pests and Diseases: Rarely.
Uses: Houseplant for a light, warm position.

Polianthes tuberosa

POLIANTHES TUBEROSA
Tuberose

Family: Agave, *Agavaceae*
Native Habitat: Originally Mexico
Flowering Time: Summer through to late fall

Tuberoses have an intense, sweet scent. This annual has fleshy tubers, ribbonlike green leaves and white, waxy, usually double, funnel-shaped flowers that open in spikes along a stalk 20–40 in. (50–100 cm) high. The tubers usually offered are those of 'The Pearl,' a variety that grows 16 in. (40 cm) high and has double blossoms. The tubers have to be sprouted.
Location: Very light to full sun.
Care: In spring, place three tubers in a 6 in. (15 cm) pot and cover

them with 0.8–1 in. (2–3 cm) of soil. Place the pots in a protected spot (a cold frame). After they sprout, increase water and food gradually. It takes five months till they flower. Tubers can be planted at intervals and brought indoors with the cold: this will give you flowering plants for cool rooms till Christmas. In the temperate zone, the tubers will not sprout again after they have flowered once.
Propagation: Not applicable.
Pests and Diseases: Rarely.
Uses: A flowering potted plant for your home.

The Most Beautiful Plants from A to Z

Polyscias scutellaria

Polystichum tsus-simense

POLYSTICHUM TSUS-SIMENSE
Holly fern

Family: Polypody, *Polypodiaceae*
Native Habitat: Japan, Korea, China
Flowering Time: Not a flowering plant

Polyscias scutellaria is far more robust than the species with compound leaves or deeply incised foliage.

Species other than *Polystichum tsus-simense* are available, but they are better suited for planting in a warm greenhouse. One such species is *Polystichum auriculatum*.

POLYSCIAS
Polyscias

Family: Ginseng, *Araliaceae*
Native Habitat: Tropical Asia, Polynesia
Flowering Time: Seldom blooms in cultivation.

These small evergreen trees or shrubs have intricate, finely divided leaves that can take a variety of forms. The tiny inflorescences are racemous umbels, heads, or spikes. *P. cumingiana*, formerly *Aralia filicolia*, has compound leaves like fern fronds, with the leaflets incised in turn. The best-known species is the more robust *P. scutellaria* syn. *P. balfouriana*. Its heart- or kidney-shaped leaves are narrowly edged in white. This

species has a good-looking cultivar 'Pennockii' that has yellow-spotted or marbled foliage. *P. guilfoylei's* leaves are simple to pinnately compound and variegated in white; it grows very fast.
Location: Light to partial shade all year; humid; at least at 64°F (18°C).
Care: Keep moderately moist with lukewarm, soft water. Feed biweekly from early spring to the end of summer; in winter, monthly.
Propagation: By tip cuttings at 77–86°F (25–30°C); difficult.
Pests and Diseases: Scale insects, aphids if air is too dry from heating.
Uses: *P. scutellaria* for the windowsill; the others for a window green-house or a warm conservatory. Suited to hydroponics.

Holly ferns grow well in the temperate zone. Only *P. tsus-simense*, a small species with dark green, leathery fronds, is cultivated as a houseplant. It reaches a diameter of about 8 in. (20 cm) and a height of 12 in. (30 cm). Dark brown scales crowd along the petiole, and the sporangia are arranged in two parallel rows.
Location: Light to partial shade; in winter nct under 41°F (5°C).
Care: Water evenly; in winter reduce watering according to the temperature. Spring through fall feed very lightly. Repot only if needed in very loose soil high in bark chips.
Propagation: By division or from spores.
Pests and Diseases: Scale insects.
Uses: A charming little fern for the windowsill or the terrarium.

I have seen polyscias thrive as part of an indoor fountain planting. Their pots were in the water, held in larger containers, filled with clay granular.

Portulaca – Psidium

Portulaca is a versatile plant: it will grow between flagstones or make a very nice border along the garden path. It looks fine in a patio planter, as well.

"Primula" translates as "the first of the year," a good description of the colorful abundance primulas bring to the cool days of early spring.

Portulaca grandiflora

PORTULACA GRANDIFLORA
Portulaca

Family: Purslane, *Portulacaceae*
Native Habitat: Argentina, Brazil, Uruguay
Flowering Time: All summer

Portulaca is an annual plant that forms a dense carpet. Its leaves are small, fleshy, and nearly cylindrical. The terminal flowers are large, simple or double, and vividly colored in all shades from white, through yellow, orange, and pink, to crimson. The flowers open only when the sun shines. As a rule, you can only buy "mixes" of plants with simple or double flowers in all colors, such as, for example, 'Calypso Mix.'
Location: In summer outdoors and sunny; best protected from rain.
Care: In early spring, sow seeds directly into loose, sandy soil in pots or dishes. Water very moderately and hardly feed at all.
Propagation: From seed.
Pests and Diseases: Rarely.
Uses: Low, mounding plant for balcony planters or dishes.

I place bowls planted with portulaca between the cacti in my collection, to add color in that area even when none of the cacti are in bloom.

Primula vulgaris *hybrid*

PRIMULA
Primrose

Family: Primrose, *Primulaceae*
Native Habitat: Asia, Europe
Flowering Time: Varies with the species

As houseplants, the following *Primulas* have significance:

The annual *P. malacoides*, originally from China, has simple or double white, red, or pink flowers that stand above the leaves. It blooms from late fall to early spring. Good varieties are: 'Pink Panther' and 'Wadenswyler type.'

Another Chinese species is *P. obconica*. Its flowers cluster in spherical umbels, white, pink, red, or lavender, above large, lobed, dark green leaves. This species can be carried over to the next year. Some people are allergic to it.

Yet another Chinese *Primula, P. sinensis*, has hand-shaped leaves covered with downy hair. It blooms in spring, white, pink, red, orange, or even blue. It is not worthwhile to carry it over to the next season.

Finally, *P. vulgaris* (syn. *P. acaulis*) is sold in its many hybrid forms. Its flower has a short stalk, a central eye, and comes in all colors of the rainbow. It is suitable for balcony planters and dishes for early spring bloom. After flowering it can be planted in the garden.
Location: Light to partial shade; no strong noon sun. In bloom, keep cool at 50–59°F (10–15°C); the cooler it is, the longer the flowers last. If warmer, increase humidity. *P. obconica* is most heat-resistant.
Care: Keep evenly moist; avoid sogginess. Before and during flowering, feed lightly every two weeks. If you overwinter *P. obconica*, feed it till the fall.
Propagation: From seed; difficult.

Pests and Diseases: Aphids; spider mites if too warm and dry; yellow leaves are a sign of iron deficiency due to hard water; gray mold if too wet.

Uses: A houseplant for cool rooms.

Psidium guajava

PSIDIUM
Guava

Family: Myrtle, *Myrtaceae*
Native Habitat: Central and South America
Flowering Time: In spring

The genus *Psidium* contains trees and shrubs with elongated oval leaves, smooth or matted, and pinnately nerved. The flowers open on axial stalks singly or in clusters.

The guava tree, *P. guajava*, is evergreen, a large shrub with oval leaves 6 in. (15 cm) long. When they first sprout, they are salmon-colored; the veins are so deeply set that the leaf looks wrinkled. In spring, white flowers with protruding stamina appear. In five months, they develop into edible, yellow, pear-shaped, fruit, high in vitamin C.

P. littordle (formerly *P. cattleianum*) has smaller leaves and red, edible fruit without much taste. Planted in the conservatory, the tree will bear fruit in the third year.

Older guava trees bear fruit regularly, but it is smart to help them out with a fine brush, especially if they are not outdoors.

Location: Full sun and very warm in summer; outdoors if well protected. In winter light at 34°F (1°C).

Care: Keep moderately moist; during growth, feed every two weeks. *P. guajava* loses some of its leaves in the winter. The fruit ripens in the winter, so keep watering the tree to prevent the fruit from falling.

Propagation: From seed or by cuttings at 72–77°F (22–25°C) under plastic.

Pests and Diseases: Root rot if too wet in winter.

Uses: Container plant for the conservatory and greenhouse. Young plants for the house.

Primula malacoides is lovely while its flowers last. After it has bloomed, it has to be discarded.

Mature plants of the genus *Psidium* will bear fruit every year, but it is wise to help them out with a small brush, particularly if your guava trees do not spend any time outdoors.

Primula malacoides

Pteris – Radermachera

Pteris cretica

Brake ferns seem to be made for a terrarium.

Pomegranates can withstand frost down to 14°F (–10°C). It is possible to take them outdoors early in the spring and leave them there till late fall.

PTERIS
Brake fern

Family: Polypody, *Polypodiaceae*
Native Habitat: Tropics and subtropics of the world
Flowering Time: Not a flowering plant

The brake fern has a bushy habit; its bipinnately compound fronds may also be split and curled at the tips. The dark brown spore spots (sori) form lines along the undersides of the fronds.

The species *P. cretica* is quite robust with many varieties, e.g., 'Albolineata,' with broader fronds and a greenish white band down the center; 'Alexandreae,' with white variegation and frond tips

that are incised and curled; 'major,' with fronds very deeply incised, broad, and united at the base; 'Parkeri,' with broad, rough fronds, the tip not curled; and 'Wimsettii,' with light green, unevenly compound fronds that have curly tips.

P. ensiformis is unquestionably a tropical fern. It has two pretty cultivars: 'Victoriae,' white-striped, and 'Evergemensis,' with a silvery gloss.

P. tremula is a fast-growing Australian species with twice-compound fronds up to 3.2 ft. (1 m) long.

Location: Light to partial shade and humid; species and varieties with green foliage somewhat darker and in winter at 54–57°F (12–14°C). Variegated ones lighter and at 60–64°F (16–18°C). Never place them near any heating unit.
Care: Keep evenly moist with soft water. Never allow the root ball to dry out. Adjust water to temperature. Provide humidity, direct and indirect. Administer highly diluted plant food once a week: salts will kill the plant. Repot if needed in low-calcium soil mix.
Propagation: By division or from spores, at 77°F (25°C) under glass.
Pests and Diseases: Scale insects and aphids if too dry; black spots indicate the presence of leaf nematodes.
Uses: A beautiful foliage plant for cool greenhouses, enclosed window gardens and glass cases, terraria, or cool rooms.

Punica granatum

PUNICA GRANATUM
Pomegranate

Family: Pomegranate, *Punicaceae*
Native Habitat: Asia Minor, established in the Mediterranean region
Flowering Time: Late summer

The pomegranate is one of the oldest of container plants. Hieronymus Bosch painted cultivated *Punica* plants in the Germany of 1539. Since the fruit-bearing species will not set fruit in northern latitudes, even in greenhouses, only ornamental varieties will be mentioned here. These grow fast, bloom longer, and have hardly any thorns. The plant flowers only after the 3rd or 5th year, so they are expensive. The most notable variety is 'flore peno,' sometimes called 'flore rubro.' The loveliest is 'legrelliae' with double, terminal, yellow-red blossoms 4 in. (10 cm) wide. The flowers of 'albo pleno' are white, those of 'flore luteo' orange-yellow. The 3.2 ft.- (1 m-) high 'nana' starts blooming as a cutting, its flower orange-red to dark red. Occasionally, it will set fruit. One variety, with double blossoms, grows slowly: 'nana racemosa.' Only 3.2 ft. (1 m) high, it is the most handsome compact form.

Location: All year sun and warm; in summer outdoors. Winter minimum 35–43°F (2–6°C).

Care: Keep evenly moist. Water less after the end of summer, to let the wood mature. Till late summer, feed every two weeks. Prune back by one-third before retiring it for winter, when it should be kept dry.

Propagation: By cuttings in midsummer; they will root in six to eight weeks. 'Nana' varieties can be started from seed.

Pests and Diseases: Scale insects and spider mites.

Uses: A gorgeous container and conservatory plant.

Punica granatum

Radermachera sinica

RADERMACHERA SINICA
Stereospermum

Family: Trumpet Creeper, *Bignonia-ceae*

Native Habitat: China

Flowering Time: Seldom blooms in cultivation

Radermachera, formerly *Stereospermum sinicum*, has twice-compound leaves. In a container it can reach 5 ft. (1.5 m). Its varieties differ in habit as well as in leaf size.

Location: Light and airy all year; in summer outdoors. In winter humid and at 54–59°F (12–15°C).

Care: Keep moderately moist with soft water. In winter, water just to keep the leaves from falling. Spray often. In summer, feed every two weeks.

Propagation: From seed (they need light to sprout). Home gardeners report success with cuttings.

Pests and Diseases: Aphids, scale insects; the plant loses its leaves if continuously exposed to concentrated cigarette smoke.

Uses: A very good-looking foliage plant for a light position. Suited to hydroponics.

The magnificent pomegranate shrub below is several years old.

In the wild, *Radermachera* bears large, sulfur-yellow bell flowers, but as a houseplant it never blooms. 'Daniella' is a variety that is particularly attractive.

Keeping the pomegranate cool in the winter is very important for the production of flowers.

Rebutia – Rhapis

The name "rebutia" derives from that of the French vintner and cactus collector Pierre Rebut. The two rebutias here depicted are *Rebutia (Aylostera) hoffmannii* and *R. krainziana*. These and other members of the genus can start to produce flowers when they are no more than 0.4 in. (1 cm) across.

In addition to the species described in the text, there are rehmannias that are more rare, such as *R. angulata*, 30 in. (75 cm) high, with scarlet flowers, and the 12 in.- (30 cm-) high, rosette-forming species *R. glutinosa*, that bears reddish brown or yellow flowers.

Fresh air is important to rebutias. They are better off in a cold frame than in a greenhouse. My own plants have been outdoors at 17.6°F (-8°C). They suffered no damage as long as they were kept completely dry.

Rebutia (Aylostera) hoffmannii

REBUTIA
Rebutia

Family: Cactus, *Cactaceae*
Native Habitat: Argentina, Bolivia
Flowering Time: Spring; sometimes a second time in the fall

Rebutia rarely grows above 4 in. (10 cm). A flattened globe, this cactus produces many offsets. Instead of ribs, it bears a spiral arrangement of warts, tufted with short, white thorns. The colorful flowers, usually a shade of red, often appear on very young plants. There also are flowers in yellow and white. The genus *Rebutia* now includes *Aylostera* and *Mediolobivia*, as well as the *Sulcorebutias*.
　Red-flowering rebutias: *R. chrysacantha*, *R. minuscula*, and *R. wessneriana*.
　Yellow-flowering: *R. marsoneri*, *R. einsteinii*, and *R. kesselringiana*.
　Orange-flowering: *R. hoffmannii*. White-flowering: *R. albiflora*, *R. eos*, and *R. krainziana*.

Pink-flowering: *R. narvaecense*, *R. perplexa*, and *R. xanthocarpa* var. *salmonea*.
Location: Sunny, airy; in summer outdoors. In winter light and dry at 37–46°F (3–8°C).
Care: Start watering only when the buds are clearly visible in the spring. Apply cactus food every two weeks. Stop watering and feeding at the beginning of autumn.
Propagation: By offsets or from seed.
Uses: Easy-to-keep cactus; ideal for a collection.

Rebutia krainziana

Rehmannia elata

REHMANNIA ELATA
Rehmannia

Family: Gesneriad, *Gesneriaceae*
Native Habitat: China
Flowering Time: Early summer; in the conservatory, early spring

This gesneriad has 8–12 in.- (20–30 cm-) long, hairy leaves; it can reach up to 5 ft. (1.5 m) in height. The thimble-shaped flowers are pink to scarlet in color, their yellow throats dotted with red. Although a shrub, rehmannia is grown from seed, like an annual.
Location: Very light, no strong noon sun; in summer outdoors. In winter light at 41–50°F (5–10°C).
Care: Water moderately and feed every two weeks till late summer. In winter, water sparingly.
Propagation: From seed in early spring at 72–77°F (22–25°C). It takes 14 months for new plants to bloom.
Pests and Diseases: Rarely.
Uses: A rare summer-flowering container plant. If you have a garden room or conservatory that is cold but never below freezing, you can overwinter rehmannias.

THE MOST BEAUTIFUL PLANTS FROM A TO Z

Reinwardtia indica

REINWARDTIA INDICA
Indian yellow flax

Family: Flax, *Linaceae*
Native Habitat: India
Flowering Time: Late fall to early spring

Indian yellow flax is a subshrub about 35 in. (90 cm) high. On its short shoots it carries golden-yellow flowers. The petals are united at their base into a short trumpet.
Location: Light, but no strong sun all year; relatively cool and airy. If outdoors in summer, partial shade. In winter, at 50–54°F (10–12°C).
Care: During the growth phase, water generously; otherwise, moderately. Feed every two weeks. Prune young plants to force them to branch out. Older plants tend to lose their lower leaves and to bloom less: grow new replacement plants annually.
Propagation: From seed or by cuttings of shoots at ground level. They root at 54–59°F (12–15°C).
Pests and Diseases: Root rot is a danger: do not overwater.
Uses: An exquisite flowering plant for cool, light rooms.

Rhapis humilis

RHAPIS
Lady palm

Family: Palm, *Arecaceae*
Native Habitat: China, Japan
Flowering Time: Seldom blooms in cultivation

Rhapis is a bamboolike, bushy palm that grows offshoots.

R. humilis, a short lady palm, has many tubular stems covered with reddish brown fibers. They grow in a dense group out of their underground rhizome. This species will reach about 3.2 ft. (1 m) in a pot and more in a large container. The leaves spread like fingers and are deeply incised.

R. excelsa can grow twice that size, is coarser in all respects, and seems less elegant. With maturity, this species builds a dense bush; it is more robust than *R. humilis*, which means that as a mature container plant, it can even bring forth white or ivory flowers, given optimal care.

Location: Light to partial shade, in summer outdoors. In winter light at 41–50°F (5–10°C). (In a pinch up to 61°F (16°C).)
Care: The plant needs a lot of water in summer, but in winter very little. Feed weekly from late spring to early fall.
Propagation: From seed; sprouting takes two to three months. Division works, too, but the parts need a long time to recover.
Pests and Diseases: Spider mites if kept too dry and warm; yellow leaves if too much sun.
Uses: A handsome foliage plant for the conservatory, lobbies, and staircases.

The name *Reinwardtia* was given to the Indian yellow flax to honor Caspar Georg Carl Reinwardt (1773-1854), who founded the famous Bogor Botanical Gardens on Java.

Planted freely in the garden, *R. excelsa* can, under favorable conditions, withstand short spurts of light frost down to 17.6°F (–8°C).

Rhipsalis baccifera

Species of Easter cactus till recently considered part of the genus *Rhipsalidopsis* are now assigned to *Hatiora*. Since it will take time for this change to filter down through the horticultural community, we have presented this plant here under its well-known name *Rhipsalidopsis*.

Rhipsalis baccifera means "the berry-bearing rod cactus." The berries develop out of the white flowers.

RHIPSALIDOPSIS
Rhipsalidopsis

Family: Cactus, *Cactaceae*
Native Habitat: Brazil
Flowering Time: Through spring

Rhipsalidopsis resembles the Christmas cactus, *Schlumbergera*. The small, flat, about 0.8 in.- (2 cm-) long leaf segments form a dense, bushy plant. The flowers, red to lavender-pink, sit at the ends of the segments. The most significant species and varieties are:
R. gaertneri, R. rosea, and *R. x graeseri* (now all under *Hatiora*).
Location: Light to partial shade all year; humid and warm; in summer outdoors.
Care: Keep slightly moist all year with lukewarm, soft water; feed every two weeks after buds have set. Keep cooler and drier in winter.
Propagation: By shoot segments.
Pests and Diseases: Root rot if too wet; buds drop if too cold.
Uses: A houseplant or container plant.

Rhipsalidopsis - hybrids

RHIPSALIS
Rhipsalis

Family: Cactus, *Cactaceae*
Native Habitat: Brazil
Flowering Time: Winter

Cacti of this genus tend to be epiphytic and to vary in form. Some have shoot segments that are thin and tubular; others, flat or edged, or even covered with scales. The small flowers last several days and turn into little berrylike fruits, red, white, or black.
R. baccifera has light green, very thin shoots and whitish flowers.
R. cereuscula has long shoots in dark green and short shoots in light green. The flowers are white.

R. clavata at first grows upright, then becomes intricately branched. It has white flowers, tinged in red.
R. pachyptera has elliptical to almost-round leaves. They are 8 x 5 in. (20 x 12 cm), grooved, coarsely veined, and dark green dramatically shaded in scarlet.
The yellow flowers give off a strong smell.
R. megalantha used to be *Lepismium; R. pilocarpa, Erythrorhipsalis pilocarpa.*
Location: Light and humid; in summer in the open shade of a tree. In winter at 50–59°F (10–15°C).
Care: Water frequently with soft water; immersing is a possibility. Never let the plant dry out. In winter, water only once the soil is dry on top. Feed every two weeks

Rhipsalis megalantha

Rhipsalis pilocarpa

Rhodochiton atrosanguineus

Rhipsalis megalantha used to be classified under the genus *Lepismium*. As the picture on the left shows (and its Greek name implies) *R. pilocarpa* bears a hairy fruit. Depending on its position, it may be advantageous to give rhipsalis some artificial plant lighting, since it needs lots of light but cannot tolerate sun.

The bell vine used to be largely unknown, and only a few avid houseplant lovers had one; now it is possible to find them in special nurseries.

with normal flower fertilizer. Because of the long shoots, position the plant high or hang it up. Epiphytic supports or orchid baskets are ideal.

Propagation: From seed or by cuttings at 77°F (25°C). If kept at high humidity, the young plants produce aerial roots very soon.

Pests and Diseases: Rarely.

Uses: An exotic hanging plant.

RHODOCHITON ATROSANGUINEUM
Bell vine

Family: Figwort, *Scrophulariaceae*
Native Habitat: Mexico
Flowering Time: Late summer

The bell vine is an evergreen climber that grows up to 10 ft. (3 m). Its leaves are heart-shaped with tapering points. The singular flower is about 2 in. (5 cm) long and has a dark red, tubular corolla that emerges from the light red calyx. The five sepals of the calyx suggest a star.

Location: Full sun, warm; in summer outdoors. In winter light at 41–50°F (5–10°C). An optimal position

would be by the south wall of a building.

Care: Water generously and feed every two weeks during the summer. In winter, water just to keep the soil from drying out. High humidity is good for the plant. Provide climbing support. Plants that were outside for the summer should be pruned before the first frost and brought inside. At temperatures over 59°F (15°C), the plant will continue to bloom.

Propagation: From seed or by cuttings.

Pests and Diseases: Aphids.

Uses: A climbing plant for the conservatory or a container; suited to hanging baskets.

If the light gets too intense, the shoots of rhipsalis will take on a red tinge. This in no way affects the plant's health.

Rhododendron – Rhoicissus

There are so many azaleas usable as houseplants that it is not necessary to remember their names. So rich is the selection of varieties on sale that everyone can find a suitable color or form. Azaleas trained as standards come in all sizes; there are narrow, tall forms and round, bushy ones; colors include all shades of pink, red, and mauve, as well as white. Plants with two-colored flowers are also available.

Close-up of a rhododendron flower

White Rhododendron-simsii *hybrid*

RHODODENDRON
Azalea, rhododendron

Family: Heath, *Ericaceae*
Native Habitat: China, Japan, Himalayas, eastern North America
Flowering Time: Varies with the species and variety, between late fall and late spring

Azaleas are among the loveliest of winter-blooming houseplants. Two species must be considered for use as houseplants: *R. x obtusum*, the "Japanese azalea," and *R. simsii*, the "Indian azalea." The latter is the parent of our houseplants, has many hybrids, and is not hardy in temperate regions. The "Japanese azalea" can be planted in the garden after it has bloomed in the house and, for years after, one can enjoy its flowers, which are simpler and closer to the wild form. The flowers of this small treelike shrub come double and semi-double, in white, pink, and red, or two-toned. The small leaves are leathery, green, and shiny. There is a wealth of varieties to choose from.

Location: Light to partial shade; cool, humid, airy.

Care: Water freely in summer with soft water. Once a week add azalea food. In the fall, keep drier to encourage buds. Bring the plant indoors and keep cool and light. Spray occasionally. When the buds have thickened or the first ones have opened, move the plant to a slightly warmer spot. Remove dead flowers regularly. Azaleas can remain in a heated room for only short periods. After they have bloomed, lower the posts into a garden bed. Shoots that grow during or just after blooming are snipped out. Prune the plants in early summer several times. For repotting use only azalea or rhododendron soil mix.

Propagation: By tip cuttings with bottom heat; difficult.

Pests and Diseases: Spider mites if too dry and warm; crinkled leaf tips indicate the work of the azalea moth larva; dropping buds mean that the plant was warmed up too soon.

Uses: A wonderful winter-blooming plant for cool rooms or a cool conservatory. Outstanding for standard training and suited to bonsai. By the way, more and

The Most Beautiful Plants from A to Z

Pink-blooming hybrid rhododendron

Rhoicissus capensis

An azalea in a container: as lovely on the terrace as inside the conservatory.

In some parts of the United States, they call rhoicissus the evergreen grapevine. The plant was taken into commercial cultivation only in 1960, so it is a relatively "new" plant, though in southern countries they use this vigorous climber to cover the walls of buildings.

more hardy rhododendrons, considered garden plants, are now planted in containers and placed on the balcony or terrace. Especially well suited to this treatment are the hybrids of *Rhododendron repens*. They bloom early in the spring in shades of red and pink, and they can grow 3.2 ft. (1 m) high and as broad again.

You can buy these plants in any good nursery. They can spend the winter outdoors, but they need protection from strong sun. Their care is essentially the same as that of the species discussed above.

RHOICISSUS CAPENSIS
Rhoicissus

Family: Grape, *Vitaceae*
Native Habitat: South Africa
Flowering Time: Hardly blooms in cultivation

Rhoicissus is a strong creeper. Its leaves are 8 in. (20 cm) wide, almost heart-shaped, toothed, thick and leathery. On top, they are metallic emerald green; on the bottom they are matted with fine, brown hair. Their petioles are long.
Location: Light or partial shade all year; in summer outdoors in the shade. In winter at 46–54°F (8–12°C).
Care: In summer, keep wet with soft water; spray often if exposed to heated air in winter. Offer strong climbing support and tie the shoots to it, as the plant lacks its own gripping organ. Pruning is tolerated.
Propagation: By shoot cuttings at 64°F (18°C). Trim leaves to smaller size to reduce evaporation.
Pests and Diseases: Mealybugs, spider mites; brown or falling leaves indicate over- or underwatering.
Uses: A robust climbing plant for cool hallways, entrances, stairwells, or very light, sunless conservatories.

When repotting it, give *Rhoicissus capensis* a larger container than you would think it needs: in addition to the roots, it also has tuberlike storage roots that take up space.

Ricinus – Rosmarinus

The amazing powers inherent in plants are well demonstrated by *Ricinus communis*. It is awesome to see a small seed develop into a 10 ft.- (3 m-) high giant with huge leaves in the short span of a summer.

The picture below shows the plant's fruit, characteristic of the species, as is the fact that it is poisonous.

Flower of Ricinus communis

RICINUS COMMUNIS
Castor bean

Family: Spurge, *Euphorbiaceae*
Native Habitat: Probably tropical Africa
Flowering Time: Late summer

The castor bean forms a treelike, 10 ft.- (3 m-) high plant. The lobes of its huge leaves spread like fingers; depending on the variety, they are dark red, green with red veining, or shiny dark green. Late in the summer, the flower spikes appear. The fruit can be dried on stem cuttings before it is ripe and used in flower arrangements. Good varieties are 'Gibsonii' (dark red leaves); 'sanguineus' (leaves green with red veins); 'zanzibarensis' (the largest variety, with huge, dark, shiny green leaves).

Warning! *Ricinus* is a deadly poisonous plant, including its fruit and seeds.
Location: Full sun, warm; outdoors.
Care: This marvelous plant is grown as an annual in northern latitudes. It needs a very large container, a great deal of water, and lots of fertilizer, administered weekly, to be able to achieve its full potential.
Propagation: From seed; the seeds need to be soaked before sowing.
Pests and Diseases: Rarely.
Uses: A decorative, annual container plant.

Ricinus communis

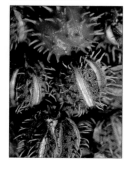

ROSA
Rose

Family: Rose, *Rosaceae*
Native Habitat: In cultivation just about worldwide
Flowering Time: Summer through fall

The rose, the queen of flowers, puts down deep roots, so it is difficult to grow in a container. There are, however, dwarf forms, so-called miniature roses, that are sold in pots. This group includes plants that are 8–12 in. (2–30 cm) high, such as, 'Minima' (red-flowering); 'Bubikopf' (light pink, large flowers); 'Daniela' (vivid shell pink, double); 'Guletta' (lemon yellow, double, very profuse); 'Zwergkonig 78' (dark red, double compact); and 'Zwergkonigin 82' (bright pink, double, large flowers).

If you have very deep containers, we particularly recommend grafted, standard-trained creeping roses, such as, 'The Fairy' (pink); 'Swany' (white); or 'Pink Bells' (pink).
Location: Light, sunny, airy; in summer outdoors. Miniature roses in winter at 50°F (10°C).
Care: Water regularly during growth; prevent waterlogging through good drainage. In winter, wet only enough to avoid a dry root ball. Till midsummer, feed every two weeks to allow the wood to mature. Remove all dead flowers or they will turn into rosehips, which use the energy the plant needs for further flowering. Standard-trained plants can overwinter outside in their containers, if these are large enough. They can be free-standing or sunk into a garden

THE MOST BEAUTIFUL PLANTS FROM A TO Z

Dwarf rose variety

Rosmarinus officinalis

ROSMARINUS OFFICINALIS
Rosemary

Family: Mint, *Laminaceae*
Native Habitat: Mediterranean region, Spain, Portugal
Flowering Time: Late spring, early summer

Rosemary is a shrub, 3.2 ft. (1 m) high, with needlelike, gray-matted leaves and pale blue labiate flowers. It is a characteristic part of the scenery around the Mediterranean.
Location: In summer, sun, hot, and protected outdoors. In winter, light at 35–46°F (2–8°C).
Care: Water sparingly, but never let it dry out. Feed, if possible organically, from spring to the end of summer. Prune back by one-third after it has bloomed.
Propagation: By cuttings in summer. Growing it from seed is lengthy and difficult.
Pests and Diseases: Rarely.
Uses: Container, balcony, or houseplant; in a container it can grow very old.

In the nineteenth century, growing roses in containers was a very important part of gardening. In fact, it was considered a distinct horticultural art. Today, dwarf roses are sold in the spring in grocery stores, even the supermini varieties.

If the tub is sufficiently deep, even weakly growing roses can be cultivated in a container.

Rosemary is an excellent balcony plant. It can be used in the kitchen, as an aromatic herb that stimulates digestion. Rosemary is also a healing herb; it invigorates the heart and the circulation. For this reason, it is often used as a bath additive. Simmered in white wine, it makes an invigorating drink for people with low blood pressure.

Garden rose in a tub

bed. Protect the graft union against cold. Loose garden soil with clay and sand added is an ideal planting medium. Renew the top layer of soil each spring. In late winter, move miniature roses to a warmer location to let them sprout.
Propagation: By cuttings or by grafting (which is not that easy for an amateur gardener). It is fairly easy to raise roses from seed.
Pests and Diseases: Aphids, powdery mildew, black spot.
Uses: The rose has limited use as a houseplant. It is better suited to dishes or balcony planters.

Ruscus – Saintpaulia

Ruscus, the butcher's broom, can withstand some frost, so that there is no hurry taking it indoors in the fall. Planted in the ground, it can even survive mild winters in the warmer regions of the north.

It would seem that *Sabal minor* grows quite large, despite the "minor" in its name. Only when it is compared to another species, *S. blackburniana*, which is only occasionally offered in nurseries specializing in container plants, can we understand the "minor": the less minor plant grows to 40 ft. (12 m) in height, and its leaves, on 6.5 ft.- (2 m-) long petioles, are spheres 6.5–10 ft. (2–3 m) across.

Ruscus aculeatus

Sabal minor

RUSCUS
Butcher's broom

Family: Lily, *Liliaceae*
Native Habitat: Mediterranean region, the Orient
Flowering Time: Spring

Butcher's broom grows to about 3.2 ft. (1 m) in a container. This long-lived evergreen is valued for its leathery foliage and its decorative fruit. The "leaves" are actually flattened shoots, so-called cladodes. It is dioecious, i.e., there are male and female plants. *R. aculeatus*, a prickly *Ruscus*, has pointed, 1.4 in.- (3.5 cm-) long, shiny, dark green cladodes. The more uncommon *R. hypoglossum* grows to 16 in. (40 cm) in height, but has 3–8 in.- (8–20 cm-) long "leaves," without points. Its fruit is red.

Location: Light to shade; in summer outdoors. In winter light and just above freezing.
Care: Water freely in summer and feed every two weeks. Reduce watering in winter. Pruning is tolerated.
Propagation: By division; by rooted offshoots; from seed (sprouting takes one year).
Pests and Diseases: Rarely.
Uses: Container plant for shady spots.

SABAL
Palmetto

Family: Palm, *Arecaceae*
Native Habitat: Subtropical America
Flowering Time: Seldom blooms in cultivation

This palm has a bushy or treelike habit. It has long leaf petioles and deeply incised leaf blades. The veins often end in threads. Flower clusters are intricately branched, hanging or upright.

S. minor grows bushy and about 6.5 ft. (2 m) high.

S. palmetto grows taller. The petioles open and flatten, covering the stem with a characteristic design.
Location: Very light, but not sunny, all year; in summer warm, outdoors. In winter at 50–59°F (10–15°C).
Care: Water generously in summer; in winter just enough to prevent the root ball from drying out. Feed lightly, from spring to late summer, every week.
Propagation: From seed or by offshoots.
Pests and Diseases: Rarely.
Uses: A very handsome green plant for the house or the conservatory.

Saintpaulia ionantha *flower*

SAINTPAULIA IONANTHA
African violet

Family: Gesneriad, *Gesneriaceae*
Native Habitat: East Africa
Flowering Time: Any time of year

The African violet is a small flowering plant. Its fleshy, hairy leaves form a rosette. They are pale green underneath, darker on top. The violet-like flower can be white, pink, or violet. Deacons of a German mission to the Usambara region of East Africa brought the plant back to Germany a hundred years ago. *S. ionantha* was discovered in 1892 by W. von Saint Paulliaire, who was stationed in the Usambara district. *S. confusa*, a very similar plant, was first found in 1895. These species can be looked at as the parents of today's innumerable varieties. In 1993, the hundredth birthday of the plant was celebrated in Germany.

African violets now come in all shades of pink, red, and blue. There are hybrids with multicolored, simple, double, curled, and rippled flowers. In addition we now also have the so-called minis, with small leaves and flowers.

Saintpaulia ionantha *hybrids*

Location: Light to partial shade and warm; no strong sun.
Care: Keep moist with soft water; avoid soggy roots. Keep the leaves dry, since water will spot them. Water either right under the rosette with a long-necked can or pour the water in the saucer, removing what is left over after the plant has had time to absorb what it needs. Feed very lightly every two weeks; if the plant grows too fast, switch to cactus food. In winter, keeping the plant rather dry and cool for a while gives it a rest. Remove all wilted flowers regularly.
Propagation: By leaf cuttings with bottom heat. Young plants will bloom after six months.
Pests and Diseases: Aphids, mealybugs if the air is too dry. Powdery mildew, gray mold, and root rot.

Uses: Flowering houseplant; very effective planted in groups of three or more in a large dish.

The African violet was first brought to and cultivated in Germany, but it enjoys the greatest popularity in the United States. The African Violet Society of America had 15,000 members back in 1955, and the abundance of varieties available is impossible to survey. These pictures show some of the different shapes, sizes, and colors available.

Salvia – Sansevieria

The bright red flowers of the scarlet sage are indispensable to the roster of balcony flowers. *Salvia officinalis*, the sage used as a herb, also contributes colors. The foliage of the variety 'Tricolor,' for example, plays between gray-green, violet, and a reddish pink; 'Aurea' is variegated in golden yellow, and 'Variegata' has leaves spotted yellow-green.

TIP

Red and blue salvia planted together make for good color. *Salvia farinacea* goes well with scarlet sage. You might wish to try either 'Victoria' or 'Blue Bedder.'

Salvia splendens

SALVIA SPLENDENS
Scarlet sage

Family: Mint, *Lamiaceae*
Native Habitat: Brazil
Flowering Time: Late spring to late fall.

The fire-engine-red racemes of scarlet sage are among the showiest of balcony flowers. The bushy plant has light green, oval, serrated leaves and square stems. It is grown as an annual. For balcony gardening, the compact varieties are best, such as 'Blaze of Fire' (brilliant scarlet, 15 in. (38 cm)); 'Red Cardinal' (intense red, 10 in. (25 cm)); 'Laser Purple' (dark violet to blue, 10 in. (25 cm)) and 'Melba' (salmon pink, 8 in. (20 cm)).

Another member of the same genus is *Salvia officinalis*. This sage grows well in containers, can winter outdoors, and its silvery-green foliage looks especially good against terra cotta.
Location: In summer, sunny and, if possible, protected from rain, outdoors.
Care: Keep evenly moist, not too wet. Feed lightly once a week. Snip off dead flowers, so the plant can produce more.
Propagation: From seed in early spring. Plant seedlings one per pot.
Pests and Diseases: Spider mites.
Uses: For balcony planters, dishes, and borders.

SANSEVIERIA TRIFASCIATA
Snake plant

Family: Agave, *Agavaceae*
Native Habitat: Tropical Africa
Flowering Time: Early spring

Sansevieria has 3.2 ft.- (1 m-) long, fleshy, upright, sword leaves. On both sides they are marked with light or dark green cross-stripes. The very fragrant, small flowers are greenish white and arranged in clusters 20 in. (50 cm) high. Many varieties are available.

Location: Very sunny and warm all year. In winter not under 59°F (15°C).

Care: Water only when the soil has dried to the touch; less in winter when it is cool. Standing in water can kill the plant. Give cactus food once a month; overfeeding softens the leaves. Repot each spring into a flat container, one size larger. *Sansevieria*s have been known to break their pots, they grow so fast.

Propagation: By division; by leaf cuttings of about 2 in. (5 cm). Cuttings from yellow-striped varieties revert to green.

Pests and Diseases: Corky growths on leaves if too wet; leaves falling over is also a sign of wetness.

Uses: An ideal plant for beginners.

Sansevieria trifasciata

The long, narrow leaves of *Sansevieria* have a clear, simple beauty. Grouped apart, maybe somewhat elevated, they have great dignity. One common variety of *Sansevieria trifasciata* is 'Laurentii,' with yellow-edged leaves. 'Craigii' has several yellow-white longitudinal stripes. The leaves of 'Hahnii' form a funnel-shaped rosette; in 'Golden Hahnii,' this is enhanced by broad, yellow stripes.

TIP

Underwatering will not hurt *Sansevieria*, but overwatering can kill it.

Sanvitalia – Schizanthus

Sanvitalia procumbens 'Goldteppich' blooms abundantly and looks good with *Ageratum* and annual ornamental grasses.

Saxifraga stolonifera forms offshoots, small plants that hang over the edge of the pot on thin stems, making this an unusual hanging plant.

Sanvitalia procumbens

SANVITALIA PROCUMBENS
Trailing zinnia

Family: Aster, *Asteraceae*
Native Habitat: Mexico, Guatemala
Flowering Time: Late spring through fall

Trailing *Sanvitalia* is a herbaceous annual with a branching habit. It spreads into mounds 6–8 in. (15–20 cm) high. Its blossoms look like miniature sunflowers. Two very nice varieties are the orange 'Mandarin Orange' and the yellow, double 'plena.' The plant blooms very amply and for a long time; it deserves more attention.
Location: Sunny.
Care: Plant seedlings 10 in. (25 cm) apart in loose, fertile soil. Water moderately and feed lightly every two weeks. Prune back mounds that have finished blooming by half; this encourages more flowers.
Propagation: From seed in early spring at 59–64°F (15–18°C).
Pests and Diseases: Rarely.
Uses: A good-looking hanging plant for balcony planters, dishes, and hanging baskets, and for underplanting tubs and troughs.

Saxifraga stolonifera

SAXIFRAGA STOLONIFERA
Saxifrage

Family: Saxifrage, *Saxifragaceae*
Native Habitat: Japan, China
Flowering Time: All summer

The leaves of the saxifrage form rosettes. They are round to kidney-shaped, and hairy. Their green surface is set off by white veins; underneath they are red. Saxifrage grows many young plants at the ends of long, thin runners. Numerous small light pink flowers open in summer in racemes. The variety 'Tricolor' has somewhat smaller, white-variegated leaves, tinged with pink when young.
Location: Light to partial shade; in summer outdoors. In winter 55–64°F (13–18°C). 'Tricolor' never under 59°F (15°C).
Care: Keep moderately moist, drier in winter, if it is cool. Feed weekly early spring to late summer.
Propagation: By offshoots; often they develop roots while still on the plant. Put several in one pot.
Pests and Diseases: Spider mites, mealybugs; root rot if too cold and wet; uneven habit and long petioles are signs that it needs fertilizer.
Uses: A pretty hanging plant; can be used as ground cover for the conservatory.

Saxifrage becomes unsightly after two to three years; it is a good idea to grow a replacement plant in the meantime.

THE MOST BEAUTIFUL PLANTS FROM A TO Z

SCHEFFLERA
Schefflera

Family: Ginseng, *Araliaceae*
Native Habitat: Taiwan, Australia, New Guinea
Flowering Time: Seldom blooms in cultivation

Schefflera can be a shrub or a tree. Its evergreen, long-petioled leaves are shaped like a hand. They have a polished look and change as they mature. The best-known species, *Schefflera actinophylla*, is also called *Brassaia*. Its 12 in.- (30 cm-) wide leaves are four-lobed in youth, but have up to sixteen lobes when mature.

Recently, a species with smaller leaves and habit, *S. arboricola*, has come on the market. It has some multicolored varieties, e.g., 'Gold Capella,' and 'Green Gold.'

Further varieties are 'Renate,' 'Henriette,' and 'Compacta.' Schefflera contains substances that can irritate skin and mucous membranes.

Location: Light to partial shade all year; in summer outdoors 59–70°F (15–21°C). Humid. In winter 59–70°F (15–21°C); variegated plants, somewhat warmer.
Care: Keep lightly moist; feed every two weeks from early spring to the end of summer. Pruning larger plants encourages branching. If in a warm place, spray often. Repot every two years.
Propagation: By tip cuttings at 72°F (22°C). By air layering; from seed.
Pests and Diseases: Spider mites if too warm and dry in winter; stunted growth and pale leaves indicate a need for fertilizing; leaves fall if the plant is too cold.
Uses: A house plant and container plant for cool stairwells and conservatories. Suited to hydroponics.

Hybrid Schizanthus wisetonensis

SCHIZANTHUS WISETONENSIS HYBRIDS
Butterfly flower hybrids

Family: Nightshade, *Solanaceae*
Native Habitat: Chile
Flowering Time: Summer through fall

These hybrids are annual, shrubby, flowering plants with light green, compound leaves and large, delicate flowers in clusters. Crossing several wild species, chiefly *S. grahamii* and *S. pinnatus*, has produced hybrids with flowers in white, yellow, pink, scarlet, and violet.

The plant is poisonous.

Location: Light to sunny; airy and warm; outdoors, starting in late spring. In winter, sun and fresh air for young plants; 50°F (10°C).
Care: Keep evenly moist; feed weekly. Remove dead flowers to encourage further blooms.
Propagation: From seed in late winter, at 64°F (18°C) under glass.
Pests and Diseases: Root rot if the plant is too wet.
Uses: For balcony planters, dishes, and for the house.

Today, *Schefflera arboricola* is a very popular house plant, maybe because it does so well in hydroponics.

Varieties of *Schizanthus* are offered in mixes, such as the 8 in.- (20 cm-) high 'Hit Parade' and 'Star Parade.' A very good 16 in.- (40 cm-) high mix also exists. Sown in late summer, plants will flower in late winter or spring.

My scheffleras grow in containers that are moved outside and placed under trees for the summer. Because of their upward-reaching habit, I secure them to the tree trunks.

Schefflera arboricola

Schlumbergera – Scutellaria

Schlumbergera hybrids make cheerful Christmas presents that continue to give pleasure for years to come. If you are able to put these plants in open shade in the garden or on the balcony for the summer, you will find that they will grow many new shoot segments by fall.

The painted ivy arum thrives in an enclosed glass case, where it can grow on an epiphytic support. *Scindapsus* also does well in hydroponics if the water is not too cold.

TIP

Experienced home gardeners can train a standard Christmas cactus after grafting it on *Pereskia aculeata*, *Selenicereus*, or *Hylocereus*.

Hybrid Schlumbergera

Scindapsus pictus

SCINDAPSUS PICTUS
Painted ivy arum

Family: Arum, *Araceae*
Native Habitat: Malaysia
Flowering Time: Seldom blooms in cultivation

Painted ivy arum is a climbing plant with dark green heart-shaped leaves, marked with white spots. The foliage of the variety `argyraeus` is very dark green, sprinkled and edged in silver. Often you will find *Scindapsus aureus* for sale, a species with yellow-marbled leaves, but this is now *Epipremnum pinnatum* `aureum.`
Location: Light to partial shade all year; humid and warm: soil and air never under 61°F (16°C).
Care: Keep evenly moist with soft, lukewarm water; spray frequently. Feed every two weeks; reduce to once a month in winter.
Propagation: By shoot cuttings in spring with bottom heating and high humidity; can be rooted and grown in water.
Pests and Diseases: Scale insects; brown leaf spots if too wet and too cool.
Uses: A good climbing or hanging plant.

SCHLUMBERGERA HYBRIDS
Christmas cactus

Family: Cactus, *Cactaceae*
Native Habitat: Originally, Brazil
Flowering Time: Late fall to midwinter

The Christmas cactus is sometimes offered as *Epiphyllum* or *Zygocactus*. These two epiphytic cacti were used to create the hybrids we call Christmas cacti in white, pink, red, and violet. The cultivar `Gold Charm` even has yellow flowers. Hardly any pure species are sold today.
Location: Light to partial shade all year; in summer outdoors. The plants rest at 54–59°F (12–15°C).

Care: Three months before you wish the plant to bloom, cut back watering and lower temperature. After one month, move to a warmer place. When buds show, increase watering and feed every two weeks. Spray occasionally without wetting the flower. After it has bloomed, allow another period of rest.
Propagation: By multisegmented leaf cuttings with bottom heating. Allow cuttings to dry a little before planting.
Pests and Diseases: Root rot if too wet. If exposed to sun, the shoot segments take on a reddish color.
Uses: Lovely flowering plant for the home and the conservatory; larger specimens make good hanging plants.

Scirpus cernuus

Scutellaria costaricana

SCIRPUS CERNUUS
Weeping bulrush

Family: Sedge, *Cyperaceae*
Native Habitat: Mediterranean region, tropics and subtropics
Flowering Time: Summer

Weeping bulrush is a grasslike plant with thin, slightly arching blades. In the wild, it grows in marshes and other wet areas. The brownish, pinhead flowers open at the tips of the threadlike blades. The plant may bloom all year. In recent years it has often been sold with its blades enclosed by a brown plastic tube; this gives it the "grass palm" look.
Location: Light to partial shade all year; no direct sun; humid; warm, at room temperature.
Care: Keep evenly moist; water in the saucer is tolerated, except in a cool winter position. At times, immerse the clay pot to the rim in water to soak. Provide indirect atmospheric humidity. Feed monthly.
Propagation: By division or from seed.
Pests and Diseases: Aphids; brown leaf tips if kept too dry.
Uses: A hanging plant for a humid environment; excellent terrarium plant and good for hydroponics.

SCUTELLARIA COSTARICANA
Scutellaria

Family: Mint, *Lamiaceae*
Native Habitat: Costa Rica
Flowering Time: Late spring to midsummer

Scutellaria is a bushy perennial with pointed, oval, dark green leaves. It blooms in bright red, terminal spikes. The throat of the long, tubular flower is yellow. Altogether, the plant is 12–16 in. (30–40 cm) high, but it grows leggy in seeking the light. Consequently, it is treated with growth-retardants.
Location: Very light and airy all year; no direct sun. In summer warm, in winter not under 59°F (15°C).
Care: Keep moderately moist. Feed weekly from spring to fall, monthly in winter. Prune back specimens that have no lower leaves. Grow a replacement plant and keep in reserve.
Propagation: By tip cuttings in autumn with bottom heat and high humidity.
Pests and Diseases: Spider mites if kept too dry and warm.
Uses: Flowering plant for greenhouse or window greenhouse.

Scirpus cernuus is a good plant for a bathroom because the recurring humidity is what it needs. It is much more resistant to aphids under such conditions. By the way, when fighting aphids, you should know that the plant has poor tolerance for the usual insecticides.

Scutellaria does not thrive when its soil is colder than the air.

Weeping bulrush is often sold compressed into a plastic sleeve (as shown below). This is not the plant's natural habit but an inappropriate commercialization.

Scirpus cernuus

Sedum – Selenicereus

Sedum morganianum

Growing it out of the bottom of its pot and thus letting it hang without any obstructions is the best way to protect the brittle shoots of the burro's tail, *Sedum morganianum.*

Though considered a bedding plant, *Sedum telephium* looks very decorative in a bowl, especially the variety 'Herbstfreude.'

The leaves of *Sedum rubrotinctum* are tinged in red.

Sedum telephium *'Herbstfreude'*

Sedum x rubrotinctum

SEDUM
Stonecrop

○ ☼ 🖐 🔔

Family: Stonecrop, *Crassulaceae*
Native Habitat: Diffused worldwide.
Flowering Time: Varies with the species

With about 500 species growing in the temperate zone, *Sedum* is the largest of the stonecrop genera. For the house and balcony, the best species are as follows:

The Mexican *S. morganianum* is one of the most attractive with its bluish white shoots almost 3.2 ft. (1 m) long. Densely set along the shoot, like roof tiles, are the small, cylindrical leaves. Unfortunately, the leaves can fall off at the slightest touch. Those of the variety *S. morganianum* 'Buretti' are shorter and cling better.

S. pachyphyllum has 1.5 in.- (4 cm-) long, thick, fleshy, club-shaped leaves. Their tips are dyed red. Similarly tinted by exposure to the sun are the cylindrical leaves of *S. x rubrotinctum,* which break off very easily. The variety 'Aurora,' of more compact habit, has salmon-colored leaves tinged in silver.

S. sieboldii blooms in October and makes a good hanging plant for a cool room. It can be planted in the garden as well, since it is quite hardy. Other interesting species are *S. bellum, S. griseum, S. platyphyllum,* and *S. stahlii.*

The scarlet *S. telephium* grows to 24 in. (60 cm) in height. Its abundant umbellate flowers make it a frequently used perennial for the conservatory, but it looks very stately in a container, as well.

Location: Light and sunny all year; in summer outdoors; not too warm. In winter, 41–50°F (5–10°C). Some species can withstand frost.
Care: Water sparingly in summer, not at all in winter. Administer cactus food once a month during growth.
Propagation: By shoot or leaf cuttings that have dried a little before being planted.
Pests and Diseases: Root rot in winter if it is too wet.
Uses: A foliage plant for bright, cool rooms, a greenhouse, or the conservatory. Well suited for hanging baskets.

Various Selaginella *species*

SELAGINELLA
Selaginella

Family: Spike moss, *Selaginellaceae*
Native Habitat: Tropical rain forests
Flowering Time: Not a flowering plant

Selaginella is a tough, low-growing plant with straight or forked stems set with small, relatively coarse leaves. The feathery, almost leathery shoots of *S. kraussiana* form a dense carpet. Equally attractive is *S. martiensii* 'Watsonia,' with silvery shoots, slightly arching at the tips.
Location: Partial shade; humid and warm all year. In winter at least 61°F (16°C).
Care: Water generously with tepid, soft water and spray. Feed with half-diluted plant food once a month. If plant is kept in a room, lower its pot into another, larger one, filled with wet clay granular.
Propagation: By division or stem cuttings.
Pests and Diseases: Slugs in the conservatory.
Uses: A ground cover for enclosed window greenhouses, warm conservatories, enclosed glass cases, and terraria.

Selenicereus grandiflorus

SELENICEREUS GRANDIFLORUS
Queen of the night

Family: Cactus, *Cactaceae*
Native Habitat: Jamaica, Cuba, Haiti, Mexico
Flowering Time: Summer through fall

This cactus grows twining, gray-green shoots with four or five ribs. The ribs are set with needlelike thorns. The magnificent, large flower opens in the evening and wilts with the dawn. It is white; its strong fragrance is of vanilla. Larger specimens have several flowers a year.

The large flowers of *S. pteranthus,* the princess of the night, are without fragrance.

Location: Year-round light but protected from direct noon sun. In winter 50–59°F (10–15°C).
Care: In summer, water with soft, tepid water and spray from time to time until the buds are set. In winter, hardly water at all. Feed every three weeks, large specimens every week, with cactus food. The long shoots need some support, and they need to be tied to it as they grow.
Propagation: By stem cuttings about 6 in. (15 cm) long with bottom heat.
Pests and Diseases: Mealybugs.
Uses: A cactus that is easy to take care of, but needs a lot of room.

High humidity is a necessity for the *Selaginella* species that are used as houseplants.

The fast-growing queen of the night may have to be pruned now and then.

317

Sempervivum – Senecio

A pair of old shoes with healthy *Sempervivum* rosettes in them: in travelling across the European countryside one often encounters unusual gardening ideas.

Senecio rowleyanus (right) is an example of the incredible variety of forms offered by this species.

Below, a miracle of symmetry: a *Sempervivum* rosette.

An unusual Sempervivum *planting*

Senecio rowleyanus

Sempervivum rosette

SEMPERVIVUM
House leek

Family: Stonecrop, *Crassulaceae*
Native Habitat: Mountainous regions of the Mediterranean and of Asia Minor.
Flowering Time: Summer into fall

Sempervivum grows in rosettes that form a dense mound. Its leaves are fleshy, green, red, or bluish, usually with a clear point. Some species also are covered with a fine network of spider-weblike threads. Older plants produce branched, umbellate clusters of usually red or pink flowers, though some bloom white or yellow. After blooming, the rosette dies but leaves behind many offsets. Some good species are *S. arachnoideum* (covered with gossamer threads); *S. ciliosum* (pure green and hairy); *S. soboliferum,*

now *Jovibarba soboliferum* (gray-green, tinged with red). The variety 'Commander Hay' has spectacular dark red rosettes.

S. tectorum ssp. *tectorum* has many hybrids that differ in leaf shape and color.

House leek·used to be considered the best protection against lightning, and a thatched roof on which it took root was thought to be supremely blessed.
Location: Sunny; outdoors all year.
Care: None.
Propagation: From seed or by offsets.
Pests and Diseases: Rarely.
Uses: For dishes and troughs on the terrace and on the roof.

SENECIO
Groundsel

Family: Aster, *Asteraceae*
Native Habitat: Africa, India, Mexico
Flowering Time: Seldom blooms in cultivation

The genus *Senecio* includes some very strange, creeping or upright succulent plants.

S. hawarthii has thin shoots with pointed, fleshy, white-matted leaves. The plant reaches only 8 in. (20 cm).

S. herreanus, string of pearls, has spherical leaves, in size and color like peas, attached to long, thin, hanging shoots.

S. kleiniae is a stem-forming succulent plant with a plume of leaves at the top, a bit like a palm.

S. macroglossus looks much like ivy. This climbing succulent's variegated form, 'Variegatus,' can only be differentiated from ivy by feeling the thickness of the leaves.

Also an ivy lookalike is *S. mikanioides*, which produces, in addition to the green leaves, others that are variegated white or pink.

S. rowleyanus is a fast-growing,

spreading species with leaves like peas on long, thin shoots.

Location: Light, sun to partial shade, in summer outdoors. In winter, 50–54°F (10–12°C) or warmer.

Care: Water rather lightly in summer, somewhat more if warm in winter. Ivylike species need climbing support and are repotted yearly in standard soil mix with a clay additive; for other species use cactus soil mix. Fast-growing species need fertilizer every two weeks; slower ones, cactus food at longer intervals.

Propagation: By shoot cuttings.

Pests and Diseases: Aphids.

Uses: A climbing or hanging plant for the home, the conservatory, or the greenhouse.

Senecio herreanus

Senecio mikanioides

Senecio bicolor

SENECIO BICOLOR
Senecio

Family: Aster, *Asteraceae*
Native Habitat: Mediterranean region
Flowering Time: Mature plants only: spring through summer

Senecio is usually grown as an annual. This silver-matted evergreen plant with deeply incised leaves is now sold in spring and again in autumn because it looks good with *Erica gracilis* and pine boughs. It is half-hardy in the temperate zone. 'Silverdust' is a compact variety, 8 in. (20 cm) high, with silvery-white foliage. The large, bulging leaves of 'Cirrus' have a blue luster and are covered with white, woolly hair.

Warning: the plant contains poisonous alkaloids.

Location: Sunny, outdoors, protected from rain.
Care: Keep lightly moist and feed every two weeks;
Propagation: From seed with bottom heat at 64°F (18°C).
Pests and Diseases: Aphids, powdery mildew, and downy mildew.
Uses: For summer and winter planting of dishes and boxes.

In its native South Africa, *Senecio mikanioides* climbs up to 16 ft. (5 m) high.

Senecio herreanus is a somewhat odd plant that will attract attention in any collection of succulents.

The small yellow flowers of *Senecio bicolor* appear only on mature plants. By the time a plant reaches 31 in. (80 cm), however, it is several years old and will have lost its youthful, bushy form; the insignificant flowers do not justify carrying it for that many winters.

Senecio – Skimmia

Senecio cruentus hybrids impress with the wealth and the intense colors of their flowers.

If a sesbania has become uneven and thin, cutting it right to the ground will encourage it to grow back bushy and full.

Hybrid Senecio cruentus

Sesbania punicea

SENECIO CRUENTUS HYBRIDS
Cineraria

Family: Aster, *Asteraceae*
Native Habitat: Canary Islands
Flowering Time: Spring

Cineraria is a herbaceous plant, 12 in. (30 cm) high, with large, soft leaves, their undersides matted with grayish hair. The daisylike flowers cluster in numerous umbels. Formerly, the flowers were vividly colored, but now softer shades are available. Some flowers are double; others are marked with a white ring. A dwarf form is available, called 'Scarlet'; it is only 6 in. (15 cm) high. Cinerarias are grown as annuals.

Location: Light, airy, humid at 61–64°F (16–18°C). Young plants in winter at 41–50°F (5–10°C).
Care: Water generously, for even short periods of dryness cut down on flowering. Provide indirect humidity. Fertilizer not required.
Propagation: From seed in late summer or by tip cuttings, about 4 in. (10 cm) long, in the spring.
Pests and Diseases: Aphids (plant seedlings far apart and provide insecticide sticks right from the start); powdery mildew; gray mold.
Uses: Colorful spring flower for bright, cool rooms.

SESBANIA PUNICEA
Sesbania

Family: Bean, *Fabaceae*
Native Habitat: Argentina, Brazil
Flowering Time: Spring to fall

In England this plant is called the scarlet glyzina tree, a very good description. The 10 ft.- (3 m-) high shrub has dark green, pinnately compound leaves and bears scarlet flowers in clusters of ten per hanging raceme.
Location: In summer, sunny and warm, outdoors. In winter, 39–50°F (4–10°C), light or dark, since the leaves fall anyway.
Care: During growth, water moderately. In winter, avoid waterlogging. Until the end of summer, feed weekly. If stored dark in winter, keep almost dry.
Propagation: By semihardwood cuttings in summer.
Pests and Diseases: Powdery mildew, root rot if too wet in the winter.
Uses: Container or conservatory plant; easy to train as a standard.

TIP

I have placed potted cinerarias at my entrance door in early spring for years. A little late frost never seems to hurt them.

Hybrid Sinningia

SINNINGIA HYBRIDS
Gloxinia

Family: Gesneriad, *Gesneriaceae*
Native Habitat: Brazil
Flowering Time: Any time of year

The gloxinia is a spectacular flower, large, bell-shaped, and velvety. The tuberous plant grows 8-12 in. (20-30 cm) high; its long, rounded leaves are dark green, soft, and hairy.

The parent species of all *Sinningia* hybrids is *S. speciosa.* Crossing it with other species, for example, *S. regina,* created a multitude of cultivars with flowers in white, pink, red, and violet, as well as multicolored and double varieties.

Location: Light all year, no direct sun; humid and warm.
Care: Keep evenly moist with tepid, soft water; feed weekly. Provide indirect humidity, since the leaves cannot tolerate spraying. After it has flowered, store the tuber dry at about 55°F (13°C). Repot it in the spring into slightly acid soil, not planting it too deep. Once it has sprouted, water generously.
Propagation: By leaf or shoot cuttings at 68°F (20°C) in wet sand.
Pests and Diseases: Aphids, spider mites, thrips; rolled-up leaves are due to dry air; rot indicates that the plant is too cold and wet.
Uses: A great flowering houseplant.

Skimmia japonica

SKIMMIA JAPONICA
Japanese skimmia

Family: Rue, *Rutaceae*
Native Habitat: Japan, Ryukyu Islands, Taiwan
Flowering Time: In the spring

Skimmia's leaves are shiny and dark green, reminiscent of laurel. In spring, the plant bears racemes of white blooms; autumn into winter, it has lacquer-red berries. This evergreen shrub reaches 3.2 ft. (1 m) in height.
Location: Light but not full sun all year; in summer outdoors. In winter, airy at 50°F (10°C). In milder regions, skimmia can also be planted in the garden.
Care: In summer, keep evenly moist with soft water; feed every two weeks. In winter, water less.
Propagation: By tip cuttings in late summer, but it is difficult and slow. Cuttings can be put in the cold frame in autumn, but it takes about a year for them to root.
Pests and Diseases: Rarely.
Uses: Container plant.

With large-blooming gloxinias that have small tubers, there is no point in carrying them over to the next year.

Beautiful varieties of *Skimmia japonica* are, among others, 'Nymans,' light red fruit; 'Scarlet Queen,' tall-growing with red fruit; and 'Kew White,' with white fruit.

Smithianta – Solanum

If you have several pieces of *Smithianta* rhizome available, you can prolong the periods of bloom by planting one every week and thus producing a series of flowering houseplants.

Solandra is a plant that needs room and sunlight. The best place for it is in the sunny conservatory, planted right in the ground.

Smithianta *hybrid*

SMITHIANTA HYBRIDS
Smithianta

Family: Gesneriad, *Gesneriaceae*
Native Habitat: South America
Flowering Time: Summer through fall

Smithianta is a herbaceous plant with a creeping, scaly runner. The soft, green, heart-shaped leaves are veined and marked in red. The bell-shaped flowers are orange and stand in racemes at the ends of leafless stalks. It is hard to find pure species, but the hybrids of *S. multiflora* and *S. zebrina* are plentiful. The plant used to be called *Naegelia*.
Location: In summer, light, warm, and humid. In winter, dry at 54°F (12°C).
Care: During growth keep evenly moist with soft water; feed every two weeks. In winter do not feed or water.
Propagation: By division of the rhizomes or from seed.
Pests and Diseases: Waterlogging is a danger.
Uses: A very lovely foliage and flowering plant for warm, humid positions.

Solandra will bloom only if it goes through a dry period first. The leaves should wilt or even fall. Only then does the plant set many new buds, when watering can resume.

Solandra guttata

SOLANDRA
Chalia vine

Family: Nightshade, *Solanaceae*
Native Habitat: Mexico, Jamaica
Flowering Time: Summer through fall; at other times, too

Some of the plants in the genus *Solandra* are 4 in.- (10 cm-) high climbing shrubs with evergreen, leathery, shiny leaves. The large funnel flowers unfold in the leaf axils; they release their fragrance at night.

The leaves of *S. grandiflora* are large and elliptical. Its flowers, about 6 in. (15 cm) across, at first are greenish white, then turn a brown-yellow color.

S. guttata's leaves are 6 in. (15 cm) long and softly hispid (covered with rough hairs) below. The yellow petals of the funnel flower curl up at the tips. A scarlet stripe runs down the inside center of each petal.

The flowers of *S. maxima* are similar yellow funnels with red markings on the inside. Possibly, the plant is poisonous.
Location: Year round, light to full sun; in the conservatory it can be planted right by the window; warm and airy.
Care: Keep evenly moist; spring through summer, feed weekly. Prune as required.
Propagation: From seed or by shoot cuttings with bottom heating.
Pests and Diseases: Aphids.
Uses: Climbing plant or ground cover for large, warm greenhouses or conservatories.

Solanum rantonnetii

SOLANUM
Nightshade

Family: Nightshade, *Solanaceae*
Native Habitat: Tropics and sub-tropics
Flowering Time: Late spring through fall, or longer, depending on species

Some interesting plants belong to the genus *Solanum*. There is, first of all, the potato, *S. tuberosum*, which on closer inspection turn out to have a pretty flower. Then there are the forms of *S. melangena*, egg-plant, from Africa, Arabia, and northwest India. Another member of *Solanum* is *S. dulcamara*, the woody nightshade, called "witch's plant" in its native Europe. As house and container plants, *S. pseudocapsicum* and *S. muricatum* are significant (described separately in this book), as well as white- or blue-flowering tropical species.

One Brazilian nightshade, *S. jasminoides*, is evergreen, fast-growing, and will reach 50 ft. (10 m) if planted in the ground. The narrow leaves are about 3 in. (8 cm) long; the flower resembles that of the potato.

The Argentine *S. rantonnetii*, by contrast, is deciduous; its flower is abundant and violet-blue with a yellow center. Especially profuse is the variety 'grandiflorum.' It is easy to standard train, but looks its best planted in the conservatory, climbing up a trellis. Considered the most handsome is the Costa Rican nightshade, *S. wendlandii*. It uses its hooked thorns to climb up to 16 ft. (5 m) high. Its leaves are up to 10 in. (25 cm) long; its flowers are pink or lilac and form large clusters. Its foliage falls in the winter.

All species of *Solanum* are poisonous in all their parts.
Location: Sun to partial shade; in summer outdoors. In winter 39–50°F (4–10°C). *S. jasminoides* can be stored dark in the winter.
Care: During growth, water freely; feed weekly. In winter, water sparingly if stored light, hardly at all if stored dark. Before moving the plant to its cooler winter position, prune it to about 20 in. (50 cm) above the rim of the container.
Propagation: By semihardwood cuttings in the spring.
Pests and Diseases: Aphids, whiteflies.
Uses: A good-looking container plant or climbing plant for the terrace or the conservatory .

Of all available exotic *Solanum* species, the most widely accepted is *S. rantonnetii*, hardly surprising in view of the abundance of its flowers, summer through fall. The flexible, up to 6.5 ft.- (2m-) long shoots will develop a tendency to climb, if not prevented.

Solanum jasminoides is among the fastest-growing container plants, particularly if it is well fertilized.

Solanum jasminoides

Solanum – Sparmannia

While the fruit of *Solanum pseudocapsicum*, on the right, is poisonous, *S. muricatum* is raised for the sake of its tasty fruit (below). In the temperate zone, fruit begins to ripen in late summer and tastes of pears and melons.

Baby's tears is a plant that thrives near water, as here, by a fountain.

Solanum pseudocapsicum

Soleirolia soleirolii

Solanum muricatum

SOLANUM PSEUDOCAPSICUM
Jerusalem cherry

Family: Nightshade, *Solanaceae*
Native Habitat: Madeira
Flowering Time: Summer

The Jerusalem cherry is a small shrubby plant with little dark green leathery leaves. Its flower is greenish white. The spherical fruit turns from green to yellow and then to coral red. It is very decorative and lasts for months.

Varieties to look at are 'Dwarf Red' and 'New Patterson' for orange fruit and 'Goldball' for large yellow fruit. The fruit of 'Snowfire' starts out white and then turns red. The fruit is poisonous. A new hanging plant is the perennial *Solanum muricatum* 'Pepino Gold.' It flowers violet-blue, forms edible fruit, and is cared for like the Jerusalem cherry.
Location: Light to full sun all year; airy and not too warm (about 59°F (15°C)); in summer outdoors.

Care: These plants are usually bought in late fall, when they are covered with fruit, and tended until the fruit loses its luster. The cooler they stand, the longer the fruit will last. To carry the plant to the next year, prune it in the fall and place it in a light, cool location. Keep the soil barely moist. Starting in late winter, sprout it again and keep watering it well all through summer. Feed biweekly. With a bit of work, you can train a standard. Although the plant is usually discarded, I have heard of Jerusalem cherries ten years old.
Propagation: From seed or by cuttings in spring. Prune young plants twice.
Pests and Diseases: Aphids and spider mites if too warm; yellow leaves if too dark; leaves fall if drafty or too wet.
Uses: House and container plant for cool rooms.

Family: Nettle, *Urticaceae*
Native Habitat: Majorca, Corsica, Sardinia
Flowering Time: Seldom blooms in cultivation

Baby's tears, sometimes still sold under its old name, *Helxine soleirolii*, is a small carpet-forming plant with shoots thin as threads on which tiny, round or oval leaves grow. Besides the green form, you can find the varieties 'argentea,' with silvery foliage, and 'aurea,' with gold-green leaves.
Location: Year-round light to partial shade; cool or at room temperature.
Care: Keep well moistened, but water only by the saucer; spring through summer, feed monthly. Water less if it is cooler; spray often if it is much warmer.
Propagation: By division.
Pests and Diseases: Protect both from dryness and waterlogging.
Uses: A ground cover for enclosed glass cases or window green-houses and for the conservatory. A trouble-free houseplant.

SOLEIROLIA SOLEIROLII
Baby's tears

THE MOST BEAUTIFUL PLANTS FROM A TO Z

SPARMANNIA AFRICANA
African sparmannia

Family: Linden, *Tiliaceae*
Native Habitat: South Africa
Flowering Time: Midwinter to early spring

The light green, lobed leaves of the African sparmannia are evergreen, up to 10 in. (25 cm) across, and hairy on both sides. It has now been a houseplant in Europe for 200 years. Today, it is often bought for the conservatory, where it can reach 6.5 ft. (2 m) in height if planted in the ground. Under favorable light conditions, umbellate clusters of simple, white flowers appear in late winter. Each flower bears a starburst of yellow and brown stamina.

The double variety 'Plena' is actually less lovely than the simple species.

Location: Very light and airy all year; in summer outdoors. In winter 43–54°F (6–12°C) or somewhat warmer.
Care: Water very generously, as much evaporation takes place through the large, velvet-soft leaves. From spring to fall, feed weekly. In winter, in a cool position, water more sparingly, if warm, spray often with soft water. Outdoors or when it grows very fast, it can be repotted once or twice a year into a larger container. Prune at any time.
Propagation: By cuttings at 68°F (20°C).
Pests and Diseases: Thrips, whiteflies, aphids; yellow leaves can be due to cigarette smoke or soil that is too cold or too wet in the winter; leaves fall because of drafts or dry air.

Sparmannia africana

Sparmannia blossoms

Uses: A substantial pot or container plant for large, bright, and if possible, cool rooms, especially in winter; for large conservatories, verandahs, hall-ways, and lobbies. An ideal candidate for a single specimen plant, for by timely pruning of the side shoots, it can be shaped into a "tree." Suited to hydroponics.

The African sparmannia has very beautiful flowers, but individual plants differ as to their ability to put forth blooms. Take cuttings for propagation only from a plant that has bloomed profusely.

African sparmannia can be planted in a wire basket and then lowered into the ground in the garden. Planted in this fashion, it will develop into a huge specimen in one growing season. In the fall, the roots can be cut around the wire basket, the plant itself can be pruned back and then moved, as a container plant, into a light, cool location.

Spathiphyllum – Stapelia

If you do not have the space for the large-blooming varieties, consider buying hybrids of the compact species, *Spathiphyllum wallisii*.

There are numerous varieties of *Stapelia variegata*; the species is often used in creating new hybrids.

Spathiphyllum wallisii *hybrids*

Stapelia variegata

SPATHIPHYLLUM
Spathiphyllum

Family: Arum, *Araceae*
Native Habitat: Tropical Americas
Flowering Time: Spring through summer

Spathiphyllum has pointed, oval, shiny green leaves on long petioles. The flower is typical of the arum family, a white or yellow spadix set off by a spathe. It floats far above the leaves on a thin stalk. The flower lasts for weeks, though the white spathe turns green in time. Beautiful varieties include 'Mauna Loa,' 'Marion Wagner,' 'Cleveland,' and 'McCoy.'

Commercially, now only hybrids of this exotic species are available.
Location: Light to partial shade; warm and humid.
Care: In summer keep moderately moist and spray occasionally, using only tepid, soft water. Water somewhat less in winter. Spring to fall, feed lightly every week.
Propagation: By division, when repotting.
Pests and Diseases: Aphids, spider mites; brown spots on the leaves are usually due to too highly concentrated fertilizer; yellowing leaves indicate too strong sun; failure to set flowers points to a need for fertilizer.
Uses: Houseplant. One of the best plants for hydroponics.

STAPELIA
Carrion flower

Family: Milkweed, *Asclepiadaceae*
Native Habitat: South Africa
Flowering Time: Summer

Stapelia is a low-growing, succulent plant, seldom higher than 8 in. (20 cm). The plant has square stems that are sometimes hairy. The flower forms a five-pointed star, and is usually large, intricately marked, and downy. For short periods, it gives off a carrion smell that attracts horseflies; these take care of pollination. Some beautiful species are:

S. gigantea has the largest flowers (10–14 in. (25–35 cm) across). It is light yellow, marked with red cross-stripes.

The flower of *S. grandiflora* is 6 in. (15 cm) wide, brownish red, mantled with red or white down.

S. hirsuta has a brown-violet flower 4 in. (10 cm) wide; the cross-stripes are yellow; the down shimmers violet.

S. nobilis has flowers 8-10 in. (20-25 cm) wide, red on the outside, striped with ochre yellow inside.

S. pillansii grows dark scarlet-brown flowers covered with scarlet down.

S. semota has chocolate flowers with light markings. The variety *S. semota* var. *lutea* blooms yellow.

S. variegata, now a part of the genus *Orbea*, is an extremely variable species. Its flower, 3 in. (8 cm) wide, is yellow with spots in red to dark brown.

Location: Light to sun all year, but not strong noon sun. In winter at 50°F (10°C).

Care: In summer, water very sparingly; in winter, in a cool location, do not water at all. The shoots, however, should not shrink. Feed only in summer and that only once a month with cactus food.

Propagation: By division or by cuttings that have dried before being planted. This vegetative way of propagation is generally the one recommended because *Stapelia* has such a strong tendency to mutate that propagation from seed is unreliable. It is not impossible, though, so if you want to try it, just be prepared to get a form of the plant that you did not expect.

Pests and Diseases: Root rot if the plant stands in water. One danger is a fungus called "the black death." It causes black spots to appear, especially at the base of the shoots, which then die off, There is no cure.

Uses: Attractive, flowering succulent. Suited to hydroponics.

Stapelia grandiflora

Stapelia grandiflora

As the name implies, *Stapelia grandiflora* has large flowers.

The intense odor of *Stapelia* blossoms serves to attract certain pollinators. It is not present in all species.

The root system of *Stapelia* is shallow; it grows well in flat dishes.

Stephanotis – Streptocarpus

Stephanotis floribunda

In winter, when it rests, keep cool and just barely moist (this is important for flowering). After the buds have set, mark the pot to make sure it is always facing the light the same way. Tie shoots to the trellis, pruning ones that have become too long.

Propagation: By tip cuttings, at 77–86°F (25–30°C).

Pests and Diseases: Aphids if too warm in the winter; yellow leaves if light is insufficient; buds dry before opening if the plant is kept too dry.

Uses: A houseplant; to twine in large window gardens, small greenhouses, and conservatories.

Bird of paradise, official flower of the City of Los Angeles, is a stemless member of the banana family with leathery, evergreen leaves about 16 in. (40 cm) long on long petioles. The long-lasting flower is surrounded by a bract folded into a boat shape. The bright orange and sky-blue petals emerge from it. Since it takes years for the plant to first bloom, *S. reginae* is expensive, sold as a cut flower or as a precious container plant.

Location: Sunny, protected from wind, outdoors in summer. In winter, light at 46–59°F (8–15°C).

Care: Keep evenly moist all year. Feed every two weeks. In winter, avoid waterlogging. After it has bloomed, repot in heavy but well-draining soil.

Propagation: By division of older plants, when repotting; from seed. Seedlings bloom only after three or four years.

Pests and Diseases: Scale insects and aphids.

Uses: A spectacular specimen plant for the conservatory or a container.

Stephanotis needs to be unobstructed by curtains or other plants. It needs an airy, open position. It has to have soft water; otherwise the leaves will turn yellow.

In southern regions, bird of paradise needs to be partially shaded because the sun is so intense.

STEPHANOTIS FLORIBUNDA
Stephanotis

Family: Milkweed, *Asclepiadaceae*
Native Habitat: Madagascar
Flowering Time: Late spring through summer

Stephanotis is a twining plant. Its leaves are leathery and dark green, a bit like those of the rubber tree. In the leaf axils it puts out loose umbels of white, fragrant, star flowers. The plant's 3.2 ft.- (1 m-) long shoots need a trellis, but if there is no room for one, it will grow on circular wires. Planted in a conservatory bed, it can cover an area 13–20 ft. (4–6 m) square.

Location: Very light and airy, but not sunny. In summer at 64–72°F (18–22°C); in winter at 54–61°F (12–16°C).

Care: Early spring to late summer, water and spray with tepid, soft water and feed every two weeks.

STRELITZIA REGINAE
Bird of paradise

Family: Banana, *Musaceae*
Native Habitat: South Africa
Flowering Time: Late winter to midsummer

Strelitzia reginae

Streptocarpus *hybrid*

Graceful *Streptocarpus* hybrids look like a delicate bouquet.

Streptocarpus saxorum is a relatively new, pleasing hanging plant.

STREPTOCARPUS
Cape primrose

Family: Gesneriad, *Gesneriaceae*
Native Habitat: Tropical Africa
Flowering Time: Late spring to fall

The leaves of the Cape primrose grow in a rosettelike formation on the ground. They are long and soft. The tubular flowers rise above them, white, pink, red, light or dark blue, or violet. Some forms have a contrasting throat or curly petals. Some hybrids have leaves without petioles, as does the blue variety 'Constant Nymph,' a parent of many further varieties. There are also 'Rosa Nymph,' pink; 'Maassens Wit,' white; and 'Margaret,' a dark violet flowering variety.

Well known and popular are the Wiesmoor and the Wendiandii hybrids. Occasionally, you will find the very rare species *S. wendiandii* and *S. grandis.* They form only one single leaf, which in the case of *S. wendiandii,* is scarlet underneath and—under optimal conditions—can grow to 3.2 ft. (1 m). Since the plant has no other surface for photosynthesis, it is vital to preserve this one leaf. Thus, for example, it cannot lie on the ground, because of the danger of fungal infections.

New on the market is the hanging or trailing Cape primrose, *S. saxorum.* It has small, almost round leaves and flowers on long stalks. It blooms from spring to fall and is good in a hanging basket. It can even tolerate the dry air in heated rooms.

The seed capsule of *Streptocarpus* is twisted or turned, which gives rise to its Latin name.
Location: Light to partial shade all year at 59–68°F (15–20°C).
Care: Keep evenly but moderately moist with soft, tepid water; if quite warm, increase humidity. In winter,

keep cooler and water less. Early spring to the end of summer, feed weekly; in winter rarely. Older plants become ungainly; it is good to raise young plants as replacements. The plant looks its best in the second year.
Propagation: By division, from seed, or by leaf cuttings.
Pests and Diseases: Aphids, spider mites, and thrips if air is too dry; leaf edges turn brown if too wet; chlorosis if hard water is used.
Uses: Richly blooming houseplant. Suited to hydroponics.

Streptocarpus saxorum

TIP

The sap of Streptocarpus has been known, in rare cases, to cause mild skin irritation.

Syngonium – Tecomaria

Here are some very attractive varieties of *Syngonium podophyllum*, such as 'Albolineatum,' with white leaf veins; 'Emerald Gem,' shiny green; 'Imperial White,' edged in white and green; and 'Trileaf Wonder,' which has dark green leaves with white veining.

The low-growing *Tagetes patula* hybrids are well suited to balcony planters and dishes.

Syngonium podophyllum

Hybrid Tagetes patula

SYNGONIUM
Syngonium

Family: Arum, *Araceae*
Native Habitat: Central and South America
Flowering Time: Early summer

This member of the arum family has much in common with philodendron. There are climbing and creeping species, with green or variegated foliage. The leaves undergo a transformation: in youth they are arrow-shaped; their mature form, varying with the species, is divided or lobed. Usually the youthful form is offered for sale. Only mature plants bloom: the inside of the bract of the green inflorescence is scarlet. Most frequently seen is *S. podophyllum*, which has some handsome varieties with colored and marked leaves. The plant contains substances irritating to the skin and mucous membranes.

Location: Light to partial shade all year; warm and humid.
Care: Keep moderately moist and spray with soft, tepid water year-round; feed every two weeks.
Propagation: By tip or shoot cuttings with bottom heating.
Pests and Diseases: Scale insects.
Uses: Twining or hanging plant for the house or for a window greenhouse. Suited to hydroponics.

TAGETES HYBRIDS
Marigold

Family: Aster, *Asteraceae*
Native Habitat: Mexico, Guatemala
Flowering Time: Late spring through fall

The annual marigold came to Europe 400 years ago and has become a favorite summer flower. The dark green, compound leaves make a strong contrast to the velvety flower, be it yellow, yellow-brown, or orange. The plant has a strong smell, which has given it humorous common names all over the world. The plants on sale now are hybrids, such as the *Tagetes erecta* hybrids, the *Tagetes patula* hybrids, and the *Tagetes tenuifolia* varieties.

Location: Sun or partial shade outdoors.
Care: Keep evenly moist and feed weekly. Remove dead flowers regularly to encourage new ones.
Propagation: From seed in the spring. Pinch out young plants to promote bushy form.
Pests and Diseases: Slugs.
Uses: A very lovely flowering plant for planters, dishes, and troughs.

Tagetes excretes a sap that kills root nematodes. For this reason it is often used in mixed plantings.

Tecoma stans

Tecomaria capensis

TECOMARIA CAPENSIS
Cape honeysuckle

Family: Trumpet creeper, *Bignoniaceae*
Native Habitat: South Africa
Flowering Time: Summer and fall

The most remarkable feature of the Cape honeysuckle is the brilliant flowers, usually orange but sometimes yellow, that appear at the ends of the shoots. The pinnately compound leaves are a deep green, smaller than on other trumpet creepers. In bright, warm conservatories, the plant keeps its foliage and blooms on into winter.
Location: Full sun and warm; in summer outdoors. In winter at 41–50°F (5–10°C), it can be stored dark, but then prune it back to the ground.
Care: Until the end of summer, water freely and feed once a week. Provide strong climbing support. Prune vigorously if required.
Propagation: From seed; by tip or shoot cuttings with bottom heat; by tip layering.
Pests and Diseases: Aphids.
Uses: Container and conservatory plant.

The trumpet shrub will bloom almost all year if it is kept warm, so the conservatory bed is the best place for it. It is important to remove seed capsules as they are formed, or they will cause the plant to cease blooming.

The Cape honeysuckle, *Tecomaria capensis*, is ideal for standard training. Specimens, kept bright and relatively cool in the spring, bloom about four weeks earlier than those kept in a greenhouse.

TECOMA STANS
Trumpet shrub

Family: Trumpet creeper, *Bignoniaceae*
Native Habitat: Florida, Texas, Mexico, Central America
Flowering Time: In summer

The trumpet shrub can reach 20 ft. (6 m) when fully grown. It blooms very profusely, producing veritable bouquets of pale yellow flowers. This evergreen shrub or small tree has compound leaves.
Location: Full sun, warm; in summer outdoors, protected from rain. In winter, light, at least at 50–54°F (10–12°C).
Care: In summer, feed weekly and water moderately; in winter only enough to keep the leaves from falling. Prune vigorously after it has flowered, to maintain the bushy habit. Remove the seed capsules.
Propagation: By tip or stem cuttings with bottom heating; seed.
Pests and Diseases: Spider mites, whiteflies.
Uses: A beautiful container and conservatory plant for collectors looking for something new. The trumpet shrub can be standard trained fairly easily.

331

Tetrastigma – Tibouchina

Tetrastigma voinierianum

Tetrastigma voinierianum, the ayo, is often used for greening the walls surrounding a pool. Even in dark corners it grows and spreads vigorously.

Thunbergia grandiflora (below) is known for the unique blue of its flowers. In contrast to the related Black-eyed Susan vine, *T. alata*, shown on the right, it is neither easy to find nor easy to tend.

Tetrastigma is a climbing plant with five-lobed toothed leaves, matted densely brown on the underside. The plant spreads too vigorously for a living room. It regularly adds several meters per season to the length of its shoots. The leaf can grow up to 10 in. (25 cm) wide.

Location: Light to partial shade and warm all year. In winter at 50–59°F (10–15°C).

Care: In summer water freely; in winter, if its position is cooler, water less. Feed weekly. Repot every spring into ever-larger containers, or better still plant in the ground. Prune energetically as needed. Provide strong climbing support.

Propagation: By cuttings with at least one eye, with bottom heat.

Pests and Diseases: Rarely.

Uses: Ideal for large, bright, not-too-cold stairwells, greenhouses, conservatories, and pool areas.

TETRASTIGMA VOINIERIANUM
Ayo

Family: Grape, *Vitaceae*
Native Habitat: Tonkin, Vietnam
Flowering Time: Seldom blooms in cultivation

Thunbergia alata

THUNBERGIA ALATA
Black-eyed Susan vine

Family: Acanthus, *Acanthaceae*
Native Habitat: South Africa
Flowering Time: Summer through fall

Black-eyed Susan vine, a perennial climbing plant, is generally grown as an annual. The funnel-shaped flowers, usually yellow, sometimes orange, have a black center. They glow among the dark green, cordate leaves, on their long petioles. The variety 'Alba' blooms white, with black center; 'Fryeri' is yellow with a white center; and 'lutea' blooms pure yellow.

Location: Light to sunny, outdoors; indoors only with lots of fresh air.

Care: In summer, water freely; avoid waterlogging. Feed every two weeks. Provide a trellis. Overwintering is not worthwhile.

Propagation: From seed, starting in late winter.

Pests and Diseases: Aphids, spider mites, whiteflies.

Uses: A popular annual climber for large pots, containers, planters, or for underplanting container plants.

Thunbergia grandiflora

THE MOST BEAUTIFUL PLANTS FROM A TO Z

Thymophylla tenuiloba

THYMOPHYLLA TENUILOBA
Dyssodia

Family: Aster, *Asteraceae*
Native Habitat: Southern United States, Mexico
Flowering Time: Summer through fall

The name of this member of the aster family has been changed from *Thymophylla tenuiloba* to *Dyssodia tenuiloba*. It is a 6 in.- (15 cm-) high balcony plant that spreads out; its leaves are finely lobed and delicate. The daisylike flowers are yellow, about 0.8 in. (2 cm) wide, and very abundant.
Location: Sunny and warm, outdoors.
Care: During growth, keep moderately moist and feed lightly every week. Remove dead blooms to encourage new ones.
Propagation: From seed in late winter, at 64–68°F (18–20°C).
Pests and Diseases: Aphids, powdery mildew.
Uses: A beautiful long-flowering hanging plant for the terrace or the balcony. Use in planters or as underplanting for container plants.

Tibouchina urvilleana

TIBOUCHINA URVILLEANA
Glory bush

Family: Melastome, *Melastomataceae*
Native Habitat: Brazil
Flowering Time: Midsummer to late spring

The glory bush has remarkable flowers: they are 3 in. (7.5 cm) wide, velvety, and violet-blue. They sit in groups on the branches and keep on opening over the period from midsummer to late spring. The leaves, 5 in. (12 cm) long and deeply veined, also look as if covered with velvet. Their edges turn red when it is cold. Only one thing is not quite perfect with *Tibouchina*—its attenuated, unbranched habit. Pruning it several times can correct this to some extent.
Location: In summer, light to sunny, but no strong noon sun; outdoors. In winter, light, 50–59°F (10–15°C).
Care: Water well in summer; keep somewhat drier in winter. Feed weekly until the end of summer; in winter, if you carry the plant to the next season, feed monthly. Pinch out the plant several times in the summer to encourage branching.
Propagation: By semiwoody cuttings at 77°F (25°C) and with high humidity.
Pests and Diseases: Rarely.
Uses: A winter-flowering plant for not-very-cold glass structures.

After a mild winter, dyssodia will reproduce itself from seeds.

Because of its leggy form, *Tibouchina* looks best if planted three or more cuttings to one container.

The containers of flowering *Tibouchina* should not be moved about: the buds sit rather lightly on the branches and are prone to fall off.

Tillandsia – Tolmiea

Tillandsia lindenii is one of the green tillandsias.

In Holland, *Tolmiea menziesii* is called "baby on mother's lap."

Picture next page: An epiphytic support, richly set with diverse gray tillandsias.

Tillandsia lindenii

TILLANDSIA
Tillandsia

Family: Bromeliad, *Bromeliaceae*
Native Habitat: Tropical and subtropical Americas
Flowering Time: Spring or summer, according to species

Tillandsia can grow in very different climatic conditions: in tropical rain forests, in dry savannas, in mountainous regions and their misty forests, and even higher up, beyond the tree line. There are gray and green tillandsias. The epiphytic gray ones grow on trees, cacti, or naked rocks, holding on with their roots. Their whitish-gray color is imparted to these tillandsias by the nutrients they take up using their suction cups. One well-known species is *T. usneoides*, Spanish moss, which looks like a dense beard of thin, gray threads. Even more beautiful are *T. argentea, T. funckiana, T. ionantha,* and *T. lorentziana.*

Green, terrestrial tillandsias are seldom seen in cultivation. The most common member of this group is *T. cyanea*; its narrow, green leaves form a 16 in.- (40 cm-) wide rosette. The inflorescence comprises greenish to red bracts set like roof tiles in an oval shape; between them short-lived blue flowers appear.

T. lindenii is very similar, but the stalk of its flower is taller.
Location: Gray tillandsias: full sun to light; in summer outdoors; in winter 50–59°F (10–15°C). Green tillandsias: light, warm, and humid all year; not under 59°F (15°C).
Care: Gray tillandsias are attached to cork or bark. Mist them, using soft water, once or twice a day through spring and summer; once or twice a week in winter. Once a month, mist with a very weak solution of plant food. Keep green tillandsias lightly moist and provide atmospheric humidity. Feed once a month with half-diluted flower fertilizer. Repot in orchid soil when needed.
Propagation: By offsets; Spanish moss by shoots of any length.
Pests and Diseases: Rarely. Green tillandsias tend to rot if too wet.
Uses: Gray tillandsias for epiphytic supports; green tillandsias for enclosed glass cases and window greenhouses.

TOLMIEA MENZIESII
Tolmiea, piggyback plant

Family: Saxifrage, *Saxifragaceae*
Native Habitat: North America down to California
Flowering Time: Seldom blooms in cultivation

The piggyback plant is a small perennial, 8–12 in. (20–30 cm) high, with heart-shaped, hairy leaves. In the hollow at the leaf base, new plants are grown. The plant's shoots will creep or hang. It is hard now to find a specimen in a nursery, but in the countryside, it is still passed from one plant lover to the next.
Location: Light to partial shade all year; in summer outdoors. In winter at least at 50°F (10°C).
Care: Water generously in summer and feed every two weeks. Keep moderately moist in winter.
Propagation: By plantlets on the leaves; by offshoots.
Pests and Diseases: Aphids.
Uses: A foliage plant for pots and hanging baskets.

Tolmiea menziesii

Trachelospermum – Tradescantia

To enjoy the flowers of the Chinese star jasmine in the winter, keep it in a container and leave it outdoors until the real, cold frosts begin.

In their oriental habitats, windmill palms reach up to 40 ft. (12 m) in height.

Trachelospermum jasminoides

TRACHELOSPERMUM JASMINOIDES
Chinese star jasmine

Family: Dogbane, *Apocynaceae*
Native Habitat: Japan, Korea, China
Flowering Time: Summer; in the conservatory much earlier

Trachelospermum is a slow-growing, evergreen shrub. Its leaves are dark green, leathery, and shiny. Its white, jasminelike flowers exude a strong perfume. The plant is poisonous in all its parts, and the scent of the flowers can cause headaches.
Location: Sun to shade; in summer outdoors. In winter 41–50°F (5–10°C); can be stored dark.
Care: During growth, water moderately. To the end of summer, feed weekly. Train to a trellis or into a pyramid. The plant has to stand cool in winter in order to set flowers.
Propagation: By tip cuttings.
Pests and Diseases: Scale insects, aphids, spider mites, whiteflies.
Uses: Climbing plant for cool conservatories; ground cover for containers. Suited to bonsai.

Trachycarpus fortuneï

TRACHYCARPUS FORTUNEI
Windmill palm

Family: Palm, *Arecaceae*
Native Habitat: China, Japan
Flowering Time: Early summer

The windmill palm is easy to grow and relatively hardy. The diameter of the leaves can be 35 in. (90 cm), and the plant can reach 10 ft. (3 m) in a container. The leaf petioles are finely toothed, and the trunk is covered with a network of fibers. The windmill palm has become completely established in warmer regions of Europe, England, and North America. It can be planted fairly far north, but must be well protected against frost when the mercury drops below 14°F (–10°C).

Location: In summer, sun to partial shade; In winter, keep either dormant and dark 23–32°F (–5–0°C), or light and warm.
Care: During growth, keep moderately moist and feed once a week to the end of summer. If the plant was overwintered in the dark, it needs to be moved into the light very gradually. Sunburn can be a danger.
Propagation: From seed; sprouting takes one to four months.
Pests and Diseases: Spider mites and scale insects; heart rot in winter storage with insufficient air circulation.
Uses: Young plants for the house; otherwise, a container plant.

TIP

Wear gloves when cutting the Chinese star jasmine: its sap is poisonous.

THE MOST BEAUTIFUL PLANTS FROM A TO Z

TRADESCANTIA
Tradescantia; spiderwort

Family: Spiderwort, *Commelinaceae*
Native Habitat: South America
Flowering Time: From spring to late summer

Tradescantia is one of the easiest of house plants; it is widely used in hanging baskets.

Most common is *T. fluminensis*, (formerly *T. albiflora*), which has small pointed, oval leaves. Its varieties are 'aurea-vittata,' with yellowish, longitudinal stripes; 'Rochford Silver,' strongly marked in snow white; and the cultivar 'tricolor,' a three-colored form.

T. cerinthoides (*T. blossfeldiana*) has shaggy, brownish leaves, red underneath. Its 'Variegata' form displays cream-colored stripes.

T. navicularis (*Callisia navicularis*), the "Moses in the cradle," is an item that only collectors would want.

T. pallida's variety 'Purple Heart' is without doubt the star among tradescantias. Formerly *Setcretia purpurea*, it grows 16 in. (40 cm) high and bears tapering scarlet leaves with hairy edges. Their beautiful color develops best in very bright light with little exposure to sun. Sad to say, the shoots are rather fragile. The axial blossoms of this variety are white and small. The leaves of *T. zebrina* (syn. *Zebrina pendula*) are red beneath and striped lengthwise in silver on top.

Location: Light, airy, and at room temperature all year. Variegated

Tradescentia fluminensis

forms need more light; green ones can, if necessary, be in partial shade.

Care: Keep lightly moist; feed every two weeks through spring and summer. In a heated room, spray frequently. Raise new plants every year, as the shoots will become spindly and leafless.

Propagation: By tip cuttings in soil or water; several cuttings to one pot.

Pests and Diseases: Aphids; brown leaf tips indicate too wet or too dry treatment.

Uses: A problem-free hanging plant for the house; rich ground cover for the conservatory.

Tradescantias are easy foliage plants with many beautiful varieties to choose from. Inspected up close, the small flowers turn out to be interesting and colorful, like the blossom of the "Moses in the cradle," *Tradescantia navicularis*, below.

Tradescentia blossfeldiana

Flowering Tradescentia navicularis

TIP

Always position *T. pallida* (*Setcretia*) away from traffic because its shoots break easily under a careless touch. Water without wetting the leaves, because water leaves unsightly spots.

Tropaeolum – Tulipa

Vivid orange nasturtiums look good with purple petunias. Many people do not know that nasturtium is an edible plant; the leaves can be added to a salad, and the buds make decent "capers," pickled in vinegar and oil.

Tropaeolum hybrids
Nasturtium

Family: Nasturtium, *Tropaeolaceae*
Native Habitat: Chile, Peru, Ecuador
Flowering Time: Late spring through fall.

Nasturtium, *T. majus,* is raised as an annual. It has shieldlike leaves. The colors offered include yellows, oranges, and velvety reds; these also occur in the many varicolored flowers. In addition to the species, which grows shoots about 6.5 ft. (2 m) long, there are compact varieties, such as 'nanum,' and double varieties, such as the yellow 'Nanum Plenum,' not to mention many hybrids.

T. peregrinum, the canary vine nasturtium, is a species that climbs up to 13 ft. (4 m) high. Its flowers are canary yellow and have fringed edges; its leaves have five to seven lobes.

Location: Full sun.
Care: Water freely; no fertilizer required. Climbing varieties need a support, the most appropriate one being chicken wire.
Propagation: From seed, in early spring if indoors; or sow in late spring directly into balcony planters and dishes.
Pests and Diseases: Aphids are strongly attracted; spider mites.
Uses: Twining plant for creating a screen or to color a wall. Low-growing species for balcony boxes, dishes, and as an underplanting.

Tropaeolum *hybrids*

Several low-growing potted tulips

Tulipa
Tulip

Family: Lily, *Liliaceae*
Native Habitat: Asia Minor, Asia
Flowering Time: In the spring

The tulips best suited to balcony planters and dishes are the simple or double, early-blooming varieties. These usually grow 10-12 in. (25-30 cm), at most 16 in. (40 cm) high and thus are not so susceptible to wind damage. The selection among the varieties and hybrids is endless, covering every color except blue.

Also good for planters are the various wild or botanical tulips, such as *T. fosteriana, T. greigii,* or *T. kaufmanniana*. These also have numerous hybrids.

T. tarda, an interesting tulip with several blossoms, grows only 4 in. (10 cm) high, as does *T. humilis* (syn. *T. pulchelia, T. violacea*).

Finally, there is the possibility of forcing tulip bulbs to bloom indoors during the Christmas season. For this purpose, the early tulips mentioned are well suited, as well as Mendel, Triumph, and species tulips.

Location: Sun to partial shade; cool indoors; outdoors free of frost.
Care, in general: Store bulbs of potted tulips after the leaves have dried and plant in the garden during autumn. Keep forced tulips cool, light, and slightly moist after they have finished blooming. After foliage wilts, store dry bulbs till fall and plant them in the garden. From after sprouting until the leaves wilt, keep moderately moist. Feed once or twice between sprouting and flowering.
Forcing bulbs to flower indoors in winter: Start the process in early fall for Christmas; for later flowering, start anytime till late fall. Plant bulbs three or four to a pot, with

Tulipa tarda

tips just showing above the soil. Water very well and bury in the garden under 8 in. (20 cm) of soil. Place a layer of loose material on top to make sure that the pots can be dug up despite frost. Alternatively, the pots can be kept in a cool cellar buried inside a box of sand. Keep the soil lightly moist. After two months, take up the pots from the garden and move to a cool, dark place. When shoots are about 4 in. (10 cm) long, move the pots to a bright spot at room temperature.
Planting tulips in balcony boxes and dishes: Plant the bulbs in their final receptacles to the depth of 4 in. (10 cm). Place them in a dark, cool place that does not freeze. After they have sprouted, move them to brighter quarters, increase watering, and add liquid fertilizer to the water once.
Propagation: By bulbs.
Pests and Diseases: Bulbs will rot if they are too wet in the winter.
Uses: Spring display for rooms, balconies, and patios.

After a long winter, forced tulips in their pots are a welcome reminder of spring to come.

A dwarf among tulips, *Tulipa tarda* is only 4 in. (10 cm) high. Because it produces many flowers, it still fills up a pot very quickly.

TIP

In early spring, you can buy forced tulips in bud that can be placed or planted in boxes, dishes, or troughs.

Vanda – Viola

The aerial roots of vandas are remarkably long and thick: they are really nutritional storage organs. In the wild, the epiphytic plant sends these from the tall tree where it is attached all the way down to the ground.

Verbena is a very frequently seen balcony plant. The selection of varieties is correspondingly large.

TIP

A new verbena variety, 'Imagination,' bears blue-violet flowers on densely branched shoots. Since these grow to about 20 in. (50 cm) long, the plant is ideal for hanging baskets. 'Imagination' has received many prizes, and its seeds are also for sale.

Vanda coerulea

Verbena hybrid

VANDA
Vanda

Family: Orchid, *Orchidaceae*
Native Habitat: Tropical Asia, India, China, the Philippines,
Flowering Time: Varies with the species

Vanda is a magnificent epiphytic orchid that can grow 3.2 ft. (1 m) high. Its straplike leaves, arranged in two ranks, are rough and leathery. The aerial roots are very thick. The upright inflorescence reaches sideways out of the axil. Perhaps the most lovely species is *V. coerulea*, its flower about 4 in. (10 cm) wide, pale blue, with darker veins. The flower of *V. cristata* is about 2 in. (5 cm), waxy and fragrant; it is colored yellow-green and blood

red. *Vanda* hybrids are easier to keep and have larger flowers. For windowsill gardens, the hybrids of *Vanda* and *Ascocentrum* are recommended.
Location: Light to sun all year; humid and warm at 64–68°F (18–20°C). Always shield from the noon sun.
Care: Water generously with soft, tepid water in the summer. Spray often, including the aerial roots. During growth, add orchid food to water every two weeks. Repot only every three years to protect the roots. Because of the long aerial roots, vandas are best planted in orchid baskets.
Propagation: By careful division.
Pests and Diseases: Buds will fall if too cool in winter; roots rot if they are injured.
Uses: For large, enclosed, window greenhouses, warm and humid greenhouses, or conservatories.

VERBENA HYBRIDS
Verbena

Family: Verbena, *Verbenaceae*
Native Habitat: South America
Flowering Time: Late spring to midfall

Verbena can be a herbaceous perennial or a subshrub; it is raised as an annual. It blooms profusely. The parent species of modern hybrids are first of all *Verbena peruviana*, responsible for the vivid verbena red, and *V. phlogifolia* and *V. incisa*, which contributed the pink and violet tones.

As for their fragrance, the hybrids owe it to *Verbena platensis*. The hybrids' flowers open in dense, umbellate spikes. They bloom white, pink, red, purple, blue, or violet, with or without a white eye. Most varieties do not grow taller than 10–12 in. (25–30 cm).

Some pretty varieties are 'Kristall' (white); 'Blaze' (scarlet); 'Amethyst' (blue); 'Madame Dubarry' (burgundy red); and 'Defiance' (deep red with an eye).

Some verbenas have long, hanging shoots. Descendants of *V. tenera*, they include the 'Kleopatra' or Italian verbenas.

These verbenas stand out by their ability to withstand rain; they can even tolerate standing in water for prolonged periods.

Location: Sunny, shielded from wind, outdoors.

Care: Water freely, but avoid waterlogging; give diluted fertilizer once a week. Remove dead flowers to promote more blooms.

Propagation: From seed. The seed's ability to sprout is limited: you may get fewer seedlings than expected.

Pests and Diseases: Aphids, spider mites, whiteflies, powdery mildew.

Uses: A good-looking flowering plant for balconies, dishes, and hanging baskets.

Viola x wittrockiana 'Velour Bleu'

VIOLA WITTROCKIANA HYBRIDS
Pansy

Family: Violet, *Violaceae*
Native Habitat: Europe, Siberia
Flowering Time: Varies with the species, fall to spring

The pansy is the most beloved of all spring-flowering plants. Over 100 years of breeding have produced well-formed and beautifully colored flowers and amply blooming, hardy plants. There are early or late bloomers, large or small flowers, single or many-colored blooms, flowers with or without an eye. The selection is so vast that it is easiest to go to the nursery and pick out the plants or seeds that one likes. One new hybrid worth mentioning is the F_1— a miniature pansy with many varieties of its own.

Location: Sun to partial shade outdoors. The plant is hardy.

Care: During growth, never allow the plants to dry out; feed every two weeks. Remove wilted flowers. In very mild regions it is possible to plant pansies in the fall, but if you want early blooms for dishes and planters, wait till spring to plant.

Propagation: From seed in summer. Seeds harvested at home will not reproduce true to the variety.

Uses: An old-fashioned spring bloomer for planters, boxes, dishes, troughs, and beds.

Italian verbenas

Italian verbenas produce cascading shoots. They are known for their ability to tolerate rain.

The parent species of our garden pansy are: *Viola tricolor*, Johnny-jump-up, *V. cornuta*, *V. lutea*, and *V. altaica*, a wild form from the Altai Mountains.

Viola Wittrockiana hybrids

TIP

Pansies planted in the fall need to be fertilized; do this when the soil is able to absorb the plant food during a thaw.

Vriesea – Vuylstekeara

The green-leafed *Vriesea* hybrids with their bright red flower spikes are always found in nurseries, along with the ever-present *Vriesea splendens*. You can also find some hybrids with varicolored flowers, products either of *V. carinata* or *V. psittacina*, the parrot bromelia.

VRIESEA
Vriesea

Family: Bromeliad, *Bromeliaceae*
Native Habitat: Central and South America
Flowering Time: The hybrids will bloom any time of year

Most vrieseas are plants with a tight rosette of long, narrow, green leaves. The leaves tend to be banded, spotted, or marbled. The flower spike comprises small blossoms and bright bracts in one or several colors. The little flowers between the bracts wilt in a few days, but the vivid yellow or red bracts will last for months. The plant dies back after it has bloomed, but it usually has produced offsets to replace itself. It does take years until these will in turn bloom and, with some species, the offsets never will flower in the home.

The best-known species is *V. splendens*, its leaves cross-striped, its flat flower spikes a shimmering red. Particularly gorgeous varieties are: 'Flammendes Schwert,' 'Major,' 'Meyers Favorite,' and 'Splendid.' The *Vriesea* hybrids are best suited to being maintained in the living room; they are less sensitive than the pure species, and there are many to choose from, e.g., 'Angelina,' 'Chantrieri,' 'Christiane,' 'Favorite,' 'Flame Gigant,' 'Gnom,' 'Illustris,' 'Rex,' or 'Vigeri.'

Location: Light to partial shade all year; warm and humid. Bottom heat of at least 64°F (18°C) is important.

Care: In summer, keep lightly moist with soft, tepid water. Add well-diluted fertilizer to the water every two weeks. Spray often. Except in winter, the leaf cup can be filled with water. In winter, water less, but continue to provide indirect humidity.

Propagation: By offsets, which are removed only when they are half as large as the original plant.

Pests and Diseases: Leaves are damaged by excessive wetness, as well as by hot, dry air.

Uses: For window greenhouses; hybrids for the windowsill. Suited to hydroponics.

Vriesea splendens

Vriesea *hybrid*

x Vuylstekeara

X Vuylstekeara was introduced in 1912. The unpronounceable name derives from that of its breeder, Vuylsteke. The loveliest and best-known hybrids are x V. Cambria and x V. Cambria 'Plush.'

X VUYLSTEKEARA
Vuylstekeara

Family: Orchid, *Orchidaceae*
Native Habitat: South America
Flowering Time: Winter through spring

One of the most beautiful of orchids, x. *Vuylstekeara* is a horticultural cultivar with starlike blossoms. The flower was created as far back as 1912; it received several international awards. The parent species were *Miltoniopsis, Odontoglossum*, and *Cochlioda*. The most significant variety is 'Plush'; it grows 30 in. (75 cm) high and has a dark red flower with a large, red-and-white lip. Other lovely varieties are Cambria 'Orange,' Edna 'Stamperland,' and 'Estella Jewel.'

Another spectacular cultivar is Cambria 'Lensings Favorit.' It was bred in 1931. Its magnificent red color is due to its connection to *Cochlioda noezliana*, while the lip clearly shows its ties to *Odontoglossum harryanum* and *Miltoniopsis vixillaria*. It is not possible to isolate the contribution made to this hybrid by *Odontoglossum crispum*. Edna 'Stamperland,' which was created ten years earlier, also bears the characteristic red color of *Cochlioda noezliana*.

Location: Shade to partial shade all year; humid. In summer outdoors at 50–61°F (10–16°C).
Care: In summer, keep evenly moist with soft water. Never have the plant in standing water Add well-diluted orchid food to the water every third time. In winter, water just to prevent the pseudobulbs from drying out. Every third year, when the pseudobulbs have grown over the rim of the pot, repot the plant into orchid soil.

Propagation: By division when repotting the plant; three to four pseudobulbs per pot.
Pests and Diseases: Rarely.
Uses: An undemanding orchid for living areas and for conservatories.

TIP

It is possible to hang x Vuylstekeara in the open shade of a tree in the garden during the summer.

Washingtonia – Yucca

Both species of *Washingtonia* are ideal container plants. They can tolerate light frost. Planted in the ground, *W. filifera* can withstand cold down to 12°F (–11°C).
Contrary to its name, *W. robusta* is less tough: it is hardy to 27°F (–3°C). The genus is named after George Washington (1732–1799).

To enjoy *Xanthosoma lindenii*, you will have to put it in a window greenhouse or warm conservatory. In a living room, the plant cannot survive because to fulfill its complex needs in that environment is almost impossible.

Washingtonias planted on the Côte d'Azur

Xanthosoma lindenii

XANTHOSOMA LINDENII
Xanthosoma

Family: Arum, *Araceae*
Native Habitat: Colombia
Flowering Time: Seldom blooms in cultivation

Xanthosoma, nowadays classed with *Caladium*, grows out of a tuberlike rhizome. The dark green, arrow-shaped leaves stand on long petioles and are dramatically marked in white along the veins. The variety 'magnificum' is especially attractively patterned in green and white. The plant contains substances irritating to the skin and mucous membranes.
Location: Partial to complete shade; warm and humid all year (64–72°F (18–22°C).)
Care: During growth, spring to fall, keep lightly moist and feed every two weeks. In winter during its rest, keep the plant cooler (not under 64°F (18°C)) and reduce watering. Do not allow root ball to dry out
Propagation: By division.
Pests and Diseases: Spider mites if the air is too dry; rot if waterlogged.
Uses: A beautiful foliage plant for dark, warm places.

WASHINGTONIA
Washington Palm

Family: Palm, *Arecaceae*
Native Habitat: Arizona, California, Mexico
Flowering Time: Seldom blooms in cultivation

There are only two species of Washington palm. Native to California and Arizona is the *W. filifera*, with foliage colored gray-green and rather noticeable fibrous threads that hang from its leaf-frond segments.

The foliage of *W. robusta* is shiny green. In its native Mexico, when the leaves dry and sag downward, they are allowed to remain and cover the trunk. This mantle of dead leaves leads to the common name "petticoat palm." Both of these fan palms grow well in containers.
Location: Light to sun all year; airy; in summer outdoors. Never near heating units. In winter, 41–46°F (5–8°C).
Care: Water moderately in summer; avoid waterlogging. Reduce water in winter. Feed every two weeks from spring to late summer. Cut off dead leaf fronds. Repot into deeper containers as needed.
Propagation: From seed; sprouting takes about two months.
Pests and Diseases: Spider mites and thrips if too dry in winter; plant will rot if too wet in winter.
Uses: A very good-looking fan palm for warm conservatories.

Yucca aloifolia

Yucca gloriosa

Every now and then, you will run across a short-stemmed *Yucca gloriosa*. It takes many years of care for the plant to develop its mighty inflorescence consisting of innumerable white bells.

Yucca tends to be quite tolerant of frost. *Yucca aloifolia* and *Yucca elephantipes* can withstand quite low temperatures.

Propagation: By stem cuttings, each piece no shorter than 4 in. (10 cm); by leaf batches; by offsets.

Pests and Diseases: Scale insects; yellow leaves are due to dark position; stem rot is a sign of excessive wetness.

Uses: Container plant; indoor tree for cool rooms, stairwells, and conservatories.

YUCCA
Yucca

Family: Agave, *Agavaceae*
Native Habitat: United States, Mexico
Flowering Time: Seldom blooms in cultivation

Yuccas form trunks that carry a dense batch of strong, dark green leaves. The two species generally offered are *Y. aloifolia*, with narrow leaves that taper to a point, and *Y. elephantipes*, which has slightly arching leaves, somewhat wider. *Y. aloifolia* usually builds a single, tall trunk. The leaves are about 20 in. (50 cm) long, 1 in. (3 cm) wide, and sharply serrated at the edges. The tip is sharp enough to cause injury. This species has several handsome variegated forms, regrettably rare in nurseries, such as: 'quadricolor,' 'tricolor,' and 'purpurea.'

The most commonly found species, *Y. elephantipes*, has a shorter trunk, thickened at the base; it branches occasionally. The leaves, shaped like a sword, grow 20–40 in. (50–100 cm) long.

Location: Full sun and fresh air all year; in summer outdoors. In winter not over 50°F (10°C).

Care: Water regularly spring to fall, only sporadically in winter. Avoid waterlogging. Allow the root ball to dry before watering again. Feed weekly, spring to late summer.

Yucca elephantipes

Zantedeschia – Zebrina

Zantedeschia aethiopica, the white calla lily, is the one most commonly found and is hardy in mild parts of the temperate zone. *Z. elliothiana* (with yellow flowers) and *Z. rehmannii* (with pink flowers) are becoming better known; they bloom in summer.

It is possible to use *Zebrina pendula* as a ground cover. The small flowers are purplish on top, whitish underneath.

Large picture on the right: *Amorphophallus titanum*, the giant's root, clearly shows a family resemblance to other arums, like *Zantedeschia*, *Monstera*, and *Anthurium*. The largest inflorescence of the plant kingdom, *Amorphophallus titanum* was discovered in the mountains of Sumatra in 1878. It alternates between growing either a single giant leaf or a single giant inflorescence each year. The huge inflorescence, which grows 6.5 ft. (2 m) high in a few days, gives off a dreadful stench. This sensational plant is closely related to many of our common houseplants.

ZANTEDESCHIA AETHIOPICA
Calla lily

Family: Arum, *Araceae*
Native Habitat: South Africa
Flowering Time: Late winter to summer

The calla lily grows about 31 in. (80 cm) high, out of a fleshy, stemlike root stock. The rich green leaves, shaped like arrowheads, have long, upright petioles. The inflorescence, up to 3.2 ft. (1 m) high, consists of a yellow spadix surrounded by a large, white bract. Different varieties include, among others, 'Crowborough,' a fragrant form with good tolerance of cold; it is hardy in milder regions of the temperate zone, but if planted outside, it blooms in summer; the compact 'Perle von Stuttgart,' which grows only 12–16 in. (30–40 cm) high and flowers very profusely; as well as 'Little Gem.' An extra tall variety is 'White Hercules.'

Location: Light to partial shade all year; in summer outdoors. In winter cool, at 50°F (10°C).
Care: During growth, water generously and fertilize up until it blooms. Stop both after it has bloomed. After midsummer, shake out the root ball, repot it, and very gradually let it sprout.
Propagation: By division of rootstock in summer.
Pests And Diseases: Spider mites, aphids.
Uses: Houseplant; suited to hydroponics.

Zantedeschia aethiopica

Zebrina pendula

ZEBRINA
Zebrina; zebra spiderwort

Family: Spiderwort, *Commelinaceae*
Native Habitat: Central America
Flowering Time: Seldom blooms in cultivation

Zebrina is a herbaceous perennial with creeping shoots, set with pointed, oval, fleshy leaves. They are green and silver on top and reddish underneath. The plant looks like tradescantia. *Z. flocculosa* has a white, hairy covering. *Z. pendula* (now *Tradescantia zebrina*), is available in a four-colored variety, 'quadricolor.' *Z. purpusii* is altogether more robust and shows no stripes on its leaves.
Location: Light but no sun and airy, all year, at 59–68°F (15–20°C).
Care: Year round, keep moderately moist, avoid waterlogging. Early spring to late summer, feed biweekly.
Propagation: By cuttings.
Pests and Diseases: Aphids; leaves fall if kept too cool; spindly form indicates need for fertilizer.
Uses: A hanging plant.

Picture on the right: Amorphophallus titanum

Acokanthera – Ansellia

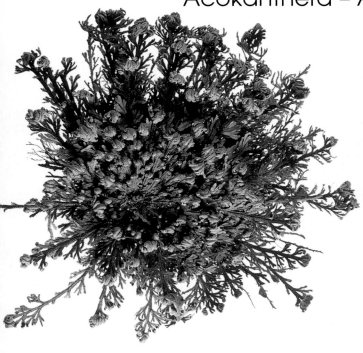

ACOKANTHERA OBLONGIFOLIA
Bushman's poison

Family: Dogbane (*Apocynaceae*).
Habitat: South Africa. **Flowering:** Late winter to spring. **Location, Care, Propagation:** Very bright, also sunny. In winter, keep at 54–59°F (12–15°C). Water with soft water and fertilize every 14 days. If possible, keep in a temperate hothouse. The plants can be cut back. Propagate using tip cuttings, at 77–86°F (25–30°C), under glass. **Highly poisonous!**

ACTINIOPTERIS AUSTRALIS
Actiniopteris

Family: Polypody (*Polypodiaceae*).
Habitat: Tropical Africa and Asia.
Location, Care, Propagation: Sun to shade all year long, humid, at room temperature. Uniform moisture with good drainage is important. Soft water. Fertilize lightly every month. Propagate from spores or careful division in spring. Ideal for bottle gardens.

Anastatica hierochuntica

This section presents brief descriptions of 166 plants that are not part of the customary stock of gardeners specializing in houseplants or container plants. Some of them are only for enthusiasts with special facilities. Others were popular once, then disappeared, but are now making a "comeback." Still others have been introduced only recently. Finally, you will find some botanical curiosities, as well as several plants that are particularly decorative or useful.

ALSOBIA DIANTHIFLORA
Alsobia

Family: Gesneriad (*Gesneriaceae*).
Habitat: Mexico, Costa Rica.
Flowering: Summer to early fall.
Location, Care, Propagation: Part shade, no full sun, warm all year. Keep moderately moist with soft water; fertilize every two weeks through the growth period. Cultivate at high humidity in a hothouse or tropical window. Propagate from runners or cuttings.

ALYOGYNE HUEGELII
Alyogyne

Family: Mallow (*Malvaceae*). **Habitat:** Australia. **Flowering:** Summer.
Location, Care, Propagation: Full sun outdoors, overwintering in a light location, at 41–50°F (5–10°C). Water heavily during growth period; fertilize every two weeks from spring to late summer. The plant, with typical mallow blooms, should be pinched out to achieve compact growth. Propagate from tip cuttings in early summer.

ADROMISCHUS MACULATUS
Adromischus

Family: Stonecrop (*Crassulaceae*).
Habitat: South and southwest Africa.
Flowering: Nearly all year round.
Location, Care, Propagation: Very sunny and warm. Light in winter, never below 50°F (10°C). Water regularly and thoroughly in summer, hardly at all in winter. Fertilize with cactus fertilizer monthly during the summer. Propagates easily from leaf cuttings in peat-sand mix.

AERANGIS FASTUOSA
Aerangis

Family: Orchid (*Orchidaceae*).
Habitat: Madagascar. **Flowering:** Spring. **Location, Care, Propagation:** Very bright but not full sun; humid. In winter not under 59°F (15°C). Keep in a greenhouse if possible, preferably in a slatted basket because of its long aerial roots, or tie onto cork bark. Fertilize weekly in summer. Propagation is for professionals.

AERIDES MULTIFLORUM
Aerides

Family: Orchid (*Orchidaceae*).
Habitat: Himalayas to south Vietnam.
Flowering: Summer to early fall.
Location, Care, Propagation: Very light all year but not sunny. Warm (68–72°F (20–22°C)), slightly cooler at night. Keep moderately moist with soft water. Cultivate in hothouse or tropical window in slatted baskets. Because of its fragile roots, repot infrequently. Propagation is for professionals.

SPECIAL COMMENT

The rose of Jericho is also called "resurrection plant" because it survives the dry season in its African homeland as a withered tangle that springs to life only when moistened.

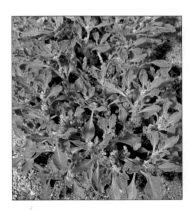

ANASTATICA HIEROCHUNTICA
Rose of Jericho

Family: Mustard (*Brassicaceae*).
Habitat: Morocco to southern Iran.
Flowering: Midsummer. **Location, Care, Propagation:** The dry, rolled-up rosettes are placed into soft water at room temperature, where they become full of moisture, open, and soon turn green. Occasionally, there are seeds which germinate at around 64°F (18°C). This annual also thrives outdoors in sunny locations.

ANGRAECUM EBURNEUM
Angraecum

Family: Orchid (*Orchidaceae*).
Habitat: Madagascar. **Flowering:** Winter. **Location, Care, Propagation:** Light all year, but not sunny; warm, humid, in a tropical window or hothouse. Water moderately with soft water and supply orchid fertilizer every two weeks. Let all protruding roots hang out of the plant basket. Propagation by division; difficult.

ANSELLIA AFRICANA
Ansellia

Family: Orchid (*Orchidaceae*).
Habitat: West Africa. **Flowering:** Winter.
Location, Care, Propagation: Very bright and warm all year. Best cultivated in a hothouse. During the growing period, keep moderately moist (soft water); in the rest period from late summer keep fairly dry. Feed weekly during the summer with orchid fertilizer. Propagation by division.

ARACHIS HYPOGAEA
Peanut, groundnut

Family: Bean (*Fabaceae*). **Habitat:** Brazil. **Flowering:** Summer. **Location, Care, Propagation:** Sunny, outdoors. This annual reacts negatively to excessive moisture, so be sure the soil is well drained. Fertilize every two weeks. Propagate from seed or use unpeeled peanuts from the vegetable counter, potted in early spring at around 68°F (20°C).

ARACHNIODES ARISTATA
Leather fern

Family: Polypody (*Polypodiaceae*). **Habitat:** Asia, Australia. **Flowering:** Nonflowering plant. **Location, Care, Propagation:** Shade, but warm, not under 61°F (16°C) even in winter. Keep uniformly moist with soft water. If air is dry from heating, spray occasionally. Fertilize lightly once a week. Propagation by division or seeding spores at a soil temperature of 64–68°F (18–20°C).

ARCHONTOPHOENIX CUNNINGHAMIANA
King palm

Family: Palm (*Arecaceae*). **Habitat:** Australia. **Flowering:** Seldom flowers under cultivation. **Location, Care, Propagation:** Light to part-shade, humid. In summer between 59–64°F (15–18°C), in winter at 50–59°F (10–15°C). Keep uniformly moist, without water build-up. From spring to late summer, fertilize every two weeks. Propagation from seed. Germination in six weeks to three months.

SPECIAL COMMENT

The way the peanut or groundnut bears fruit is interesting: after pollination, the flower stem penetrates into the ground, continues to grow horizontally on reaching the desired depth of 2–4 in. (5–10 cm), and develops groundnuts. If it fails to make contact with the soil, the plant doesn't bear fruit (see also page 75).

BANKSIA COCCINEA
Banksia

Family: Protea (*Proteaceae*). **Habitat:** Australia. **Flowering:** Winter and spring. **Location, Care, Propagation:** Light all year, but not in full sun. In the summer, may be outdoors. In winter, around 50°F (10°C). Keep uniformly moist with soft water. Be sure to avoid water build-up. Fertilize lightly and infrequently. Propagation from cuttings, but difficult.

BARKERIA SPECTABILIS
Barkeria

Family: Orchid (*Orchidaceae*). **Habitat:** Central America. **Flowering:** Winter. **Location, Care, Propagation:.** Very light but not sunny; humid. In winter, not below 54°F (12°C). In a closed plant window. Keep well moistened during the growing period, but almost dry for several months in late summer. From spring to late summer use orchid fertilizer every two weeks. Propagate by division.

BAUHINIA VARIEGATA
Purple orchid tree, mountain ebony

Family: Bean (*Fabaceae*). **Habitat:** China, India, subtropics. **Flowering:** Spring and summer. **Location, Care, Propagation:** Very light but not full sun. In winter around 41°F (5°C). Water well in the summer, and fertilize weekly until fall. Propagation from seed or cuttings at high soil temperature, but difficult.

SPECIALTIES AND RARITIES

ARIOCARPUS FISSURATUS
Livingrock cactus

Family: Cactus (*Cactaceae*). **Habitat:** Mexico. **Flowering:** Only after many years, usually in fall. **Location, Care, Propagation:** Warm, full sun. In winter, at 41–50°F (5–10°C). In summer, water infrequently but thoroughly; then let the soil dry out well. Fertilize sparingly. Keep dry in winter. Propagation by seed.

ARISAEMA CANDIDISSIMUM
White jack-in-the-pulpit

Family: Arum (*Araceae*). **Habitat:** Western China. **Flowering:** June. **Location, Care, Propagation:** Part-shade and moderately warm to about 64°F (18°C). In summer, keep uniformly moist and fertilize weekly until blooming begins. Overwinter the tuber cool (not under 50°F (10°C)) and dry, after the leaves have withered. Propagate from side tubers.

ARISTOLOCHIA GIGANTEA
Giant Dutchman's pipe

Family: Birthwort (*Aristolochiaceae*). **Habitat:** South America. **Flowering:** Summer. **Location, Care, Propagation:** All year, partly shady and warm (garden room, greenhouse). In summer, fertilize weekly and keep uniformly moist with soft water. In winter, keep nearly dry. Tie to a support. Propagation from cuttings.

BERTOLONIA HOUTTEANA
Bertolonia

Family: Melastome (*Melastomataceae*). **Habitat:** Brazil. **Flowering:** Seldom blooms under cultivation. **Location, Care, Propagation:** Light or part shade all year, no direct sun, warm (72–77°F (22–25°C)) and humid (closed plant window). Water moderately with soft water at room temperature and fertilize monthly. Propagate from tip cuttings or seed, at 86–95°F (30–35°C) soil temperature.

BIDENS FERULIFOLIA
Fernleaf beggarstick

Family: Aster (*Asteraceae*). **Habitat:** Mexico. **Flowering:** Summer to late fall. **Location, Care, Propagation:** This annual or biennial needs a sunny, warm outdoor location. Water regularly and thoroughly in summer, and fertilize weekly. Propagate from tip cuttings or seed.

BIFRENARIA HARRISONIAE
Bifrenaria

Family: Orchid (*Orchidaceae*). **Habitat:** Brazil. **Flowering:** Depends on the species. **Location, Care, Propagation:** Light all year, but not sunny; warm and humid. In a controlled-temperature greenhouse or closed plant window. In the growth period water thoroughly—and always with soft water; apply orchid fertilizer every three weeks. Propagate by dividing.

SPECIAL COMMENT

The blooms of the tropical giant Dutchman's pipe are enormous! In South America, Alexander von Humboldt saw children wearing the gigantic flowers as caps. The flowers of *Aristolochia gigantea*, or *A. gigantea* var. *hookeri*, a variety of *A. grandiflora*, are about 12 by 14 in. (30 by 35 cm). Whereas the pure species reeks indescribably of carrion, the variety has no odor.

Bignonia – Caralluma

BIGNONIA CAPREOLATA
Crossvine bignonia

Family: Bignonia (*Bignoniaceae*).
Habitat: United States. **Flowering:** Early summer. Only some specimens flower.
Location, Care, Propagation: Bright to full sun. In summer also outdoors, In winter, cool. Water thoroughly in the growth period and fertilize weekly. In winter, reduce water and do not fertilize. Propagate from cuttings or seed.

BLOSSFELDIA LILIPUTANA
Blossfeldia

Family: Cactus (*Cactaceae*). **Habitat:** South America. **Flowering:** Summer. **Location, Care, Propagation:** All year, light to lightly sunny, also outdoors, but not under 46°F (8°C). Roots easily from offsets. Such plants do not live long, so should be grafted onto *Selenicereus*. Water with caution and fertilize rarely. Keep totally dry from the end of October. Propagation through seed.

BOWIEA VOLUBILIS
Common bowiea

Family: Lily (*Liliaceae*). **Habitat:** South Africa. **Flowering:** Winter. **Location, Care, Propagation:** In winter, sunny and warm. During the growth period water sparingly and give weak fertilizer monthly. In summer—during the rest period—do not water. Propagation through division of the side bulbs, or from seed. Rare plant treasure for connoisseurs.

SPECIAL COMMENT

Two plants that are like David and Goliath: the blossfeldia, which reaches a maximum diameter of 0.6 in. (1.6 cm), and the Brazilian butiapalm, whose leaves grow to a length of 10 ft. (3 m). Fortunately, this plant grows slowly in a container.

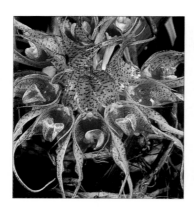

BULBOPHYLLUM BINNENDIJEKI
Bulbophyllum

Family: Orchid (*Orchidaceae*).
Habitat: Africa, Asia. **Flowering:** Depends on the species. **Location, Care, Propagation:** Light all year, but not sunny, moderately warm to hot, humid (closed plant window). In winter, never under 61°F (16°C). Water generously with soft water until the pseudobulbs form; fertilize sparingly. Propagate by dividing.

BUTIA CAPITATA
Brazilian butiapalm

Family: Palm (*Arecaceae*). **Habitat:** South America. **Flowering:** Seldom flowers under cultivation. **Location, Care, Propagation:** Sunny. Outdoors in summer. Overwinter light at 46–50°F (8–10°C). Water regularly, but only moderately in winter. In summer, fertilize every two weeks. Propagate from seed, previously slit and soaked in warm water. Very long germinating period, to 24 months.

CAESALPINIA PULCHERRIMA
Caesalpinia

Family: Caesalpinia (*Caesalpinaceae*). **Habitat:** Tropics and subtropics of the Americas and Asia. **Flowering:** Summer. **Location, Care, Propagation:** Full sun and warm, outdoors also in summer. In winter, minimum 54°F (12°C). In the growth period, fertilize every two weeks; keep lightly moist. In winter, keep somewhat drier. Propagate from seed, cuttings, or tip-layering at a soil temperature of 77–86°F (25-30°C).

SPECIALTIES AND RARITIES

BRACHYCHITON RUPESTRIS
Barrel bottletree

Family: Cacao (*Sterculiaceae*).
Habitat: Australia. **Flowering:** Seldom under cultivation. **Location, Care, Propagation:** Light to sunny, warm; cooler in winter, but not under 54°F (12°C). Only water in moderation. Without fail, avoid water build-up. In summer, fertilize every two weeks. In winter, keep almost dry. Propagation by tip cuttings or seed.

BRASSAVOLA NODOSA
Brassavola

Family: Orchid (*Orchidaceae*).
Habitat: Central and northern regions of South America. **Flowering:** October to December. **Location, Care, Propagation:** Very light, but no full midday sun in summer; warm and humid. Water and spray generously with soft water; apply fertilizer with a high potash content every two weeks. Rest period extends over several weeks from late summer. Propagation by division.

BRASSIA VERUCOSA
Spider orchid

Family: Orchid (*Orchidaceae*).
Habitat: Tropical South America.
Flowering: Spring through to late summer. **Location, Care, Propagation:** Light, warm, and humid, somewhat cooler in the rest period but never under 57°F (14°C). Except during the rest period of about two weeks after blooming, water moderately with soft water at room temperature. Propagation by division.

CALANTHE VESTITA HYBRID
Hybrid calanthe

Family: Orchid (*Orchidaceae*).
Habitat: Tropical Africa, Asia, Australia.
Flowering: Fall through spring.
Location, Care, Propagation: Light, warm, and humid (closed plant window). In winter at 59°F (15°C). During the growth period, water generously with soft water and fertilize every two weeks. After flowering, keep dry. Propagation by division.

CAPPARIS SPINOSA
Common caper

Family: Caper (*Capparaceae*).
Habitat: Southern Europe, Middle East, Asia. **Flowering:** Summer. **Location, Care, Propagation:** Full sun and warm in summer. Does best in the cracks of a natural stone wall in a conservatory. In winter, light and 50–59°F (10–15°C). Water sparingly and apply weak fertilizer only occasionally. Propagation by tip cuttings.

CARALLUMA JOANNIS
Caralluma

Family: Milkweed (*Asclepiadaceae*).
Habitat: South Africa, Asia. **Flowering:** Summer. **Location, Care, Propagation:** Light, but not sunny; warm. In summer water moderately from below and assure good drainage. Only fertilize occasionally. In winter, cooler—to 50°F (10°C)—and keep dry. Propagate by planting tip cuttings in sandy soil, or from seed.

SPECIAL COMMENT

Did you know that the buds of the caper bush contain the same active ingredient as horseradish, mustard, and cress, namely, ethereal mustard oil? To preserve capers in vinegar or oil, do not use opened buds. Before processing them, allow the buds to wither a little. This permits the aromatic materials to develop optimally.

Carissa – Conophytum

CARISSA MACROCARPA
Carissa, Natal plum

Family: Dogbane (*Apocynaceae*).
Habitat: South Africa. **Flowering:**
Blooms only appear on plants over 26
ft. (8 m) tall. **Location, Care,**
Propagation: Full sun, well aired, in
summer also outdoors; in winter at
41–50°F (5–10°C). Water evenly and
fertilize every four weeks. In winter,
keep drier. Propagation by tip cuttings
at high soil temperature. **The plant is**
extremely poisonous!

CARNEGIA GIGANTEA
Saguaro cactus

Family: Cactus (*Cactaceae*). **Habitat:**
Central and South America. **Flowering:**
Only plants over 26 ft. (8 m) tall will
bloom. **Location, Care, Propagation:**
Sunny; cool in winter, but at least 41°F
(5°C). In summer, water very little and
apply just a minimum of fertilizer. In
winter, keep completely dry.
Propagation from seed. The plant
hardly grows at all, about 3.2 ft. (1 m)
in 30 years.

CARPOBROTUS ACINACIFORMIS
Carpobrotus

Family: Fig-marigold (*Aizoaceae*).
Habitat: South Africa. **Flowering:**
Summer to early winter. **Location,**
Care, Propagation: Warm and sunny,
also outdoors in summer if protected
from rain. In winter, light and cool, not
under 41°F (5°C). Water sparingly,
keeping plant nearly dry in winter.
Propagation by tip cuttings that have
been allowed to dry for a week before
planting.

SPECIAL COMMENT

In its mature form, the
saguaro cactus, which
grows to 50 ft. (15 m), is
known to every fan of
western films. It is the
trademark of Arizona,
which has created a
special sanctuary, the
well-known Saguaro
National Monument,
for this strictly
protected cactus
species.

CHRYSOTHEMIS PULCHELLA
Chrysothemis

Family: Gesneriad (*Gesneriaceae*).
Habitat: Central America. **Flowering:**
Summer. **Location, Care, Propagation:**
Very light, but not sunny; warm, humid
(in a closed plant window or warm
greenhouse). Water moderately with
soft water and fertilize every two
weeks. Rest period in fall. Overwinter
the tubers cool and dry. Propagation
by cuttings or small side tubers.

CHYSIS AUREA
Chysis

Family: Orchid (*Orchidaceae*).
Habitat: Central and South America.
Flowering: Late spring, early summer.
Location, Care, Propagation: Very light
and warm, but no full midday sun in
summer; in winter cooler but above
54°F (12°C). Water generously with soft
water in summer, and fertilize every
two weeks. After the formation of new
pseudobulbs, allow to rest at 54–59°F
(12–15°C). Propagation by division.

COCCOLOBA UVIFERA
Common seagrape

Family: Buckwheat (*Polygonaceae*).
Habitat: Florida. **Flowering:** Seldom
blooms under cultivation. **Location,**
Care, Propagation: Light and warm all
year, but not sunny. In winter, at least
59°F (15°C). In summer, water
generously and fertilize every week; in
winter, water less often and fertilize
only once a month. In spring, repot in
large pots. Propagation by tip cuttings
at a soil temperature of 77°F (25°C).

SPECIALTIES AND RARITIES

CARYOTA MITIS
Tufted fishtail palm

Family: Palm (*Arecaceae*). **Habitat:** Southeast Asia, Malaysian archipelago. **Flowering:** Seldom blooms under cultivation. **Location, Care, Propagation:** Light but not sunny all year, warm (72–77°F (22–25°C)), humid (hothouse plant). Always keep moderately moist, but take greatest care to avoid water build-up. In summer, fertilize every month. Propagation through seed or side shoots, at high soil temperature.

CEPHALOCEREUS SENILIS
Old man cactus

Family: Cactus (*Cactaceae*). **Habitat:** Mexico. **Flowering:** Seldom blooms under cultivation, and only when around 16 ft. (5 m) tall. **Location, Care, Propagation:** Sunny, warm, and humid. In summer, despite the resting period, at 59–64°F (15–18°C). In summer, water moderately and fertilize every two weeks. In winter, keep nearly dry, only spraying occasionally with a fine spray. Propagation by seed.

CERATONIA SILIQUA
Carob tree, St. Johnsbread tree

Family: Caesalpinia (*Caesalpinaceae*). **Habitat:** Mediterranean region. **Flowering:** Early summer through fall. **Location, Care, Propagation:** In summer, sun to part shade, warm, also outdoors. In winter, light at 35–50°F (2–10°C), or even warmer if very light. Water and fertilize with restraint; occasional drying out is tolerated. Propagation by seed at high soil temperature.

COCHLIOSTEMA ODORATISSIMUM
Cochliostema

Family: Spiderwort (*Commelinaceae*). **Habitat:** Tropical Central America. **Flowering:** Late winter, but also at other times under cultivation. **Location, Care, Propagation:** Very light, warm, and humid all year, but not sunny (hothouse plant). Keep moderately moist with soft water and spray frequently; fertilize every two weeks. Propagate using newly imported seed at 68–72°F (20–22°C).

COELOGYNE CRISTATA
Coelogyne

Family: Orchid (*Orchidaceae*). **Habitat:** Southeast Asia, Himalayas, Burma. **Flowering:** All year, depending on the species. **Location, Care, Propagation:** Light and airy all year, but not sunny and not too warm (57–61°F (14–16°C)). In winter, coolish. Keep moderately moist in the growth period (soft water at room temperature), and apply a low-lime fertilizer every month. Water less in winter. Propagation by division.

CONOPHYTUM BILOBUM
Living stones

Family: Fig-marigold (*Aizoaceae*). **Habitat:** South Africa. **Flowering:** Late summer. **Location, Care, Propagation:** Sunny and airy. In summer, outdoors if protected against rain. In winter, not under 41°F (5°C). Keep nearly dry during the summer rest period; from the fall, water sparingly and fertilize lightly once a month. Propagate from seed or by dividing off individual small plants.

SPECIAL COMMENT

In former times the 0.006 oz. (0.18 g) seeds of the St. Johnsbread or carob tree were used to measure the weight of gems and gold. The word "carat" comes from *Ceratonia*. Nowadays, the fruits are mostly used to make ersatz coffee (carob coffee) and, by the food industry, as St. Johnsbread flour, for thickening and as a stabilizer.

355

Coprosma – Darlingtonia

COPROSMA X KIRKII
Coprosma

Family: Madder (*Rubiaceae*). **Habitat:** New Zealand. **Flowering:** Seldom blooms under cultivation. **Location, Care, Propagation:** Light but not sunny all year long. Also outdoors in summer, and in winter at 41–50°F (5–10°C). In the summer, keep moderately moist, but allow the root ball to dry out before watering again; fertilize weekly. Propagate from semihardwood stem cuttings. Trim young plants more frequently.

COROKIA COTONEASTER
Cotoneaster corokia

Family: Saxifrage (*Saxifragaceae*). **Habitat:** New Zealand. **Flowering:** Summer. **Location, Care, Propagation:** Sun to part shade, in summer also outdoors. In winter, not below 41°F (5°C). In summer, fertilize every two weeks and keep moderately moist. Avoid water build-up. Propagate from cuttings at 61–68°F (16–20°C).

CORYNOCARPUS LAEVIGATUS
New Zealand karakanut

Family: Karaka (*Corynocarpaceae*). **Habitat:** New Zealand. **Flowering:** Seldom blooms under cultivation. **Location, Care, Propagation:** All year, light to sunny, humid. In summer also outdoors, in winter at 37–57°F (3–14°C). Fertilize weekly in summer, keep moderately moist; drier in winter. Propagate by tip cuttings at 64–68°F (18–20°C). **The seeds of this plant are extremely poisonous.**

SPECIAL COMMENT

The seed of the karaka tree is bitter and very poisonous. In its homeland, it is eaten by the Maoris after special treatment. Elsewhere, this evergreen shrub is regarded as an ideal container plant because it is exceptionally decorative and not at all prone to disease.

CRINODENDRON PATAGUA
Red lilytree

Family: Elaeocarpus (*Elaeocarpaceae*). **Habitat:** Chile. **Flowering:** Late fall and winter. **Location, Care, Propagation:** In summer, airy and part shade outdoors. Cannot tolerate heat very well. In winter, light at 41–50°F (5–10°C), or warmer under glass if summer flowering is desired. Water with soft water and fertilize every two weeks. Propagate from seed or cuttings in a warm propagating bed.

CRINUM X POWELLII
Crinum

Family: Lily (*Liliaceae*). **Habitat:** South Africa. **Flowering:** Summer to early fall. **Location, Care, Propagation:** In summer, sun to part shade. In winter, light and cool. Pot the bulbs in spring and water very little. During the growing period, water more frequently and fertilize every two weeks. Propagation from bulblets or side bulbs. **The plant is poisonous.**

CUNONIA CAPENSIS
Cape cunonia, red alder

Family: Cunonia (*Cunoniaceae*). **Habitat:** South Africa. **Flowering:** Summer. **Location, Care, Propagation:** All year, light but not sunny; in winter at 46–54°F (8–12°C). From the early summer, place outdoors, water well, and fertilize weekly. In winter, water very little. Propagate from fresh, imported seed or from soft cuttings, at 68°F (20°C) under glass.

SPECIALTIES AND RARITIES

CORYPHANTHA VIVIPARA
Coryphantha

Family: Cactus (Cactaceae). **Habitat:** North America, Mexico. Flowering: Summer. **Location, Care, Propagation:** In summer, light, airy and warm. In winter, light and cool at around 44˚F (5˚C) From spring, water sparingly. Keep completely dry in winter. Fertilize monthly in summer. Propagate by separating and rooting side shoots, or from seed (but then one must graft).

COSTUS CUSPIDATUS
Spiralflag

Family: Ginger (*Zingiberaceae*). **Habitat:** Brazil. **Flowering:** All year, usually fall and winter. **Location, Care, Propagation:** Very light but not sunny, warm, all year. Keep moderately moist with soft water, and fertilize every two weeks. In spring, cut back and force anew. Propagation from tip cuttings at 77˚F (25˚C) under glass, from seed or by division.

COTYLEDON ORBICULATA
Cotyledon

Family: Stonecrop (*Crassulaceae*). **Habitat:** South Africa. **Flowering:** Summer. **Location, Care, Propagation:** All year, sunny and warm. Water moderately and carefully, without damaging the newest growth. Fertilize weekly with cactus fertilizer. Propagate from cuttings that have been thoroughly dried before planting, or from seed.

CUSSONIA SPICATA
Spiked cabbage tree

Family: Ginseng (*Araliaceae*). **Habitat:** South Africa. **Flowering:** Seldom blooms under cultivation. **Location, Care, Propagation:** All year, light to shady; in summer, warm, outdoors if protected against wind and rain. In winter at 41–50˚F (5–10˚C). Water moderately in summer and fertilize every two weeks. In winter, don't allow the root balls to dry out, but water very little. Propagation from seed.

CYPHOSTEMMA JUTTAE
Cyphostemma

Family: Grape (*Vitaceae*). **Habitat:** Namibia. **Flowering:** Summer. **Location, Care, Propagation:** In summer, sunny and warm; in winter at 50–53˚F (10–12˚C). Water moderately and fertilize monthly during the growth period. Water hardly at all in winter, when the leaves will drop. The best soil mix is cactus soil with sandy-lime supplements to 50 percent. Propagate from seed.

DARLINGTONIA CALIFORNICA
California pitcher-plant

Family: Pitcher-plant (*Sarraceniaceae*). **Habitat:** California. **Flowering:** Late spring to mid-summer. **Location, Care, Propagation:** All year in part shade or shade, cool, airy and humid. In summer, if possible, airy and cool outdoors. Keep the root balls damp (soft water), do not fertilize as these insect-catching plants see to their own food requirements. Propagate by division or from seed.

SPECIAL COMMENT

The Darlingtonia demonstrates how cunningly plants drive insects to certain death. Their emerald-green hoselike leaves are twisted and, at their tips, are equipped with a domed cover that arches over the mouth opening. Attracted by honey glands inside the leaves, the insects land on a transparent tissue, fly around in search of light until weary, and eventually, exhausted, fall through the hose into a slimy fluid that decomposes them.

Dasylirion – Duchesnea

SPECIAL COMMENT

The blooms of the dorstenia are morphologically unique because flowers of both sexes appear on a single outspread, flat, flower base and are melded together into a single layer. The male flowers, with their stamens, are more numerous than the females, which are also smaller. When the fruit is ripe, it is flung well clear of the plant.

DASYLIRION SERRATIFOLIUM
Sawtooth sotal

Family: Agave (*Agavaceae*). **Habitat:** Mexico. **Flowering:** Summer. **Location, Care, Propagation:** In summer, sunny, also outdoors. In winter, as light as possible and cool, to the frost threshold. Water moderately in summer; keep relatively dry in winter. From spring to early fall, fertilize every two weeks. Propagation from seed at a soil temperature of 68–77°F (20–25°C).

DICHORISANDRA THYRSIFLORA
Dichorisandra

Family: Spiderwort (*Commelinaceae*). **Habitat:** Brazil. **Flowering:** Fall. **Location, Care, Propagation:** All year, light or part-shade, warm and humid, but avoid full sun (hothouse). In summer, water moderately and fertilize every two weeks. In winter, keep drier at 59–64°F (15–18°C). During this rest period, the foliage is thrown off. Propagation from cuttings or by division.

DIONAEA MUSCIPULA
Venus flytrap

Family: Sundew (*Droseraceae*). **Habitat:** North America. **Flowering:** Late spring to midsummer. **Location, Care, Propagation:** All year long, humid. In summer, cool and shaded, also outdoors. In winter, light, to 41–50°F (5–10°C). Keep moist with soft water. Fertilize sparingly once a month in summer. Propagation by division or from leaf cuttings or seed. Insect-eating plant.

Dorstenia flower

DORSTENIA ELATA
Torusherb, dorstenia

Family: Mulberry (*Moraceae*). **Habitat:** Tropical Africa and America. **Flowering:** Summer. **Location, Care, Propagation:** All year light to part shade, but no full sun; warm and humid (hothouse plant). Water moderately, spray often, fertilize every two weeks. Propagation from seed or tip cuttings at 77–86°F (25–30°C) under glass.

DORYANTHES PALMERI
Spear lily

Family: Agave (*Agavaceae*). **Habitat:** Australia. **Flowering:** Seldom flowers under cultivation. **Location, Care, Propagation:** Full sun, also outdoors in summer. In winter, light, at 50°F (10°C). Keep well moistened in summer, but avoid water build-up. Fertilize every two weeks. In winter, keep drier. Propagation from shoots that form after flowering, or from seed.

SPECIALTIES AND RARITIES

DIOSPYROS KAKI
Kaki persimmon

Family: Ebony (*Ebenaceae*). **Habitat:** Japan, China. **Flowering:** Early summer. **Location, Care, Propagation:** Outdoors all summer, light and sheltered from the wind. Overwinter at about 41°F (5°C). Water moderately with soft water, and fertilize every two weeks from the time of flowering. Propagation from seed (cold and wet treatment of the seed).

DISA UNIFLORA
Disa

Family: Orchid (*Orchidaceae*). **Habitat:** South Africa. **Flowering:** Summer. **Location, Care, Propagation:** Cool and humid all summer, airy, in a shaded greenhouse. Not for beginners! In summer, give soft water generously, fertilize every month, and assure good drainage. In the winter rest period, keep at 41–50°F (5–10°C). Propagate by separating off bulblets.

DISCHIDIA PECTENOIDES
Urn plant

Family: Milkweed (*Asclepiadaceae*). **Habitat:** Philippines. **Flowering:** Varies. **Location, Care, Propagation:** All year very light to part shade, but never sunny; warm and humid (in a shaded hothouse). Water with soft water (occasionally enriched with fertilizer) and spray often. An epiphyte, but soil culture is possible, using a bromeliad mix. Propagation by division.

DORYOPTERIS PALMATA
Doryopteris

Family: Polypody (*Polypodiaceae*). **Habitat:** Tropical America. **Flowering:** Not a flowering plant. **Location, Care, Propagation:** Shady, warm, and humid all year, not under 54°F (12°C) in winter. Keep uniformly moist with soft water, and fertilize every two weeks. Repot in loose soil with a crumbly texture. Propagate from seed or bulbils, or by division.

DROSERA DIELSIANA
Sundew

Family: Sundew (*Droseraceae*). **Habitat:** Distributed worldwide. **Flowering:** From late spring to late summer. **Location, Care, Propagation:** Light, airy, and humid (small greenhouse). Water regularly with soft water (water may stand in the saucer), but omit fertilizer, as this is an insect-eating plant. Propagation from seed (light-sensitive seed) or from adventitious shoots.

DUCHESNEA INDICA
Barren strawberry

Family: Rose (*Rosaceae*). **Habitat:** East Asia, India. **Flowering:** Early summer to fall. **Location, Care, Propagation:** Light but not sunny. In winter, rest period at 50–54°F (10–12°C). In summer, water generously and fertilize once a week. In winter, keep drier. Hanging plant or ground cover. Propagate from rooted runners or from seed.

SPECIAL COMMENT

If one eats the red fruits of the *Duchesnea*, which resemble wild strawberries, nothing will happen, but once may be enough: they have so little taste that it is not worthwhile to repeat the experiment.

Dudleya – Fenestraria

DUDLEYA PULVERULENTA
Echeveria

Family: Stonecrop (*Crassulaceae*). **Habitat:** California, Mexico. **Flowering:** Early summer, summer. **Location, Care, Propagation:** Sunny in summer, also outdoors if sheltered from rain. In winter, light and cool (not below 59°F (15°C)). Water moderately in summer (mature specimens should be watered from below), and fertilize monthly with weak fertilizer. Keep dry in winter. Propagation from leaf cuttings or from seed.

DYCKIA MARNIERI-LAPOSTOLLEI
Dyckia

Family: Bromeliad (*Bromeliaceae*). **Habitat:** South America. **Flowering:** Spring to summer. **Location, Care, Propagation:** Sunny in summer, also outdoors if sheltered. In winter, light and cool (not below 41°F (5°C)). Water sparingly in summer and fertilize every two weeks. Keep dry in winter. Remove dead plant parts. Propagation by separating off side rosettes.

ECHINOFOSSULOCACTUS PENTACANTHUS
Stenocactus

Family: Cactus (*Cactaceae*). **Habitat:** Mexico. **Flowering:** Spring. **Location, Care, Propagation:** Sun to part shade, also outdoors in summer. Overwinter at 46–50°F (8–10°C). Water generously in summer, but keep nearly dry in winter. Omit fertilizer during the annual repotting. Propagation from seed.

ESCOBARIA TUBERCULOSA
Coryphantha

Family: Cactus (*Cactaceae*). **Habitat:** Texas, New Mexico. **Flowering:** Summer. **Location, Care, Propagation:** Sunny and warm in summer, also outdoors if protected against rain. Overwinter at 43–50°F (6–10°C). Water sparingly in summer, fertilizing lightly every one or two months. In winter, keep dry. Propagation from seed or by separating off sideshoots.

ESPOSTOA LANATA
Pilocereus

Family: Cactus (*Cactaceae*). **Habitat:** Ecuador, Peru. **Flowering:** Seldom blooms under cultivation. **Location, Care, Propagation:** All year under glass, full sun, humid, and warm. Water at high temperatures only, but spray frequently. In winter, keep dry and cool. In spring, top up with loose, nutrient-rich substratum as needed.

EUTERPE EDULIS
Euterpalm

Family: Palm (*Arecaceae*). **Habitat:** South America. **Flowering:** Seldom flowers under cultivation. **Location, Care, Propagation:** All year, very light, humid, and at 68–77°F (20–25°C) (for warm greenhouses or garden rooms). Water moderately and apply weak fertilizer every two weeks. Keep humidity high. Propagation from seed at a soil temperature of 77°F (25°C).

ELETTARIA CARDAMOMUM
Cardamom

Family: Ginger (*Zingiberaceae*).
Habitat: Ceylon, India, Southeast Asia.
Flowering: Seldom blooms under cultivation. **Location, Care, Propagation:** All year, as light and warm as possible, but shielded from full sunshine. Keep the root ball moderately moist; fertilize every two weeks. Propagation from seed or tip cuttings at a soil temperature of 68–77°F (20–25°C).

EMBROTHRIUM COCINEUM
Chilean firebush

Family: Protea (*Proteaceae*). **Habitat:** Chile, Argentina. **Flowering:** Main flowering early summer. **Location, Care, Propagation:** In summer, light to part shade, also outdoors; in winter, light and cool. Ideal in a coldhouse. Water with soft water, fertilize every two weeks. Make sure, too, that the soil contains no lime. Propagation from offsets or seed.

ERANTHEMUM PULCHELLUM
Eranthemum

Family: Acanthus (*Acanthaceae*).
Habitat: India. **Flowering:** Winter.
Location, Care, Propagation: Light to part-shade and not too warm (around 61°F (16°C)) all year. In summer, also outdoors. Keep moderately moist all year and fertilize every two weeks. Propagation from tip cuttings at a soil temperature of 68–77°F (20–25°C).

FASCICULARIA BICOLOR
Fathead tree

Family: Bromeliad (*Bromeliaceae*).
Habitat: Chile. **Flowering:** Summer.
Location, Care, Propagation: All year, light to sunny; in summer also outdoors if protected against rain. In winter at around 41°F (5°C). Water moderately in summer (assure good drainage), and fertilize every two weeks. In winter, keep nearly dry. Propagate by division in spring, or by removing offsets.

FAUCARIA TIGRINA
Faucaria

Family: Fig-marigold (*Aizoaceae*).
Habitat: South Africa. **Flowering:** Early fall. **Location, Care, Propagation:** In summer, light to sunny, also outdoors; in winter at 50°F (10°C). Water moderately in summer, and apply cactus fertilizer monthly. From the beginning of the winter rest period, gradually water less and then cease watering entirely. Propagation by division or from seed.

FENESTRARIA AURANTIACA
Fenestraria, baby toes

Family: Fig-marigold (*Aizoaceae*).
Habitat: South Africa. **Flowering:** Late summer. **Location, Care, Propagation:** In summer, very sunny and warm, also outdoors; after flowering, light, at 54–59°F (12–15°C). Water moderately in summer and apply cactus fertilizer once a month. Keep dry in winter. Repot in cactus soil in spring. Propagate by division.

SPECIAL COMMENT

The fenestraria is not only one of the most interesting succulents; it is also a prime example of mimicry—the protective adaptation of plants. In accordance with the motto "Fool and camouflage," the plant evades predators by using its sap-filled leaves to almost totally bury its splendor in the sand. The only thing to peek out is its upper end, which looks like a glittering piece of quartz. This effect is due to a transparent outer skin that acts like an assemblage of tiny windows.

Ferocactus – Hakea

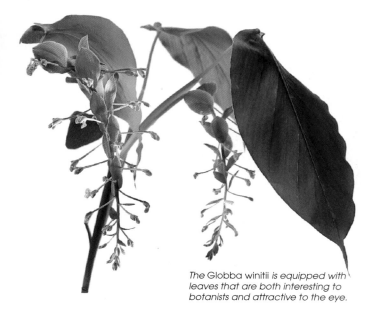

The Globba winitii *is equipped with leaves that are both interesting to botanists and attractive to the eye.*

FEROCACTUS ACANTHODES
California barrel cactus

Family: Cactus (*Cactaceae*). **Habitat:** United States, Mexico. **Flowering:** Summer. **Location, Care, Propagation:** In summer, full sun and warm; outdoors, too, if protected against rain. In winter, light at 50–57°F (10–14°C). From early spring to fall, water regularly but sparingly. Be sure to avoid water build-up, and fertilize infrequently. This is followed by a dry rest period. Repot in cactus soil. Propagation from seed.

FREMONTODENDRON CALIFORNICUM
California fremontia

Family: Cacao (*Sterculiaceae*). **Habitat:** California, Arizona. **Flowering:** Spring to fall. **Location, Care, Propagation:** Light to full sun, and airy; in summer also outdoors if sheltered from rain. Overwinter at 39–50°F (4–10°C). Water moderately in summer (avoiding water build-up) and fertilize weekly. Propagation from cuttings or seed.

SPECIAL COMMENT

The *Goethea cauliflora*, named after the German poet Goethe, is a remarkable plant: its flowers develop from the sides of the stem. This rare phenomenon, called cauliflowering or stem-flowering, also occurs in the cacao tree, *Theobroma cacao*. Characteristically, the buds form on the old wood rather than on the new shoots.

GOETHEA CAULIFLORA
Goethea

Family: Mallow (*Malvaceae*). **Habitat:** Brazil. **Flowering:** Early summer to fall. **Location, Care, Propagation:** All year, part shade, warm, and humid, preferably in a greenhouse or flower window. In summer, water moderately with soft water. Keep fairly dry in winter. Repot in acidic substratum. Propagation from top cuttings under glass at a soil temperature of 86°F (30°C).

GONGORA QUINQUENERVIS
Gongora

Family: Orchid (*Orchidaceae*). **Habitat:** Central America. **Flowering:** Spring to early summer. **Location, Care, Propagation:** All year, part shade, warm, and humid; nighttime temperatures lower, around 35–39°F (2–4°C). Does best in a greenhouse that is lightly shaded in summer. Water moderately in summer, still less in winter, and assure good drainage. Propagation by division. Not a plant for beginners!

GRAPTOPETALUM BELLUM
Letterpetal

Family: Stonecrop (*Crassulaceae*). **Habitat:** Mexico. **Flowering:** Spring to midsummer. **Location, Care, Propagation:** All year, very light to sunny, but shade from full midday sun. Warm in summer, also outdoors. In winter at 41–50°F (5–10°C). Water moderately in summer and apply cactus fertilizer twice. In winter, keep dry. Propagation from parts at a soil temperature of 68–77°F (20–25°C).

SPECIALTIES AND RARITIES

GIBBAEUM PUBESCENS
Gibbaeum

Family: Fig-marigold (*Aizoaceae*).
Habitat: South Africa. **Flowering:** Late
winter to early spring. **Location, Care,
Propagation:** Light to sunny all year;
also outdoors in summer if sheltered
from rain. During the summer rest
period, keep totally dry. The rest of the
time, water very little. Apply cactus
fertilizer occasionally. Propagation
from parts or seed.

GLOBBA WINITII
Globba

Family: Ginger (*Zingiberaceae*).
Habitat: Asia, Oceania. **Flowering:**
Summer. **Location, Care, Propagation:**
All year, very light but not sunny, warm,
and humid (hothouse plant). In
summer, keep moderately moist; even
in winter, when the leaves have fallen,
never let it dry out completely and
maintain high humidity. Propagate by
dividing the tubers or from tuber
sections.

GLOTTIPHYLLUM LINGUIFORME
Glottiphyllum

Family: Fig-marigold (*Aizoaceae*).
Habitat: South Africa. **Flowering:** Late
summer through winter. **Location,
Care, Propagation:** Full sun all year,
outdoors in summer if sheltered. In
winter at 46–54°F (8–12°C). Water little.
Apply nitrogen-poor fertilizer weekly in
the two months before flowering
begins. Keep completely dry during
the winter and early spring. Propagation from leaf cuttings or by division.

SPECIAL COMMENT

Globba winitii is one of
many beauties that
have emerged from
the ginger family. The
genus includes over
100 species. Because
of the marvelous
structure of its flowers
and bracts, which
often carry bulbils—
that is, material for
propagation—
botanical gardens like
to feature the globba
in their displays.

GREENOVIA AUREA
Greenovia

Family: Stonecrop (*Crassulaceae*).
Habitat: Canary Islands. **Flowering:**
Early spring. **Location, Care,
Propagation:** Sunny, warm in summer,
outdoors if sheltered from rain. In
winter, light at 41–50°F (5–10°C). Water
sparingly in summer (avoid water
build-up), and apply weak fertilizer
every six weeks. Keep nearly dry in
winter. Propagation from small side
rosettes.

HAAGEOCEREUS VERSICOLOR
Haageocereus

Family: Cactus (*Cactaceae*). **Habitat:**
Peru, Chile. **Flowering:** Seldom blooms
under cultivation. **Location, Care,
Propagation:** Full sun all year, very
warm in summer, and not below 50°F
(10°C) in winter. Water with soft water
at room temperature in summer, and
apply cactus fertilizer with added lime.
When repotting in spring, use cactus
soil with added lime. Propagate from
seed.

HAKEA OLEIFOLIA
Olive-leaf hakea

Family: Protea (*Proteaceae*). **Habitat:**
Australia. **Flowering:** Varies. **Location,
Care, Propagation:** Sunny all year,
outdoors in summer if protected
against rain. In winter at 41–50°F
(5–10°C). During the growth period,
water moderately and fertilize every
two weeks. In winter, keep dry.
Propagate from semihardwood
cuttings in summer, or from seed.

Hardenbergia – Juanulloa

HARDENBERGIA VIOLACEA
Purple coral tree

Family: Bean (*Fabaceae*). **Habitat:** Australia, Tasmania. **Flowering:** Early spring. **Location, Care, Propagation:** All year part shade to sun. Warm in summer, also outdoors if sheltered. Cooler in winter, not above 50°F (10°C). Let the soil dry out between waterings. In summer, fertilize every four weeks. Propagation from seed or tip cuttings in spring.

HECHTIA
Hechtia

Family: Bromeliad (*Bromeliaceae*). **Habitat:** Mexico. **Flowering:** Seldom flowers under cultivation. **Location, Care, Propagation:** Full sun all year, outdoors also in summer. In winter, not below 41°F (5°C). Water generously with decalcified water in summer (avoid water build-up) and fertilize every two weeks. In winter, keep nearly dry. Propagate from offshoots.

HEDYCHIUM GARDNERIANUM
India gingerlily

Family: Ginger (*Zingiberaceae*). **Habitat:** Eastern Himalayas, Nepal, Sikkim. **Flowering:** Midsummer to early fall. **Location, Care, Propagation:** Sunny in summer, also outdoors. Dark in winter, at 46–50°F (8–10°C). During the growth period, water generously and fertilize every week. In fall, cut back to ground level. Repot in spring. Force light and warm. Propagate by dividing the rhizome.

SPECIAL COMMENT

The tall-growing and strong India gingerlily (*Hedychium*) has thick fleshy shoots and cannalike tubers, leaves that reach 19 in. (45 cm) in length, and large, upright, yellow-gold flower spikes with an agreeable fragrance. Unfortunately, the flowers appear somewhat late in the year, but for the possessor of a garden room, this is an advantage.

HOHENBERGIA STELLATA
Hohenbergia

Family: Bromeliad (*Bromeliaceae*). **Habitat:** Central and South America. **Flowering:** Late winter. **Location, Care, Propagation:** Needs a lot of space. All year, very light to sunny, in summer also outdoors, in winter not below 41°F (5°C). In summer, keep uniformly moist with soft water; in winter, spray rather than watering. Propagation from offshoots.

HOMALOCLADIUM PLATYCLADUM
Ribbonbush

Family: Buckwheat (*Polygonaceae*). **Habitat:** Solomon Islands. **Flowering:** Summer. **Location, Care, Propagation:** All year very light to full sun (cold or lukewarm house), in summer also outdoors if sheltered. In winter at 46–61°F (8–16°C). Water moderately in summer and fertilize every two weeks. Propagate from soft-wood cuttings at a soil temperature of 68°F (20°C) under glass.

HOODIA GORDONII
Hoodia

Family: Milkweed (*Asclepiadaceae*). **Habitat:** South Africa. **Flowering:** Summer to fall. **Location, Care, Propagation:** Full sun all year, warm in summer and at 50–59°F (10–15°C) in winter. Water sparingly in summer and only occasionally apply cactus fertilizer. Keep nearly dry in winter. Propagate from seed or cuttings, but you may have to wait up to a year for roots to form.

SPECIALTIES AND RARITIES

HELICONIA WAGNERIANA
Heliconia

Family: Banana (*Musaceae*). **Habitat:** Tropical America. **Flowering:** The entire year, except for rest periods. **Location, Care, Propagation:** Very light, humid, and never below 64°F (18°C) all year (hothouse plant). Always water with soft water at room temperature and fertilize once a week. Repot annually in standard potting soil. Propagation from rhizomes.

HEMIGRAPHIS REPANDA
Hemigraphis

Family: Acanthus (*Acanthaceae*). **Habitat:** South and East Asia. **Flowering:** Summer. **Location, Care, Propagation:** Warm and humid all year. In summer light to part shade, in winter light (for closed plant windows and terrariums). Water moderately but regularly, spray frequently, fertilize every two weeks. Repot annually. Propagation from tip cuttings at a soil temperature of about 77°F (25°C).

HEMIONITIS ARIFOLIA
Hemionitis

Family: Polypody (*Polypodiaceae*). **Habitat:** Tropical Asia. **Flowering:** Seldom blooms under cultivation. **Location, Care, Propagation:** Light or part shade, warm and humid all year (for hothouse, terrarium, tropical window). Keep uniformly moist and fertilize infrequently. Because root formation is minimal, repot very rarely. Propagate from bulbils in the axils of the pinnate leaves.

SPECIAL COMMENT

Huernias are succulents, low-growing, often turf-forming plants with sharp stems that are usually serrated. The large blooms are marvelously beautiful, but, unfortunately, smell really unpleasant.

HUERNIA MACROCARPA
Huernia

Family: Milkweed (*Asclepiadaceae*). **Habitat:** South Africa, Kenya, Ethiopia. **Flowering:** Summer and fall. **Location, Care, Propagation:** Light, sunny, and warm all year, but shelter from full midday sun. In summer, water sparingly and apply cactus fertilizer once a month. In winter, keep nearly dry. Propagation by separated shoots planted in sandy soil at 68–77°F (20–25°C).

ILLICIUM VERUM
Truestar anisetree

Family: Star anise (*Illiciaceae*). **Habitat:** Japan, Korea, China. **Flowering:** Spring. **Location, Care, Propagation:** Light all year, warm in summer, minimum of 41°F (5°C) in winter (coldhouse, garden room). Always keep root ball moderately moist with lime-free water. During the growth period, until late summer, fertilize weekly. Propagate from tip cuttings or seed.

JUANULLOA AURANTIACA
Juanulloe, guaramaya

Family: Potato (*Solanaceae*). **Habitat:** Peru. **Flowering:** Summer to fall. **Location, Care, Propagation:** Light, not sunny, and warm all year. Grows best planted out in a shaded hothouse. Water and fertilize in moderation. To encourage branching, prune often. Propagate from semi-hard cuttings at high soil temperature under glass. **The plant is poisonous.**

Kohleria – Metrosideros

KOHLERIA X HYBRIDA
Kohleria

Family: Gesneriad (*Gesneriaceae*).
Habitat: Mostly Colombia. **Flowering:**
Spring, summer, and fall. **Location,
Care, Propagation:** All year light but
not in full sun, humid. Warm in summer,
50–54°F (10–12°C) in winter. Water
moderately in summer, but in winter
water only enough to keep the foliage
from withering. Fertilize monthly during
the growth period. Propagate by
division or from tip cuttings.

LACHENALIA ALOIDES
Cape cowslip

Family: Lily (*Liliaceae*). **Habitat:** South
Africa. **Flowering:** Late summer until
spring. **Location, Care, Propagation:**
Sunny and airy in summer, also
outdoors. In winter, light, at 43–50°F
(6–10°C). In early fall, place the bulbs
in sandy potting soil. During the winter,
water moderately, more when putting
forth buds, and fertilize weekly until
flowering. Propagation from bulblets.

LOCKHARTIA OERSTEDII
Lockhartia

Family: Orchid (*Orchidaceae*).
Habitat: Mexico, Panama. **Flowering:**
Summer. **Location, Care, Propagation:**
Very light but not sunny all year, not
too warm, airy, and humid. Water
moderately but always with soft water;
assure high humidity and apply orchid
fertilizer every month. Propagation is a
matter for professionals.

MALVAVISCUS ARBOREUS
South American wax-mallow

Family: Mallow (*Malvaceae*). **Habitat:**
Mexico, Peru, Brazil. **Flowering:** Winter.
Location, Care, Propagation: Sunny
and warm, from spring also outdoors if
protected against rain. Minimum
winter temperature of 54°F (12°C).
Keep moderately moist and fertilize
every two weeks. In spring, cut back
the shoots. Propagation from seed or
cuttings at a soil temperature of 77°F
(25°C).

MASDEVALLIA KIMBALLIANA
Masdevallia

Family: Orchid (*Orchidaceae*).
Habitat: South America. **Flowering:**
Varies between species. **Location,
Care, Propagation:** Temperate, shady,
and humid all year. In winter, not
above 63°F (17°C), nights at 54–56°F
(12–13°C). Keep uniformly moist using
soft water, somewhat less in winter,
and assure high humidity. From early
spring to fall, fertilize monthly.
Propagation by division.

MATUCANA WEBERBAUERI
Matucana

Family: Cactus (*Cactaceae*). **Habitat:**
Peru. **Flowering:** Summer. **Location,
Care, Propagation:** Light and sunny all
year, also outdoors in summer if
protected against rain. In winter, cool
at 41–50°F (5–10°C). During the growth
period, water moderately and apply
cactus fertilizer now and then. The soil
should be lightly acidic and porous.
Propagation from seed.

SPECIALTIES AND RARITIES

LOPHOPHORA WILLIAMSII
Mescal-button peyote

Family: Cactus (*Cactaceae*). **Habitat:** Mexico, Texas. **Flowering:** summer. **Location, Care, Propagation:** Very sunny and warm in summer, also outdoors if shielded from wind and rain. In winter around 41˚F (5˚C). During the growth period, water generously and fertilize every month or two. From fall, keep completely dry. Needs a deep pot (turnip roots). Propagation from seed.

LYCASTE SKINNERI
Lycaste

Family: Orchid (*Orchidaceae*). **Habitat:** Mexico to Honduras. **Flowering:** Winter to early spring. **Location, Care, Propagation:** Bright but not full sun all year long. In summer, warm; after the leaves fall, at 41-54˚F (5-12˚C). In summer apply weak fertilizer once a week, and keep evenly moist with soft water. In winter, only give enough water to keep the pseudobulbs from drying out. Propagation by division.

LYSIMACHIA CONGESTIFLORA
Loosestrife

Family: Primrose (*Primulaceae*). **Habitat:** China. **Flowering:** Summer to fall. **Location, Care, Propagation:** In summer, sunny, outdoors in hanging planters and boxes. Water generously and fertilize weekly. The herbaceous perennial, which is not winter hardy, is grown as an annual in the temperate zone. Regularly remove finished blooms to encourage new flowers. Propagation from tip cuttings in summer.

MAXILLARIA SANDERIANA
Maxillaria

Family: Orchid (*Orchidaceae*). **Habitat:** Ecuador, Peru. **Flowering:** Late summer to fall. **Location, Care, Propagation:** Part shade, warm (59-64˚F (15-18˚C)), and humid all year. Water rather sparingly, spray after bud formation has ceased, and apply orchid fertilizer monthly during the growth period. Over the summer, also in an orchid basket in a tree with light foliage. Propagate by division.

MELOCACTUS MAXONII
Melon cactus

Family: Cactus (*Cactaceae*). **Habitat:** Central and South America. **Flowering:** Summer. Under cultivation, only after many years. **Location, Care, Propagation:** All year, sunny, warm, and humid. Water with soft water, more in summer than in winter, and spray often. In the growth period, fertilize every four weeks. Propagation from seed at a soil temperature of 82-86˚F (28-30˚C).

METROSIDEROS EXCELSA
Irontree

Family: Myrtle (*Myrtaceae*). **Habitat:** New Zealand, Australia, Polynesia. **Flowering:** Spring, but only after about 10 years. **Location, Care, Propagation:** From the beginning of summer, outdoors in full sun, but sheltered; from early fall, light and at 41-50˚F (5-10˚C). Throughout the summer, water generously with soft water. Fertilize weekly until the end of summer. Propagation from cuttings at 77˚F (25˚C) or from seed.

SPECIAL COMMENT

The peyote is an interesting but somewhat dangerous representative of the cactus family. The South American Indians regarded it as a god. The strong intoxicants that it contains evoke hallucinations with bad side-effects, which is why California and Mexico have outlawed it.

Microlepia – Pinguicula

MICROLEPIA SPELUNCAE
Cupfern

Family: Polypody (*Polypodiaceae*).
Habitat: Old World tropics, South
Africa. **Flowering:** Nonflowering plant.
Location, Care, Propagation: Shady,
warm, and humid all year. Water
generously with soft water at room
temperature, but avoid water build-up
at all costs. Weak fertilizer once a
month. Propagation by division or by
seeding the spores at a soil
temperature of 68°F (20°C).

MIKANIA TERNATA
Mikania

Family: Aster (*Asteraceae*). **Habitat:**
Brazil. **Flowering:** Seldom flowers under
cultivation. **Location, Care,
Propagation:** All year, light to sunny,
humid, in summer also outdoors. In
winter at least 54°F (12°C). Keep
moderately moist but ensure high
humidity; fertilize monthly. Propagation
by division or tip cuttings at 68-77°F
(20-25°C).

MURRAYA PANICULATA
Common orange jasmine

Family: Rue (*Rutaceae*). **Habitat:** Asia,
Australia. **Flowering:** All year,
depending on location. **Location,
Care, Propagation:** Light to part shade
and humid all year. In winter, a
minimum of 54°F (12°C). Water with
soft water; keep drier in winter, without
letting the leaves fall off. During the
growth period, fertilize every two
weeks. Propagate from seed or tip
cuttings at a soil temperature of 86°F
(30°C).

PHAEDRANTHUS BUCCINATORIUS
Mexican bloodtrumpet

Family: Trumpet creeper (*Bignoniaceae*). **Habitat:** Mexico. **Flowering:**
High summer. **Location, Care,
Propagation:** Sunny and warm in
summer. In winter, light at 41-50°F
(5-10°C) (or more in the garden room).
Give plenty of water and fertilizer, but
reduce both in cool winter quarters.
Offer a climbing support. Propagation
from seed or soft-wood cuttings.

PHAJUS TANKERVILLEAE
Phajus

Family: Orchid (*Orchidaceae*).
Habitat: Asia, Australia. **Flowering:** Late
winter to early summer. **Location,
Care, Propagation:** Very light, warm,
and humid all year; partly shield
against full midday sun in summer. In
winter, at a minimum of 59°F (15°C).
Water generously with soft water, and
apply orchid fertilizer monthly.
Propagation from pseudobulbs.

PHLEBODIUM AUREUM
Golden cupfern

Family: Polypody (*Polypodiaceae*).
Habitat: Tropical South America.
Location, Care, Propagation:. Light all
year, but not sunny; warm and humid.
Water generously with soft water but
avoid water build-up. From spring to
fall, apply weak fertilizer once a week.
Propagation by division or spore
seeding at a soil temperature of 68°F
(20°C).

SPECIALTIES AND RARITIES

NEMATANTHUS STRIGILLOSUS
Pouch plant

Family: Gesneriad (*Gesneriaceae*).
Habitat: Brazil. **Flowering:** Spring.
Location, Care, Propagation: Light but
not sunny all year; cooler in winter, but
at least 54°F (12°C) to encourage bud
formation. Fertilize every two weeks
and keep moderately moist with soft
water, drier in winter. Propagation from
shoot or tip cuttings at a soil
temperature of 68–77°F (20–25°C).

OCHNA SERRULATA
Ochna

Family: Orchid (*Orchidaceae*).
Habitat: Tropical Africa. **Flowering:**
Late winter through spring. **Location,
Care, Propagation:** All year, light to
sunny, in summer also outdoors. In
winter at 41–50°F (5–10°C). Keep
moderately moist and fertilize every
two weeks. Prune as needed.
Propagation from seed or cuttings at a
soil temperature of 77°F (25°C).

PERILEPTA DYERIANA
Perilepta

Family: Acanthus (*Acanthaceae*).
Habitat: Burma. **Flowering:** Summer.
Location, Care, Propagation: All year,
part shade, warm, and humid, in
summer also outdoors if sheltered.
Always keep moderately moist and
assure high humidity. Ideal for closed
plant windows and terrariums. Start
new cuttings every year. Occasionally
trim young plants.

SPECIAL COMMENT

The butterwort
(*Pinguicula*) constitutes
a botanical
contradiction.
Although this small,
insect-eating plant
belongs among the
plants with two seed-
leaves (cotyledons),
during propagation
from seed it
germinates with only
a single seed-leaf. If
propagating from
individual leaves, be
careful not to injure
them. Sand is suitable
as the propagating
medium. Propagation
has succeeded when
the leaves have rooted
and developed
adventitious shoots.

PHYLLANTHUS ANGUSTIFOLIUS
Phyllanthus

Family: Spurge (*Euphorbiaceae*).
Habitat: Jamaica, Florida. **Flowering:**
Summer. **Location, Care, Propagation:**
Light to part shade all year, no full sun,
warm, and humid (hothouse plant).
Water rather sparingly, fertilize monthly,
repot rarely. Propagation from seed or
cuttings at a soil temperature of 86°F
(30°C) in a closed propagating bed.

PINGUICULA MEXICANA
Butterwort

Family: Bladderwort (*Lentibularia-
ceae*). **Habitat:** Mexico. **Flowering:**
Varies. **Location, Care, Propagation:**
Part shade, cool, and humid, e.g., in a
terrarium or shaded coldhouse. Keep
somewhat drier in winter at 46–50°F
(8–10°C). Insect-trapping plant.
Fertilizing unnecessary. Propagation
from seed or leaf cuttings.

Pinguicula mexicana

Pisonia – Sarcocaulon

PISONIA UMBELLIFERA
Pisonia

Family: Four o'clock (*Nyctaginaceae*).
Habitat: New Zealand, Norfolk Islands, Queensland. **Flowering:** Seldom blooms under cultivation. **Location, Care, Propagation:** Bright but not sunny all year, never under 64°F (18°C). Keep moderately moist all the time and spray often. In summer fertilize every one to two weeks, monthly in winter. Propagation from tip cuttings.

PITYROGRAMMA ASTROAMERICANA
Goldfern

Family: Polypody (*Polypodiaceae*)
Habitat: Tropical America. **Location, Care, Propagation:** Very light but not sunny, airy, and all year at 54–64°F (12–18°C). The lighter the location, the more silver or gold powder develops. Keep root ball lightly moist. Never spray! The plant ages quickly, so start new ones every year. Propagate by sowing spores.

PLUMERIA ALBA
White frangipani

Family: Dogbane (*Apocynaceae*).
Habitat: Puerto Rico, Lesser Antilles.
Flowering: Summer to early fall.
Location, Care, Propagation: Full sun, warm, and humid all year (hothouse plant). From early spring to late fall, water moderately. Fertilize once a week. Keep dry in winter. Propagation from leaf cuttings at 77°F (25°C) or from seed. **The plant is poisonous.**

SPECIAL COMMENT

In a garden room, the flowers of the frangipani appear from spring through to fall. People who have once seen a flowering frangipani tree in the tropics can never forget the picture, and want to possess one themselves. As early as 1770, the species is said to have bloomed every year in the imperial gardens in Vienna.

PSEUDERANTHEMUM ATROPURPUREUM
Purplespot pseuderanthemum

Family: Acanthus (*Acanthaceae*).
Habitat: Polynesia. **Flowering:** Summer to early fall. **Location, Care, Propagation:** All year, part shade, humid, and warm. Also in winter never under 61–64°F (16–18°C) air and soil temperature. Water only with soft water at room temperature. During the growing period, lightly fertilize every two weeks. Propagate from cuttings.

PTYCHOSPERMA ELEGANS
Solitaire palm

Family: Palm (*Arecaceae*). **Habitat:** Australia. Flowering: Seldom blooms under cultivation. **Location, Care, Propagation:** Light, no direct sun, all year at 68–77°F (20–25°C) and humid. Preferably place in a warm garden room. Water generously and fertilize weekly during the growth period. Propagation from seed. Germination in two to three months.

RHOEO SPATHACEA
Rhoeo, Moses in the cradle

Family: Spiderwort (*Commelinaceae*).
Habitat: Mexico, Guatemala.
Flowering: Spring to midsummer.
Location, Care, Propagation: Light but not sunny, room temperature all year, and humid. Water moderately with soft water, fertilize once a week. Propagation from seed or tip and stem cuttings. The plant is now offered as *Tradescantia spathacea*.

SPECIALTIES AND RARITIES

PODOCARPUS MACROPHYLLUS
Southern yew, Buddhist pine
Podocarpus

Family: Podocarp (*Podocarpaceae*).
Habitat: East Asia. **Flowering:** Summer.
Location, Care, Propagation: Sunny to
light shade, from late spring also
outdoors, protected from rain. In
winter, lighter, at 41–50°F (5–10°C) in a
coldhouse or stairwell. Water
moderately. Keep drier in winter.
Fertilize every two weeks. Propagation
from seed or tip cuttings. **The plant is
poisonous.**

PORPHYROCOMA LANCEOLATA
Porphyrocoma

Family: Acanthus (*Acanthaceae*).
Habitat: Brazil. **Flowering:** Late spring.
Location, Care, Propagation: All year
light, warm, and humid, but not sunny.
In summer, water generously, less in
winter, but assure high humidity. During
the growth period, fertilize every week.
Propagation from tip cuttings at a soil
temperature of 68–77°F (20–25°C). Trim
the young plants frequently.

PORTULACARIA AFRA
Portulacaria

Family: Purslane (*Portulacaceae*).
Habitat: South Africa. **Flowering:**
Summer. **Location, Care, Propagation:**
Full sun all year, in summer also
outdoors, protected from wind and
rain; warm. Water sparingly, fertilize
every four weeks. Keep dry in winter.
Propagation from tip cuttings, but first
dry these for two to three weeks. Ideal
bonsai plant.

RUSSELIA EQUISETIFORMIS
Coral plant

Family: Figwort (*Scrophulariaceae*).
Habitat: Central and South America.
Flowering: Late spring to fall. **Location,
Care, Propagation:** All year light but
not full sun, in summer also outdoors,
at 59–64°F (15–18°C) (garden room
plant). Supply with ample water and
fertilize weekly. Occasionally remove
old—never new—branches.
Propagation from runners or cuttings.

SANCHEZIA PARVIBRACTEATA
Sanchezia

Family: Acanthus (*Acanthaceae*).
Habitat: South America. **Flowering:**
Seldom flowers under cultivation.
Location, Care, Propagation: All year
light to part shade, warm, and humid,
preferably in a terrarium or closed
plant window. Water moderately and
fertilize every two weeks during the
growth period. Propagate from tip
cuttings at a minimum of 68°F (20°C).

SARCOCAULON PATERSONII
Bushman's candles

Family: Geranium (*Geraniaceae*).
Habitat: Southwest Africa. **Flowering:**
Fall to winter. **Location, Care,
Propagation:** All year, full sun and
warm. Only during the growth period
(from late summer) water moderately
and fertilize lightly once a month.
Otherwise, keep totally dry.
Propagation from seed or cuttings,
which must be allowed to dry out
thoroughly before planting.

SPECIAL COMMENT

The *Sarcocaulon* is one
of the most remarkable
beings in the plant
kingdom, and a model
for the modesty of its
requirements. It is to be
found in the extremely
arid regions of
southwest Africa. There
it can remain dormant,
without a single leaf,
for years on end.

Sauromatum – Tacca

Forced tubers of the veiny lizard arum

SAUROMATUM VENOSUM
Veiny lizard arum

Family: Arum (*Araceae*). **Habitat:** Subtropical Asia, Sudan. **Flowering:** Winter to spring. **Location, Care, Propagation:** Force the tuber in early winter. Keep the inflorescence somewhat moist and fertilize occasionally. When the leaf has withered, preserve the tuber frost-free and dry until the next forcing. Propagation from side tubers.

SARRACENIA X HYBRIDA
Hybrid pitcher plant

Family: Pitcher plant (*Sarraceniaceae*). **Habitat:** North America. **Flowering:** Early summer. **Location, Care, Propagation:** All year, light to sunny, airy, humid, and moderately warm. Always use decalcified water. Very rarely fertilize with diluted organic fertilizer, as this insect-catching plant looks after most of its own nutritional needs. Propagate by division or from seed.

SPECIAL COMMENT

The veiny lizard arum, *Sauromatum venosum*, develops the typical arum stalk from a totally dry tuber—for example, one lying on a plate. This inflorescence can grow to a height of 14–16 in. (35–40 cm) in a matter of two to four weeks, but emits an unpleasant smell reminiscent of carrion.

SONERILA MARGARITACEA
Sonerila

Family: Melastome (*Melastomataceae*). **Habitat:** Java. **Flowering:** Fall. **Location, Care, Propagation:** All year, very light, humid, and warm (closed plant window). Water moderately with soft water at room temperature. Fertilize every week in summer. Assure high humidity. Propagation from tip cuttings at a soil temperature of 68–77°F (20–25°C).

SOPHRONITIS FLORALIA
Sophronitis

Family: Orchid (*Orchidaceae*). **Habitat:** Brazil. **Flowering:** Winter. **Location, Care, Propagation:** Light to part shade and airy all year. In summer, warm in the daytime, cooler at night. In winter, around 63°F (17°C) during the day, and 57°F (14°C) at night. Keep lightly but uniformly moist, and never allow to dry out. Always water with decalcified water and apply orchid fertilizer every two to three months. Propagate by division.

SPREKELIA FORMOSISSIMA
Aztec lily

Family: Lily (*Liliaceae*). **Habitat:** Mexico. **Flowering:** Spring. **Location, Care, Propagation:** At the time of flowering, light and warm; in the rest period, dry, dark, around 59°F (15°C). When growth begins, water moderately. Later, water generously and fertilize every week. Propagation from side bulbs. **The plant is poisonous.**

SERISSA FOETIDA
Tree of a thousand stars

Family: Madder (*Rubiaceae*). **Habitat:** Southeast Asia. **Flowering:** Spring, summer. **Location, Care, Propagation:** All year, very light and humid, but protect from the midday sun. In summer, also outdoors; in winter at 50–59°F (10–15°C). Water generously and only with soft water. Avoid water build-up. In summer, fertilize every two weeks. Propagation from tip cuttings in a heatable propagating bed.

SETARIA PALMIFOLIA
Palm grass

Family: Grass (*Poaceae*). **Habitat:** Tropical Asia. **Flowering:** Seldom blooms under cultivation. **Location, Care, Propagation:** Light and at room temperature all year; in summer, also outdoors. Keep lightly and uniformly moist and fertilize every two weeks in summer. In spring, repot in lime-rich soil. Propagate by separating off side shoots or from seed in a heatable propagating bed.

SIDERASIS FUSCATA
Siderasis

Family: Spiderwort (*Commelinaceae*). **Habitat:** Brazil. **Flowering:** Seldom blooms under cultivation. **Location, Care, Propagation:** All year, light to shady and humid, never under 61°F (16°C) (hothouse plant). Keep the root ball lightly and uniformly moist, but make certain there is indirect humidity. Fertilize monthly. Propagation by division and cultivation from seed in a warm propagating bed.

SPECIAL COMMENT

The epiphytic stanhopeas are perhaps the most unusual orchids under cultivation. Their relatively large, almost unpleasantly fragrant flowers are fleshy and equipped with complicated passageways through which crawl the insects that pollinate them.

STANHOPEA TIGRINA
Stanhopea

Family: Orchid (*Orchidaceae*). **Habitat:** Mexico, Brazil, Guatemala. **Flowering:** Summer. **Location, Care, Propagation:** All year, light to part shade, in summer also outdoors. In winter at 55–63°F (13–17°C). Spray generously in summer with decalcified water. At every third watering, add orchid fertilizer. From late summer to winter, give less water. Propagation by division.

SYNADENIUM GRANTII
Grant's milkbush

Family: Spurge (*Euphorbiaceae*). **Habitat:** Uganda, Tanzania. **Flowering:** Seldom flowers under cultivation. **Location, Care, Propagation:** Light to full sun, warm. In winter at 46–50°F (8–10°C). In summer water regularly, but only a very little in winter. From spring to early fall, fertilize every two weeks. Propagation from cuttings in spring or summer at a soil temperature above 72°F (22°C). **The plant sap that oozes out is highly toxic.**

TACCA INTEGRIFOLIA
Tacca

Family: Tacca (*Taccaceae*). **Habitat:** Northeast India, Malaysia, Sumatra, Borneo, Java, Thailand. **Flowering:** Spring. **Location, Care, Propagation:** All year, light to part shade, humid, and warm. Keep lightly and uniformly moist with decalcified, water at body temperature. During the growth period, apply orchid fertilizer every month. Propagate by dividing.

Testudinaria – Zygopetalon

TESTUDINARIA ELEPHANTIPES
Hottentot bread, Tortoise plant

Family: Yam (*Dioscoreaceae*). **Habitat:**
South Africa. **Flowering:** Winter.
Location, Care, Propagation: Sunny to
part shade all year, and not too warm.
In summer and when bearing foliage,
keep moderately moist and use
cactus fertilizer every two weeks. At
other times, spray only now and then.
This comical climbing plant was
formerly called *Dioscorea*, then
Testudinaria, and now, once again,
Dioscorea.

TETRANEMA ROSEUM
Tetranema, allophyton

Family: Figwort (*Scrophulariaceae*).
Habitat: Mexico, Guatemala.
Flowering: Late winter through to fall.
Location, Care, Propagation: Light but
not sunny and at room temperature all
year. Keep only lightly moist and
fertilize every two weeks during the
growth period. Propagation in spring
from seed or by dividing older plants.

THEVETIA PERUVIANA
Thevetia

Family: Dogbane (*Apocynaceae*).
Habitat: Tropical America. **Flowering:**
Summer. **Location, Care, Propagation:**
All year, light to sunny. Warm in
summer, also outdoors. In winter, never
below 59°F (15°C). Water little in
summer and hardly at all in winter.
Avoid water build-up at all costs. In
summer, fertilize every two weeks.
Propagation from seed or cuttings. **This
plant is very poisonous.**

SPECIAL COMMENT

In their South African
habitat *Testudinaria*,
with their 3.2 ft.- (1 m-)
long looped branches,
develop tubers that
reach 3.2 ft. (1 m) in
diameter. The hard
tuber, covered with
edgy humps,
resembles the
carapace of a tortoise.

VALLOTA SPECIOSA
Scarboro lily

Family: Lily (*Liliaceae*). **Habitat:** South
Africa. **Flowering:** High summer.
Location, Care, Propagation: In
summer, sunny and warm; in winter
light, at 46–50°F (8–10°C). Force bulbs
in spring, and gradually water more
and more. After flowering, water
somewhat less. Propagation from side
bulbs or from seed. Today the plant is
called *Cyranthys purpureus*. **The plant
is very poisonous.**

VANILLA PLANIFOLIA
Mexican vanilla

Family: Orchid (*Orchidaceae*).
Habitat: Tropical America. **Flowering:**
High summer. **Location, Care,
Propagation:** Light but not sunny,
humid, and warm all year; ideal for
humid and warm garden rooms.
During the growth period, water
generously, in winter somewhat less.
Every week, fertilize more heavily than
other orchid species. Supply a
climbing support. Propagation from
root cuttings.

VIBURNUM TINUS
Laurestinus

Family: Honeysuckle (*Caprifoliaceae*).
Habitat: Southern Europe, Mediterranean region. **Flowering:** Spring to
summer. **Location, Care, Propagation:**
In summer, sunny to part shade, in
winter light at 39–46°F (4–8°C). Keep
moderately moist to the beginning of
growth and fertilize weekly to the end
of summer. In winter, give less water.
Propagation in summer from semihardwood cuttings.

TRICHODIADEMA DENSUM
Trichodiadema

Family: Fig-marigold (*Aizoaceae*). **Habitat:** South Africa. **Flowering:** Late winter to early spring. **Location, Care, Propagation:** Keep very sunny and airy, also outdoors in summer. During the growth period, water generously. Overwinter dry, light, and above 46°F (8°C). Propagation from seed or cuttings.

TURNERA SUBULATA
Turnera

Family: Turnera (*Turneraceae*). **Habitat:** Tropical America. **Flowering:** Spring to fall. **Location, Care, Propagation:** Very light, humid, and warm all year, but not full sun. Also in winter, never under 61–64°F (16–18°C). Keep moderately moist and fertilize every two weeks. In spring, cut back shoots as required. Propagation from seed or soft-wood cuttings at a soil temperature of 68–77°F (20–25°C).

UEBELMANNIA PECTINIFERA
Uebelmannia

Family: Cactus (*Cactaceae*). **Habitat:** Brazil. **Flowering:** Seldom blooms under cultivation. **Location, Care, Propagation:** In summer, full sun and hot; in winter, light, cool, but never below 50°F (10°C). Water carefully with soft water at room temperature, make sure the drainage is good, and avoid water build-up at all costs. Spray often. Propagation from seed.

WHITFIELDIA LATERITIA
Whitfieldia

Family: Acanthus (*Acanthaceae*). **Habitat:** West Africa, Sierra Leone. **Flowering:** Winter to spring. **Location, Care, Propagation:** Light to part shade and warm all year, never under 64°F (18°C). From spring through summer, fertilize every two weeks. Propagation from soft-wood cuttings in a heatable propagating bed. Pinch out young plants two or three times.

ZAMIA PUMILA
St. John's coontie

Family: Cycad (*Cycadaceae*). **Habitat:** Florida, Bahamas, West Indies. **Flowering:** Seldom flowers under cultivation. **Location, Care, Propagation:** Very light and humid, but not sunny; outdoors in summer if sheltered. In winter, never below 54°F (12°C). Water moderately; even less in winter. Propagate from fresh seed at a soil temperature of 86–95°F (30–35°C). Long germination period.

ZYGOPETALON CRINITUM
Zygopetalon

Family: Orchid (*Orchidaceae*). **Habitat:** Brazil. **Flowering:** Usually in winter. **Location, Care, Propagation:** All year, light to part-shade, humid, airy, at 59–64°F (15–18°C). Keep moist with soft water. From spring to fall, apply low doses of fertilizer every two weeks. Support the heavy inflorescences in good time. Propagate by separating off leafy pseudobulbs.

SPECIAL COMMENT

The uniqueness of *Zamias*, which date from prehistoric times, lies in their "coral roots," which are immediately under or above the surface of the soil, and are colonized by a blue alga.

Useful Addresses

MAIL-ORDER NURSERIES

Alpenflora Gardens
17985—40th Avenue
Surrey, BC, Canada V3S 4N8
Rock garden and alpine plants.

Borbeleta Gardens
13980 Canby Avenue
Faribault, MN 55021
Lilies, day lilies, Siberian and bearded iris.

The Bovees Nursery
1737 S.W. Coronado
Portland, OR 97219
Hybrid and species rhododendrons, shrubs, and alpines.

Canyon Creek Nursery
3527 Dry Creek Road
Oroville, CA 95965
Wide range of perennials.

Colorado Alpines, Inc.
P.O. Box 2708
Avon, CO 81620
Alpine and rock garden plants.

Dominion Seed House
115 Guelph Street
Georgetown, ON, Canada
L7G 4A2
Wide range of seeds.

Fancy Fronds
1911—4th Avenue West
Seattle, WA 98119
Wide range of hardy ferns—worldwide.

Gardenimport Inc.
P.O. Box 760
Unit 5, 2 Essex Avenue
Thornhill, ON, Canada L3T 4A5
Annuals, perennials, and bulbs.

Glasshouse Works
P.O. Box 97
10 Church Street
Stewart, OH 45779-4097
Exotic, tropical, and variegated plants.

Gossler Farm Nursery
1200 Weaver Road
Springfield, OR 97478-9663
Magnolias, daphnes, stewartias, and other unusual trees and shrubs.

Heronswood Nursery
7530—288th Street N.E.
Kingston, WA 98346
Wide range of unusual woody and perennial plants.

Holbrook Farm and Nursery
Route 2, Box 223B
Fletcher, NC 28732
Wide range of perennials and native species.

Klehm Nursery
Route #5, Box 197
Penny Road
South Barrington, IL 60010-9555
Hostas, day lilies, herbaceous and tree peonies, and perennials.

Kline Nursery Co.
17401 S.W. Bryant Road
Lake Oswego, OR 97035
Perennials, hardy cyclamen, ferns, and species lilies. Alpines.

Lamb Nurseries
E.101 Sharp Avenue
Spokane, WA 99202
Perennials, rock garden plants, and violets.

Lilypons Water Gardens
P.O. Box 10
6800 Lilypons Road
Lilypons, MD 21717-0010
Water lilies, lotus and bog plants.

Logee's Greenhouses
141 North Street
Danielson, CT 06239
Begonias and other greenhouse exotics.

Grant Mitch Novelty Daffodils
P.O. Box 218
Hubbard, OR 97032
Choice hybrid daffodils.

Oregon Trail Daffodils
3207 S.E. Mannthey Road
Corbett, OR 97019
Choice hybrid daffodils.

Park Seed Co., Inc.
P.O. Box 46
Highway 254 North
Greenwood, SC 29648-0046
Wide range of flower and vegetable seed. Plants and bulbs.

Plant Delights Nursery
9241 Sauls Road
Raleigh, NC 27603
Hostas and many unusual shrubs and perennials.

Prairie Nursery
P.O. Box 365, Rt. 1
Westfield, WI 53564
Native prairie plants.

Rice Creek Gardens
1315—66th Avenue N.E.
Minneapolis, MN 53432
Alpine and rock garden plants.

Roses of Yesterday and Today
802 Brown's Valley Road
Watsonville, CA 95076-0398
Wide range of "Old Garden" roses.

Schriner's Gardens
3625 Quinaby Road N.E.
Salem, OR 97303
Fine modern iris hybrids.

Siskiyou Rare Plant Nursery
2825 Cummings Road
Medford, OR 97501
Wide range of alpine and rock garden plants.

Anthony Skittone
1415 Eucalyptus
San Francisco, CA 94132
Spring and summer bulbs—worldwide.

Thompson and Morgan
P.O. Box 1308
Farraday and Gramme Avenues
Jackson, NJ 08527
Wide selection of seeds—all types.

Andre Viette Farm and Nursery
Route 1, Box 16
State Route 608
Fisherville, VA 22939
Broad selection of perennials.

Wayside Gardens
1 Garden Lane
Hodges, SC 29695-0001
Wide selection of trees, shrubs, perennials, and bulbs. Roses.

We-Do Nurseries
Route 5, Box 724
Marion, NC 29801
Rock garden, woodland plants. Unusual Asiatic selections.

Useful Addresses

Woodlanders, Inc.
1128 Colleton Avenue
Aiken, SC 29801
Southern U.S. natives and hard-to-find exotics.

Yucca Do Nursery
P.O. Box 655
Waller, TX 77484
Unusual trees, shrubs, and perennials for Zones 8 and 9. Native Texan plants and their Mexican and Asiatic counterparts.

SPECIALIST SOCIETIES

African Violet Society of America
Box 1326
Knoxville, TN 37901

Alpine Garden Club of British Columbia
13751—56A Avenue
Surrey, BC, Canada V3W 1S4

American Begonia Society
8302 Kittyhawk Avenue
Los Angeles, CA 90045

American Bonsai Society
228 Rosemont Avenue
Erie, PA 16505

American Conifer Society
P.O. Box 242
Severna Park, MD 21146

American Daffodil Society Inc.
1686 Grey Fox Trails
Milford, OH 45150

American Fern Society Inc.
Dept. of Botany
University of Tennessee
Knoxville, TN 37996-1100

American Fuchsia Society
Hall of Flowers
Golden Gate Park
San Francisco, CA 94122

American Gloxinia/Gesneriad Society
P.O. Box 174
New Milford, CT 06776

American Herb Association
P.O. Box 353
Rescue, CA 95672

American Hibiscus Society
P.O. Box 491F, Rt. 1
Fort Myers, FL 33905

American Hosta Society
5300 Whiting Ave.
Edina, MN 55435

American Iris Society
7414 E. 60th Street
Tulsa, OK 74145

American Ivy Society
National Center for American Horticulture
Mount Vernon, VA 22121

American Orchid Society
Botanical Museum of Harvard University
Cambridge, MA 02138

American Peony Society
250 Interlachen Road
Hopkins, MN 55343

American Plant Life Society
P.O. Box 985
National City, CA 92050

American Rhododendron Society
P.O. Box 1380
Gloucester, VA 23061

American Rock Garden Society
15 Fairmead Road
Darien, CT 06820

Bromeliad Society
P.O. Box 3279
Santa Monica, CA 90403

Cactus and Succulent Society of America
P.O. Box 3010
Santa Barbara, CA 93105

California Horticultural Society
1847—34th Avenue
San Francisco, CA 94122

California Native Plant Society
909—12th Street, #116
Sacramento, CA 95814

Cymbidium Society of America
1250 Orchid Drive
Santa Barbara, CA 93111

Epiphyllum Society of America
P.O. Box 1395
Monrovia, CA 91016

Gesneriad Society International
P.O. Box 549
Knoxville, TN 37901

Herb Society of America
300 Massachusetts Avenue
Boston, MA 02115

Holly Society of America
407 Fountain Green Road
Bel Air, MD 21014

Indoor Light Garden Society of America
423 Powell Drive
Bay Village, OH 44140

International Cactus and Succulent Society
P.O. Box 1452
San Angelo, TX 76901

International Geranium Society
6501 Yosemite Drive
Buena Park, CA 90620

Los Angeles International Fern Society
2423 Burritt Avenue
Redondo Beach, CA 90278

The Magnolia Society
907 S. Chestnut Street
Hammond, LA 70403-5102

National Fuchsia Society
c/o Bonita Doan, Dept. DH
774 Forest Loop Drive
Point Hueneme, CA 93041

New England Wild Flower Society
Hemenway Road
Framingham, MA 01701

North American Heather Society
62 Elma-Monte Road
Elma, WA 985541

North American Lily Society, Inc.
P.O. Box 272
Owatonna, MN 55060

Palm Society
1320 South Venetian Way
Miami, FL 33139

The Perennial Plant Association
Dept. of Horticulture
Ohio State University
2001 Fyffe Court
Columbus, OH 43210

Rhododendron Species Foundation
P.O. Box 3798
Federal Way, WA 980603-3798

Saintpaulia International
P.O. Box 549
Knoxville, TN 37901

Terrarium Society
57 Wolfpit Avenue
Norwalk, CT 06851

Index

Index

Index

Index